Dante Alighieri

PURGATORIO

Translated by
Stanley Lombardo

Introduction by
Claire E. Honess and
Matthew Treherne

Notes and Headnotes by
Ruth Chester

D1226160

Hackett Publishing Company, Inc.
Indianapolis/Cambridge

19 18 17 16   1 2 3 4 5 6 7

For further information, please address
Hackett Publishing Company, Inc.
P.O. Box 44937
Indianapolis, Indiana 46244-0937

www.hackettpublishing.com

Cover design by Brian Rak
Interior design by Carrie Wagner
Composition by William Hartman

Library of Congress Cataloging-in-Publication Data

Names: Dante Alighieri, 1265–1321 author. | Lombardo, Stanley,
    1943–   translator. | Honess, Claire E., author of introduction. |
    Treherne, Matthew, author of introduction. | Dante Alighieri,
    1265–1321. Purgatorio.
    English.
Title: Purgatorio / Dante Alighieri ; translated by Stanley Lombardo ;
    introduction by Claire E. Honess and Matthew Treherne ; notes and
    headnotes by Ruth Chester.
Description: Indianapolis : Hackett Publishing Company, Inc., 2016. |
    English translation and Italian original text on facing pages. |
    Includes bibliographical references and index.
Identifiers: LCCN 2016002492| ISBN 9781624664915 (pbk.) |
    ISBN 9781624664922 (cloth)
Subjects: LCSH: Purgatory--Poetry.
Classification: LCC PQ4315.3 .L66 2016 | DDC 851/.1--dc23
LC record available at https://lccn.loc.gov/2016002492

Contents

Introduction   vii
Translator's Preface   xxxvii
Note on the Text   xxxix
Abbreviations   xl
Bibliographical Note   xli
Geography of the *Purgatorio* (diagram)   xliii
Structure of the *Purgatorio* (chart)   xliv

Purgatorio   1

Notes   329
Index of the Penitent   423

Introduction

In many respects the *Purgatorio* is the most original of the three *cantiche* of Dante's *Commedia*. Unlike the concepts of Heaven and Hell—firmly established within the Judeo-Christian tradition and clearly defined in the popular imagination—the notion of Purgatory as a place of cleansing after death had come late to Christian orthodoxy. Indeed, the Church did not issue its first statement of belief regarding Purgatory until 1274, and the doctrine would not be finally formalized until the Council of Florence in 1439. This allowed Dante's theologically informed poetic imagination free rein in the design and elaboration of a second realm of the afterlife that bridges the gap between Hell's abyss and Heaven's heights in strikingly creative ways.

Purgatory, in the simplest terms, is an intermediate realm of waiting and suffering where those souls who have died repentant are cleansed (purged) of all traces of sin (imagined as a stain left on the soul) in order to be made fit to enter Heaven. While the doctrines of Heaven and Hell both draw on numerous (albeit loosely defined) biblical references to punishment and reward after death, Purgatory is not mentioned at all in the Bible but rather develops organically through the coming together of two key biblical ideas in conjunction with a series of more practical considerations.

The first of the biblical ideas that influenced the development of the doctrine of Purgatory is that of prayer for the dead, which has its roots in 2 Macc., where Judas Maccabeus makes offerings to counteract the sins of his soldiers killed in battle and where it is noted, "If he had not hoped that they that were slain should rise again, it would have seemed superfluous and vain to pray for the dead" (2 Macc. 12:44). This tradition seems to have quickly passed into Christian practice, as is attested by exhortations to pray for the deceased found in inscriptions on early Christian tombs and by the presence of prayers for the dead in liturgical contexts dating from at least the fourth century.

The second biblical idea that contributed to the conception of an intermediate state of cleansing punishment after death derives from a series of passages that suggest that the souls of the righteous will be tested by fire at the Last Judgment as a means of freeing them from their sins. Of particular relevance here is a passage in the first letter to the Corinthians, which makes clear that, while all who build on the foundation of Christ will be saved, some will achieve this salvation only by passing through a cleansing fire:

> Now if any man build upon this foundation [Christ], gold, silver, precious stones, wood, hay, stubble: every man's work shall be manifest; for the day of the Lord shall declare it, because it shall be revealed in fire; and the fire shall try every man's work, of what sort it is. If any man's work abide, which he hath built thereupon, he shall receive a reward. If any man's work burn, he shall suffer loss; but he himself shall be saved, yet so as by fire. (1 Cor. 3:12–15)

The interpretation of this passage as indicating the existence of purgatorial suffering following the death of the body but before the Last Judgment was taken up by St Augustine in his *City of God* (XXI.26) and soon became the standard accepted reading, so that by the time of St Thomas Aquinas it could be cited as self-evident proof of the existence of Purgatory (as it is, e.g., in his *Summa contra Gentiles* IV.xci.6–7).

These more strictly theological approaches to Purgatory combined, as the medieval period proceeded, with other, more practical concerns, which influenced the way in which the doctrine and surrounding traditions subsequently developed. The huge social change that characterized the twelfth and thirteenth centuries, and in particular the growth of mercantile economies based in the rapidly expanding cities, led to a certain unease with "black-and-white" categories of good and bad, saved and damned. Christian merchants, well aware that they were guilty of the sins of Avarice and Usury (no doubt among others), sought a way to expiate their sins without necessarily needing to abandon their lucrative profession. At the same time, the existence of a temporal intermediate place of punishment was useful to the Church, which saw, in the belief that punishment after death could be abbreviated by the penitential prayers and good deeds of the faithful, an opportunity to fill its own coffers by accepting "indulgences"—essentially payment by the faithful in lieu of the performance of such acts of penance. Finally, this period also witnessed the growth of the practice of individual confession, which led to further reflection on the "debt" owed by the sinner and the means in which it might be repaid during the sinner's life and in the afterlife.

Against the background of these social, economic, political, and theological developments, the notion of Purgatory *as a place*, distinct from either Heaven or Hell, began to enter the popular imagination. Jacques Le Goff, in his seminal study of the "birth" of Purgatory, dates the first emergence of the noun *purgatorium* to mean "the place where purgatorial punishment in the afterlife is enacted" to somewhere between 1170 and 1180, and, while this precise dating has been questioned by later commentators, there can be no doubt that toward the end of the twelfth century this relative newcomer to Judeo-Christian eschatology comes to take on a much greater degree of concreteness.

Nonetheless, there is, in accounts of visions of the afterlife before Dante, little by way of a fully worked out description of the place where purgation takes place and the process by which it is effected, and there is certainly no consistency in those accounts that do exist. In most cases, Purgatory is nothing more than a waiting area—a place between Heaven and Hell where those not good enough for the former and not bad enough for the latter, or those who repented late in life await the Last Judgment, after which they will finally be admitted to Paradise. Variously described as a valley of fire and ice, as the bosom of Abraham, as an "upper" (as opposed to an eternal "lower") Hell, as a pit of darkness, and as a bridge between Hell and Heaven, the two constants appear to be testing by, or suffering in, fire, and the request for prayers on the part of the living. In some accounts, Purgatory is associated with a mountain site, as it is in Dante's *Purgatorio*, although in many more cases mountains (and especially volcanoes) are associated with eternal punishment, and perhaps seen as the gateway to Hell.

The most famous of the purgatorial mountains is St Patrick's Purgatory, a mountain in Ireland on which penitents would spend the night, enduring torment in return for cleansing from sins; unlike in

Dante's poem, however, this cleansing happens during the sinner's lifetime, and not after her or his death. More significantly, perhaps, there is a well-developed tradition, both learned and popular, that suggests a mountain site for the Earthly Paradise, found, in Dante's account, at the top of the mountain of Purgatory, and it seems plausible that it is on this that Dante draws in conceptualizing the geography and structure of his Purgatory—a realm formulated perhaps from the top down rather than from the bottom up.

Purgatory in the Cosmology of the *Commedia*

It is from the top down, then, that we will now consider the structure of Dante's Purgatory, for it is from the unique perspective of the Earthly Paradise, the Garden of Eden at the top of Mount Purgatory, that the cosmology not only of the *Purgatorio* but of the *Commedia* as a whole comes to make sense.

At the end of his journey through Purgatory, his sins cleansed and his soul pure, Dante's traveler comes full circle, back to that place where not only his own journey but that of the whole human race had begun, the place lost through original sin and now reachable only through the acknowledgement, understanding, and thorough rejection of sin: through the process illustrated in the *Inferno* and the *Purgatorio*. It is sin, as we discover at the end of the *Inferno*, that creates the very mountain of Purgatory itself, pushed up out of the Earth's Southern Hemisphere when the abyss of Hell was formed by the dramatic fall of Lucifer (*Inf.* XXXIV.124–26). It is sin, then, that causes Mount Purgatory to rise out of the great ocean, just as it is sin that exiles the human race from the idyllic garden at its summit; it is therefore no coincidence that a straight line joins Eden in the Southern Hemisphere to Lucifer, punished immobile at the Earth's very core. And the significance of this line does not stop here, as Lucifer himself makes clear when he says:

> And now you are beneath the hemisphere
>   opposite the one that arches over
>   the great land mass, under whose zenith
> The Man was slain who was born and lived without sin.
>   (*Inf.* XXXIV.112–15)

Rather, we find, at the antipodes of the Earthly Paradise, the city of Jerusalem, the place where, on the Cross, Christ took on himself the sins of humanity. Along this line, then, the whole of salvation history situates itself: the sin that came into the world with Lucifer, who in Eden tempted Adam and Eve in the guise of the serpent, is punished and redeemed; human beings, having been exiled from their true home, are, through the redemption effected by Christ, and via their own faith and repentance, enabled to return whence they came.

Dante thus gives a concrete geographical shape and trajectory to a number of medieval legends linking Adam with Christ and original sin with redemption: the legend, for example, that links Golgotha, "the place of the skull" (see Matthew 27:33), with the burial place of Adam or that which claims that the Cross of the Crucifixion was made from the wood of the Tree of Knowledge. He also ensures that the journey of his character along this line—from the earthly world via the depths of Hell and the slopes of Mount Purgatory to the Earthly Paradise—takes on a significance that goes far beyond the fate of any one individual, for a journey that has these as its key coordinates cannot but represent, on some level, the whole story of the human relationship with God.

Viewing the second *cantica* of the *Commedia* from this perspective also highlights both the originality and the coherence of the vision that Dante creates for his afterlife, and specifically for its second realm. While we have seen that, in the popular medieval imagination, mountains were frequently associated with the Earthly Paradise and occasionally seen as places of purgation, it is significant that there is no precedent for the bringing together, on a mountain site, of these two staging posts on the journey to God, which tend, rather, to be polarized: the Earthly Paradise acting as a sort of antechamber to Heaven and Purgatory being a continuation of, and sometimes indistinguishable from, Hell.

Dante, in contrast, reasserts the earthly nature of Eden, situating it at the highest point of the Earth's surface, and at the same time raises Purgatory out of Hell's abyss, fundamentally altering its emotional and spiritual impact. For Purgatory, in Dante's conception, is precisely the path that leads the soul to Heaven, and the Earthly Paradise is that path's end point as well as the starting point for the new, celestial, journey recounted in the *Paradiso*. And if Purgatory is that realm "where the human soul is cleansed/and becomes worthy to leap up to the sky" (*Purg.* I.5–6), then an incontrovertible logic connects it with Eden, that place where the human soul was created clean, which humanity lost through sin and can regain only through true repentance and the cleansing journey that Dante's second *cantica* describes. The Earthly Paradise episode is not, therefore, we suggest, a sort of extended postscript to the *Purgatorio* but rather the necessary culmination and goal of this realm's moral structure.

The Moral Structure of the *Purgatorio*

How, then, is Dante's Purgatory organized in order to purify those souls who undertake its cleansing journey so that they are made fit to reenter Eden and regain all that sin first took from them?

It is immediately apparent that the structure of Dante's *Purgatorio* is much simpler than that of the *Inferno*, with its multiple circles, subcircles, *gironi* and *bolge*, reflecting the apparently almost infinite variety and complexity of human sinfulness. Purgatory, instead, is structured around just seven main categories of sin, punished on the seven terraces that encircle the mountain at different distances from its summit. Each of these terraces corresponds to one of the seven so-called deadly sins, or, more properly "capital vices": in order, as Dante encounters them, Pride, Envy, Wrath, Sloth, Avarice, Gluttony, and Lust. From the earliest Christian times, thinkers had attempted to create taxonomies of human sinfulness, but these were first systematized and reduced to seven main categories by Gregory the Great in the second half of the sixth century. Such was the authority of Gregory that his categories were refined but not substantively changed during the course of the centuries that followed. However, they came to greater prominence after the Fourth Lateran Council of 1215, at which rules of confession were formalized, leading to a rapid growth in the production of handbooks for confessors and penitential manuals; these drew widely on this system, which was simple without being simplistic as well as convenient and memorable.

The differences in structure and complexity between Dante's Hell and his Purgatory can be explained by the different purposes of the two realms. Hell exists to punish sins—specifically sinful *deeds*—and is purely retributive in nature. The souls in Hell do not—indeed *cannot*—hope to benefit from their punishment, for change and development is impossible there; they suffer for deeds done and not repented, and the futility of the eternally reiterated punishment itself forms part of their suffering. In contrast to his *Inferno*, and in contrast also to most contemporary visions of Purgatory where, as we have seen, the punishments were frequently distinguished from those of Hell only by their temporary nature, Dante's Purgatory is a place of education far more than a place of punishment. This does not, of course, mean that it is not a place of suffering, for the pain inflicted on the souls here is every bit as real and as horrible as that inflicted in Hell. However, here the pain is, as it were, pain with a purpose—not mere retribution, but a means to an end, freely chosen by the souls, to the extent that they are able to speak of it not as pain but as solace:

> I say our pain,
>   but I really ought to say our solace,
> For the same desire leads us to the trees
>   as led Christ to say *"Eli"* gladly
>   when he made us free with blood from his veins.
> (*Purg.* XXIII.71–75)

In imitation of Christ, who suffered and died gladly in order to remove from the world the stain of original sin, the souls accept their suffering willingly in the knowledge that they are thereby removing from their own souls the stains of their individual sins.

And this explains also the simpler structure of Purgatory compared to Hell, because here this corrective and educational process is applied not to the souls' individual sinful actions, which have already been repented and forgiven as a prerequisite for entry into the realm, but to those character traits, those sinful inclinations or dispositions that led the soul to behave sinfully. It is immediately clear that one sinful disposition may lie at the root of a whole series of sinful deeds. For example, Pride, a sense of being better than one's neighbor, may induce the sinner to oppress his neighbor and treat him unfairly; it may lead him to commit acts of violence against his neighbor or to take from him what is rightfully his; it may show itself in deception, hypocrisy, or even betrayal. And conversely any one sinful action—a murder, say—may be committed from any one of a number of sinful inclinations: Pride, Envy, Anger, Lust, and so on. The simpler structure of Dante's Purgatory compared to his Hell does not, therefore, suggest a narrowing of the poet's understanding of the ways in which human beings can offend God and their neighbors but rather reflects an attempt to look beneath the surface of such offenses in order to understand their deeper motivations.

Moreover, it is clearly apparent that this desire to understand both sin and the causes of sin applies also to the souls in Purgatory, who accept their punishments willingly and with open acknowledgement of what they have done wrong; this is evident from the very beginning of the *cantica* when Manfred freely admits that his sins were "horrible" (*Purg.* III.121). Indeed, the reader of the *Purgatorio* comes to understand that the souls not only accept their punishments but actively choose them, as the character of Statius reveals when he explains what happens when a soul is freed from punishment on the mountain and allowed to rise up to God:

> The will alone gives proof of its purity,
>   when, wholly free to change its cloister,
>   it surprises the soul and empowers it to will.
> It wills before, indeed, but is thwarted by desire,
>   which Divine Justice sets, counter to the will,
>   toward punishment in accordance with its sin.
>   (*Purg.* XXI.61–66)

All the souls in Purgatory desire, first and foremost, to enter Heaven, their true "cloister." This is the choice they made at the moment of their death, if not before, when they chose to repent and turn to God. However, since nothing imperfect can enter Heaven, this desire can only be realized once every stain and remnant of the inclination to sin has been removed by punishment. Thus, the choice that turns the souls' will to God becomes also the choice of suffering to which God turns the souls' desires—against, but as the only possible means to, their desire for salvation.

Statius' explanation picks up and illustrates the earlier account of Purgatory's structure and functioning provided in the central cantos of the *Purgatorio*, which are also, of course, the central cantos of the

Comedy as a whole, and in many ways (not least from the point of view of our understanding of the poem's moral structure) the fulcrum around which the whole poem turns. Here, Virgil explains that Creation is an act of love and that all created things therefore have an innate ability to love, which is turned, first and foremost, toward that which created them. This love Virgil refers to as "natural," and it is literally "inerrant" (*Purg.* XVII.94) in the sense that it can never be deflected from the creator. Created human souls, however, also possess another kind of love, referred to by Virgil as "of the mind" (*Purg.* XVII.93), that is, controlled and directed by the human intellect through the use of free will and under the guidance of reason. This love is far from inerrant. Indeed, thanks to human weakness, it has an almost inevitable tendency to stray, to turn, as the character of Marco, a Lombard, says in the previous canto, "to whatever delights it" (*Purg.* XVI.90); this leads the soul away from the true good, which is God, toward other, deceptive, secondary goods, goods that may, in fact, only *seem* good while leading the soul off the "straight way" (cf. *Inf.* I.3) and toward perdition. It is on the basis of *this* love that the human soul is judged and assigned its place in the afterlife, for judgment can only take place on the basis of that love that the soul itself controls; otherwise, as Marco explains, "and it would not be just to have joy/for goodness, or feel grief for evil" (*Purg.* XVI.71–72), and Heaven and Hell themselves would be unjust.

In canto XVII, Virgil goes on to explain how it is that "love of the mind," when misdirected (twisted toward evil), too weak, or too focused on secondary ends (*Purg.* XVII.100–101), can lead to each of the sinful inclinations cleansed in Purgatory. Love directed toward evil rather than good must, Virgil explains, necessarily have as its focus another person, since it is impossible to hate either oneself or God, and this can be enacted in three different ways, corresponding to the first three sinful inclinations cleansed on the mountain.

An individual may wish harm to his neighbor because he hopes thereby to be exalted himself in comparison: this is the sin of Pride. Alternatively, a soul may wish ill upon his neighbor because of some good (possession, status, or quality) that the neighbor has and that he desires for himself: this is the sin of Envy. Or a sinner may sin against his neighbor by wishing injury upon him because of some perceived slight or offense: this is the sin of Wrath. Love that is too weak in its focus on God and virtue is indicative of an inclination toward Sloth, punished on the fourth terrace of the mountain of Purgatory. And, finally, Virgil explains that love that is too focused on secondary goods—money and possessions, food and drink, another person—is not wrong in itself, since to love these things in due proportion is proper to the human condition and acceptable to God, but becomes sinful when due proportion is not observed and the love of these secondary goods replaces or overshadows the love of God. This leads to the sins of Avarice, Gluttony, and Lust, punished on the mountain's final three terraces.

Following this explanation, it is possible to see the function of the process of purgation in a new light, as a righting of love. Through the cleansing processes that Dante's character is allowed to witness, the souls' "love of the mind" is brought back into alignment with their "inerrant" natural love, so that by the end of their journey—when they reach that moment of utter freedom and purity that Statius describes—their entire potential to love, both natural and of the mind, is focused wholly and joyfully on God so that they are able, at last, to return to Him.

Training the Soul to Love

An understanding of purgation as a righting of love, a positive learning process, changes profoundly also the way in which the *contrapasso*, the unique way in which Dante makes the punishment fit the sin, works in Purgatory. In Hell, the *contrapasso*, which forces the sinners to confront their behavior by reenacting it—either through analogy or contrast—or by having it reenacted upon them, forms part of the souls' punishment: not only do they suffer for their sins, but the form that this suffering takes acts as a perpetual reminder of the reason for their damnation, a reminder that only exacerbates the pain inflicted by ensuring that no denial or evasion is possible. In contrast, while the *contrapasso* functions practically in exactly the same way in the *Purgatorio* as in the *Inferno*, and while here too it serves to remind the souls of the true nature of their sinful tendencies, in Purgatory the *contrapasso* serves a fundamentally educative purpose: by facing up to the sinful dispositions that caused them to misuse the love that God created in them, by recognizing them for what they are, owning and understanding them, the souls in Purgatory learn to reject sin and to embrace its opposite, and their misdirected love is thereby transformed into the inerrant love of God.

Thus, if the souls on the terrace of Pride carry heavy boulders on their backs that force them to stoop in a posture evoking humility, this is no coincidence, for this is precisely the quality that their earthly lives had lacked and that they must learn in the course of their purgatorial journey. Their punishment forces them to embody that which they must, in time, actually become: humble souls from whom all trace of Pride has been eradicated. Likewise the envious, whose eyes are sewn shut with wire, learn not to cast covetous glances at their neighbors but instead to support them; the slothful learn the virtue of zeal through time spent in eager forward motion; the gluttons, who endure constant temptation by fruit that they cannot and must not eat, learn the virtue of abstemiousness, and so on.

Moreover, the process of spiritual change that takes place in Purgatory is not effected, as the process of punishment is in Hell, through pain alone but rather works on the souls' sinful tendencies on a series of levels—physical, mental, and spiritual—combining the negative reinforcement of the *contrapasso* with positive encouragement toward virtue. Thus, on each of Purgatory's terraces the souls are presented with a series of examples that illustrate both the sin being cleansed and the moral virtue that opposes it and that the soul is being trained to adopt. This technique is very much in keeping with medieval techniques of writing and preaching on the subject of vice and virtue, whereby short memorable tales or anecdotes, which might be taken from the Bible, from folk tales, from history, or from hagiography, were used as exempla to illustrate a particular vice or virtue and its comeuppance or reward.

In the *Purgatorio* these exempla are compared to whips and bridles (see *Purg.* XIII.37–42): the latter to restrain the souls' inclination toward vice, the former to spur the souls on toward the opposing virtue. As a clear sign of the way in which Purgatory is more concerned with training the soul to virtue than with punishing its vices, in each case the exempla of virtue precede those of vice. This reflects that contrast with Hell that has already been highlighted in relation to the contrapasso: the souls are not here forced to contemplate their own abjectness but instead choose to meditate on their immediate (the specific virtue that opposes their sinful tendency) and ultimate (God and Heaven) learning goals.

These exempla are presented to the souls in a variety of formats: on the terrace of Pride they are sculpted into the ground on which the souls walk and on the rock walls in front of which they pass with a lifelike artistry that only the Creator Himself could exhibit; on the terraces of Envy, Wrath, and Gluttony they are presented through disembodied voices or ecstatic visions; and on those of Sloth, Avarice, and Lust they are variously shouted out or repeated prayerfully by the penitent souls themselves. As the mountain is ascended, therefore, we see the souls' increasingly active engagement with their own moral change. While initially the examples are merely set before the souls for their benefit and edification, once the penitents have progressed in understanding and purity they are able to become, as it were, their own teachers, articulating and reiterating the models for what they once were and what they must now become.

In keeping with the syncretic vision that Dante exhibits throughout the poem, these models of both vice and virtue are taken from classical as well as from biblical and Christian sources; in all cases, however, the first example with which the souls are presented, standing almost synecdochically as the sum of all virtue, is taken from the life of the Virgin Mary. Thus her humility in declaring herself the "handmaid of the Lord" (*ancilla Dei*; Lk. 1:38; and cf. *Purg.* X.44) stands in contrast to the sin of Pride, her charity at the wedding at Cana in Galilee opposes the sin of Envy, her zeal in rushing to visit her relative Elizabeth on hearing of her pregnancy contrasts sharply with the sin of Sloth, her chastity in declaring herself a virgin (*virum non cognosco*; Lk. 1:34; and cf. *Purg.* XXV.128) provides an example for those guilty of the sin of Lust, and so on. It is no coincidence that it is through the intercession of Mary that Dante will eventually be allowed his final and ineffable vision of God (*Par.* XXXIII), for we see, throughout the *Purgatorio*, that the path to God is waymarked, from beginning to end, by the life and example of the Virgin.

Time Is of the Essence: Antepurgatory

Purgatory is, then, a place of education and reordering. It is also, of course, a place of anticipation. It should come as no surprise therefore to find that time is a constant theme of the *Purgatorio*, evoked repeatedly not only with regard to the waiting period that the penitent souls must undergo but also in relation to earthly time and its passing, for it is precisely the passing of time—the fact that purgation, like earthly life, has a beginning, a duration, and an end—that gives Purgatory its unique status within the structure of the afterlife. In Purgatory, then, the sun rises and sets, alternating periods of light (which look forward to the pure and constant light of Heaven) and darkness (which recall the everlasting darkness of Hell), and this becomes a pretext for a series of lengthy temporal periphrases in which the poet contrives to tell the time in Purgatory by comparing the position of the sun there, in the Southern Hemisphere, to its position at various points on the Earth's surface and, perhaps most importantly, for the reasons we have already highlighted, at the city of Jerusalem, standing at Purgatory's antipodes, as is the case in the opening lines of canto II:

> The sun now had reached that horizon
> the zenith of whose great circling arc
> stands directly above Jerusalem,
> And Night, revolving on the other side,
> was rising from the Ganges with the Scales
> that fall from her hand when she grows in might,
> So that, where I was, the rose and white cheeks
> of lovely Aurora were slowly changing
> to a pale orange as she showed her age.
> (*Purg.* II.1–9)

This complex way of saying that the sun was setting in Jerusalem while it was rising at the foot of Mount Purgatory draws explicit attention to time and its passing by forcing the reader to work out the puzzle of the poet's complex temporal allusions. And a similar effect is also achieved through the frequently reiterated references to the position of the sun as it strikes the Dante-character's physical body, casting the shadow that most frequently in this *cantica* gives away his status as a living human being.

And Purgatory must needs exist in time, for without the passing of time it could not function as a temporal and temporary place of punishment, in contrast to the eternal suffering of Hell. In fact, Heaven and Hell are both eternal; they admit of no progression and no change (save, until the Last Judgment, for the addition of new souls), whereas Purgatory is entirely built around the possibility of change, even after death, and the need for spiritual progress in order to be made fit to see God. This spiritual progress, as we have seen, depends wholly on the penitent soul itself, who owns and directs its own reeducation and the realignment of its own love. This means that the souls in Purgatory do not receive a fixed "sentence," the fulfillment of which will buy their freedom; rather, they wait, as Statius explains, for the will to rise to "surprise" them (*Purg.* XXI.63) with their own release. Time, in Purgatory, can be measured passively (as on Earth) in days, weeks, months, and years; waiting time, however, is for the souls an active phenomenon, not a mere ticking-off of days on a calendar but something to be embraced and engaged with as a series of steps, however small, toward an ultimate goal that is worth the wait.

There is one group of souls in Purgatory, however, that does experience the passing of time as a sentence to be endured rather than as a process to be embraced. For the souls in Ante-Purgatory, a waiting area situated on the lowest slopes of the mountain below the gate that marks the entry into Purgatory proper with its healing terraces, time constitutes their only—and sufficient—punishment, and this is appropriate, even under the terms of the *contrapasso*. For these are the souls who delayed repentance in life, some until their very last dying breath: the excommunicated, those who died unexpectedly or violently, the busy, the negligent, the plain lazy. Ante-Purgatory, as its location outside the gate would suggest, is an area separate and distinct from the rest of this realm morally as well as physically. Here no cleansing occurs, but rather a punishment that appears to be as retributive, in intent if not in severity, as any of those inflicted on the souls in Hell.

The souls in Ante-Purgatory, as the character of Belacqua explains, must wait outside Purgatory proper, delaying the undertaking

of their reeducation and cleansing, for as long as they put off repen-
tance in life (*Purg.* IV.130–32) or, in the case of the souls who had
been excommunicated by the Church, such as Manfred, for thirty
times the time that the soul spent outside of the Church's author-
ity (Purg. III.136–40). This waiting serves no useful purpose; it is
accompanied by no edifying exempla and nothing is learned from
it—it is a punishment pure and simple, albeit a singularly appropriate
one. For these souls who delayed their turning to God in repentance
are now themselves delayed in undertaking that journey that will
eventually lead them to Him.

   These souls, who are forced to wait outside the gates powerless to
help themselves, can, however, hope that their prescribed "sentence"
may be shortened by the prayers of the living and specifically, as Be-
lacqua also clarifies, by prayers that come "from a heart in a state of
grace" (*Purg.* IV.134). As we have seen, the belief in the efficacy of
prayer for the dead lies at the heart of the development of the Chris-
tian conception of Purgatory. In Dante, the prayers of the faithful
have the power to speed the progress of souls throughout the second
realm, as is illustrated, for example, by the character of Forese Donati,
a friend of Dante who turned to God late in his life. When Dante
expresses surprise at seeing him already on the terrace of Gluttony a
mere four years after his death, Forese explains that his cleansing has
been expedited by the prayers of his virtuous wife, Nella, who "with
her devoted prayers" has freed him not only from Ante-Purgatory
("the slope where one must wait") but also from the other terraces
of the mountain (*Purg.* XXIII.88–90).

   In Ante-Purgatory, however, the need for prayer becomes all the
more urgent, in accordance with the role of time there as a source of
real psychological torment. Lacking the willing acceptance of suffer-
ing that comes only once the process of cleansing has begun, these
souls jostle desperately for the attention of the Dante-character, this
living man who can take back news of them to their loved ones
and request their prayers and who may even be induced to pray for
them himself. In the memorable metaphor that opens canto VI, for
example, the character is compared to the winner in a game of dice
who finds himself suddenly everyone's best friend, surrounded by
crowds hoping to benefit from his winnings while the loser slips
quietly away unheeded (*Purg.* VI.1–12). The fervor of these souls,

"whose only prayer [is] that others pray/for their speedy progress on to sainthood" (*Purg.* VI.26–27) is clearly reflected in this metaphor, for, in fact, in Purgatory there are no losers and each soul is assured of its eventual place in Heaven; yet time is of such pressing importance here that the souls may even momentarily forget this in their desperation to shorten the time of their waiting.

The Church Penitent

The souls in Purgatory do not only, however, request the prayers of the living; they also pray for themselves, for their loved ones on Earth, and for the world. Indeed, prayers, psalms, and hymns characterize every part of Dante's Purgatory, from the singing of "In exitu Isräel de Aegypto" (Ps. 113; *Purg.* II.46) by the souls newly arrived at the foot of the mountain, to that of "Deus venerunt gentes" (Ps. 78; *Purg.* XXXIII.1) as the traveler prepares to enter the waters of the Eunöe in the *cantica*'s final canto. Unlike the souls' requests for the prayers of the living, these prayers are not aimed at shortening the souls' time in Purgatory but rather seem to function as part of that educative process that we have already highlighted as essential to the moral structure of Dante's second realm. Thus, the souls of the proud pray a version of the Lord's Prayer that seems to have been adapted in order to make it particularly relevant to their vice and its correction:

> Our Father, who art in Heaven,
>   circumscribed only by the greater love
>   Thou hast for Thy primal works on high,
> Praised be Thy name and Thy power
>   by every creature, as is meet and just
>   to render thanks for Thy sweet breath.
> May the peace of Thy kingdom come to us,
>   for we cannot attain it of ourselves
>   if it come not on its own, for all our wit.
>   (*Purg.* XI.1–9)

As they turn toward humility, the souls emphasize in their prayers the greatness of God's love for Creation and the appropriateness of praise as Creation's response to that love and acknowledge the necessarily limited nature of the souls' own capacities to attain Heaven.

Likewise, the souls of the wrathful pray the Agnus Dei, repeating the prayer "for peace and for mercy/from the Lamb of God who takes away our sins" (*Purg.* XVI.17–18) over and over, as they inculcate in themselves the virtue of forbearance. The avaricious pray, "Adhaesit pavimento anima mea" (Ps. 118:25; *Purg.* XIX.73), making their words (my soul hath cleaved to the pavement) echo the posture that constitutes their punishment, a literal reflection of their sin, which turned their souls away from heavenly things in their embrace of earthly ones. Similarly the gluttons chant, "Labia mea domine. . ." (Ps. 50:17; *Purg.* XXIII.11), with the continuation of the verse—". . . aperies, et os meum annuntiabit laudem tuam" (O Lord, thou wilt open my lips: and my mouth shall declare Thy praise)—understood. This reflects the way in which their punishment retrains them to use the organ of their sin (their mouths, which they used to take in excess food and drink) to the praise and glory of God.

Just as in life on Earth Christians gather to praise and worship God and gain in both faith and fellowship by making this a communal activity, so too in Purgatory progress toward God is not undertaken by the souls in isolation from one another but as part of a group—the Church Penitent—joined in a common aim. St Augustine had famously distinguished between the City of God—the souls of the blessed in Heaven, the Church Triumphant—and the City of Man—those iniquitous souls who reject God, whether during their earthly lives or, beyond them, in Hell. He had also, however, acknowledged that before the Last Judgment at any given time a part of the City of God might be living on Earth alongside, but not part of, the City of Man: this he referred to as "the City of God on pilgrimage in this life." Purgatory, since it is not yet Heaven but another stage of the journey toward that celestial home, can be understood as a continuation of that earthly pilgrimage, and there is a great deal of continuity between the Church Militant and the Church Penitent, not least in terms of the ways in which the communal relationship with God finds its outward expression. If the shared experience of a formal liturgy is necessary and useful to the spiritual growth of Christians on Earth, then this is shown here to be true also of the penitent souls in Purgatory as they complete their pilgrimage.

And the prayers of the penitent souls find their response in the blessings pronounced over them, not by priests but by the angelic guardians of Purgatory. The passage from one terrace to the next is marked in each case by the pronunciation of a beatitude appropriate to the sinful tendency being cleansed: "Blessed are the poor in spirit" for the proud (*Purg.* XII.110), "Blessed are the merciful" on the terrace of Envy (*Purg.* XV.38), "Blessed are the peacemakers" for the wrathful (*Purg.* XXII.69), "Blessed are the pure in heart" on the terrace of Lust (Purg. XXVII.8), and so on. This is accompanied by the removal of one of the seven Ps (standing for the seven *peccata*, or sins, cleansed on the mountain) inscribed on the Dante-character's forehead at the moment of his passing into Purgatory proper in canto IX—a moment marked by a formal ritual of penitence that recalls perhaps the marking of penitents' foreheads with the sign of the Cross, as a reminder of sin and of the fragile and temporary status of human life, which takes place on Ash Wednesday. Indeed, it may not be insignificant that the garments of the angel who inscribes the Ps on the character's forehead are described as being the color of ashes (*Purg.* IX.115–16).

Ultimately, these rituals have their purgatorial culmination in the Earthly Paradise, where the metaphor of cleansing that has been present throughout ("See that you wash/all these wounds away," the angel tells the Dante-character) is fully realized and perfected through the process of the souls' washing in the rivers Lethe and Eunoe, which acts as a renewal of the sacrament of baptism. While baptism frees the soul from original sin and inducts it into membership of the Church Militant, immersion in the rivers of the Earthly Paradise marks the soul's complete purity, free from any trace of the stain of its personal sins and vices, and its transition from the Church Penitent to the Church Triumphant. And just as in baptism the soul is symbolically reborn in Christ, so the Dante-character, at the end of the *Purgatorio*, is "as if newly created,/pure and made ready to ascend to the stars" (*Purg.* XXXIII.144–45).

A Model Community: Purgatory and Politics

The time spent in Purgatory (for the Dante-character as much as for the penitent souls themselves) presents itself, then, as an otherworldly reflection of the life of the Church, marked by prayer, song, meditation on the Bible (as well as other worthy *exempla*), ritual, blessing, and sacrament. More specifically, it presents itself as the reflection of a life in which all these things are undertaken *in common* by a community working together toward a shared goal. And this notion of Purgatory as a model community applies, in fact, not only on the religious level but also on the political one. In many ways, it can be argued that Purgatory represents Dante's blueprint for the ideal earthly community: a model of cooperation, of support for one's fellow citizens, of peace, harmony, and progress. This is facilitated, of course, by the many parallels between Purgatory and life on Earth already noted (existence in time, the possibility of development and growth through learning, the temporary nature of the realm from the perspective of eternity, etc.). It also reflects Dante's deep interest, evident throughout the *Commedia*, in human beings in their social context and his growing concern, which reaches a peak of fervor around the time of the writing of the *Purgatorio*, with politics more narrowly understood as the right and proper way in which life on Earth should be governed and led.

In the *Inferno*, Dante's political views, while not being restricted to his own hometown, are focused very explicitly through a Florentine lens. The main "political" episodes of the *cantica* involve Florentine characters and deal either with Florence herself or with cities like it: Lucca, Pisa, Genoa, Pistoia, and so on. In the immediate aftermath of Dante's exile from the city, Florence dominates Dante's thoughts, and his practical experience as a political leader in his hometown governs to a very large extent the way in which he thinks about the life of the community and the way in which he sees this being corrupted in his own time. In the *Purgatorio*, while Florence remains (as it will until the very end of the poem) a subject close to the poet's heart, there is a clear sense that Dante's approach to politics has moved on and substantially expanded its remit.

That the *Purgatorio* will be a text that engages with the political context in which it was written emerges clearly from early in the *cantica*. Still in Ante-Purgatory, Virgil and his protégé meet the soul of Sordello, a Mantuan poet who inquires about the provenance of these newcomers and, on hearing that Virgil is himself from Mantua, leaps up to embrace him, exclaiming: "O Mantuan/I am Sordello, from your country" (*Purg*. VI.73–74). This spontaneous outburst of patriotic feeling, elicited by nothing more than the name of a shared hometown (for Sordello has no idea who Virgil may be at this stage), inspires a lengthy and impassioned invective that sets the tone for the political commentary that will characterize the *Purgatorio* as a whole and lays out clearly Dante's political convictions as they stand toward the end of the first decade of the fourteenth century.

Three main strands of political engagement seem to emerge from the invective. In the first place, we see the conviction that the city-states that have sprung up and come to flourish in northern and central Italy in particular are, without exception, corrupt; indeed, there is not one city among them all that is not at war (*Purg*.VI.82). These conflicts are not only between cities but also within them: "they gnaw at one another even when/enclosed within a single wall and moat" (*Purg*. VI.83–84). As these cities are torn apart by civil wars and factional strife, the reader is reminded by Dante's graphic turn of phrase of Ugolino, who, in Hell, gnaws eternally at the brains of his fellow Pisan Archbishop Ruggieri—a more different embrace from the patriotic one of Virgil and Sordello would be hard to imagine.

The situation described here and in the closing lines of the canto, where the poet's darkly sarcastic attention falls on his own city of Florence, "a sick woman who in vain/tried to find rest upon her feather bed" (*Purg*.VI.149–50), is no different from that hinted at in the *Inferno*, where citizen turns on fellow citizen, city on city, and exile—the fate of Dante himself and perhaps the prompt that led him to reassess both his political views and his literary ambitions—is the alienating sentence ordinarily handed down to detractors and opponents. It is when the poet begins to look more deeply into the causes of such rampant corruption that we see his views begin to take up a new, and more systematic, position. If the cities are corrupt, Dante argues, this is because there is no greater power set above them with the authority to keep their own ambitions in check and to ensure peace among them, and there is, in the poet's view, only one possible candidate for such an overarching authoritative political role: the empire, and specifically an empire that is both holy and Roman.

Dante's views on Rome and on empire are laid out in all their theoretical detail in both book IV of the *Convivio* and in the *Monarchia*. While the *Purgatorio's* treatment of the issue is more poetic and less philosophical, the essence of the view put forward remains consistent across all three works. Fundamentally, a universal world Empire whose ruler, by virtue of already holding *all* possible power and goods, is immune from the promptings of *cupiditas*—that ceaseless and inevitable human desire for more possessions, more might, and more power than one's neighbors—is presented by the poet as the only possible guarantor of peace in Italy and beyond. Such an Empire certainly does not exist at the time of the writing of the *Purgatorio*, for Dante describes it as a horse without a rider, turned untamed and wild, and its putative ruler, Albert of Hapsburg, as "German Albert" (*Purg.*VI.97), the scornful adjective lamenting his patent lack of concern with anything south of the Alps. It has existed in the past, however, as it did at the time of Christ's coming to Earth in human form, when the Son of God submits himself to the census ordered by Augustus and thus registers himself as a Roman citizen, acknowledging Roman authority over him—even unto death. Dante clearly sees the hand of God in the bringing about of the earthly political peace—the biblical *plenitudo temporis*, or "fullness of time" (Gal. 4:4)—that permits the realization of the Incarnation, and not only in the immediate context of the Augustan era: Rome is seen as having been divinely predestined to rule since its earliest beginnings, and the city thus becomes, for Dante, the only possible seat of the world Empire that he dreams of seeing recreated. Albert's "Germanness," in this light, comes to seem all the more serious: it is not only that his limited ambitions prevent the realization of peace among the warring Italian cities but, much more fundamentally, that in neglecting Rome as the rightful seat of Empire he is also neglecting God's will. No wonder, then, that in the invective Rome is implicitly compared to the Jerusalem of Jeremiah: "widowed and alone" (*Purg.*VI.113; and compare Lam. 1:1).

However, if Rome has been abandoned by its Emperor this is not only the fault of Albert's own lack of ambition. For that position of authority that should be his and his alone is occupied by a different power altogether: that of the Church. Dante's feelings about the involvement of the Papacy in political affairs, in Italy and beyond, have already been made patently clear in the *Inferno*, where, in the context of the condemnation of the sin of Simony, the poet attacks those contemporary churchmen who are interested only in the acquisition of personal power and wealth and who, in pursuing these ends, prostitute the Church and betray their office. In the invective of *Purgatorio* VI, these Church leaders are ironically referred to as "people who *should* [but, it is implied, do not] remain devoted" (*Purg.* VI.91; emphasis ours), but a stronger condemnation is found in canto XVI, where Marco the Lombard explains more fully the problem of *cupiditas* and situates this specifically political discussion in the context of the *cantica*'s broader concern with the causes of and remedies for human sinfulness.

Thus Marco sets out the way in which the "simple little soul, which knows nothing/. . ./. . . turns eagerly to whatever delights it," "beguiled" by "trivial goods" that will lead it astray "if it is not guided or its love reined in" (*Purg.* XVI.88–93). Sin and corruption come into the world when *cupiditas* is not "reined in" in this way, and this happens when those institutions that should guide humanity to the correct way are themselves allowed to become corrupt. And corruption, for institutions as much as for individuals—as for the Dante-character in the dark wood with which his poem opens—derives from not following the "straight way" that leads to God. Now, if the empire, in Dante's view, is divinely predestined to be universal, the only seat of political authority over the whole world, then any infringement on that authority on the part of the Church must necessarily lead to corruption.

Dante conceives of the Church and the Empire as equal, but entirely separate, authorities, the one secular and political, the other wholly religious, each functioning within its own sphere to create those conditions that allow the human soul to fulfill the loving potential with which it was created and to turn to God. If the Papacy had argued that the Empire was dependent on the Church for its authority in the same way that the moon depended for its light on the light of the sun, here Marco, polemically, describes the Church and the Empire as "two suns":

Rome, which made the world good, once had two suns,
each illuminating a different road,
the road of the world and the road of God.
One extinguished the other, and the sword
is now joined to the crook, and these two,
forced to go together, can only go bad.
(*Purg.* XVI.106–11)

The extent and seriousness of the corruption that sets in when
"the sword" (the Empire) is joined to "the crook" (the Church) is
illustrated in a no less authoritative place than the Earthly Paradise
itself, in a complex and striking episode that raises as many questions
as it answers but whose fundamental meaning is plain. In the Earthly
Paradise, Dante is reunited with his beloved, Beatrice, who appears at
the head of a chariot, which represents the Church. In canto XXXII
of the *Purgatorio*, the Dante-character is instructed to watch as the
chariot undergoes a series of dramatic attacks and transformations
that represent the traumatic history of the Church from its estab-
lishment to Dante's day. After having survived its early persecutions
from without and the threat of heresies from within, the Church is
attacked by an eagle (the symbol of empire), which represents the
Donation of Constantine, at which moment, as Dante has lamented
in *Inferno* XIX, the Church received "the dowry that first/made a
pope rich" (*Inf.* XIX.116–17). From here on, tainted by the political
power that it has obtained, the chariot starts to become monstrous,
sprouting feathers like those of the eagle that had attacked it and at
length being transformed into a hideous seven-headed, ten-horned
beast like that which emerges from the sea in the book of Revela-
tion (Rv. 13:1).

Finally, there appears upon the chariot a "disheveled whore"
(*Purg.* XXXIII.149) who recalls the apocalyptic Whore of Babylon,
not only in her appearance but also in the way in which she flirts
with a giant (probably representing the French monarchy), just as the
biblical prostitute is described as the one "with whom the kings of
the Earth have committed fornication" (Rv. 17:2), who eventually
conspires with her to drag the chariot away into the woods. There
can be no clearer illustration of how low the Church has sunk in
Dante's eyes, and even if, in the following canto Beatrice prophesies

"a time/safe from all delay and free of obstacles" when a mysterious heavenly messenger "will slay the thievish woman/and the giant who sins alongside her" (*Purg.* XXXIII.41–45), the seriousness of the current situation—a situation akin to that of the biblical "end times"—is portrayed with extraordinary vividness.

Pagan Poetry, Vernacular Poetry, Christian Poetry

The importance of Rome within the political vision expounded by Dante in the *Purgatorio* helps to explain also the continued presence of Virgil as his character's guide through this second realm. While in Hell Virgil is able to speak authoritatively and from experience, even if he does not always have all the answers (see *Inf.* VIII–IX and XXI–XXII), in Purgatory he is in uncharted territory: as he tells the newly arrived souls on the shore of the mountain in canto II, both he and the Dante-character are here "strangers like yourselves" (*Purg.* II.63). In this wholly Christian realm, Virgil does not—and cannot—have all the answers, and his guidance of the traveler is that of a trusted friend rather than a maestro or teacher. However, as the great classical prophet of Rome and, specifically, of the greatness of Augustan Rome, the Rome under whose authority the *plenitudo temporis* was achieved, Virgil clearly remains a key figure for Dante's understanding of history and of the close connections that he perceives between secular and salvation histories.

Virgil's importance, however, is not limited to the historical perspective, for, as we discover, he can be read not only as a prophet of Rome but also of that very Incarnation that the peace achieved under Augustus' rule allowed to occur, and this despite his having been a pagan and despite his own eternal fate among the damned souls in Limbo. On the terrace of Avarice, the Dante-character and his guide encounter a soul who appears to be strangely out of place: the soul of the Latin poet Statius. Statius had died in 96 AD, making it theoretically possible that he would have had the opportunity to hear the "new preachers" (*Purg.* XXI.80) of the Christian faith and to have been converted and baptized (in secret for fear of persecution).

However, it is important to emphasize that there is no trace, either in historical records or in his own writings, of any evidence to suggest that Statius really was a Christian: the story appears to have been entirely invented by Dante for the purposes of his poem. And it quickly becomes clear to the reader that the purpose that Statius serves in the poem is not really about Statius himself at all, but about Virgil. When Statius realizes that the soul guiding this living man through Purgatory is none other than the great Virgil himself, he is so overcome that he momentarily forgets that he is nothing more than an insubstantial soul as he kneels and tries (in vain) to embrace him.

This embrace is not a mere act of poetic homage: Virgil is a poetic maestro for Statius, as he is for Dante, but he is more than this. For just as he guides Dante through the darkness and confusion of Hell and on through the order and growth of Purgatory to the Earthly Paradise, so, we learn, does Virgil guide Statius away from the errors of the pagan world (the only world that Virgil himself could have known) and toward the truths of the Christian faith, through which the way to Purgatory and ultimately Heaven are opened up to him. Statius tells him solemnly, "I was a poet through you, through you a Christian" (*Purg.* XXII.73). More specifically, he tells how Virgil's *Eclogue* IV had served to open his eyes to the truth of this new faith when he read Virgil's prophecy that history would renew itself and that a new age of "Virgin Justice" would be initiated when new progeny would descend from the heavens.

It is not difficult to see how Virgil's poem could have been read by a reader with an awareness, even in outline, of the story of the birth of Christ as a prophecy of the Incarnation: the Virgin, the offspring, the renewal of history, and the new understanding of justice are all present in Virgil's text, and, indeed, the notion that Virgil had been an unknowing prophet of Christianity was a common one in the Middle Ages. Dante here uses a very memorable image to convey this when he compares Virgil to a traveler in the night who carries a lantern behind himself so that, although he himself cannot see, the way of those who follow is illuminated (*Purg.* XXII.67–69).

From Virgil to Statius to Dante, in poetic terms as in moral ones, the *Purgatorio* is a realm of transition, as we witness in this episode something akin to the handing-on of a baton, from the classical poet, inspired perhaps to include Christian truths in his writings but unable himself to benefit from his insights, to the Christian convert, hiding his faith under the veil of poetry on classical themes, and finally to the Christian poet, who can still draw on the great poetry of the past but who uses it only as the foundation for a greater poetic edifice, which, like the mountain of Purgatory itself, stretches up to God. It should come as no surprise, therefore, that poetry, and in particular the way in which poetry can lead the soul either toward or away from God, is one of the most frequently recurring themes of the *Purgatorio*.

This theme emerges in the text as early as the second canto, where, on the shores of Mount Purgatory, the Dante-character and his guide encounter the soul not of a poet but of a musician, Casella, whom Dante had known in life. On being asked to sing for the travelers, Casella begins to sing one of Dante's own poems "Love that converses with me in my mind" (Amor che ne la mente mi ragiona; *Purg.* II.112). No sooner has he begun, however, than Purgatory's guardian, Cato, appears to break up the song's audience and send them on their way up the mountain. It is not, however, that singing is banned in Purgatory, for, as we have seen, it forms an integral part of the purgatorial experience. Indeed, this song, interrupted as soon as it has begun, stands in contrast with the singing of Ps. 113 recounted earlier in the same canto, where we are told that the souls "went on to chant the rest of that psalm" in its entirety. Nor, it seems, is the contrast only between the religious and the secular; rather, the difference appears to lie in the use to which the two songs are put, for while the psalm, with its account of the Exodus, serves as a model for the arduous journey through Purgatory to the "Promised Land" at its summit, Casella's song serves only as a distraction, delaying the souls on their journey to God and turning their minds away from their ultimate goal.

It may also be relevant that the poem that Casella chooses for his song is one of the *canzoni* that Dante had selected for inclusion in the *Convivio*. There, he had interpreted the poem as reflecting his new love of learning, allegorized as a lady, "Lady Philosophy," who has, he claims, comforted him after the death of Beatrice and replaced that earlier love. It seems plausible to assume that it is to this turning-away from his first love and all that she stands for that the poet refers to later in the text, when he has Beatrice herself reproach the character, explaining that "when . . . /I exchanged my life, this man deserted me/and gave himself over to other causes" (*Purg.*

XXX.124–26). If this abandonment of Beatrice is at the root of the sin that led the Dante-character to the dark wood, it is little wonder that a poem exalting this very desertion should find no favor on the threshold of Purgatory.

This reading appears to be confirmed when, on the terrace of Gluttony, the Dante-character meets the soul of Bonagiunta da Lucca, a poet of the previous generation who identifies Dante precisely as the author, not of the *Convivio* or of "Amor che ne la mente. . ." but of "Ladies who have intelligence of love" (Donne ch'avete intelletto d'amore; *Purg.* XXIV.51). This is the *canzone* that marks the turning point of the *Vita Nova*, the moment when the work's protagonist discovers the pure joy that comes from poetry of praise—poetry that is unselfish, asking for nothing more than the freedom to praise its object. "Donne ch'avete . . ." represents the point in the text at which a clear parallel begins to be drawn between the protagonist's love for Beatrice and the Christian love of God, for in both cases the aim of the lover is only to honor, glorify, and worship the beloved—not in the hope of gaining anything in return (as the Dante-character had previously desired to receive Beatrice's greeting) but simply because the beloved deserves to be honored, glorified, and worshipped.

In this poem, where a human woman becomes one of the ways in which God works in the world to refine the poet's understanding of love, Dante anticipates the refocusing of the souls' capacity to love away from secondary ends and onto God that is described in the *Purgatorio*. Yet despite this he rejects Beatrice after her death, allowing his love to be turned away from her and from all that she stands for. Despite having been "so blessed in his youthful life [literally, *vita nova*, "new life" in a clear reference to the earlier work]/ . . . that every sound disposition/would have been marvelously borne out in him" (*Purg.* XXX.115–17), he fails to fulfill his potential and finds himself in a dark wood, forced to start the process of righting his love all over again.

The journey recounted in the *Purgatorio* is, then, also a poetic journey that rewrites the author's poetic biography in reverse, taking him back, on the spiritual level, from "Amor che ne la mente . . ." to "Donna ch'avete . . . ," the starting point from which he had, by 1300, so dramatically fallen away. Yet the poetry of the *Purgatorio* is not retrograde: the intense focus on poets and poetry, especially in the last third of the *cantica*, also illustrates what it is that distinguishes the poetry of the *Commedia* from that of the *Vita Nova*. For in this vast and varied plurilingual text Dante not only draws on the love lyric of his youth (also epitomized by the character of Guido Guinizelli whom he meets in canto XXVI) but also, as we have seen, on the themes and language of the poets of the classical past and on those of the Bible.

He draws on the moral and political verse of Sordello, whose embrace of Virgil inspires his invective, and even on the language of the playful and scurrilous poetic exchanges that he had enjoyed with his friend Forese Donati, encountered on the terrace of Gluttony and still using down-to-earth language to describe the "brazen-faced" and "barbarous" Florentine hussies who "go around bare-breasted, flaunting their nipples" (*Purg.* XXIII.101–3). He peppers his writing with multiple biblical and liturgical phrases in Latin, alongside occasional references to Virgil (Manibus ... date lilia plenis; *Purg.* XXX.20; cf. *Aen.*VI.883), and even has one of his poets, Arnaut Daniel, speak in his Occitan mother tongue (*Purg.* XXVI.140–47). Above all, he corrects and rewrites his own earlier misguided ideas on both love and poetry itself, returning the former to a perfected (because seen now *sub specie aeternitatis*) version of the spiritualized love described in the *Vita Nova* while expanding the latter exponentially to allow it to take onboard all styles, all registers, and all languages in a reflection of the diversity and complexity of God's own Creation.

An Antechamber of Heaven

As we hope to have shown in this brief introduction, Dante's *Purgatorio* is a work that brings together a number of the theological, social, and cultural phenomena that were current in the first decade of the fourteenth century (new ideas about the realm here being described, about penitence and confession, about the best way to govern a city, about the art and poetry of the past and present, about political hopes and apocalyptic fears for the future) and melds them into a single coherent and meaningful text. Taking that part of the Christian afterlife that had been least often described and about which his readers and listeners could be expected to have fewest preconceptions, Dante produces a vision that is clear, consistent, and compelling, giving solidity to what had previously been nebulous, and systematizing what had previously been haphazard. In so doing, he also provides himself with a mouthpiece for some of his own most deeply held beliefs and with a model for a new, more flexible, more ambitious, and more all-encompassing form of poetry.

Above all, the *Purgatorio* is a work governed by hope, for like the citizens of Augustine's "City of God on pilgrimage in this life," every single denizen of Purgatory has her or his true home elsewhere, as the character of Sapìa, a Sienese woman being cleansed of the sin of Envy, makes abundantly clear in her response to the traveler's question as to whether any of the souls being punished on this terrace is Italian:

> O my brother, we are all citizens
>   of the one true city. You mean to ask
>   who lived in Italy while still a pilgrim.
>   (*Purg.* XIII.94–96)

Every single soul to whom we are introduced in Purgatory is *already* a citizen of this "true city," and for every one of them the time spent in Purgatory will ultimately come to an end. For the gate of Purgatory is also the gate of Heaven, and its angel guardian holds its keys directly from St Peter himself (*Purg.* IX.127); this gate having been opened, no soul can turn back, and neither dissent nor transgression is now possible. The people of Purgatory are all "people assured/ . . . of seeing the exalted light/that is the sole object of [their] desire" (*Purg.* XIII.85–87); they are, even in Ante-Purgatory, "spirits who have ended well, spirits already/among the elect" (*Purg.* III.74–75). Purgatory is, certainly, a place of pain and suffering, but it is a place where "the souls . . . are content/to stay in the fire" (*Inf.* I.118–19), where they suffer gladly, accepting their pain as a means to an end and understanding that it can be only temporary, as Purgatory itself, for all its solidity of construction, is, in fact, temporary and provisional.

After the Last Judgment, to which the symbolic and apocalyptic events of the Earthly Paradise look forward, Purgatory, like the Earth on which it stands, will no longer exist. Then, any soul who, at the hour of its death if not sooner, has turned to God in genuine sorrow and repentance will be with God in Paradise, the realm that, having completed his own journey through the cleansing terraces, and having confessed his sins with a truly contrite heart in the Earthly Paradise, the Dante-character will now go on to visit. For the Dante-character, and for Dante's readers, however, Heaven can only really make sense in the light of what has been learned on the journey up the mountain. Perfection, as the reader of the *Paradiso* soon comes to discover, can be difficult and confusing, and to come to it unprepared would be overwhelming. Purgatory ensures that no soul, no traveler, and no reader arrives in Heaven unprepared. Rather, the second realm prepares for the third, not only through the obvious means of ensuring that the souls being prepared to meet God are free from all stain of sin, but also by ensuring that they have learned how to live as members of a community, that they have grasped—and rehearsed—the importance of prayer and worship, and that, perhaps most importantly of all, they have learned how to love God in the same perfect way in which He loves them.

Claire E. Honess and Matthew Treherne
University of Leeds

Translator's Preface

My approach to translating the *Purgatorio* has been substantially the same as that outlined in the Translator's Preface to my translation of the *Inferno*: a close, nearly line-for-line rendering in an American poetic vernacular. I have relied upon Charles Singleton's comprehensive commentary to the *Commedia* as my main guide to the Italian text, especially in resolving the meaning of the many disputed passages. Meaning of course is paramount in translation, but it is matters of style, insofar as style is distinguishable from meaning, that confront the translator with the critical choices that will define his translation as art.

The main stylistic choices I have made in recreating Dante's poem in English may be separated into matters of diction, tone, and verse form. Dante's range of diction and tone in the *Inferno*, rising to outraged and sometimes austere dignity at times but equally at home with hellish obscenities, maps well onto the vernacular of contemporary American speech and poetry. (One reviewer has compared the language of my translation of the *Inferno* to the edgy dialogue in a typical Martin Scorsese film.) Dante's range of diction and rhetorical tone in the *Purgatorio*, while still vernacular, is largely contained in a higher register than in the *Inferno*—we no longer have the colorful speech of the damned, but diatribes of various sorts continue, and Beatrice's memorable tongue-lashing of Dante on the summit of Mount Purgatory is in a register of its own. Throughout the range of his registers Dante himself is a sure guide to the translator who pays close attention to his author's shifts in tone and subtle modulations of style.

The choice of verse form presents its own problems. Dante's signature interlocking triple rhyme scheme throughout the *Commedia*—ABA BCB CDC etc.—can and has been replicated in English with some success, but at the cost of frequent unnatural inversions, archaisms, and loose or padded translation. Rhymed translation is always a difficult fit in translation into English; triple rhyme sustained over thousands of lines (the *Commedia* is 14,233 lines long) is extremely compromising. Another consideration is that English rhyme tends to be on the final syllable, calling attention to itself in a way that rhyme in Italian, which tends to be over the last two syllables and as a natural by-product of grammatical inflection and word suffixes, does not. Hearing Dante recited in Italian, one is aware of but not overpowered by the rhymes. At the same time it would be a mistake to ignore rhyme entirely in a translation that aims to give some sense of the poetics of the original text. I have opted to use rhyme where I think it counts the most: to provide closure to each of the *Commedia*'s one hundred cantos, segueing into rhyme toward the end of each canto and concluding with interlocked final rhymes.

Just as important as rhyme in the dynamics of Dante's verse is the tercet structure and the rhythmic integrity of each line, both of which I work to preserve in translation. Dante's eleven-syllable line tends to have three accentual beats with several relatively un-stressed syllables between each beat and one or more word-ending vowels elided—features that I have incorporated into my verse line, although I have allowed the lines to vary in length from nine to twelve syllables. This is very nearly a line-for-line translation, cer-tainly tercet-for-tercet, matching up as closely as possible with the facing Italian text and its rhetorical and verse structure.

In spite of the fact that in the text of his poem he occasionally addresses the reader, Dante's intended audience included listeners. The poem was composed to be heard as well as read. A tradition of solo performers arose and has continued to this day (Roberto Be-nigni being the latest and perhaps the most famous). I have followed suit, composing my translations of the *Inferno* and the *Purgatorio* for performance and, as far as I could, revising the translation in the light of live readings for audiences with attention at this stage especially to sentence and verse rhythm (a major determinate of tone) and overall poetic force. The translation is addressed to a number of audi-ences: undergraduate students and their instructors, Dante scholars, the general reader, and the community of American poets. I have tried to take into account the interests of all of these constituents.

I am grateful to Claire Honess and Matthew Treherne for the fine Introduction they have provided to the poem and to Ruth Ches-ter for her notes and headnotes to each canto. My thanks also to

Regina Psaki and Claire Honess for reading the translation and making numerous suggestions to improve it. Thanks also to Rebekah Curry for her work in compiling the Index of the Penitent. And my warmest gratitude to Anne Shaw and Dee Johnson for our weekly meetings to read aloud and discuss the Italian text of the *Purgatorio*. Finally, as ever, I am grateful to Brian Rak and the staff at Hackett for seeing this project through. The *Paradiso* awaits.

Note on the Text

The Italian text of the *Purgatorio* substantially accords with Giorgio Petrocchi's critical edition (*La Commedia secondo l'antica vulgata*, Milan: Mondadori, 1966). New conventions for line indentation and verse paragraphing have been adopted.

Abbreviations

Aen.	*Aeneid*	Kgs.	Kings
Apoc.	Apocalypse	Lam.	Lamentations
Cant.	Canticles	Lev.	Leviticus
Conv.	*Convivio*	Lk.	Luke
Cor.	Corinthians	Macc.	Maccabees
Dn.	Daniel	Mk.	Mark
Deut.	Deuteronomy	Matt.	Matthew
DVE	*De vulgari eloquentia*	*Met.*	*Metamorphoses*
Eccl.	Ecclesiastes	*Mon.*	*Monarchia*
Est.	Esther	Num.	Numbers
Ez.	Ezekiel	*Par.*	*Paradiso*
Gal.	Galations	Prov.	Proverbs
Gen.	Genesis	Ps.	Psalms
Hos.	Hosea	*Purg.*	*Purgatorio*
Inf.	*Inferno*	Rv.	Revelation
Is.	Isaiah	Sam.	Samuel
Jdt.	Judith	Sg.	Song of Songs
Jgs.	Judges	*Theb.*	*Thebaid*
Jn.	John	Tim.	Timothy
Jo.	Joshua		

Bibliographical Note[1]

Recommended translations of Dante's minor works are *Dante's Lyric Poetry* (ed. and trans. Kenelm Foster and Patrick Boyde, 2 vols., Oxford University Press, 1967), *Vita nuova* (ed. Dino S. Cervigni and Edward Vasta, University of Notre Dame Press, 1995), *De vulgari eloquentia* (trans. and ed. Steven Botterill, Cambridge University Press, 1996), *Il Convivio* (trans. Richard Lansing, New York: Garland, 1990), and *Monarchia* (trans. and ed. Prue Shaw, Cambridge University Press, 1995). The standard reference work in Italian, usually dubbed "monumental," is the six-volume *Enciclopedia Dantesca* (Roma, Treccani, 1970–1975), whose compilation was directed by Umberto Bosco.

In English, Paget Toynbee's *Dictionary of Proper Names and Notable Matters in the Works of Dante* (1898), revised by Charles S. Singleton (Oxford: Clarendon Press, 1968) is still useful. More recent is the one-volume *Dante Encyclopedia* (New York: Garland Press, 2000), compiled under the general editorship of Richard Lansing. More recently still, medievalist and Dante scholar Christopher Kleinhenz edited the two-volume *Medieval Italy: An Encyclopedia* (New York and London: Routledge, 2004). The authoritative reference work for classical lore is Hubert Cancik and Helmuth Schneider (eds.), *Brill's New Pauly Encyclopedia of the Ancient World*, vols. 1 (A–ARI) through 10 (OBL–PHE) (Leiden and Boston: Brill, 2002–2007).

Exegesis of Dante's *Comedy* got off to an early start soon after the author's death with the commentary on the *Inferno* by his son Jacopo Alighieri and has since continued unabated. Convenient online searchable editions of more than seventy of the major Italian and English commentaries are available through the Dartmouth Dante Project (https://dante.dartmouth.edu/). Italian Dante scholarship privileges readings of single cantos by individual critics. This is the format followed in the periodical *Lectura Dantis: A Forum for Dante Research and Interpretation*, edited by the late Tibor Wlassics, with its

---

1. Adapted from Dante, *Inferno*, translated by Stanley Lombardo, with Introduction by Steven Botterill and Notes by Anthony Oldcorn (Indianapolis and Cambridge: Hackett Publishing Co., 2009).

three one-volume supplements (I: *Inferno* [Spring 1990]; II: *Purgatorio* [1993]; III: *Paradiso* [1995]) as well as in the two published volumes of the University of California Press's *Lectura Dantis* (*Inferno*, 1998; *Purgatorio*, 2008). A very useful topical survey of recent scholarship is Rachel Jacoff (ed.), *The Cambridge Companion to Dante* (2nd ed., Cambridge University Press, 2007). The annual *Dante Studies*, the organ of the American Dante Society, publishes state-of-the-art essays in English on specific cantos and topics.

The Holy Bible is usually cited in the Douay-Rheims 1899 American edition text, translated from Jerome's Latin Vulgate, the version that Dante was familiar with.

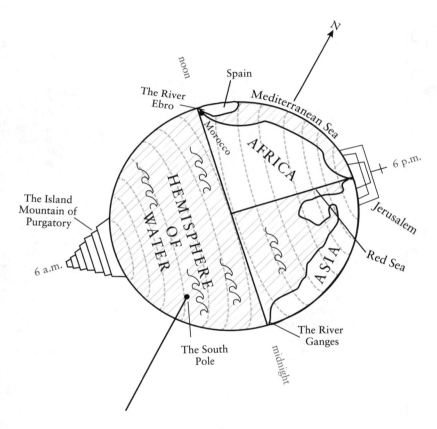

Geography of the *Purgatorio*, with time coordinates as given in canto II, 1–6. Not drawn to scale.

STRUCTURE OF THE PURGATORIO

Location, Landmark, or Means of Purgation	Class of Penitent	Sub-class of Penitent	Representative Penitents	Agents of God	Canto
Ante-Purgatory: The Shores of Mt. Purgatory				Cato	I
			Casella	The Angel-Pilot	II
	The Excommunicated		Manfred		III
The First Fissure in the Rock					IV
Ante-Purgatory: The Open Slope	The Late-Repentant	The Indolent	Belacqua		IV
	The Late-Repentant	Grouped with those who died violently	Jacopo del Cassera		V
			Buonconte del Montefeltro		V
			Pia dei Tolomei		V
			Benincasa da Laterina		VI
			Federico Novello		VI
			Orso degli Albert		VI
			Farinata degli Scornigiani		VI
			Pierre de la Brosse		VI
			Sordello da Goito		VI
Ante-Purgatory: The Valley	The Late-Repentant	The Negligent Princes	Rudolph I of Hapsburg		VII
			Ottokar of Bohemia		VII
			Philip III of France		VII
			Henry I of Navarre		VII
			Peter III of Aragon		VII
			Charles of Anjou		VII
			Alfonso III of Aragon		VII
			James of Aragon		VII
			Frederick of Aragon		VII
			Henry III of England		VII
			William of Montferrat		VII
			Nino Visconti	The Angel-Sentinels	VIII
			Currado Malaspina		VIII
The Gate of Purgatory				St. Lucy/The Angel of the Church	IX

Region	Terrace	Sin	Souls	Angel	Canto
The Second Fissure in the Rock					X
	1st Terrace	The Proud			X
			Omberto Aldobrandesco		XI
			Oderisi da Gubbio		XI
			Provenzan Salvani		XI
				The Angel of Humility	XII
	2nd Terrace	The Envious	Sapia		XIII
			Guido del Duca		XIV
			Rinieri da Calboli		XIV
The Blinding Light					XV
	2nd Terrace			The Angel of Generosity	XV
The Cloud of Darkness					XV
	3rd Terrace	The Wrathful	Marco Lombardo	The Angel of Meekness	XVI
				The Angel of Meekness	XVII
	4th Terrace	The Slothful	The Abbot of San Zeno		XVIII
	4th Terrace/5th Terrace	The Slothful/The Avaricious			
	5th Terrace	The Avaricious	Pope Adrian V	The Angel of Zeal	XIX
	5th Terrace	The Prodigal	Hugh Capet		XX
			Statius		XXI
				The Angel of Liberality	XXII
	6th Terrace	The Gluttonous	Foresi Donati		XXIII
			Bonagiunta of Lucca		XXIV
			Pope Martin IV		XXIV
			Ubaldino dalla Pila		XXIV
			Bonifazio of Ravenna		XXIV
			Marchesi di Forli		XXIV
	6th Terrace/7th Terrace	The Gluttonous/The Lustful	Guido Guinizelli		XXVI
			Arnaut Daniel		XXVI
				The Angel of Chastity	XXVII
The Wall of Flames					

7th Terrace: The Earthly Paradise

Matelda

Beatrice

XXVIII
XXIX
XXX
XXXI

XXXII

XXXIII

The River Lethe

The Tree of the Knowledge of Good and Evil

The River Eunoe

PURGATORIO

Canto I

THE FIRST CANTO OPENS WITH *a promise of the new poetic project to come, followed by an invocation to the classical Muses asking them to help Dante fulfill his aim. Dante and his guide, the Roman poet Virgil, find themselves on the shores that surround the mountain of Purgatory. A detailed description of the cosmos tells us that we are at dawn on Easter day in the year 1300. The travelers encounter an old man, the Roman Cato of Utica, who is the first guardian of this realm. Cato demands to know how the travelers have escaped from Hell, apparently breaking the divine laws. Virgil makes Dante kneel before the old man and explains the pilgrim's divinely instigated journey, describing the intervention of a heavenly lady and their passage through Hell. To attain permission to pass through Purgatory, he calls on Cato's love of freedom, which the pilgrim also seeks,*

Per correr miglior acque alza le vele
omai la navicella del mio ingegno,
3   che lascia dietro a sé mar sì crudele;
e canterò di quel secondo regno
dove l'umano spirito si purga
6   e di salire al ciel diventa degno.
Ma qui la morta poesì resurga,
o sante Muse, poi che vostro sono;
9   e qui Calïopè alquanto surga,
seguitando il mio canto con quel suono
di cui le Piche misere sentiro
12   lo colpo tal, che disperar perdono.

Dolce color d'orïental zaffiro,
che s'accoglieva nel sereno aspetto
15   del mezzo, puro infino al primo giro,
a li occhi miei ricominciò diletto,
tosto ch'io usci' fuor de l'aura morta
18   che m'avea contristati li occhi e 'l petto.

2

and appeals to his love for his wife Marcia. Cato can no longer be moved by love for Marcia, who dwells in Limbo, but agrees to let the travelers pass for the sake of the Lady from Heaven. Cato describes the rushes that grow along the shores of the island mountain of Purgatory and advises Virgil to gird Dante with one and to wash from his face the dirt of Hell. The travelers walk on to a place where the morning dew has not yet evaporated. Virgil dips his hands into it and uses this to wash the pilgrim's face, revealing his natural color. Then, following Cato's instructions, Virgil picks a rush and ties it around the pilgrim's waist. A new plant immediately appears to take its place.

Now the little boat of my native wit
   hoists its sail to run through milder waters,
      leaving behind that sea so merciless.   *3*
I will sing now of the second kingdom,
   the realm where the human soul is cleansed
      and becomes worthy to leap up to the sky.   *6*
Here let poetry rise from the dead,
   O sacred Muses, for I am yours,
      and here let Calliope ascend somewhat higher,   *9*
Accompanying my song with the same strains
   that made the wretched daughters of Pierus
      so feel their guilt that they despaired of pardon.   *12*

The sweet color of oriental sapphire
   that suffused the clear sky at the meridian
      and stayed pure down to the horizon's rim   *15*
Once more filled my eyes with delight
   as soon as I had escaped the dead air
      that had afflicted both my eyes and my heart.   *18*

Lo bel pianeto che d'amar conforta
faceva tutto rider l'orïente,
21   velando i Pesci ch'erano in sua scorta.
I' mi volsi a man destra, e puosi mente
a l'altro polo, e vidi quattro stelle
24   non viste mai fuor ch'a la prima gente.
Goder pareva 'l ciel di lor fiammelle:
oh settentrïonal vedovo sito,
27   poi che privato se' di mirar quelle!

Com' io da loro sguardo fui partito,
un poco me volgendo a l'altro polo,
30   là onde 'l Carro già era sparito,
vidi presso di me un veglio solo,
degno di tanta reverenza in vista,
33   che più non dee a padre alcun figliuolo.
Lunga la barba e di pel bianco mista
portava, a' suoi capelli simigliante,
36   de' quai cadeva al petto doppia lista.
Li raggi de le quattro luci sante
fregiavan sì la sua faccia di lume,
39   ch'i' 'l vedea come 'l sol fosse davante.
"Chi siete voi che contro al cieco fiume
fuggita avete la pregione etterna?"
42   diss' el, movendo quelle oneste piume.
"Chi v'ha guidati, o che vi fu lucerna,
uscendo fuor de la profonda notte
45   che sempre nera fa la valle inferna?
Son le leggi d'abisso così rotte?
o è mutato in ciel novo consiglio,
48   che, dannati, venite a le mie grotte?"
Lo duca mio allor mi diè di piglio,
e con parole e con mani e con cenni
51   reverenti mi fé le gambe e 'l ciglio.
Poscia rispuose lui: "Da me non venni:
donna scese del ciel, per li cui prieghi
54   de la mia compagnia costui sovvenni.

The beautiful planet that urges us to love
  made the whole eastern sky smile, her light
    veiling the Fishes that escorted her. 21
I turned to the right, and setting my mind
  on the other pole, I saw those four stars
    no one since earth's first people had seen. 24
The sky seemed to revel in the brilliance
  of those points of light. O widowed North,
    deprived forever of that glorious sight! 27

Once I had withdrawn my gaze from there
  and turned a little toward the opposite pole,
    where the Wagon's stars had already set, 30
I saw beside me an old man, alone,
  whose looks were so deserving of reverence
    that no son could owe his father more. 33
He had a long beard that was flecked with white,
  and his hair, colored in much the same way,
    fell onto his chest in two flowing strands. 36
The rays of light from those four most holy stars
  shone on his face so beautifully
    that it looked to me as if it basked in the sun. 39
"Who are you to have made your escape
  from the eternal prison and up the dark stream?"
    he said, as he shook his venerable locks. 42
"Who was your guide, or what was the lantern
  that brought you out of the deep midnight
    that shrouds Hell's valley in eternal darkness? 45
Have the laws that govern the Abyss been broken,
  or has a new decree been passed in Heaven,
    that you, the damned, come to my rocky shore?" 48
At this my Master reached out for me
  and by words and gestures and with his hands
    made me bow my head and genuflect. 51
Then he answered him, "I came not on my own.
  A Lady descended from Heaven; at her entreaty
    I offered this man my company and aid. 54

Ma da ch'è tuo voler che più si spieghi
di nostra condizion com' ell' è vera,
57   esser non puote il mio che a te si nieghi.
Questi non vide mai l'ultima sera;
ma per la sua follia le fu sì presso,
60   che molto poco tempo a volger era.
Sì com' io dissi, fui mandato ad esso
per lui campare; e non lì era altra via
63   che questa per la quale i' mi son messo.
Mostrata ho lui tutta la gente ria;
e ora intendo mostrar quelli spirti
66   che purgan sé sotto la tua balìa.
Com' io l'ho tratto, saria lungo a dirti;
de l'alto scende virtù che m'aiuta
69   conducerlo a vederti e a udirti.
Or ti piaccia gradir la sua venuta:
libertà va cercando, ch'è sì cara,
72   come sa chi per lei vita rifiuta.
Tu 'l sai, ché non ti fu per lei amara
in Utica la morte, ove lasciasti
75   la vesta ch'al gran dì sarà sì chiara.
Non son li editti etterni per noi guasti,
ché questi vive e Minòs me non lega;
78   ma son del cerchio ove son li occhi casti
di Marzia tua, che 'n vista ancor ti priega,
o santo petto, che per tua la tegni:
81   per lo suo amore adunque a noi ti piega.
Lasciane andar per li tuoi sette regni;
grazie riporterò di te a lei,
84   se d'esser mentovato là giù degni."

"Marzïa piacque tanto a li occhi miei
mentre ch'i' fu' di là," diss' elli allora,
87   "che quante grazie volse da me, fei.
Or che di là dal mal fiume dimora,
più muover non mi può, per quella legge
90   che fatta fu quando me n'usci' fora.

But if you want a further explanation
  of the true nature of our presence here,
    I cannot very well deny your wish.   *57*
This man has not seen his final sunset,
  although his own madness brought it so close
    that little time remained for him to turn back.   *60*
As I said, I was sent to his aid,
  and there was no other way to rescue him
    than by the very road that I have taken.   *63*
I have shown him all of the damned below
  and now intend to show him those spirits
    who cleanse themselves under your jurisdiction.   *66*
It would take long to tell how I have led him.
  A power from above has assisted me
    in bringing him to see and listen to you.   *69*
May it please you now to welcome his coming:
  he goes in search of liberty, and how dear that is
    one who has given his life for it knows.   *72*
You know it, since you did not find death
  bitter in Utica, where you left behind
    the garment that will shine on that glorious day.   *75*
We have not broken the eternal decrees,
  for he is alive, and Minos does not bind me.
    I am from that circle where your Marcia   *78*
Prays with chaste eyes that you, saintly heart,
  still hold her as yours. By her love for you,
    and yours for her, I implore you,   *81*
Grant us passage through your seven realms.
  I will bring word of your kindness to her,
    if you consent to be mentioned there below."   *84*

"Marcia was so pleasing to my eyes,"
  he said, "when I was alive in the world,
    that whatever she asked of me I did.   *87*
Now that she dwells beyond the evil river
  she no longer has any power to move me,
    as was ordained at my deliverance.   *90*

Ma se donna del ciel ti move e regge,
  come tu di,' non c'è mestier lusinghe:
93   bastisi ben che per lei mi richegge.
Va dunque, e fa che tu costui ricinghe
  d'un giunco schietto e che li lavi 'l viso,
96   sì ch'ogne sucidume quindi stinghe;
ché non si converria, l'occhio sorpriso
  d'alcuna nebbia, andar dinanzi al primo
99   ministro, ch'è di quei di paradiso.
Questa isoletta intorno ad imo ad imo,
  là giù colà dove la batte l'onda,
102   porta di giunchi sovra 'l molle limo:
null' altra pianta che facesse fronda
  o indurasse, vi puote aver vita,
105   però ch'a le percosse non seconda.
Poscia non sia di qua vostra reddita;
  lo sol vi mosterrà, che surge omai,
108   prendere il monte a più lieve salita."

Così sparì; e io sù mi levai
  sanza parlare, e tutto mi ritrassi
111   al duca mio, e li occhi a lui drizzai.
El cominciò: "Figliuol, segui i miei passi:
  volgianci in dietro, ché di qua dichina
114   questa pianura a' suoi termini bassi."

L'alba vinceva l'ora mattutina
  che fuggia innanzi, sì che di lontano
117   conobbi il tremolar de la marina.
Noi andavam per lo solingo piano
  com' om che torna a la perduta strada,
120   che 'nfino ad essa li pare ire in vano.
Quando noi fummo là 've la rugiada
  pugna col sole, per essere in parte
123   dove, ad orezza, poco si dirada,
ambo le mani in su l'erbetta sparte
  soavemente 'l mio maestro pose:
126   ond' io, che fui accorto di sua arte,

But if, as you say, a Lady from Heaven
  directs your actions, there is no need of flattery.
    It is enough that you ask me in her name.   *93*
Go then, and see that you gird this man
  with a smooth reed, and that you wash his face
    so that it is cleansed of all defilement;   *96*
For it would not be fitting for him to go
  with his eyes tainted by any shred of mist
    before the first minister from Paradise.   *99*
At the lowest point of this little island,
  down there where the waves beat on the shore,
    some reeds grow in a patch of soft mud.   *102*
No other plant can take root there
  or become hardy enough to hold on long
    against the battering of those breakers.   *105*
When you have done that, do not return here.
  The sun, which is now beginning to rise,
    will show you an easier ascent up the mountain."   *108*

And with that he vanished. I rose to my feet
  without speaking a word, and drawing myself
    close to my leader, turned my eyes toward him.   *111*
"My son," he began, "follow my steps.
  Let's turn back now. You can see that the plain
    slopes down from here to its lowest edge."   *114*

Dawn was overcoming the twilight hour,
  which fled before it, so that I could make out,
    off in the distance, the trembling sea.   *117*
We picked our way along the lonely plain
  like travelers who have left the road
    and wander lost until they find it again.   *120*
When we came to a place that was shaded
  and fanned by a breeze, and where the morning dew
    still fought the sun and had not evaporated,   *123*
My master gently ran his hands through
  the long grass that grew there, and I,
    understanding what he intended to do,   *126*

porsi ver' lui le guance lagrimose;
  ivi mi fece tutto discoverto
129   quel color che l'inferno mi nascose.

Venimmo poi in sul lito diserto,
  che mai non vide navicar sue acque
132   omo, che di tornar sia poscia esperto.
Quivi mi cinse sì com' altrui piacque:
  oh maraviglia! ché qual elli scelse
135   l'umile pianta, cotal si rinacque
subitamente là onde l'avelse.

Offered my tear-stained cheeks to him;
  and he uncovered all the color in my face
    that the grime of Hell had obliterated.   *129*

Now we came to the deserted shore.
  No man has ever sailed upon that sea
    and then sailed back to where he was before.   *132*
There, as pleased Another, he girded me.
  And then, how marvelous! The humble sprout
    that he selected grew back instantly   *135*
In the very spot where he had plucked it out.

CANTO II

THE CANTO OPENS WITH A *celestial and geographical description of sunrise over Mount Purgatory, which sits at the exact opposite side of the globe from Jerusalem. Dante and Virgil are standing on the shores of the mount deciding where to go when, looking west over the sea, they see a distant white light that grows stronger as it swiftly moves toward them. The light is revealed to be a heavenly winged messenger bringing the souls of those who have been saved to Purgatory. Virgil tells Dante that he will see many such angelic representatives on his journey up Purgatory. The souls sing together Ps. 113, which describes the exodus from Egypt of the Israelites, and as they leave the boat they are marked with the sign of the Cross by the angel. The newly arrived souls, thinking the travelers are*

Già era 'l sole a l'orizzonte giunto
   lo cui meridïan cerchio coverchia
3   Ierusalèm col suo più alto punto;
e la notte, che opposita a lui cerchia,
   uscia di Gange fuor con le Bilance,
6   che le caggion di man quando soverchia;
sì che le bianche e le vermiglie guance,
   là dov' i' era, de la bella Aurora
9   per troppa etate divenivan rance.
Noi eravam lunghesso mare ancora,
   come gente che pensa a suo cammino,
12   che va col cuore e col corpo dimora.
Ed ecco, qual, sorpreso dal mattino,
   per li grossi vapor Marte rosseggia
15   giù nel ponente sovra 'l suol marino,
cotal m'apparve, s'io ancor lo veggia,
   un lume per lo mar venir sì ratto,
18   che 'l muover suo nessun volar pareggia.

familiar with the place, ask for directions only to be corrected by Virgil, who explains that they too are strangers here. On seeing that Dante is still alive and breathing the souls are overcome with wonder. One soul comes forward to embrace Dante, who fruitlessly attempts to return the embrace only to find he is grasping at air. This soul is his friend in life, the singer Casella. Casella explains how he has had to wait at the mouth of the river Tiber to be carried to Purgatory by the angel. Dante then asks him to sing one of his own poems. Casella's singing momentarily enraptures the souls, but almost immediately Cato arrives, berating them for their tardiness in moving toward purgation, and they scatter like doves scared away from their food.

The sun now had reached that horizon
  the zenith of whose great circling arc
    stands directly above Jerusalem,   *3*
And Night, revolving on the other side,
  was rising from the Ganges with the Scales
    that fall from her hand when she grows in might,   *6*
So that, where I was, the rose and white cheeks
  of lovely Aurora were slowly changing
    to a pale orange as she showed her age.   *9*
We were still lingering on the seashore
  like travelers who ponder the road ahead,
    their minds moving but their bodies still,   *12*
When suddenly in the mist a ruddy glow
  hovering above the sea's western rim
    like Mars shining through the morning haze,   *15*
Appeared to me—and may I see it again!—
  rushing over the water so rapidly
    that nothing could match its speed in flight;   *18*

Dal qual com' io un poco ebbi ritratto
l'occhio per domandar lo duca mio,
21   rividil più lucente e maggior fatto.
Poi d'ogne lato ad esso m'appario
un non sapeva che bianco, e di sotto
24   a poco a poco un altro a lui uscìo.

Lo mio maestro ancor non facea motto,
mentre che i primi bianchi apparver ali;
27   allor che ben conobbe il galeotto,
gridò: "Fa, fa che le ginocchia cali.
Ecco l'angel di Dio: piega le mani;
30   omai vedrai di sì fatti officiali.
Vedi che sdegna li argomenti umani,
sì che remo non vuol, né altro velo
33   che l'ali sue, tra liti sì lontani.
Vedi come l'ha dritte verso 'l cielo,
trattando l'aere con l'etterne penne,
36   che non si mutan come mortal pelo."
Poi, come più e più verso noi venne
l'uccel divino, più chiaro appariva:
39   per che l'occhio da presso nol sostenne,
ma chinail giuso; e quei sen venne a riva
con un vasello snelletto e leggero,
42   anto che l'acqua nulla ne 'nghiottiva.
Da poppa stava il celestial nocchiero,
tal che faria beato pur descripto;
45   e più di cento spirti entro sediero.
'*In exitu Isräel de Aegypto*'
cantavan tutti insieme ad una voce
48   con quanto di quel salmo è poscia scripto.
Poi fece il segno lor di santa croce;
ond' ei si gittar tutti in su la piaggia:
51   ed el sen gì, come venne, veloce.

La turba che rimase lì, selvaggia
parea del loco, rimirando intorno
54   come colui che nove cose assaggia.

And when I looked again, after turning away
   for just a moment to question my Guide,
     it was larger and brighter than before.   *21*
Then on either side of it there appeared
   something white—I couldn't say just what—
     and little by little some more white below.   *24*

All this while my Master spoke not a word,
   but when the first white spots proved to be wings
     and he recognized the pilot for what he was,   *27*
He cried, "Down on your knees! Behold
   the Angel of the Lord: fold your hands!
     From now on you will see ministers like this.   *30*
See how he scorns all human devices
   and will use no oar between shores so distant,
     nor spread any sail except his own wings.   *33*
See how he holds them straight toward Heaven
   and fans the air with eternal feathers
     that do not change like merely mortal plumage."   *36*
The radiance of that heavenly bird
   increased so much as it drew closer and closer
     that my eyes could no longer sustain its splendor,   *39*
And I lowered my gaze as it came to shore
   with a vessel that was so swift and light
     that its keel hardly drew any water at all.   *42*
The celestial pilot who stood on the stern
   would make one blissful just to hear him described.
     More than a hundred souls were on board.   *45*
"*In exitu Israël de Aegypto,*"
   they were singing as if with one voice
     and went on to chant the rest of that psalm.   *48*
The angel blessed them with the Sign of the Cross,
   at which they jumped down onto the beach, and he
     departed as swiftly as he had arrived.   *51*

The crowd that remained there looked around
   the way strangers do when in a new place,
     sizing up all the unfamiliar things there.   *54*

Da tutte parti saettava il giorno
lo sol, ch'avea con le saette conte
57   di mezzo 'l ciel cacciato Capricorno,
quando la nova gente alzò la fronte
ver' noi, dicendo a noi: "Se voi sapete,
60   mostratene la via di gire al monte."
E Virgilio rispuose: "Voi credete
forse che siamo esperti d'esto loco;
63   ma noi siam peregrin come voi siete.
Dianzi venimmo, innanzi a voi un poco,
per altra via, che fu sì aspra e forte,
66   che lo salire omai ne parrà gioco."
L'anime, che si fuor di me accorte,
per lo spirare, ch'i' era ancor vivo,
69   maravigliando diventaro smorte.
E come a messagger che porta ulivo
tragge la gente per udir novelle,
72   e di calcar nessun si mostra schivo,
così al viso mio s'affisar quelle
anime fortunate tutte quante,
75   quasi oblïando d'ire a farsi belle.

Io vidi una di lor trarresi avante
per abbracciarmi con sì grande affetto,
78   che mosse me a far lo somigliante.
Ohi ombre vane, fuor che ne l'aspetto!
tre volte dietro a lei le mani avvinsi,
81   e tante mi tornai con esse al petto.
Di maraviglia, credo, mi dipinsi;
per che l'ombra sorrise e si ritrasse,
84   e io, seguendo lei, oltre mi pinsi.
Soavemente disse ch'io posasse;
allor conobbi chi era, e pregai
87   che, per parlarmi, un poco s'arrestasse.
Rispuosemi: "Così com' io t'amai
nel mortal corpo, così t'amo sciolta:
90   però m'arresto; ma tu perché vai?"

The Sun's arrows had driven Capricorn
  from the sky's meridian and with his sure rays
    was shooting the world full with the light of day   *57*
When the new arrivals raised their faces
  toward the two of us and said, "If you know,
    show us the way to go up the mountain."   *60*
And Virgil answered, "Perhaps you believe
  that we are familiar with this place,
    but we are pilgrims here like yourselves.   *63*
We arrived just now, not long before you,
  by another road, one so rough and harsh
    that the climb now will seem like play to us."   *66*
When these spirits became fully aware,
  by the breaths I drew, that I was still alive,
    all at once they turned pale with wonder.   *69*
And as people crowd around to hear the news
  from a messenger who bears an olive branch,
    heedless of how they trample each other,   *72*
So all of these souls, souls of good fortune,
  kept their eyes fixed on my face, as if they had
    forgotten they were going to make themselves fair.   *75*

One of them I saw coming forward
  to embrace me, and with such affection
    that I was moved to do the same to him.   *78*
Oh empty shades, in all but appearance!
  Three times I clasped my hands behind him,
    and each time I drew them back onto my chest.   *81*
I think my wonder must have shown on my face.
  The shade smiled at this and took a step back
    as I pressed forward to follow him.   *84*
Speaking gently he said I should stop,
  and it was then I knew him, and I asked
    if he would stay a while and talk with me.   *87*
"Just as I loved you in my mortal flesh,
  So do I now," he said, "freed from it at last,
    so I will stay a while. But you, why this journey?"   *90*

"Casella mio, per tornar altra volta
là dov' io son, fo io questo vïaggio,"
93   diss' io; "ma a te com' è tanta ora tolta?"
Ed elli a me: "Nessun m'è fatto oltraggio,
se quei che leva quando e cui li piace,
96   più volte m'ha negato esto passaggio;
ché di giusto voler lo suo si face:
veramente da tre mesi elli ha tolto
99   chi ha voluto intrar, con tutta pace.
Ond' io, ch'era ora a la marina vòlto
dove l'acqua di Tevero s'insala,
102   benignamente fu' da lui ricolto.
A quella foce ha elli or dritta l'ala,
però che sempre quivi si ricoglie
105   qual verso Acheronte non si cala."

E io: "Se nuova legge non ti toglie
memoria o uso a l'amoroso canto
108   che mi solea quetar tutte mie doglie,
di ciò ti piaccia consolare alquanto
l'anima mia, che, con la sua persona
111   venendo qui, è affannata tanto!"
'*Amor che ne la mente mi ragiona*'
cominciò elli allor sì dolcemente,
114   che la dolcezza ancor dentro mi suona.
Lo mio maestro e io e quella gente
ch'eran con lui parevan sì contenti,
117   come a nessun toccasse altro la mente.
Noi eravam tutti fissi e attenti
a le sue note; ed ecco il veglio onesto
120   gridando: "Che è ciò, spiriti lenti?
qual negligenza, quale stare è questo?
Correte al monte a spogliarvi lo scoglio
123   ch'esser non lascia a voi Dio manifesto."

Come quando, cogliendo biado o loglio,
li colombi adunati a la pastura,
126   queti, sanza mostrar l'usato orgoglio,

"Casella," I said, "I make this journey
   to return again to where I am now.
      But why did it take you so long to get here?"   *93*
And he replied, "I have not been wronged
   if he who takes aboard whom he will and when
      has many times denied me passage,   *96*
For his will is formed by a will that is just.
   Truly, for three months he has accepted,
      without objection, all who wanted to board.   *99*
In due time I came back to the shore
   where the Tiber's waters first become salt,
      and there in mercy he gathered me in.   *102*
To that river mouth he now sets his wings,
   for that is where the souls assemble
      who do not sink down to Acheron."   *105*

Then I said, "If a new law does not take from you
   your memory or practice of the songs of love
      that used to soothe all of my sorrows,   *108*
Please console my soul with one now,
   for it is all out of breath along with my body,
      weary and spent from journeying here."   *111*
"Love that converses with me in my mind,"
   he then began, singing so sweetly
      that the sweetness resounds within me still.   *114*
My master and I and all the people
   there with Casella seemed as content
      as if nothing touched our minds but that song.   *117*
We were all enthralled, completely intent
   on his melody, when the venerable old man
      appeared and cried, "What's this, lazy spirits?   *120*
What negligence is this, what indolence?
   Run to the mountain, and there shed the burden
      that keeps God from showing Himself to you!"   *123*

Doves, when they flock to feed on a plain,
   will peck at grains of wheat or at tares,
      without their usual display of disdain,   *126*

se cosa appare ond' elli abbian paura,
    subitamente lasciano star l'esca,
129   perch' assaliti son da maggior cura;
così vid' io quella masnada fresca
    lasciar lo canto, e fuggir ver' la costa,
132   com' om che va, né sa dove rïesca;
né la nostra partita fu men tosta.

But when something that frightens them appears
  they will all at once forget their food,
    suddenly assailed by greater cares.   *129*
So did I see this new band of souls go,
  song forgotten as toward the mountain they fled
    like travelers on a road that they do not know;   *132*
And with no less haste we went where they led.

CANTO III

CATO'S ADMONITION AT THE CLOSE *of the preceding canto has driven the souls on toward the mountain. The poet Dante praises his faithful companion Virgil at the opening of a canto that significantly explores the developing roles of the two characters. Virgil is filled with remorse for having allowed Dante to waylay his journey and the two hurry toward the mountain. Dante gazes up to the mountain's heights as the rising sun casts his own shadow before him. On seeing only one shadow on the ground, Dante is afraid, fearing that Virgil has abandoned him. The ever-present Virgil reassures him, explaining that as a bodiless soul he has no shadow to cast and that the mystery of his nature is forever hidden from human understanding. On approaching the mountain they see that*

Avvegna che la subitana fuga
　　dispergesse color per la campagna,
3　　　　rivolti al monte ove ragion ne fruga,
i' mi ristrinsi a la fida compagna:
　　e come sare' io sanza lui corso?
6　　　　chi m'avria tratto su per la montagna?
El mi parea da sé stesso rimorso:
　　o dignitosa coscïenza e netta,
9　　　　come t'è picciol fallo amaro morso!
Quando li piedi suoi lasciar la fretta,
　　che l'onestade ad ogn' atto dismaga,
12　　　　la mente mia, che prima era ristretta,
lo 'ntento rallargò, sì come vaga,
　　e diedi 'l viso mio incontr' al poggio
15　　　　che 'nverso 'l ciel più alto si dislaga.

Lo sol, che dietro fiammeggiava roggio,
　　rotto m'era dinanzi a la figura,
18　　　　ch'avëa in me de' suoi raggi l'appoggio.

its sides are rough and impossible to climb; Virgil is unsure of the way to ascend. Dante sees a group of souls in the distance who turn out to be the souls of those who were excommunicated by the Church. The souls, seeing Dante's shadow, are amazed and hesitant. After reassurance from Virgil they show the travelers the way up. One soul comes forward to speak to the travelers. This is the soul of Manfred, who describes his death in battle, excommunicated. Because he retained his faith and hope in God, however, he is saved but must spend thirty times the time he spent outside of the Church's jurisdiction waiting outside Purgatory proper, unless this time is shortened by the prayers of the faithful on Earth.

Their sudden flight had scattered the crowd
   across the plain and toward the mountain
      where Justice sifts and searches our souls,   *3*
And I drew close to my faithful companion.
   How could I have ever gone on without him?
      And who would have drawn me up the mountain?   *6*
He seemed to me bitten with self-reproach.
   O noble conscience, so pure and worthy
      that the slightest fault brings bitter remorse!   *9*
When he had eased off from the hurried pace
   that robs every act of its dignity,
      my mind, that at first had been held in check,   *12*
Ranged farther now and broadened its scope.
   I directed my gaze toward that hill most high
      that rises from the sea up toward the heavens.   *15*

The sun, a flame-red ball at my back,
   had its light cut off on the ground before me
      by the shadow that my own body cast.   *18*

Io mi volsi dallato con paura
    d'essere abbandonato, quand' io vidi
21   solo dinanzi a me la terra oscura;

e 'l mio conforto: "Perché pur diffidi?"
    a dir mi cominciò tutto rivolto;
24   "non credi tu me teco e ch'io ti guidi?
Vespero è già colà dov' è sepolto
    lo corpo dentro al quale io facea ombra;
27   Napoli l'ha, e da Brandizio è tolto.
Ora, se innanzi a me nulla s'aombra,
    non ti maravigliar più che d'i cieli
30   che l'uno a l'altro raggio non ingombra.
A sofferir tormenti, caldi e geli
    simili corpi la Virtù dispone
33   che, come fa, non vuol ch'a noi si sveli.
Matto è chi spera che nostra ragione
    possa trascorrer la infinita via
36   che tiene una sustanza in tre persone.
State contenti, umana gente, al *quia*;
    ché, se potuto aveste veder tutto,
39   mestier non era parturir Maria;
e disïar vedeste sanza frutto
    tai che sarebbe lor disio quetato,
42   ch'etternalmente è dato lor per lutto:
io dico d'Aristotile e di Plato
    e di molt' altri"; e qui chinò la fronte,
45   e più non disse, e rimase turbato.

Noi divenimmo intanto a piè del monte;
    quivi trovammo la roccia sì erta,
48   che 'ndarno vi sarien le gambe pronte.
Tra Lerice e Turbìa la più diserta,
    la più rotta ruina è una scala,
51   verso di quella, agevole e aperta.
"Or chi sa da qual man la costa cala,"
    disse 'l maestro mio fermando 'l passo,
54   "sì che possa salir chi va sanz' ala?"

Seeing that the ground was darkened
  by my shadow only, I turned to my side
    with sudden fear that I had been abandoned.   *21*

Then Virgil, my solace, turned to me and said,
  "Why are you so distrustful? Don't you believe
    that I am by your side, still guiding you?   *24*
It is evening now in the place where the body
  that once cast my shadow is dead and buried.
    Taken from Brindisi, it lies in Naples.   *27*
If I cast no shadow now, do not wonder at that
  any more than that the heavenly spheres
    do not obstruct one another's rays.   *30*
The Power that disposes bodies like ours
  to suffer torments, heat and cold, wills not
    that how He does so be revealed to us.   *33*
Foolish is he who hopes that our reason
  can ever encompass the infinite path
    that One Substance in Three Persons takes.   *36*
Then be content, humankind, with the *quia*,
  for if you were able to see all for yourself,
    Mary would not have needed to give birth;   *39*
And you have seen the futile desire of some
  whose longing that their desire be fulfilled
    has been the cause of their eternal grief.   *42*
I speak of Aristotle and of Plato
  and of many others." Here he bent his head
    and said no more in his troubled state.   *45*

Now we had come to the foot of the mountain,
  where we found an escarpment that was so steep
    the nimblest legs would have been of no use.   *48*
The roughest and most desolate landslide
  between Lerici and Turbia would seem
    a wide, easy stairway by comparison.   *51*
"Now who would know where the slope is less steep,"
  my master said, as he came to a halt,
    "so that someone without wings might ascend?"   *54*

E mentre ch'e' tenendo 'l viso basso
essaminava del cammin la mente,
57   e io mirava suso intorno al sasso,
da man sinistra m'apparì una gente
d'anime, che movieno i piè ver' noi,
60   e non pareva, sì venïan lente.

"Leva," diss' io, "maestro, li occhi tuoi:
ecco di qua chi ne darà consiglio,
63   se tu da te medesmo aver nol puoi."
Guardò allora, e con libero piglio
rispuose: "Andiamo in là, ch'ei vegnon piano;
66   e tu ferma la spene, dolce figlio."
Ancora era quel popol di lontano,
i' dico dopo i nostri mille passi,
69   quanto un buon gittator trarria con mano,
quando si strinser tutti ai duri massi
de l'alta ripa, e stetter fermi e stretti
72   com' a guardar, chi va dubbiando, stassi.

"O ben finiti, o già spiriti eletti,"
Virgilio incominciò, "per quella pace
75   ch'i' credo che per voi tutti s'aspetti,
ditene dove la montagna giace,
sì che possibil sia l'andare in suso;
78   ché perder tempo a chi più sa più spiace."
Come le pecorelle escon del chiuso
a una, a due, a tre, e l'altre stanno
81   timidette atterrando l'occhio e 'l muso;
e ciò che fa la prima, e l'altre fanno,
addossandosi a lei, s'ella s'arresta,
84   semplici e quete, e lo 'mperché non sanno;
sì vid' io muovere a venir la testa
di quella mandra fortunata allotta,
87   pudica in faccia e ne l'andare onesta.
Come color dinanzi vider rotta
la luce in terra dal mio destro canto,
90   sì che l'ombra era da me a la grotta,

While he stood there with his eyes cast down,
  searching his mind to find a way ahead,
    and I was looking up scanning the rocks,   *57*
There appeared on my left a troop of souls
  moving their feet in our direction,
    yet seeming not to, so slowly did they come.   *60*

"Lift your eyes, master," I said. "Look over there!
  Some souls are coming who can give us guidance,
    if you can't discover any within yourself."   *63*
He looked up then, and with an air of relief
  replied, "Let us go there, for they are coming slowly,
    and you, dear son, hold on to that hope."   *66*
Those souls were still as far—and I mean after
  we had gone toward them a thousand paces—
    as a skilled thrower could hurl a stone,   *69*
When they all pressed up against the hard rock
  of the sheer cliff face and stood together there,
    as men who are in doubt will stop and look.   *72*

"Spirits who have ended well, spirits already
  among the elect," Virgil began, "by that peace
    which I believe awaits all of you,   *75*
Tell us where the mountain slopes down
  and can be ascended, for time lost
    is most irkful to him who knows the most."   *78*
As sheep come forth from an enclosure
  by ones, twos, or threes, and the rest stand timid
    with their eyes and muzzles turned to the ground,   *81*
And what the first one does, the others do too,
  huddling behind it if it should stop,
    simple and quiet, without knowing why,   *84*
So I saw then that happy flock's leader
  move to come forward, his expression modest,
    and dignified in all of his movements.   *87*
When those in front saw the light broken
  on my right side, so that my shadow
    ran from my feet right up to the cliff,   *90*

restaro, e trasser sé in dietro alquanto,
e tutti li altri che venieno appresso,
93   non sappiendo 'l perché, fenno altrettanto.
"Sanza vostra domanda io vi confesso
che questo è corpo uman che voi vedete;
96   per che 'l lume del sole in terra è fesso.
Non vi maravigliate, ma credete
che non sanza virtù che da ciel vegna
99   cerchi di soverchiar questa parete."
Così 'l maestro; e quella gente degna
"Tornate," disse, "intrate innanzi dunque,"
102   coi dossi de le man faccendo insegna.

E un di loro incominciò: "Chiunque
tu se,' così andando, volgi 'l viso:
105   pon mente se di là mi vedesti unque."
Io mi volsi ver' lui e guardail fiso:
biondo era e bello e di gentile aspetto,
108   ma l'un de' cigli un colpo avea diviso.
Quand' io mi fui umilmente disdetto
d'averlo visto mai, el disse: "Or vedi";
111   e mostrommi una piaga a sommo 'l petto.
Poi sorridendo disse: "Io son Manfredi,
nepote di Costanza imperadrice;
114   ond' io ti priego che, quando tu riedi,
vadi a mia bella figlia, genitrice
de l'onor di Cicilia e d'Aragona,
117   e dichi 'l vero a lei, s'altro si dice.
Poscia ch'io ebbi rotta la persona
di due punte mortali, io mi rendei,
120   piangendo, a quei che volontier perdona.
Orribil furon li peccati miei;
ma la bontà infinita ha sì gran braccia,
123   che prende ciò che si rivolge a lei.
Se 'l pastor di Cosenza, che a la caccia
di me fu messo per Clemente allora,
126   avesse in Dio ben letta questa faccia,

They came to a halt and backed up a little,
  and all of the others following behind
    did the same thing, without knowing why.   *93*
"Without your asking I confess to you
  that what you see is a human body
    cutting off the sunlight that falls on the ground.   *96*
Do not marvel at this, but do believe
  that it is not without power from heaven
    that this man attempts to surmount this wall."   *99*
Thus my master. And that worthy folk said,
  "Turn around then and go on before us,"
    gesturing with the backs of their hands.   *102*

Then one of them began, "And as you go,
  whoever you are, turn your head around
    and consider if you ever saw me back there."   *105*
I turned around and fixed my eyes on him.
  He was handsome and blond, his face noble,
    but a blow had cloven one of his eyebrows.   *108*
When I humbly denied that I had ever
  seen him before, he said, "Look now,"
    and showed me a wound at the top of his chest,   *111*
Smiling the while. "I am Manfred," he said,
  "grandson of the Empress Constance,
    and so I beg of you, when you return,   *114*
To go to my beautiful daughter, mother
  of Sicily's pride and of Aragon's,
    and tell her the truth, to offset any lies.   *117*
After I had my body pierced twice
  with mortal wounds, I delivered myself,
    weeping, to Him who willingly forgives.   *120*
My sins were horrible, but the embrace
  of the Infinite Goodness is so wide
    that it receives all who turn toward it.   *123*
If the bishop of Cosenza, who was sent
  by Pope Clement to hunt me down,
    had rightly read this aspect of God,   *126*

l'ossa del corpo mio sarieno ancora
in co del ponte presso a Benevento,
129   sotto la guardia de la grave mora.
Or le bagna la pioggia e move il vento
di fuor dal regno, quasi lungo 'l Verde,
132   dov' e' le trasmutò a lume spento.
Per lor maladizion sì non si perde,
che non possa tornar, l'etterno amore,
135   mentre che la speranza ha fior del verde.
Vero è che quale in contumacia more
di Santa Chiesa, ancor ch'al fin si penta,
138   star li convien da questa ripa in fore,
per ognun tempo ch'elli è stato, trenta,
in sua presunzïon, se tal decreto
141   più corto per buon prieghi non diventa.
Vedi oggimai se tu mi puoi far lieto,
revelando a la mia buona Costanza
144   come m'hai visto, e anco esto divieto;
ché qui per quei di là molto s'avanza."

Then the bones of my body still would lie
  near the head of Benevento's bridge
    under the guard of those heavy stones.   *129*
Now they are beaten by the wind and rain,
  beyond Naples' kingdom, along the Verde,
    where he moved them with candles snuffed out.   *132*
No one is so lost by their malediction
  that Love Eternal cannot return,
    as long as hope still flourishes green.   *135*
Still, whoever dies excommunicated
  from the Holy Church, even if he repents
    at the end of his life, must stay outside   *138*
Upon this bank for thirty times the space
  he lived in presumption, unless this sentence
    is shortened by the prayers of those in grace.   *141*
See now if you can gladden my heart
  by reporting to my good Constance where
    you have seen me and how I am kept apart.   *144*
For much is gained here through those back there."

CANTO IV

THE CANTO OPENS WITH A *description of the concentration that the pilgrim felt in listening to Manfred, whom he encountered at the end of canto III. Dante uses an idea of the unitary soul drawn from Aristotle's philosophy to describe the experience. During this conversation, the travelers have continued walking and have now come to a place where they can begin to ascend the mountain. Passing through a tiny fissure in the rock, Dante and Virgil begin the difficult climb using their feet and hands, empowered to do so only by the desire that spurs them on. Dante bemoans the difficulty of the climb, and Virgil encourages him onward to reach a ledge on the side of the mountain, where the pair sits down to rest. The pilgrim is surprised to see the sun high in the north, until Virgil reminds him, using an extended*

Quando per dilettanze o ver per doglie,
   che alcuna virtù nostra comprenda,
3   l'anima bene ad essa si raccoglie,
par ch'a nulla potenza più intenda;
   e questo è contra quello error che crede
6   ch'un'anima sovr' altra in noi s'accenda.
E però, quando s'ode cosa o vede
   che tegna forte a sé l'anima volta,
9   vassene 'l tempo e l'uom non se n'avvede;
ch'altra potenza è quella che l'ascolta,
   e altra è quella c'ha l'anima intera:
12   questa è quasi legata e quella è sciolta.
Di ciò ebb' io esperïenza vera,
   udendo quello spirto e ammirando;
15   ché ben cinquanta gradi salito era
lo sole, e io non m'era accorto, quando
   venimmo ove quell' anime ad una
18   gridaro a noi: "Qui è vostro dimando."

cosmological and geographical description, that they are now in the Southern Hemisphere. Dante inquires how much farther they have to ascend, and Virgil explains that the rule of the mountain means that the higher they climb, the easier the ascent becomes. Their conversation is interrupted at this point by the sarcastic and lethargic Belacqua, who, with his fellow late-repentant souls, sits in the shadow of a rock. He explains that, for their negligence in turning to God in life, the souls must wait outside Purgatory proper for the equivalent length of their life on Earth. This wait can be shortened, however, by the prayers of those still alive and in a state of grace. The canto concludes with Virgil spurring the pilgrim on to continue the climb as night descends.

Whenever one of our senses receives
  an impression of pleasure or of pain,
    it collects the attention of our entire soul,   3
Which seems to neglect its other powers;
  (and this argues against the erroneous view
    that soul upon soul is kindled within us).   6
And so, when anything either seen or heard
  bends the soul toward it and holds it fast,
    time goes by without our being aware,   9
For there is one faculty that notices time
  and another one possessing the soul,
    the latter locked in, the former disengaged.   12
I had a strong experience of just this kind
  as I listened to that spirit in wonder,
    for the sun had climbed a full fifty degrees   15
And I had not noticed, when we all arrived
  at a place where those souls cried out to us
    as if with one voice: "Here is what you seek."   18

Maggiore aperta molte volte impruna
  con una forcatella di sue spine
21   l'uom de la villa quando l'uva imbruna,
che non era la calla onde salìne
  lo duca mio, e io appresso, soli,
24   come da noi la schiera si partìne.

Vassi in Sanleo e discendesi in Noli,
  montasi su in Bismantova e 'n Cacume
27   con esso i piè; ma qui convien ch'om voli;
dico con l'ale snelle e con le piume
  del gran disio, di retro a quel condotto
30   che speranza mi dava e facea lume.
Noi salavam per entro 'l sasso rotto,
  e d'ogne lato ne stringea lo stremo,
33   e piedi e man volea il suol di sotto.
Poi che noi fummo in su l'orlo suppremo
  de l'alta ripa, a la scoperta piaggia,
36   "Maestro mio," diss' io, "che via faremo?"
Ed elli a me: "Nessun tuo passo caggia;
  pur su al monte dietro a me acquista,
39   fin che n'appaia alcuna scorta saggia."
Lo sommo er' alto che vincea la vista,
  e la costa superba più assai
42   che da mezzo quadrante a centro lista.
Io era lasso, quando cominciai:
  "O dolce padre, volgiti, e rimira
45   com' io rimango sol, se non restai."
"Figliuol mio," disse, "infin quivi ti tira,"
  additandomi un balzo poco in sùe
48   che da quel lato il poggio tutto gira.

Sì mi spronaron le parole sue,
  ch'i' mi sforzai carpando appresso lui,
51   tanto che 'l cinghio sotto i piè mi fue.
A seder ci ponemmo ivi ambedui
  vòlti a levante ond' eravam saliti,
54   che suole a riguardar giovare altrui.

A farmer thrusting a forkful of thorns
  into a hedge, when grapes are darkening,
    might very well plug a larger hole   *21*
Than the gap that my leader now climbed through,
  with me right behind him, he and I alone,
    when that troop had taken its leave of us.   *24*

You can climb up to San Leo and down to Noli,
  you can reach the summit of Bismontova,
    all on foot; but here a man must fly—   *27*
On the swift wings and plumes, I mean to say,
  of great desire, as I behind that leader
    who gave me hope and was a light to me.   *30*
We were climbing within a rocky cleft
  that pressed in close to us on every side,
    and the ground required both hands and feet.   *33*
When we reached the fissure's upper edge
  and were out on the open slope again,
    "Master," I asked, "what road shall we take?"   *36*
And he answered, "Don't fall back a single step,
  Just keep climbing this mountain right behind me,
    until some knowledgeable guide appears."   *39*
The summit was so high it was out of sight,
  and the slope was steeper than a line drawn
    from a circle's mid-quadrant up to its center.   *42*
I was exhausted, and ventured to say,
  "Dear, sweet father, turn around and see
    how I'll be left behind unless you pause."   *45*
"My son," he said, "drag yourself up there,"
  pointing to a ledge a little higher
    that went on to circle the entire hill.   *48*

His words spurred me on to such an extent
  that I forced myself to clamber up behind him
    until that ledge was firmly under my feet.   *51*
There the two of us sat down to rest,
  facing the east, from where we had climbed,
    for it is pleasing to see how far one has come.   *54*

Li occhi prima drizzai ai bassi liti;
poscia li alzai al sole, e ammirava
57   che da sinistra n'eravam feriti.
Ben s'avvide il poeta ch'ïo stava
stupido tutto al carro de la luce,
60   ove tra noi e Aquilone intrava.
Ond' elli a me: "Se Castore e Poluce
fossero in compagnia di quello specchio
63   che sù e giù del suo lume conduce,
tu vedresti il Zodïaco rubecchio
ancora a l'Orse più stretto rotare,
66   se non uscisse fuor del cammin vecchio.
Come ciò sia, se 'l vuoi poter pensare,
dentro raccolto, imagina Sïòn
69   con questo monte in su la terra stare
sì, ch'amendue hanno un solo orizzòn
e diversi emisperi; onde la strada
72   che mal non seppe carreggiar Fetòn,
vedrai come a costui convien che vada
da l'un, quando a colui da l'altro fianco,
75   se lo 'ntelletto tuo ben chiaro bada."

"Certo, maestro mio," diss' io, "unquanco
non vid' io chiaro sì com' io discerno
78   là dove mio ingegno parea manco,
che 'l mezzo cerchio del moto superno,
che si chiama Equatore in alcun' arte,
81   e che sempre riman tra 'l sole e 'l verno,
per la ragion che di,' quinci si parte
verso settentrïon, quanto li Ebrei
84   vedevan lui verso la calda parte.
Ma se a te piace, volontier saprei
quanto avemo ad andar; ché 'l poggio sale
87   più che salir non posson li occhi miei."
Ed elli a me: "Questa montagna è tale,
che sempre al cominciar di sotto è grave;
90   e quant' om più va sù, e men fa male.

I turned my eyes first to the shore below,
  then up toward the sun, and was amazed
    to see that its rays struck down from the left.   *57*
The poet saw that I was astounded
  at how the chariot of light in the sky
    was on a path that ran to the north of us,   *60*
And so he said, "If the luminous orb
  that moves above and below the Equator
    were in the company of Castor and Pollux,   *63*
You would see the Zodiac's ruddy glow
  turned even closer to the northern Bears,
    unless it were to leave its ancient track.   *66*
If you want to understand how this can be,
  concentrate, and picture both Zion
    and this mountain positioned on earth   *69*
In such a way that they have the same horizon
  but in different hemispheres; then you will see
    that the road that Phaethon failed to drive   *72*
Must pass this mountain on one side
  while passing Zion on the other; that is,
    .if you are able to apply your intellect."   *75*

"Indeed, my master," I said, "never before
  have I seen as clearly as I do now
    where my native wit has seemed deficient.   *78*
The mid-circle of the turning heavens,
  which a certain science calls the Equator,
    and which lies between summer and winter,   *81*
Is, for the very reason you gave,
  as far to the north from here as the Hebrews
    saw it in the sky toward the torrid regions.   *84*
But if it pleases you, I would like to know
  how far we have to go, for the slope rises
    farther than my eyes are able to climb."   *87*
And he said to me, "This mountain is such
  that the climb is hard at the beginning
    and less troublesome the more one ascends.   *90*

Però, quand' ella ti parrà soave
    tanto, che sù andar ti fia leggero
93   com' a seconda giù andar per nave,
allor sarai al fin d'esto sentiero;
    quivi di riposar l'affanno aspetta.
96   Più non rispondo, e questo so per vero."

E com' elli ebbe sua parola detta,
    una voce di presso sonò: "Forse
99   che di sedere in pria avrai distretta!"
Al suon di lei ciascun di noi si torse,
    e vedemmo a mancina un gran petrone,
102   del qual né io né ei prima s'accorse.
Là ci traemmo; e ivi eran persone
    che si stavano a l'ombra dietro al sasso
105   come l'uom per negghienza a star si pone.
E un di lor, che mi sembiava lasso,
    sedeva e abbracciava le ginocchia,
108   tenendo 'l viso giù tra esse basso.
"O dolce segnor mio," diss' io, "adocchia
    colui che mostra sé più negligente
111   che se pigrizia fosse sua serocchia."
Allor si volse a noi e puose mente,
    movendo 'l viso pur su per la coscia,
114   e disse: "Or va tu sù, che se' valente!"
Conobbi allor chi era, e quella angoscia
    che m'avacciava un poco ancor la lena,
117   non m'impedì l'andare a lui; e poscia
ch'a lui fu' giunto, alzò la testa a pena,
    dicendo: "Hai ben veduto come 'l sole
120   da l'omero sinistro il carro mena?"
Li atti suoi pigri e le corte parole
    mosser le labbra mie un poco a riso;
123   poi cominciai: "Belacqua, a me non dole
di te omai; ma dimmi: perché assiso
    quiritto se'? attendi tu iscorta,
126   o pur lo modo usato t'ha' ripriso?"

And when the climb seems as pleasant to you
  and as easy as floating in a boat
    that lets the current take it downstream,   *93*
At that point this trail will come to an end.
  Look forward to resting your weary frame there.
    I say no more, but I know this is true."   *96*

As soon as he had spoken these words,
  a voice sounded close by, saying, "Perhaps
    you will have some need to sit before then."   *99*
Hearing these words we both turned around
  and saw to our left an enormous rock
    that neither of us had noticed before.   *102*
We went over to it; some people were there
  lounging in the shade behind the boulder,
    like men settled in for a long, lazy nap.   *105*
One of them, who seemed so weary to me,
  was sitting with his arms around his knees
    and had his face pressed down between them.   *108*
"O my sweet lord," I said, "Turn your eyes
  toward the one over there, who looks as lazy
    as if Sloth herself were his little sister."   *111*
At that he turned his attention toward us,
  barely moving his face up along his thigh,
    and said, "Then you go on up if you're so strong." *114*
I knew him then, and the pain caused
  by my shortness of breath did not prevent me
    from going over to him; and then,   *117*
When I reached him, he barely lifted his head,
  saying, "Have you really seen how the sun
    drives his chariot on your left side?"   *120*
His lazy manner and his brief words
  brought a little smile to my lips, and I said,
    "Belacqua, I am not grieved for you now,   *123*
But tell me, why are you sitting here?
  Are you waiting for an escort? Or is it that
    your old ways have caught up with you again?" *126*

Ed elli: "O frate, andar in sù che porta?
ché non mi lascerebbe ire a' martìri
129   l'angel di Dio che siede in su la porta.
Prima convien che tanto il ciel m'aggiri
di fuor da essa, quanto fece in vita,
132   per ch'io 'ndugiai al fine i buon sospiri,
se orazïone in prima non m'aita
che surga sù di cuor che in grazia viva;
135   l'altra che val, che 'n ciel non è udita?"

E già il poeta innanzi mi saliva,
e dicea: "Vienne omai; vedi ch'è tocco
138   meridïan dal sole e a la riva
cuopre la notte già col piè Morrocco."

He said, "What's the use, brother, of my ascent?
  No, the angel of God who sits at the gate
    would not let me through to the place of torment.   *129*
First I must endure as many turns of the skies,
  on the outside here, as I did in my life,
    for I delayed to the end my repentant sighs,   *132*
Unless I am aided by prayers beforehand
  that arise from a heart that lives in grace,
    for what good are prayers not heard in heaven?"   *135*

But now the poet, not waiting for me,
  began to climb, saying, "We can linger no more.
    The sun is touching the meridian. See!   *138*
And Night covers with her foot Morocco's shore."

CANTO V

AS DANTE AND VIRGIL WALK *away from the group, the negligent souls notice the pilgrim's shadow for the first time and are amazed. Dante turns back to the group of the souls, for which Virgil berates him for his hesitancy, encouraging him to stick to his purpose of moving onward. The ashamed Dante immediately follows his guide. They walk toward another group of souls who are singing the penitential psalm Miserere. This group also notices Dante's shadow, and they break off their song in amazement. Virgil reassures them that the pilgrim is indeed alive and in his real body.*

Io era già da quell' ombre partito,
   e seguitava l'orme del mio duca,
3   quando di retro a me, drizzando 'l dito,
una gridò: "Ve' che non par che luca
   lo raggio da sinistra a quel di sotto,
6   e come vivo par che si conduca!"
Li occhi rivolsi al suon di questo motto,
   e vidile guardar per maraviglia
9   pur me, pur me, e 'l lume ch'era rotto.

"Perché l'animo tuo tanto s'impiglia,"
   disse 'l maestro, "che l'andare allenti?
12   che ti fa ciò che quivi si pispiglia?
Vien dietro a me, e lascia dir le genti:
   sta come torre ferma, che non crolla
15   già mai la cima per soffiar di venti;
ché sempre l'omo in cui pensier rampolla
   sovra pensier, da sé dilunga il segno,
18   perché la foga l'un de l'altro insolla."
Che potea io ridir, se non "Io vegno?"
   Dissilo, alquanto del color consperso
21   che fa l'uom di perdon talvolta degno.

The souls encourage the travelers to stop and speak with them, but Virgil tells Dante that they must keep moving and converse while walking. This group of sinners were late-repentant who met violent ends, repenting only at the moment of death. The rest of the canto is made up of encounters with three souls who describe the events of their deaths: Jacopo del Cassero, Buonconte da Montefeltro, and Pia dei Tolomei. The three scenes that they describe create an image of the violent and turbulent world of thirteenth-century Italy.

I had already parted company with those shades
  and was following the footsteps of my guide
    when one of them behind me pointed his finger   *3*
And cried, "Look at how the sun's rays can't be seen
  shining on the left side of that one below,
    and at how he seems to move as if still alive!"   *6*
I turned my eyes to where the voice came from
  and saw that they were staring in amazement
    at me, at me and the shadow that I made.   *9*

"Why is your mind so befuddled,"
  my master said, "that you have slowed your pace?
    Why do you care what they are whispering?   *12*
Just follow behind me and let people talk.
  Be as steady as a tower that always stands firm
    and never trembles during a windstorm.   *15*
When a man lets one thought after another
  well up in him, he sets his goal farther back,
    for thoughts like this only weaken each other."   *18*
What else could I reply, except, "I'm coming"?
  I said it, turning a shade of red that might
    at times make a person worthy of pardon.   *21*

E 'ntanto per la costa di traverso
   venivan genti innanzi a noi un poco,
24   cantando 'Miserere' a verso a verso.
Quando s'accorser ch'i' non dava loco
   per lo mio corpo al trapassar d'i raggi,
27   mutar lor canto in un "oh!" lungo e roco;
e due di loro, in forma di messaggi,
   corsero incontr' a noi e dimandarne:
30   "Di vostra condizion fatene saggi."
E 'l mio maestro: "Voi potete andarne
   e ritrarre a color che vi mandaro
33   che 'l corpo di costui è vera carne.
Se per veder la sua ombra restaro,
   com' io avviso, assai è lor risposto:
36   fàccianli onore, ed esser può lor caro."

Vapori accesi non vid' io sì tosto
   di prima notte mai fender sereno,
39   né, sol calando, nuvole d'agosto,
che color non tornasser suso in meno;
   e, giunti là, con li altri a noi dier volta,
42   come schiera che scorre sanza freno.
"Questa gente che preme a noi è molta,
   e vegnonti a pregar," disse 'l poeta:
45   "però pur va, e in andando ascolta."

"O anima che vai per esser lieta
   con quelle membra con le quai nascesti,"
48   venian gridando, "un poco il passo queta.
Guarda s'alcun di noi unqua vedesti,
   sì che di lui di là novella porti:
51   deh, perché vai? deh, perché non t'arresti?
Noi fummo tutti già per forza morti,
   e peccatori infino a l'ultima ora;
54   quivi lume del ciel ne fece accorti,
sì che, pentendo e perdonando, fora
   di vita uscimmo a Dio pacificati,
57   che del disio di sé veder n'accora."

And all the while some others were walking
  across the slope a little ahead of us,
    chanting the *Miserere* verse by verse.   *24*
When they came to realize that my body
  did not allow the sun's rays to pass through
    their chant trailed off to a long and hoarse "Oh!"   *27*
And two of them, dispatched as messengers,
  ran over to us with this urgent request:
    "Enlighten us as to your condition."   *30*
My master answered, "You can go back to those
  who sent you here and report to them
    that this man's body is made of real flesh.   *33*
If they stopped because they saw his shadow,
  as I suspect, they are well enough answered.
    And it may reward them to do him honor."   *36*

I have never seen meteors or lightning bolts
  cut through a clear sky in the early night,
    or through August's haze when the sun goes down,   *39*
As swiftly as these spirits went back up;
  and as soon as they arrived, the entire troop
    wheeled around and stampeded toward us.   *42*
"It is a large crowd that presses around us,
  and they come to entreat you," the poet said.
    "Just keep on moving, and listen as you go."   *45*

"O soul proceeding to your happy state
  with the very body with which you were born,"
    they came crying, "stop walking for a while.   *48*
Look if you have ever seen any of us,
  so you can take news of him back over there.
    Ah, why keep walking? Ah, why don't you stop?   *51*
We, all of us, met with violent deaths
  and were sinners up to the very last hour.
    Then light from heaven made us know what to do,   *54*
So that, repenting and granting pardon ourselves,
  we came forth from life at peace with God,
    who fills our hearts with desire to see Him."   *57*

E io: "Perché ne' vostri visi guati,
non riconosco alcun; ma s'a voi piace
60   cosa ch'io possa, spiriti ben nati,
voi dite, e io farò per quella pace
che, dietro a' piedi di sì fatta guida,
63   di mondo in mondo cercar mi si face."

E uno incominciò: "Ciascun si fida
del beneficio tuo sanza giurarlo,
66   pur che 'l voler nonpossa non ricida.
Ond' io, che solo innanzi a li altri parlo,
ti priego, se mai vedi quel paese
69   che siede tra Romagna e quel di Carlo,
che tu mi sie di tuoi prieghi cortese
in Fano, sì che ben per me s'adori
72   pur ch'i' possa purgar le gravi offese.
Quindi fu' io; ma li profondi fóri
ond' uscì 'l sangue in sul quale io sedea,
75   fatti mi fuoro in grembo a li Antenori,
là dov' io più sicuro esser credea:
quel da Esti il fé far, che m'avea in ira
78   assai più là che dritto non volea.
Ma s'io fosse fuggito inver' la Mira,
quando fu' sovragiunto ad Orïaco,
81   ancor sarei di là dove si spira.
Corsi al palude, e le cannucce e 'l braco
m'impigliar sì ch'i' caddi; e lì vid' io
84   de le mie vene farsi in terra laco."

Poi disse un altro: "Deh, se quel disio
si compia che ti tragge a l'alto monte,
87   con buona pïetate aiuta il mio!
Io fui di Montefeltro, io son Bonconte;
Giovanna o altri non ha di me cura;
90   per ch'io vo tra costor con bassa fronte."
E io a lui: "Qual forza o qual ventura
ti travïò sì fuor di Campaldino,
93   che non si seppe mai tua sepultura?"

I answered, "Even staring at your faces
  I don't recognize any. But, happy spirits,
    if there is anything I can do for you,   *60*
Tell me, and I will do it, by the very peace
  that makes me pursue it from world to world,
    following the steps of such a guide as this."   *63*

One of them began, "Each of us trusts
  in your benevolence without any oaths,
    if lack of power does not rescind your will.   *66*
So I, speaking alone before the others,
  beg you, if you ever see the country
    that lies between Romagna and Naples,   *69*
Do me the favor of asking those in Fano
  to pray for me, to offer supplication
    so that I may purge my grievous offenses.   *72*
That is where I was from, but the deep wounds
  from which my lifeblood flowed were dealt to me
    in the heartland of the Antenori,   *75*
Where I believed I was most secure.
  The man of Este had it done, angry with me
    far more than he had any right to be.   *78*
If I had only fled toward La Mira then,
  when I was overcome at Oriaco,
    I would still be back there where men draw breath;   *81*
But I ran to the marsh, where the reeds and mud
  entangled me so. I fell, and there I saw
    blood from my veins form a pool on the ground."   *84*

Then another said, "Oh, so may your desire
  to ascend this mountain be fulfilled,
    aid my own, I beg you, out of kindly pity.   *87*
I come from Montefeltro, and I am Buonconte.
  Neither Giovanna, nor anyone cares for me,
    and so I go among these with downcast brow."   *90*
I asked him, "What force or what misfortune
  carried you so far from Campaldino
    that your burial place was never known?"   *93*

"Oh!" rispuos' elli, "a piè del Casentino
   traversa un'acqua c'ha nome l'Archiano,
96   che sovra l'Ermo nasce in Apennino.
Là 've 'l vocabol suo diventa vano,
   arriva' io forato ne la gola,
99   fuggendo a piede e sanguinando il piano.
Quivi perdei la vista e la parola;
   nel nome di Maria fini,' e quivi
102   caddi, e rimase la mia carne sola.
Io dirò vero, e tu 'l ridì tra ' vivi:
   l'angel di Dio mi prese, e quel d'inferno
105   gridava: "O tu del ciel, perché mi privi?
Tu te ne porti di costui l'etterno
   per una lagrimetta che 'l mi toglie;
108   ma io farò de l'altro altro governo!"
Ben sai come ne l'aere si raccoglie
   quell' umido vapor che in acqua riede,
111   tosto che sale dove 'l freddo il coglie.
Giunse quel mal voler che pur mal chiede
   con lo 'ntelletto, e mosse il fummo e 'l vento
114   per la virtù che sua natura diede.
Indi la valle, come 'l dì fu spento,
   da Pratomagno al gran giogo coperse
117   di nebbia; e 'l ciel di sopra fece intento,
sì che 'l pregno aere in acqua si converse;
   la pioggia cadde, e a' fossati venne
120   di lei ciò che la terra non sofferse;
e come ai rivi grandi si convenne,
   ver' lo fiume real tanto veloce
123   si ruinò, che nulla la ritenne.
Lo corpo mio gelato in su la foce
   trovò l'Archian rubesto; e quel sospinse
126   ne l'Arno, e sciolse al mio petto la croce
ch'i' fe' di me quando 'l dolor mi vinse;
   voltòmmi per le ripe e per lo fondo,
129   poi di sua preda mi coperse e cinse."

"Oh," he answered, "at the Casentino's foot
a stream called the Archiano crosses.
   It rises above Ermo in the Apennines.   *96*
I reached it just where its name is lost,
wounded in my throat, spilling blood
   all over the ground as I fled on foot.   *99*
At that point I could no longer see or speak,
and ending on the name of Mary, I fell.
   All that was left of me then was my flesh.   *102*
I will tell the truth, and you repeat it
among the living. God's angel took me,
   and the one from Hell cried, 'Why do you rob me, *105*
You from Heaven? You get the eternal part
for one little tear that deprives me of him.
   But I will dispose of the rest otherwise.'   *108*
You know well how moisture in the air
condenses into water when it rises
   to a colder part of the atmosphere.   *111*
This devil, conjoining his intellect
with an evil will that seeks only evil,
   stirred the winds and mists by his natural power; *114*
And when day was done he covered with clouds
the valley that stretches from Pratomagno
   to the mountain chain, making the sky so dense *117*
That the pregnant air turned into water.
   The rain fell, and the gullies collected
   all the water the ground could not absorb,   *120*
Forming great torrents that rushed along
and down so swiftly toward the royal river
   that nothing at all could hold it back.   *123*
The roiling Archiano found at its mouth
my frozen body and swept it along
   into the Arno, loosening the cross   *126*
I had made on my breast when pain overcame me.
   The river rolled me along its banks and bottom,
   then covered me over with its debris."   *129*

"Deh, quando tu sarai tornato al mondo
e riposato de la lunga via,"
132   seguitò 'l terzo spirito al secondo,

"ricorditi di me, che son la Pia;
Siena mi fé, disfecemi Maremma:
135   salsi colui che 'nnanellata pria

disposando m'avea con la sua gemma."

When he finished speaking a third spirit said:
  "Oh, after you have finished your journey,
    returned to the world, and have rested,   *132*
Remember me. I am called la Pia.
  Siena made me, Maremma took my life,
    as is well known to him who betrothed me   *135*
With his ring, and who took me as his wife."

CANTO VI

DANTE IS SURROUNDED BY A *large group of souls all entreating his prayers and the prayers he can solicit for them back among the living. Many figures from Dante's contemporary Italy are named. Dante questions Virgil on the efficacy of prayer since this is something that Virgil's own Aeneid denies. Virgil explains that pagan prayers are ineffectual because they are disconnected from the Christian God, telling Dante that Beatrice will explain this further. The travelers encounter a solitary figure who, on*

Quando si parte il gioco de la zara,
 colui che perde si riman dolente,
3 repetendo le volte, e tristo impara;
con l'altro se ne va tutta la gente;
 qual va dinanzi, e qual di dietro il prende,
6 e qual dallato li si reca a mente;
el non s'arresta, e questo e quello intende;
 a cui porge la man, più non fa pressa;
9 e così da la calca si difende.
Tal era io in quella turba spessa,
 volgendo a loro, e qua e là, la faccia,
12 e promettendo mi sciogliea da essa.
Quiv' era l'Aretin che da le braccia
 fiere di Ghin di Tacco ebbe la morte,
15 e l'altro ch'annegò correndo in caccia.
Quivi pregava con le mani sporte
 Federigo Novello, e quel da Pisa
18 che fé parer lo buon Marzucco forte.
Vidi conte Orso e l'anima divisa
 dal corpo suo per astio e per inveggia,
21 com' e' dicea, non per colpa commisa;
Pier da la Broccia dico; e qui proveggia,
 mentr' è di qua, la donna di Brabante,
24 sì che però non sia di peggior greggia.

discovering that Virgil comes from Mantua, reveals himself as Sordello,
also a native of that area. The two souls affectionately embrace. Here the
narrative breaks off and Dante the poet pronounces a long invective against
the political strife of his contemporary Italy, attributing it to the lack of
a strong and engaged imperial leader. Florence is specifically named and
receives harsh criticism.

When a game of dice breaks up, the loser
   stays around, dejected, and going over
      all of the throws he learns in sorrow,   *3*
While the others all mill around the winner.
   One goes in front, another grabs him from behind,
      and someone at his side makes his presence felt.   *6*
The winner does not stop, but listens to this one
   and that, and those to whom he offers his hand
      leave him alone, and so he escapes the crowd.   *9*
That is how I was among that press of souls,
   turning my face this way and that
      and by making promises sloughed them all off.   *12*
The Aretine was there who met his death
   at the fierce hands of Ghino di Tacco,
      and the one who drowned as he rode in the chase.   *15*
Federico Novello was also there,
   pleading with hands outstretched, and the Pisan
      who made the good Marzucco show himself strong.   *18*
I saw Count Orso, and that soul severed
   from its body by spite and envy,
      as he said, and not for any crime committed—   *21*
Pierre de la Brosse I mean. And let her take care,
   the Lady of Brabant, while she remains on earth,
      that she not wind up in a flock far worse.   *24*

Come libero fui da tutte quante
    quell' ombre che pregar pur ch'altri prieghi,
27   sì che s'avacci lor divenir sante,
io cominciai: "El par che tu mi nieghi,
    o luce mia, espresso in alcun testo
30   che decreto del cielo orazion pieghi;
e questa gente prega pur di questo:
    sarebbe dunque loro speme vana,
33   o non m'è 'l detto tuo ben manifesto?"
Ed elli a me: "La mia scrittura è piana;
    e la speranza di costor non falla,
36   se ben si guarda con la mente sana;
ché cima di giudicio non s'avvalla
    perché foco d'amor compia in un punto
39   ciò che de' sodisfar chi qui s'astalla;
e là dov' io fermai cotesto punto,
    non s'ammendava, per pregar, difetto,
42   perché 'l priego da Dio era disgiunto.
Veramente a così alto sospetto
    non ti fermar, se quella nol ti dice
45   che lume fia tra 'l vero e lo 'ntelletto.
Non so se 'ntendi: io dico di Beatrice;
    tu la vedrai di sopra, in su la vetta
48   di questo monte, ridere e felice."
E io: "Segnore, andiamo a maggior fretta,
    ché già non m'affatico come dianzi,
51   e vedi omai che 'l poggio l'ombra getta."
"Noi anderem con questo giorno innanzi,"
    rispuose, "quanto più potremo omai;
54   ma 'l fatto è d'altra forma che non stanzi.
Prima che sie là sù, tornar vedrai
    colui che già si cuopre de la costa,
57   sì che ' suoi raggi tu romper non fai.
Ma vedi là un'anima che, posta
    sola soletta, inverso noi riguarda:
60   quella ne 'nsegnerà la via più tosta."

As soon as I was free of all those souls
  whose only prayer was that others pray
    for their speedy progress on to sainthood,   *27*
I said, "O light of my mind, it seems to me
  that you deny in a certain passage
    that prayer can bend decrees of Heaven;   *30*
And yet these people pray for that alone.
  Will their hope therefore come to nothing,
    Or are your words not really clear to me?"   *33*
And he answered, "My writing is plain,
  and their hopes are not false, if you
    consider the matter with a sound mind.   *36*
For the height of justice is not brought low
  if the fire of love achieve in an instant
    what those who stay here must satisfy.   *39*
And in the passage where I made this point
  the defect could not be amended with prayer,
    because that prayer could never reach God.   *42*
But do not concern yourself with questions
  so profound before she speaks to you,
    the light between the intellect and truth.   *45*
I do not know if you understand. I mean
  Beatrice. You will see her above,
    on this mountain's summit, smiling in bliss."   *48*
Then I said, "My lord, let us pick up the pace,
  for I am no longer as weary as I was,
    and look, the hill already casts a shadow."   *51*
"We will go on for the rest of this day,"
  he responded, "as far as we can now,
    but the facts do not match your understanding.   *54*
Before you reach the top you will see again
  the one whose rays are hidden by the slope
    and which therefore you do not interrupt.   *57*
But look at that soul there sitting all alone
  with his eyes turned in our direction.
    He will let us know the fastest route."   *60*

Venimmo a lei: o anima lombarda,
   come ti stavi altera e disdegnosa
63   e nel mover de li occhi onesta e tarda!
Ella non ci dicëa alcuna cosa,
   ma lasciavane gir, solo sguardando
66   a guisa di leon quando si posa.
Pur Virgilio si trasse a lei, pregando
   che ne mostrasse la miglior salita;
69   e quella non rispuose al suo dimando,
ma di nostro paese e de la vita
   ci 'nchiese; e 'l dolce duca incominciava
72   "Mantüa . . . ," e l'ombra, tutta in sé romita,
surse ver' lui del loco ove pria stava,
   dicendo: "O Mantoano, io son Sordello
75   de la tua terra!" e l'un l'altro abbracciava.

Ahi serva Italia, di dolore ostello,
   nave sanza nocchiere in gran tempesta,
78   non donna di province, ma bordello!
Quell' anima gentil fu così presta,
   sol per lo dolce suon de la sua terra,
81   di fare al cittadin suo quivi festa;
e ora in te non stanno sanza guerra
   li vivi tuoi, e l'un l'altro si rode
84   di quei ch'un muro e una fossa serra.
Cerca, misera, intorno da le prode
   le tue marine, e poi ti guarda in seno,
87   s'alcuna parte in te di pace gode.
Che val perché ti racconciasse il freno
   Iustinïano, se la sella è vòta?
90   Sanz' esso fora la vergogna meno.
Ahi gente che dovresti esser devota,
   e lasciar seder Cesare in la sella,
93   se bene intendi ciò che Dio ti nota,
guarda come esta fiera è fatta fella
   per non esser corretta da li sproni,
96   poi che ponesti mano a la predella.

We came up to him. O Lombard soul,
  how erect and disdainful you bore yourself,
    and in your eyes such dignity and calm!   *63*
The spirit did not say a word to us
  but let us come over as he just watched
    as if he were a lion in still repose.   *66*
Virgil nonetheless drew up to him
  and asked him to show us the best ascent.
    To this request he made no response   *69*
But asked about what country we lived in.
  My gentle guide had no sooner said,
    "Mantua . . ." when the shade who had been so aloof   *72*
Leaped up to him, crying, "O Mantuan,
  I am Sordello, from your country."
    And the two of them embraced each other.   *75*

Ah, servile Italy, hostel of sorrow,
  pilotless ship in a great hurricane,
    no mistress of provinces, but a house of whores!   *78*
How eager was that noble soul
  to welcome his fellow citizen there
    at the mere sweet sound of his city's name!   *81*
Your living now are never free from war,
  and they gnaw at one another even when
    enclosed within a single wall and moat.   *84*
Search, you wretch, all around the shores
  your seas break upon, then look within
    to see if any part of you knows peace.   *87*
What good did it do that Justinian
  repaired the harness if the saddle is empty?
    If he hadn't, at least your shame would be less.   *90*
Ah, you people who should remain devoted
  and allow Caesar to sit in the saddle,
    if you understood what God writes for you,   *93*
See how vicious this beast has become
  through not being corrected by the spurs
    ever since you took the reins in your hands!   *96*

O Alberto tedesco ch'abbandoni
   costei ch'è fatta indomita e selvaggia,
99   e dovresti inforcar li suoi arcioni,
giusto giudicio da le stelle caggia
   sovra 'l tuo sangue, e sia novo e aperto,
102   tal che 'l tuo successor temenza n'aggia!
Ch'avete tu e 'l tuo padre sofferto,
   per cupidigia di costà distretti,
105   che 'l giardin de lo 'mperio sia diserto.
Vieni a veder Montecchi e Cappelletti,
   Monaldi e Filippeschi, uom sanza cura:
108   color già tristi, e questi con sospetti!
Vien, crudel, vieni, e vedi la pressura
   d'i tuoi gentili, e cura lor magagne;
111   e vedrai Santafior com' è oscura!
Vieni a veder la tua Roma che piagne
   vedova e sola, e dì e notte chiama:
114   "Cesare mio, perché non m'accompagne?"
Vieni a veder la gente quanto s'ama!
   e se nulla di noi pietà ti move,
117   a vergognar ti vien de la tua fama.
E se licito m'è, o sommo Giove
   che fosti in terra per noi crucifisso,
120   son li giusti occhi tuoi rivolti altrove?
O è preparazion che ne l'abisso
   del tuo consiglio fai per alcun bene
123   in tutto de l'accorger nostro scisso?
Ché le città d'Italia tutte piene
   son di tiranni, e un Marcel diventa
126   ogne villan che parteggiando viene.
Fiorenza mia, ben puoi esser contenta
   di questa digression che non ti tocca,
129   mercé del popol tuo che si argomenta.
Molti han giustizia in cuore, e tardi scocca
   per non venir sanza consiglio a l'arco;
132   ma il popol tuo l'ha in sommo de la bocca.
Molti rifiutan lo comune incarco;
   ma il popol tuo solicito risponde
135   sanza chiamare, e grida: "I' mi sobbarco!"

O German Albert, who abandon her
  who has become untamable and wild
    but should instead bestride her stirrups,   99
May a just judgment fall from the stars
  upon your blood, and may it be so strange and clear
    that your successor will live in fear of it.   102
Both you and your father, detained by greed
  in that faraway land, have permitted
    the Empire's garden to become a desert.   105
Come and see the Montecchi and Cappelletti,
  the Monaldi and Filippeschi, the former
    already wretched, the latter in dread;   108
Come, cruel one, come and see the trials
  your nobles suffer, and care for their hurts.
    Then you will see how dark Santafiora is.   111
Come and see your Rome, as she sheds tears,
  widowed and alone, crying out day and night,
    "My Caesar, why are you not at my side?"   114
Come and see how your people love one another;
  and if pity for us cannot move you,
    come out of shame for your reputation.   117
And if I may ask, O Jove most high
  who was crucified here on earth for us,
    are your righteous eyes turned elsewhere now?   120
Or is this some preparation you are making
  in the abyss of your contemplation
    for some good beyond our comprehension?   123
For every city in Italy is filled
  with tyrants, and every churl who comes along
    in politics thinks he's a new Marcellus.   126
My Florence, you may be well content
  with this digression that does not touch you,
    thanks to the efforts of your people.   129
Many others have justice at heart
  but their long deliberations retard
    pulling the arrow back to the bow;   132
And many refuse the public burden.
  But your people need not even be asked,
    crying out eagerly, "I'll take it on!"   135

Or ti fa lieta, ché tu hai ben onde:
tu ricca, tu con pace e tu con senno!
138   S'io dico 'l ver, l'effetto nol nasconde.
Atene e Lacedemona, che fenno
l'antiche leggi e furon sì civili,
141   fecero al viver bene un picciol cenno
verso di te, che fai tanto sottili
provedimenti, ch'a mezzo novembre
144   non giugne quel che tu d'ottobre fili.
Quante volte, del tempo che rimembre,
legge, moneta, officio e costume
147   hai tu mutato, e rinovate membre!
E se ben ti ricordi e vedi lume,
vedrai te somigliante a quella inferma
150   che non può trovar posa in su le piume,
ma con dar volta suo dolore scherma.

So rejoice now, and with good reason,
  for you are wealthy, at peace, and wise.
    If I speak the truth, the facts cannot hide it.   *138*
Athens and Lacedaemon, which made
  the ancient laws and had such civil order,
    gave the tiniest hints of the good life   *141*
Compared to you, who in your provisions
  are so subtle that what you spin in October
    does not last until mid-November.   *144*
How many times within recent memory
  have you changed laws, coinage, offices, customs,
    and even installed a new citizenry?   *147*
And you will see, once you have reflected,
  that you are just like a sick woman who in vain
    tries to find rest upon her feather bed   *150*
And keeps tossing and turning to ease her pain.

CANTO VII

THE POET SORDELLO, WHOM THE *travelers met at the end of canto*
VI, asks to know their identities. Virgil identifies himself and Sordello is
amazed, asking where Virgil now dwells in the afterlife. Virgil gives one
of the most extended descriptions in the Commedia *of his own state*
and that of his fellow Limbo dwellers. He then asks Sordello for guidance

Poscia che l'accoglienze oneste e liete
    furo iterate tre e quattro volte,
3   Sordel si trasse, e disse: "Voi, chi siete?"
"Anzi che a questo monte fosser volte
    l'anime degne di salire a Dio,
6   fur l'ossa mie per Ottavian sepolte.
Io son Virgilio; e per null' altro rio
    lo ciel perdei che per non aver fé."
9   Così rispuose allora il duca mio.
Qual è colui che cosa innanzi sé
    sùbita vede ond' e' si maraviglia,
12   che crede e non, dicendo "Ella è . . . non è . . . ,"
tal parve quelli; e poi chinò le ciglia,
    e umilmente ritornò ver' lui,
15   e abbracciòl là 've 'l minor s'appiglia.
"O gloria di Latin," disse, "per cui
    mostrò ciò che potea la lingua nostra,
18   o pregio etterno del loco ond' io fui,
qual merito o qual grazia mi ti mostra?
    S'io son d'udir le tue parole degno,
21   dimmi se vien d'inferno, e di qual chiostra."

"Per tutt' i cerchi del dolente regno,"
    rispuose lui, "son io di qua venuto;
24   virtù del ciel mi mosse, e con lei vegno.

*on how to ascend the mountain. Sordello informs him that the souls are
unable to ascend during the night. Instead he leads the travelers to the edge
of a beautiful valley from which they can look down on a group of souls.
These are the negligent princes. Sordello describes and identifies many of the
figures they see below them.*

After these courteous and joyful greetings
  had been repeated three or four times,
    Sordello drew back and asked, "Who are you?"   *3*
"Before souls worthy of ascending to God
  were ever directed toward this mountain,
    my bones were interred by Octavian.   *6*
I am Virgil, and for no other fault
  but not having the faith did I lose Heaven."
    That was how my leader responded.   *9*
As one who suddenly sees something before him
  at which he marvels, believing it and not,
    and saying, "It is," but then, "no, it isn't,"   *12*
So seemed Sordello. He bowed his head
  and came back humbly to Virgil, bending low
    to clasp him where an inferior should.   *15*
"O glory of the Latins," he said, "through whom
  our language showed what it could accomplish,
    O everlasting honor of the place of my birth,   *18*
What merit or grace shows you to me?
  If I am worthy to hear you, tell me this:
    If you come from Hell, from which cloister there?"   *21*

"Through all the circles of the kingdom of woe
  have I made my way here," Virgil answered.
    "Power from heaven moved me, and with it I come.   *24*

Non per far, ma per non fare ho perduto
a veder l'alto Sol che tu disiri
27   e che fu tardi per me conosciuto.
Luogo è là giù non tristo di martìri,
ma di tenebre solo, ove i lamenti
30   non suonan come guai, ma son sospiri.
Quivi sto io coi pargoli innocenti
dai denti morsi de la morte avante
33   che fosser da l'umana colpa essenti;
quivi sto io con quei che le tre sante
virtù non si vestiro, e sanza vizio
36   conobber l'altre e seguir tutte quante.
Ma se tu sai e puoi, alcuno indizio
dà noi per che venir possiam più tosto
39   là dove purgatorio ha dritto inizio."

Rispuose: "Loco certo non c'è posto;
licito m'è andar suso e intorno;
42   per quanto ir posso, a guida mi t'accosto.
Ma vedi già come dichina il giorno,
e andar sù di notte non si puote;
45   però è buon pensar di bel soggiorno.
Anime sono a destra qua remote;
se mi consenti, io ti merrò ad esse,
48   e non sanza diletto ti fier note."
"Com' è ciò?" fu risposto. "Chi volesse
salir di notte, fora elli impedito
51   d'altrui, o non sarria ché non potesse?"
E 'l buon Sordello in terra fregò 'l dito,
dicendo: "Vedi? sola questa riga
54   non varcheresti dopo 'l sol partito:
non però ch'altra cosa desse briga,
che la notturna tenebra, ad ir suso;
57   quella col nonpoder la voglia intriga.
Ben si poria con lei tornare in giuso
e passeggiar la costa intorno errando,
60   mentre che l'orizzonte il dì tien chiuso."
Allora il mio segnor, quasi ammirando,
"Menane," disse, "dunque là 've dici
63   ch'aver si può diletto dimorando."

Not for what I did but what I did not do
  I lost the vision of the exalted Sun
    that you desire and I came to know too late. *27*
There is a place down there, sad not with torments
  but solely with darkness, where lamentations
    sound not as wailing but only as sighs. *30*
There I abide, with the innocent infants
  whom death sank its fangs into before they ever
    had a chance to be cleansed of human guilt. *33*
There I abide, with those who were not clothed
  in the three holy virtues, but who without fault
    knew the other four and followed them all. *36*
But if you know the way, and if you can,
  give us directions, so we may come sooner
    to where Purgatory has its true beginning." *39*

He answered, "We are not assigned a fixed place.
  I am allowed to ascend and move around,
    and I will guide you as far as I can go. *42*
But see how the day is already waning,
  and it is not possible to ascend by night.
    We should be thinking now of a good place to rest. *45*
There are some souls sequestered off to the right.
  If you agree, I will lead you to them,
    and in their acquaintance you will find delight." *48*
"How is that?" came the response. "If one should wish
  to ascend by night, would someone hinder him,
    or would he not climb because he was not able?" *51*
Good Sordello traced a line in the dust
  with his finger and said, "See? You would not cross
    even this line once the sun goes down, *54*
Not because anyone hinders the ascent,
  but the shadowy night, the darkness itself,
    enmeshes the will in helplessness. *57*
During the night one could head back down
  and wander aimlessly around the slope
    as long as the horizon locks out the day." *60*
At that my lord said with an astonished air,
  "Lead us, then, to the place where you say
    we could find delight as we take our rest." *63*

Poco allungati c'eravam di lici,
  quand' io m'accorsi che 'l monte era scemo,
66   a guisa che i vallon li sceman quici.
"Colà," disse quell' ombra, "n'anderemo
  dove la costa face di sé grembo;
69   e là il novo giorno attenderemo."
Tra erto e piano era un sentiero schembo,
  che ne condusse in fianco de la lacca,
72   là dove più ch'a mezzo muore il lembo.
Oro e argento fine, cocco e biacca,
  indaco, legno lucido e sereno,
75   fresco smeraldo in l'ora che si fiacca,
da l'erba e da li fior, dentr' a quel seno
  posti, ciascun saria di color vinto,
78   come dal suo maggiore è vinto il meno.
Non avea pur natura ivi dipinto,
  ma di soavità di mille odori
81   vi facea uno incognito e indistinto.
"*Salve, Regina*" in sul verde e 'n su' fiori
  quindi seder cantando anime vidi,
84   che per la valle non parean di fuori.

"Prima che 'l poco sole omai s'annidi,"
  cominciò 'l Mantoan che ci avea vòlti,
87   "tra color non vogliate ch'io vi guidi.
Di questo balzo meglio li atti e ' volti
  conoscerete voi di tutti quanti,
90   che ne la lama giù tra essi accolti.
Colui che più siede alto e fa sembianti
  d'aver negletto ciò che far dovea,
93   e che non move bocca a li altrui canti,
Rodolfo imperador fu, che potea
  sanar le piaghe c'hanno Italia morta,
96   sì che tardi per altri si ricrea.
L'altro che ne la vista lui conforta,
  resse la terra dove l'acqua nasce
99   che Molta in Albia, e Albia in mar ne porta:

We went on a short distance from there
  when I saw that the mountain was hollowed out,
    just as valleys hollow out mountains here.   *66*
"We will go over there," the spirit said,
  "to where the slope makes a lap of itself,
    and wait there for the new day to come."   *69*
There was a slanting path, neither steep nor level,
  that brought us over to the hollow's flank
    where its outer edge more than half died off.   *72*
Gold and fine silver, cochineal, white lead,
  wood from India gleaming and clear,
    and fresh emerald at the moment it's split,   *75*
If set in that valley would all be surpassed,
  in terms of color, by the flowers and grass
    that grew in that place, as less is by greater.   *78*
Nature had not only painted there
  but blended the sweetness of a thousand scents
    into one we had never known before.   *81*
From there I saw, seated amid the flowers
  and green grass, and singing *"Salve Regina,"*
    souls I hadn't seen from outside the valley.   *84*

"Do not ask me," began the Mantuan
  who had led us there, "to lead you among them
    before the dwindling sun goes down to its nest.   *87*
From this bank you will get to know better
  all of their faces and what they have done
    than if you were with them on the level below.   *90*
The one sitting highest, with the look of someone
  who has neglected to do what he ought to have done
    and whose lips don't move with the others in song,   *93*
Was Emperor Rudolph, who could have healed
  the wounds that killed Italy, leaving her
    to be resurrected, too late, by another.   *96*
That one, who seems to be comforting him, rules
  the land where the waters spring that the Moldau
    brings to the Elba and the Elba to the sea.   *99*

Ottacchero ebbe nome, e ne le fasce
   fu meglio assai che Vincislao suo figlio
102   barbuto, cui lussuria e ozio pasce.
E quel nasetto che stretto a consiglio
   par con colui c'ha sì benigno aspetto,
105   morì fuggendo e disfiorando il giglio:
guardate là come si batte il petto!
L'altro vedete c'ha fatto a la guancia
108   de la sua palma, sospirando, letto.
Padre e suocero son del mal di Francia:
   sanno la vita sua viziata e lorda,
111   e quindi viene il duol che sì li lancia.
Quel che par sì membruto e che s'accorda,
   cantando, con colui dal maschio naso,
114   d'ogne valor portò cinta la corda;
e se re dopo lui fosse rimaso
   lo giovanetto che retro a lui siede,
117   ben andava il valor di vaso in vaso,
che non si puote dir de l'altre rede;
   Iacomo e Federigo hanno i reami;
120   del retaggio miglior nessun possiede.
Rade volte risurge per li rami
   l'umana probitate; e questo vole
123   quei che la dà, perché da lui si chiami.
Anche al nasuto vanno mie parole
   non men ch'a l'altro, Pier, che con lui canta,
126   onde Puglia e Proenza già si dole.
Tant' è del seme suo minor la pianta,
   quanto, più che Beatrice e Margherita,
129   Costanza di marito ancor si vanta.
Vedete il re de la semplice vita
   seder là solo, Arrigo d'Inghilterra:
132   questi ha ne' rami suoi migliore uscita.
Quel che più basso tra costor s'atterra,
   guardando in suso, è Guiglielmo marchese,
135   per cui e Alessandria e la sua guerra
fa pianger Monferrato e Canavese."

His name was Ottokar, and he was better
  in diapers than his bearded son Wenceslaus,
    who feeds on luxury and idleness.   *102*
The snub-nosed one who seems engrossed
  in talk with the one who has a kindly look
    died in flight and disflowering the lily;   *105*
Look at him there, beating his breast,
  and see how the other one, sighing,
    lets him rest his cheek in the palm of his hand.   *108*
Those two are the father and father-in-law
  of the plague of France; they know his wicked life,
    his vice, and that is why grief pierces them so.   *111*
That burly one who is singing along
  with the one with the very masculine nose
    was girt with every honor for valor;   *114*
And if the youth who is sitting behind him
  had succeeded him, his worth would have been poured
    from one vessel into another,   *117*
Which cannot be said of the other heirs.
  James and Frederick possess the kingdoms;
    the better heritage neither possesses.   *120*
Human worth rarely rises through the branches,
  and the One who gives it wills it so,
    for the purpose that it may be asked of Him.   *123*
My words apply both to the large-nosed one
  and the other one, Peter, who chants with him
    and who caused Apulia and Provence to grieve;   *126*
And the plant is as inferior to the seed
  as Constance may boast more of her husband
    than Beatrice and Margaret may boast of theirs.   *129*
See over there, sitting all alone, the king
  of the simple life, Harry of England;
    his tree will branch into better offspring.   *132*
Lowest among them, his eyes lifted to the light
  as he sits on the ground, is William the Marchese,
    because of whom Alessandria's might   *135*
Makes Montferrat mourn, and Canavese."

Canto VIII

THE CANTO OPENS WITH AN *evocation of the emotions aroused by the coming of night in those away from home. As the pilgrim watches, one of the group of souls in the valley rises before the whole group begins to sing together. On finishing their song, the group watches as two angels descend toward the valley and land on each of its banks, enclosing the company between them. Sordello explains that they are sent by the Virgin Mary to protect the valley from a serpent who comes at night. Dante and his companions descend into the valley as night falls. He is approached by the*

Era già l'ora che volge il disio
  ai navicanti e 'ntenerisce il core
3   lo dì c'han detto ai dolci amici addio;
e che lo novo peregrin d'amore
  punge, se ode squilla di lontano
6   che paia il giorno pianger che si more;
quand' io incominciai a render vano
  l'udire e a mirare una de l'alme
9   surta, che l'ascoltar chiedea con mano.
Ella giunse e levò ambo le palme,
  ficcando li occhi verso l'orïente,
12   come dicesse a Dio: "D'altro non calme."
"*Te lucis ante*" sì devotamente
  le uscìo di bocca e con sì dolci note,
15   che fece me a me uscir di mente;
e l'altre poi dolcemente e devote
  seguitar lei per tutto l'inno intero,
18   avendo li occhi a le superne rote.

Aguzza qui, lettor, ben li occhi al vero,
  ché 'l velo è ora ben tanto sottile,
21   certo che 'l trapassar dentro è leggero.

soul of Nino Visconti, who requests that Dante take news of him to his daughter before bemoaning the fickleness of his wife. Their conversation is interrupted by the arrival in the valley of the serpent, who is driven away by the protecting angels. Dante takes up again his conversation with the souls, this time with that of Currado Malaspina. Dante praises Malaspina's name and family. Malaspina alludes to Dante's coming exile and the aid and refuge he will receive from the Malaspina family.

It was twilight now, the hour that turns the sailor
   homeward, and melts his heart with longing
      on the day he has told his loved ones good-bye,   *3*
The hour that pierces the new pilgrim's heart
   with love, if he happens to hear a distant bell
      that seems to mourn the dying day.   *6*
I no longer heard what Sordello was saying
   as I gazed instead on one of the souls
      who had risen up and was gesturing for silence.   *9*
He joined his palms and lifted them up,
   fixing his eyes on the East, as if he said
      to God, "For nothing else do I care."   *12*
"Te lucis ante" came from his lips
   with such devotion and with notes so sweet
      my soul left my body in ecstasy.   *15*
Then the others joined him sweetly, devoutly,
   and they finished the entire hymn together,
      keeping their eyes on the wheeling heavens.   *18*

Here sharpen well, Reader, your eyes to the truth,
   for the veil now is so transparent
      that it is surely easy to pass within.   *21*

Io vidi quello essercito gentile
    tacito poscia riguardare in sùe,
24   quasi aspettando, palido e umìle;
e vidi uscir de l'alto e scender giùe
    due angeli con due spade affocate,
27   tronche e private de le punte sue.
Verdi come fogliette pur mo nate
    erano in veste, che da verdi penne
30   percosse traean dietro e ventilate.
L'un poco sovra noi a star si venne,
    e l'altro scese in l'opposita sponda,
33   sì che la gente in mezzo si contenne.
Ben discernëa in lor la testa bionda;
    ma ne la faccia l'occhio si smarria,
36   come virtù ch'a troppo si confonda.
"Ambo vegnon del grembo di Maria,"
    disse Sordello, "a guardia de la valle,
39   per lo serpente che verrà vie via."
Ond' io, che non sapeva per qual calle,
    mi volsi intorno, e stretto m'accostai,
42   tutto gelato, a le fidate spalle.

E Sordello anco: "Or avvalliamo omai
    tra le grandi ombre, e parleremo ad esse;
45   grazïoso fia lor vedervi assai."
Solo tre passi credo ch'i' scendesse,
    e fui di sotto, e vidi un che mirava
48   pur me, come conoscer mi volesse.
Temp' era già che l'aere s'annerava,
    ma non sì che tra li occhi suoi e ' miei
51   non dichiarisse ciò che pria serrava.
Ver' me si fece, e io ver' lui mi fei:
    giudice Nin gentil, quanto mi piacque
54   quando ti vidi non esser tra ' rei!
Nullo bel salutar tra noi si tacque;
    poi dimandò: "Quant' è che tu venisti
57   a piè del monte per le lontane acque?"

Then I saw that noble army gaze
　silently upward, hushed and expectant,
　　their faces pale and with lowly looks;　24
And I saw descending from above
　two angels bearing flaming swords,
　　their blades broken short and their points blunted.　27
Their robes were as green as newborn leaves,
　and as they trailed behind, the angels' green wings
　　beat softly on them and made them flutter.　30
One of them alighted a little above us
　and the other on the opposite bank,
　　so that the company was contained between.　33
I could clearly make out their bright, blond heads,
　but their actual faces bedazzled my eyes,
　　for excess always confounds our senses.　36
"Both of them come from Mary's bosom,"
　Sordello said, "to guard the valley
　　from the serpent that will be coming this way."　39
Not knowing which way it might be coming,
　I turned around and, frozen with fear,
　　huddled closer to those trusted shoulders.　42

Sordello went on, "Let us go down now
　among the great shades and speak with them.
　　It will be very pleasing to them to see you."　45
I believe I had taken only three steps down
　when I saw one of them staring just at me
　　as if wishing he could recall who I was.　48
It was now the hour when the air grows dark,
　but not yet so dark that it could not show
　　to his eyes and mine what it had blocked before.　51
He moved toward me, and I toward him.
　Noble Judge Nino, how glad I was
　　to see that you were not among the damned!　54
No fair greeting was left unsaid between us.
　Then he asked, "How long is it since you came
　　over the far waters to the foot of this mountain?"　57

"Oh!" diss' io lui, "per entro i luoghi tristi
venni stamane, e sono in prima vita,
ancor che l'altra, sì andando, acquisti."

E come fu la mia risposta udita,
Sordello ed elli in dietro si raccolse
come gente di sùbito smarrita.
L'uno a Virgilio e l'altro a un si volse
che sedea lì, gridando: "Sù, Currado!
vieni a veder che Dio per grazia volse."
Poi, vòlto a me: "Per quel singular grado
che tu dei a colui che sì nasconde
lo suo primo perché, che non lì è guado,
quando sarai di là da le larghe onde,
dì a Giovanna mia che per me chiami
là dove a li 'nnocenti si risponde.
Non credo che la sua madre più m'ami,
poscia che trasmutò le bianche bende,
le quai convien che, misera!, ancor brami.
Per lei assai di lieve si comprende
quanto in femmina foco d'amor dura,
se l'occhio o 'l tatto spesso non l'accende.
Non le farà sì bella sepultura
la vipera che Melanesi accampa,
com' avria fatto il gallo di Gallura."

Così dicea, segnato de la stampa,
nel suo aspetto, di quel dritto zelo
che misuratamente in core avvampa.

Li occhi miei ghiotti andavan pur al cielo,
pur là dove le stelle son più tarde,
sì come rota più presso a lo stelo.
E 'l duca mio: "Figliuol, che là sù guarde?"
E io a lui: "A quelle tre facelle
di che 'l polo di qua tutto quanto arde."
Ond' elli a me: "Le quattro chiare stelle
che vedevi staman, son di là basse,
e queste son salite ov' eran quelle."

"Oh," I said to him, "I came this morning,
from the regions of woe. I am in my first life,
although by my journey I gain the other."   *60*

When they heard my answer the two of them,
Sordello and Nino, drew back from me
like men struck by sudden bewilderment.   *63*
One of them turned to Virgil, and the other
called to someone seated there, "Up, Currado,
come see what God in His grace has willed!"   *66*
Then turning to me, "By the singular gratitude
you owe to Him who hides his primal purpose
so deep that there is no ford to reach it,   *69*
When you are far from these spreading waters,
tell my Giovanna to send prayers for me
to where the guiltless have their prayers heard.   *72*
I do not think her mother loves me now
since she stopped wearing white on her head,
which in her misery she will long for again.   *75*
Her example makes it easy to understand
how long love's fire lasts in a woman
if not rekindled by frequent sight and touch.   *78*
The viper on the banner of the Milanese
will not make her tomb look nearly so fine
as the cock of Gallura would have done."   *81*

As Nino said these things his face was stamped
with a look of righteous indignation
that burns in due measure within a man's heart.   *84*

My eager eyes kept moving upward
to the part of the sky where the stars turn slowest,
as a wheel turns slowest close to the axle.   *87*
My leader said, "Son, what are you staring at?"
"At those three little torches," I replied,
"with which the pole down here is all aglow."   *90*
"The four bright stars," Virgil explained,
"you saw this morning, are now low over there,
and these have risen where those others were."   *93*

Com' ei parlava, e Sordello a sé il trasse
   dicendo: "Vedi là 'l nostro avversaro";
96   e drizzò il dito perché 'n là guardasse.
Da quella parte onde non ha riparo
   la picciola vallea, era una biscia,
99   forse qual diede ad Eva il cibo amaro.
Tra l'erba e ' fior venìa la mala striscia,
   volgendo ad ora ad or la testa, e 'l dosso
102   leccando come bestia che si liscia.
Io non vidi, e però dicer non posso,
   come mosser li astor celestïali;
105   ma vidi bene e l'uno e l'altro mosso.
Sentendo fender l'aere a le verdi ali,
   fuggì 'l serpente, e li angeli dier volta,
108   suso a le poste rivolando iguali.

L'ombra che s'era al giudice raccolta
   quando chiamò, per tutto quello assalto
111   punto non fu da me guardare sciolta.
"Se la lucerna che ti mena in alto
   truovi nel tuo arbitrio tanta cera
114   quant' è mestiere infino al sommo smalto,"
cominciò ella, "se novella vera
   di Val di Magra o di parte vicina
117   sai, dillo a me, che già grande là era.
Fui chiamato Currado Malaspina;
   non son l'antico, ma di lui discesi;
120   a' miei portai l'amor che qui raffina."
"Oh!" diss' io lui, "per li vostri paesi
   già mai non fui; ma dove si dimora
123   per tutta Europa ch'ei non sien palesi?
La fama che la vostra casa onora,
   grida i segnori e grida la contrada,
126   sì che ne sa chi non vi fu ancora;
e io vi giuro, s'io di sopra vada,
   che vostra gente onrata non si sfregia
129   del pregio de la borsa e de la spada.

As he spoke, Sordello drew him closer,
  saying, "Behold our Adversary,"
    and pointed his finger where he should look.   *96*
In the part of the little valley
  that had no bank, a serpent appeared,
    perhaps the one who gave Eve the bitter fruit.   *99*
Through grass and flowers came the evil streak,
  turning its head from time to time, and licking
    its back, like a beast that sleeks itself.   *102*
I did not see and therefore cannot tell
  just how the celestial raptors took flight,
    but I could see both plainly once in motion.   *105*
When it heard the green wings split the air,
  the serpent fled, and the angels wheeled around
    and flew back to their respective posts.   *108*

The shade who had drawn closer to the judge
  when he called to him had not at any time
    in that entire assault taken his eyes off me.   *111*
"So may the lantern that leads you above
  find enough wax in your judgment and will
    to bring you to the enameled summit,"   *114*
He began, "if you have news that is true
  of Val di Magra or of its environs,
    please tell me, for once I was a great man there.   *117*
I was called Currado Malaspina,
  not the old Currado, but his descendant.
    I bore to my own the love that is purified here."   *120*
"Well," I said to him, "I have never been there,
  in your country. But is there anywhere
    in all of Europe where it is not renowned?   *123*
The fame and honor that attend your house
  celebrate its lords and their domains.
    Even those who have not been there know them,   *126*
And, so may I go above, I swear to you
  your honored family does not neglect
    the glory of its purse or of its sword.   *129*

Uso e natura sì la privilegia,
    che, perché il capo reo il mondo torca,
132   sola va dritta e 'l mal cammin dispregia."
Ed elli: "Or va; che 'l sol non si ricorca
    sette volte nel letto che 'l Montone
135   con tutti e quattro i piè cuopre e inforca,
che cotesta cortese oppinïone
    ti fia chiavata in mezzo de la testa
138   con maggior chiovi che d'altrui sermone,
se corso di giudicio non s'arresta."

And though an evil prince may pervert the world,
  your people, through custom and nature both,
    alone go straight and scorn the wicked path.   *132*
And he said, "Now go, for not a seventh time
  will the sun lie in the zodiacal bed
    that is straddled by the four legs of the Ram,   *135*
Before events will hammer into your head
  this courteous opinion with nails much stronger
    than what you, and other men also, have said,   *138*
If Judgment's course is delayed no longer."

Canto IX

THE CANTO OPENS WITH AN *elaborate image of moonrise. The fatigued Dante falls asleep and has a frightening dream in which he is borne up into the sky by a golden eagle. They fly so high that they are burned, and this sensation of burning jolts Dante out of his sleep. He is at first frightened and unsure of where he is but is quickly comforted by Virgil. Virgil explains that they have ascended the mountain and arrived at the gate of Purgatory. While Dante slept, St Lucy came to them and carried him up to the*

La concubina di Titone antico
 già s'imbiancava al balco d'orïente,
3   fuor de le braccia del suo dolce amico;
di gemme la sua fronte era lucente,
 poste in figura del freddo animale
6   che con la coda percuote la gente;
e la notte, de' passi con che sale,
 fatti avea due nel loco ov' eravamo,
9   e 'l terzo già chinava in giuso l'ale;
quand' io, che meco avea di quel d'Adamo,
 vinto dal sonno, in su l'erba inchinai
12   là 've già tutti e cinque sedavamo.

Ne l'ora che comincia i tristi lai
 la rondinella presso a la mattina,
15   forse a memoria de' suo' primi guai,
e che la mente nostra, peregrina
 più da la carne e men da' pensier presa,
18   a le sue visïon quasi è divina,
in sogno mi parea veder sospesa
 un'aguglia nel ciel con penne d'oro,
21   con l'ali aperte e a calare intesa;

gateway, departing at the precise moment of his waking. Dante and Virgil walk toward the gate and see its angel guardian, who questions them on how they come to be there. Three steps lead up to the gate. Dante kneels before the angel, who traces seven Ps on his forehead. The angel then unlocks the gate with two keys, one gold and one silver. The gate opens with a mighty roar, and as Dante enters he believes he hears singing.

The concubine of ancient Tithonus
  was gleaming white on her eastern balcony,
    away now from her sweet lover's arms,   *3*
Her forehead enstarred with a set of jewels
  arranged in the shape of that frigid creature
    that strikes at a person with its tail.   *6*
And Night, in the place where we were then,
  had ascended two of the steps that she climbs,
    with the third already bending down its wings,   *9*
When I, who had something of Adam in me,
  Beaten by sleep, lay down on the grass
    where the five of us were already seated.   *12*

At the morning hour, when the swallow
  begins to sing her laments, remembering,
    it may be, her suffering of old,   *15*
And when our minds most go on pilgrimage
  from our bodies, and, least bound by thoughts,
    are in their visions almost divine,   *18*
I seemed to see, in a vivid dream,
  an eagle in the sky with plumes of gold
    on outspread wings and prepared to dive.   *21*

ed esser mi parea là dove fuoro
  abbandonati i suoi da Ganimede,
24   quando fu ratto al sommo consistoro.
Fra me pensava: "Forse questa fiede
  pur qui per uso, e forse d'altro loco
27   disdegna di portarne suso in piede."
Poi mi parea che, poi rotata un poco,
  terribil come folgor discendesse,
30   e me rapisse suso infino al foco.
Ivi parea che ella e io ardesse;
  e sì lo 'ncendio imaginato cosse,
33   che convenne che 'l sonno si rompesse.

Non altrimenti Achille si riscosse,
  li occhi svegliati rivolgendo in giro
36   e non sappiendo là dove si fosse,
quando la madre da Chirón a Schiro
  trafuggò lui dormendo in le sue braccia,
39   là onde poi li Greci il dipartiro;
che mi scoss' io, sì come da la faccia
  mi fuggì 'l sonno, e diventa' ismorto,
42   come fa l'uom che, spaventato, agghiaccia.
Dallato m'era solo il mio conforto,
  e 'l sole er' alto già più che due ore,
45   e 'l viso m'era a la marina torto.

"Non aver tema," disse il mio segnore;
  "fatti sicur, ché noi semo a buon punto;
48   non stringer, ma rallarga ogne vigore.
Tu se' omai al purgatorio giunto:
  vedi là il balzo che 'l chiude dintorno;
51   vedi l'entrata là 've par digiunto.
Dianzi, ne l'alba che procede al giorno,
  quando l'anima tua dentro dormia,
54   sovra li fiori ond' è là giù addorno
venne una donna, e disse: 'I' son Lucia;
  lasciatemi pigliar costui che dorme;
57   sì l'agevolerò per la sua via.'

In my dream I seemed to be in the spot
  where Ganymede left his companions behind
    when he was swept up to the highest court,   *24*
And I said to myself, "Perhaps this eagle
  is used to striking only here, and disdains
    to snatch up anyone from another place."   *27*
Then the eagle seemed, having circled a while,
  to descend as terrible as a thunderbolt
    and snatch me up to the sphere of fire,   *30*
Where it seemed the eagle and I both burned;
  and the imagined fire scorched me so
    that my sleep was disrupted and I awoke.   *33*

In just the same way as Achilles was startled
  when he turned his awakened eyes around
    without any idea of where he was,   *36*
When his mother carried him, asleep in her arms,
  from Chiron to the island of Scyros,
    from where the Greeks would later take him off,   *39*
So too was I startled, as soon as sleep
  fled from my face, and I grew pale as death,
    like a man who is frozen stiff with terror.   *42*
Only my Comfort was beside me now.
  The sun was already two hours high,
    and my face was turned away to the sea.   *45*

"Have no fear," said my lord. "Take courage,
  for we are in a good position now.
    Do not hold back, but rally all your strength.   *48*
You have now arrived at Purgatory.
  See the rock wall that encircles it,
    and the entrance where the wall looks notched.   *51*
A while ago, in the dawn before day,
  when your soul was slumbering within you,
    there came upon the flowers that adorn that place   *54*
A lady who said, 'I am Lucy.
  Let me take this man who is sleeping,
    for so will I speed him on his way.'   *57*

Sordel rimase e l'altre genti forme;
  ella ti tolse, e come 'l dì fu chiaro,
60   sen venne suso; e io per le sue orme.
Qui ti posò, ma pria mi dimostraro
  li occhi suoi belli quella intrata aperta;
63   poi ella e 'l sonno ad una se n'andaro."

A guisa d'uom che 'n dubbio si raccerta
  e che muta in conforto sua paura,
66   poi che la verità li è discoperta,
mi cambia' io; e come sanza cura
  vide me 'l duca mio, su per lo balzo
69   si mosse, e io di rietro inver' l'altura.

Lettor, tu vedi ben com' io innalzo
  la mia matera, e però con più arte
72   non ti maravigliar s'io la rincalzo.

Noi ci appressammo, ed eravamo in parte
  che là dove pareami prima rotto,
75   pur come un fesso che muro diparte,
vidi una porta, e tre gradi di sotto
  per gire ad essa, di color diversi,
78   e un portier ch'ancor non facea motto.
E come l'occhio più e più v'apersi,
  vidil seder sovra 'l grado sovrano,
81   tal ne la faccia ch'io non lo soffersi;
e una spada nuda avëa in mano,
  che reflettëa i raggi sì ver' noi,
84   ch'io drizzava spesso il viso in vano.
"Dite costinci: che volete voi?"
  cominciò elli a dire, "ov' è la scorta?
87   Guardate che 'l venir sù non vi nòi."
"Donna del ciel, di queste cose accorta,"
  rispuose 'l mio maestro a lui, "pur dianzi
90   ne disse: 'Andate là: quivi è la porta.'"
"Ed ella i passi vostri in bene avanzi,"
  ricominciò il cortese portinaio:
93   "Venite dunque a' nostri gradi innanzi."

Sordello and the other nobles remained.
  She took you, and when the day was bright
    she came up here, and I followed her steps.   *60*
She laid you down here, but not before
  her beautiful eyes showed me the entrance there.
    Then she and sleep both left you together."   *63*

And as a man who has come to see the truth
  after being in doubt exchanges his fear
    for confidence and is now reassured,   *66*
So was I changed, and when my leader saw
  that my worry was gone, he started up the path
    with me behind him, heading for the height.   *69*

Reader, you surely see that I am raising
  the level of my poem, so do not wonder
    if I reinforce it with more artifice.   *72*

We drew closer, and we reached a place
  where what had seemed a fissure before,
    a breach that causes a gap in a wall,   *75*
I now saw was a gate with three steps beneath
  leading up to it, each a different color,
    and a gatekeeper who as yet had said not a word.   *78*
And as I looked more closely I saw
  that he was seated upon the topmost step,
    and his face was too much for me to endure.   *81*
He held in his hand a naked sword
  that reflected the sun so brightly upon us
    that I tried but could not turn my eyes toward it.   *84*
"Say from there, what is it you want?"
  were his first words. "Where is your escort?
    Take care lest your ascent be harmful to you."   *87*
"A lady from heaven who knows these things well,"
  my master answered, "just a moment ago
    said to us, 'Go that way; there is the gate.'"   *90*
"And may she advance your steps to the good,"
  the courtly gatekeeper responded.
    "Come forward then, here to our stairs."   *93*

Là ne venimmo; e lo scaglion primaio
bianco marmo era sì pulito e terso,
96   ch'io mi specchiai in esso qual io paio.
Era il secondo tinto più che perso,
d'una petrina ruvida e arsiccia,
99   crepata per lo lungo e per traverso.
Lo terzo, che di sopra s'ammassiccia,
porfido mi parea, sì fiammeggiante
102   come sangue che fuor di vena spiccia.
Sovra questo tenëa ambo le piante
l'angel di Dio sedendo in su la soglia
105   che mi sembiava pietra di diamante.
Per li tre gradi sù di buona voglia
mi trasse il duca mio, dicendo: "Chiedi
108   umilemente che 'l serrame scioglia."
Divoto mi gittai a' santi piedi;
misericordia chiesi e ch'el m'aprisse,
111   ma tre volte nel petto pria mi diedi.
Sette P ne la fronte mi descrisse
col punton de la spada, e "Fa che lavi,
114   quando se' dentro, queste piaghe' disse."
Cenere, o terra che secca si cavi,
d'un color fora col suo vestimento;
117   e di sotto da quel trasse due chiavi.
L'una era d'oro e l'altra era d'argento;
pria con la bianca e poscia con la gialla
120   fece a la porta sì, ch'i' fu' contento.
"Quandunque l'una d'este chiavi falla,
che non si volga dritta per la toppa,"
123   diss' elli a noi, "non s'apre questa calla.
Più cara è l'una; ma l'altra vuol troppa
d'arte e d'ingegno avanti che diserri,
126   perch' ella è quella che 'l nodo digroppa.
Da Pier le tegno; e dissemi ch'i' erri
anzi ad aprir ch'a tenerla serrata,
129   pur che la gente a' piedi mi s'atterri."
Poi pinse l'uscio a la porta sacrata,
dicendo: "Intrate; ma facciovi accorti
132   che di fuor torna chi 'n dietro si guata."

And so we went ahead. The first step
  was white marble, so polished and clear
    that I could see my true reflection in it. *96*
The second, colored darker than purple,
  was made of a stone that was rough and scorched
    and split along both its length and breadth. *99*
The third, a massy slab at the top,
  seemed like porphyry to me, as flaming red
    as blood that spurts from an opened vein. *102*
The angel of God had both his feet planted
  on this step as he sat on the threshold,
    which seemed to me to be made of adamant. *105*
Up these three steps my leader drew me,
  with all goodwill, and then he said,
    "Beg him humbly to draw back the bolt." *108*
I threw myself devoutly at those holy feet
  and pleaded that in mercy he open the gate,
    but first beat my breast three times with my fist. *111*
Seven Ps the angel traced on my forehead
  with the point of his sword, saying, "See that you wash
    all these wounds away when you are inside." *114*
Ashes, or earth that is dug out dry,
  would be the same color as the garments he wore,
    and from within them he drew out two keys, *117*
One made of gold and the other of silver.
  What he did to the gate then, first with the white one
    and then with the yellow, left me content. *120*
"If either of these keys should ever fail,
  so that it does not turn inside the lock,"
    he said to us, "this gate does not open. *123*
One is more precious, but the other requires
  more skill and art before it will turn the lock,
    for this is the one that unties the knot. *126*
I have them from Peter, who instructed me
  to err in opening rather than keeping shut,
    if only the soul will fall down at my feet." *129*
Then he opened the door of the sacred portal,
  saying, "Enter, but I admonish you,
    he who looks back goes outside again." *132*

E quando fuor ne' cardini distorti
li spigoli di quella regge sacra,
135   che di metallo son sonanti e forti,
non rugghiò sì né si mostrò sì acra
Tarpëa, come tolto le fu il buono
138   Metello, per che poi rimase macra.
Io mi rivolsi attento al primo tuono,
e "*Te Deum laudamus*" mi parea
141   udire in voce mista al dolce suono.
Tale imagine a punto mi rendea
ciò ch'io udiva, qual prender si suole
144   quando a cantar con organi si stea;
ch'or sì or no s'intendon le parole.

And when the hinges of that sacred door,
  that are made of heavy, resounding metal,
    turned on their pins, their strident roar   135
Was louder than the sound the Tarpeian Rock made
  when the good Metellus was drawn away
    and the meager treasury was never repaid.   138
I turned aside, on that first sound intent,
  and then thought I heard *"Te Deum laudamus"*
    chanted to musical accompaniment,   141
A sound that gave me the same impression
  we have when listening to a choir chant
    to the accompanying music of an organ: 144
Now we can hear the words, and now we can't.

CANTO X

DANTE AND VIRGIL PASS THROUGH *the gate of Purgatory without looking back. They climb through a narrow and steep fissure of rock before emerging onto a terrace running around the side of the mountain. Carved into walls of the mountainside are three exemplary scenes demonstrating the*

Poi fummo dentro al soglio de la porta
  che 'l mal amor de l'anime disusa,
3   perché fa parer dritta la via torta,
sonando la senti' esser richiusa;
  e s'io avesse li occhi vòlti ad essa,
6   qual fora stata al fallo degna scusa?

Noi salavam per una pietra fessa,
  che si moveva e d'una e d'altra parte,
9   sì come l'onda che fugge e s'appressa.
"Qui si conviene usare un poco d'arte,"
  cominciò 'l duca mio, 'in accostarsi
12   or quinci, or quindi al lato che si parte."
E questo fece i nostri passi scarsi,
  tanto che pria lo scemo de la luna
15   rigiunse al letto suo per ricorcarsi,
che noi fossimo fuor di quella cruna;
  ma quando fummo liberi e aperti
18   sù dove il monte in dietro si rauna,
ïo stancato e amendue incerti
  di nostra via, restammo in su un piano
21   solingo più che strade per diserti.
Da la sua sponda, ove confina il vano,
  al piè de l'alta ripa che pur sale,
24   misurrebbe in tre volte un corpo umano;

virtue of humility: the Annunciation, David dancing before the Ark of the Covenant, and the Emperor Trajan helping the poor widow. The travelers see a group of people moving slowly toward them, bent low to the ground, and carrying huge boulders on their backs.

When we had crossed the threshold of the gate
   that is not used by souls with evil loves
      because they make the crooked seem straight,   *3*
I knew by the sound that it had slammed shut.
   And if I had turned my eyes to look,
      what excuse would have sufficed for such a fault?   *6*

We were climbing through a fissure in the rock
   that slanted first one way and then another,
      like a wave that ebbs and then comes surging back,   *9*
When my leader said, "We will have to use
   a little skill here and cling to the face
      of whichever side leans away from us."   *12*
This slowed down our halting steps so much
   that the oval of the waning moon
      had reached its bed and sunk into it,   *15*
Before we were out of that needle's eye.
   But when we were free and out in the open
      up where the mountainside withdraws,   *18*
I weary, and both of us uncertain
   of our path, we stopped on a plateau
      more solitary than a desert road.   *21*
From its edge, which borders on the abyss,
   to the foot of the sheer embankment's rise
      would measure three times the height of a man.   *24*

e quanto l'occhio mio potea trar d'ale,
  or dal sinistro e or dal destro fianco,
27   questa cornice mi parea cotale.
Là sù non eran mossi i piè nostri anco,
  quand'io conobbi quella ripa intorno
30   che dritto di salita aveva manco,
esser di marmo candido e addorno
  d'intagli sì, che non pur Policleto,
33   ma la natura lì avrebbe scorno.

L'angel che venne in terra col decreto
  de la molt'anni lagrimata pace,
36   ch'aperse il ciel del suo lungo divieto,
dinanzi a noi pareva sì verace
  quivi intagliato in un atto soave,
39   che non sembiava imagine che tace.
Giurato si saria ch'el dicesse "*Ave!*"
  perché iv'era imaginata quella
42   ch'ad aprir l'alto amor volse la chiave;
e avea in atto impressa esta favella
  "*Ecce ancilla Deï*," propriamente
45   come figura in cera si suggella.

"Non tener pur ad un loco la mente,"
  disse 'l dolce maestro, che m'avea
48   da quella parte onde 'l cuore ha la gente.
Per ch'i' mi mossi col viso, e vedea
  di retro da Maria, da quella costa
51   onde m'era colui che mi movea,
un'altra storia ne la roccia imposta;
  per ch'io varcai Virgilio, e fe'mi presso,
54   acciò che fosse a li occhi miei disposta.
Era intagliato lì nel marmo stesso
  Lo carro e ' buoi, traendo l'arca santa,
57   per che si teme officio non commesso.
Dinanzi parea gente; e tutta quanta,
  partita in sette cori, a' due mie' sensi
60   faceva dir l'un "No,' l'altro 'Sì, canta."

And as far as my eye could spread its wings,
  now to the left side, now the other,
    the terrace extended into the distance.   *27*
Our feet had not yet stepped onto it
  when I saw that the face of the encircling cliff,
    which was steep and impossible to climb,   *30*
Was made of white marble, and was adorned
  with carvings so fine they would put to shame
    not only Polyclitus but Nature herself.   *33*

The angel who came to earth to announce
  the peace that had been wept for all those years
    and opened heaven that had long been banned   *36*
Appeared before us so truly carved
  in an attitude so gentle and sweet
    that it seemed not at all like a silent image.   *39*
You would have sworn that it was saying "*Ave*,"
  for imaged there also was the woman
    who turned the key that opened Love on high;   *42*
And her expression was stamped with the words
  "*Ecce ancilla Dei*," in just the same way
    as a figure can be impressed on wax.   *45*

"Do not keep your mind on one part only,"
  said my gentle master, who had me
    on that side where we have our hearts.   *48*
And so I turned my face, and looking
  beyond Mary I saw, on the same side
    as the one who was directing me,   *51*
Another story set in the rock.
  I edged past Virgil and got closer to it
    so that my eyes could take it all in.   *54*
Carved into the marble there were the oxen
  and cart, drawing the sacred ark that makes us fear
    to assume a duty not assigned to us.   *57*
Walking ahead of it were figures divided
  into seven choirs, a scene that made
    one sense say "No!" and another "Yes, they sing!"   *60*

Similemente al fummo de li 'ncensi
    che v'era imaginato, li occhi e 'l naso
63   e al sì e al no discordi fensi.
Lì precedeva al benedetto vaso,
    trescando alzato, l'umile salmista,
66   e più e men che re era in quel caso.
Di contra, effigïata ad una vista
    d'un gran palazzo, Micòl ammirava
69   sì come donna dispettosa e trista.

I' mossi i piè del loco dov' io stava,
    per avvisar da presso un'altra istoria,
72   che di dietro a Micòl mi biancheggiava.
Quiv' era storïata l'alta gloria
    del roman principato, il cui valore
75   mosse Gregorio a la sua gran vittoria;
i' dico di Traiano imperadore;
    e una vedovella li era al freno,
78   di lagrime atteggiata e di dolore.
Intorno a lui parea calcato e pieno
    di cavalieri, e l'aguglie ne l'oro
81   sovr' essi in vista al vento si movieno.
La miserella intra tutti costoro
    pareva dir: 'Segnor, fammi vendetta
84   di mio figliuol ch'è morto, ond' io m'accoro";
ed elli a lei rispondere: "Or aspetta
    tanto ch'i' torni"; e quella: "Segnor mio,"
87   come persona in cui dolor s'affretta,
"se tu non torni?"; ed ei: "Chi fia dov' io,
    la ti farà"; ed ella: "L'altrui bene
90   a te che fia, se 'l tuo metti in oblio?";
ond' elli: "Or ti conforta; ch'ei convene
    ch'i' solva il mio dovere anzi ch'i' mova:
93   giustizia vuole e pietà mi ritene."

Colui che mai non vide cosa nova
    produsse esto visibile parlare,
96   novello a noi perché qui non si trova.

In the same way, the sculpted incense smoke
  caused discord between my eyes and my nose,
    the one saying "Yes," and the other "No."   63
Before the blessed ark the humble psalmist,
  his robe hitched up, leaped up and danced.
    There he was, both more and less than king.   66
Opposite was a figure at a window
  of a grand palace. This was Michal,
    who looked on like a woman scornful and grim.   69

I went on a few steps from where I stood
  to look more closely at another story
    that gleamed at me in white beyond Michal.   72
Depicted there was the crowning glory
  of a Roman prince, the one whose valor
    urged Gregory on to his great victory—   75
I mean of course the emperor Trajan.
  A poor widow was by his bridle,
    weeping as she stood in a posture of grief.   78
The ground around the emperor was trampled
  by a mounted troop, and above them the eagles,
    cast in gold, seemed to move in the wind,   81
While in their midst the wretched woman
  could be seen saying, "Avenge, my lord,
    my murdered son, for whom my heart grieves."   84
And he seemed to answer, "Only wait
  until I return." To which she said, "My lord,"
    with grief's urgency, "what if you don't return?"   87
To which he replied, "Then my successor
  will see to it." And she, "What use is there
    in another's goodness, if you forget your own?"   90
And then he said, "Take comfort now, for I must
  pay my debt to you before I go to war.
    Justice wills it, and compassion holds me here."   93

The One who never sees anything new
  wrought these images of speech visible,
    new to us because they are not found here.   96

Mentr' io mi dilettava di guardare
l'imagini di tante umilitadi,
99   e per lo fabbro loro a veder care,
"Ecco di qua, ma fanno i passi radi,"
mormorava il poeta, "molte genti:
102   questi ne 'nvïeranno a li alti gradi."
Li occhi miei, ch'a mirare eran contenti
per veder novitadi ond' e' son vaghi,
105   volgendosi ver' lui non furon lenti.

Non vo' però, lettor, che tu ti smaghi
di buon proponimento per udire
108   come Dio vuol che 'l debito si paghi.
Non attender la forma del martìre:
pensa la succession; pensa ch'al peggio
111   oltre la gran sentenza non può ire.

Io cominciai: "Maestro, quel ch'io veggio
muovere a noi, non mi sembian persone,
114   e non so che, sì nel veder vaneggio."
Ed elli a me: "La grave condizione
di lor tormento a terra li rannicchia,
117   sì che ' miei occhi pria n'ebber tencione.
Ma guarda fiso là, e disviticchia
col viso quel che vien sotto a quei sassi:
120   già scorger puoi come ciascun si picchia."

O superbi cristian, miseri lassi,
che, de la vista de la mente infermi,
123   fidanza avete ne' retrosi passi,
non v'accorgete voi che noi siam vermi
nati a formar l'angelica farfalla,
126   che vola a la giustizia sanza schermi?
Di che l'animo vostro in alto galla,
poi siete quasi antomata in difetto,
129   sì come vermo in cui formazion falla?

While I was taking delight in viewing
  these images of such great humility,
    dearer to see because of their Maker,   *99*
"Here come a great crowd of people,"
  murmured the poet, "but with slow steps.
    They will direct us to the next set of stairs."   *102*
My eyes, which had been perfectly content,
  were not slow to turn in his direction,
    eager as ever to view any new thing.   *105*

But, Reader, I would not have you turn
  from your good resolution when you hear how
    God means for us to pay our debt.   *108*
Do not dwell on the form of the suffering.
  Think of what follows; think that at the worst
    it cannot go beyond the final Judgment.   *111*

"Master," I began, "that which I see
  moving toward us does not look like people,
    but my sight is blurred and I can't make them out."   *114*
And he answered, "The nature of their torment
  is so grave it doubles them to the ground.
    My own eyes at first were undecided on this.   *117*
But look more closely, and disentangle
  the figures from the stones they are bent beneath,
    and you can see how each is beating his breast."   *120*

O arrogant Christians, miserable wretches,
  feeble in the vision and scope of your mind,
    you put all your trust in backward paces.   *123*
Do you not understand that we are worms
  born to become angelic butterflies
    that soar to justice without protection?   *126*
Why does your mind float up to the sky
  since you are little more than defective insects,
    worms, as it were, not yet fully formed?   *129*

Come per sostentar solaio o tetto,
per mensola talvolta una figura
132   si vede giugner le ginocchia al petto,
la qual fa del non ver vera rancura
nascere 'n chi la vede; così fatti
135   vid' io color, quando puosi ben cura.
Vero è che più e meno eran contratti
secondo ch'avien più e meno a dosso;
138   e qual più pazïenza avea ne li atti,
piangendo parea dicer: "Più non posso."

A corbel to support a ceiling or a roof
  is sometimes cast in the form of a figure
    with its knees drawn up tight against its chest,   *132*
And though unreal it creates real dismay
  in whoever sees it. When I looked closely,
    I saw these souls stooped in much the same way.   *135*
The degree to which their bodies were bent
  was in proportion to how much their backs bore,
    and even he who seemed the most patient   *138*
Seemed to say, weeping, "I can bear no more."

CANTO XI

THE CANTO OPENS WITH AN *expanded version of the Lord's Prayer, spoken by the souls of the proud, which closes with a prayer for the deliverance of those still alive on Earth. The narrator in turn exhorts his readers to pray for the souls in Purgatory. Virgil courteously addresses the souls, asking them to point the way to the easiest path up the mountain. An at first unidentified soul, hidden under his rocky burden,*

"O Padre nostro, che ne' cieli stai,
  non circunscritto, ma per più amore
3   ch'ai primi effetti di là sù tu hai,
laudato sia 'l tuo nome e 'l tuo valore
  da ogne creatura, com' è degno
6   di render grazie al tuo dolce vapore.
Vegna ver' noi la pace del tuo regno,
  ché noi ad essa non potem da noi,
9   s'ella non vien, con tutto nostro ingegno.
Come del suo voler li angeli tuoi
  fan sacrificio a te, cantando osanna,
12   così facciano li uomini de' suoi.
Dà oggi a noi la cotidiana manna,
  sanza la qual per questo aspro diserto
15   a retro va chi più di gir s'affanna.
E come noi lo mal ch'avem sofferto
  perdoniamo a ciascuno, e tu perdona
18   benigno, e non guardar lo nostro merto.
Nostra virtù che di legger s'adona,
  non spermentar con l'antico avversaro,
21   ma libera da lui che sì la sprona.
Quest' ultima preghiera, segnor caro,
  già non si fa per noi, ché non bisogna,
24   ma per color che dietro a noi restaro."

tells them the way before introducing himself as Omberto Aldobrandesco.
Dante is then recognized by the soul of Oderisi da Gubbio, an illuminator,
who gives a long speech on the transience of earthly fame with specific
reference to artists. Oderisi then describes the life of the soul who is walking
in front of him, Provenzan Salvani.

"Our Father, who art in Heaven,
   circumscribed only by the greater love
      Thou hast for Thy primal works on high,   *3*
Praised be Thy name and Thy power
   by every creature, as is meet and just
      to render thanks for Thy sweet breath.   *6*
May the peace of Thy kingdom come to us,
   for we cannot attain it of ourselves
      if it come not on its own, for all our wit.   *9*
As Thy angels make Thee sacrifice
   of their own free will, singing hosanna,
      so let men make sacrifice of theirs.   *12*
Give us this day the daily manna
   without which we who strive to advance
      go backward in this harsh wilderness.   *15*
And, as we forgive the wrong done unto us
   by others, do Thou forgive us also,
      regarding not our merit, but Thy mercy.   *18*
And do not pit our strength, easily subdued,
   against the ancient adversary
      but deliver us from him who tempts us.   *21*
This final prayer, dear Lord, is made
   not for ourselves, for there is no need,
      but for those still left behind us."   *24*

Così a sé e noi buona ramogna
  quell' ombre orando, andavan sotto 'l pondo,
27   simile a quel che talvolta si sogna,
disparmente angosciate tutte a tondo
  e lasse su per la prima cornice,
30   purgando la caligine del mondo.
Se di là sempre ben per noi si dice,
  di qua che dire e far per lor si puote
33   da quei c'hanno al voler buona radice?
Ben si de' loro atar lavar le note
  che portar quinci, sì che, mondi e lievi,
36   possano uscire a le stellate ruote.

"Deh, se giustizia e pietà vi disgrievi
  tosto, sì che possiate muover l'ala,
39   che secondo il disio vostro vi lievi,
mostrate da qual mano inver' la scala
  si va più corto; e se c'è più d'un varco,
42   quel ne 'nsegnate che men erto cala;
ché questi che vien meco, per lo 'ncarco
  de la carne d'Adamo onde si veste,
45   al montar sù, contra sua voglia, è parco."

Le lor parole, che rendero a queste
  che dette avea colui cu' io seguiva,
48   non fur da cui venisser manifeste;
ma fu detto: "A man destra per la riva
  con noi venite, e troverete il passo
51   possibile a salir persona viva.
E s'io non fossi impedito dal sasso
  che la cervice mia superba doma,
54   onde portar convienmi il viso basso,
cotesti, ch'ancor vive e non si noma,
  guardere' io, per veder s'i' 'l conosco,
57   e per farlo pietoso a questa soma.
Io fui latino e nato d'un gran Tosco:
  Guiglielmo Aldobrandesco fu mio padre;
60   non so se 'l nome suo già mai fu vosco.

Praying thus for their deliverance and ours
  those shades walked on beneath their burdens—
    not unlike those we sometimes have in our dreams—   *27*
As in disparate agony they made their way
  wearily around the entire first ledge,
    purging away the darkness of the world.   *30*
If good is always said of us up there,
  what can be said or done for them down here
    by those whose will is rooted in good?   *33*
Surely we should help them cleanse the stains
  they took from here, so that pure and light
    they might ascend to the wheeling stars.   *36*

"Ah, so may justice and pity soon relieve you
  of your burden and let you spread your wings
    to lift yourself as high as your desires,   *39*
Show us the shortest way to the stairs,
  and if there is more than one passage up,
    tell us which one has the least steep ascent,   *42*
For my companion here, because he is burdened
  with the flesh of Adam, must climb slowly
    however much he yearns to mount higher."   *45*

It was not at all clear to me at first
  by whom the words were spoken in response
    to this request that my leader had made,   *48*
But someone said, "If you keep to the right
  as you come along with us on this bank,
    you will find stairs a living man can climb.   *51*
And if I were not hindered by the stone
  that subdues my proud neck
    so that I must hold my face down low,   *54*
I would look at this man who is still alive
  and is not named, to see if I know him
    and make him pity me for my burden.   *57*
I was Italian, a great Tuscan's son.
  Guglielmo Aldobrandesco was my father.
    I do not know if you recognize his name.   *60*

L'antico sangue e l'opere leggiadre
d'i miei maggior mi fer sì arrogante,
63   che, non pensando a la comune madre,
ogn' uomo ebbi in despetto tanto avante,
ch'io ne mori,' come i Sanesi sanno,
66   e sallo in Campagnatico ogne fante.
Io sono Omberto; e non pur a me danno
superbia fa, ché tutti miei consorti
69   ha ella tratti seco nel malanno.
E qui convien ch'io questo peso porti
per lei, tanto che a Dio si sodisfaccia,
72   poi ch'io nol fe' tra ' vivi, qui tra ' morti."

Ascoltando chinai in giù la faccia;
e un di lor, non questi che parlava,
75   si torse sotto il peso che li 'mpaccia,
e videmi e conobbemi e chiamava,
tenendo li occhi con fatica fisi
78   a me che tutto chin con loro andava.
"Oh!" diss' io lui, "non se' tu Oderisi,
l'onor d'Agobbio e l'onor di quell' arte
81   ch'alluminar chiamata è in Parisi?"

"Frate," diss' elli, "più ridon le carte
che pennelleggia Franco Bolognese;
84   l'onore è tutto or suo, e mio in parte.
Ben non sare' io stato sì cortese
mentre ch'io vissi, per lo gran disio
87   de l'eccellenza ove mio core intese.
Di tal superbia qui si paga il fio;
e ancor non sarei qui, se non fosse
90   che, possendo peccar, mi volsi a Dio.
Oh vana gloria de l'umane posse!
com' poco verde in su la cima dura,
93   se non è giunta da l'etati grosse!
Credette Cimabue ne la pittura ·
tener lo campo, e ora ha Giotto il grido,
96   sì che la fama di colui è scura.

The ancient blood and gallant exploits
　of my forebears made me so arrogant
　　That, not thinking of our common mother,　　　　*63*
I held all men in such excessive scorn
　that it caused my death, as the Sienese know,
　　and every child in the Campagnatico.　　　　　*66*
I am Omberto, and not only to me
　is pride a curse, but it has dragged with it
　　all my kinfolk to calamity.　　　　　　　　　　*69*
It is for this pride I must bear this weight
　until God is satisfied, here among the dead,
　　for I did not do so among the living."　　　　　*72*

As I was listening I lowered my head,
　and one of them, not the one speaking,
　　twisted beneath the heavy load on his back,　　*75*
Saw me, knew me, and then called out,
　keeping his eyes fixed, with great effort, on me
　　as I walked hunched over in their company.　　*78*
"Oh," I said to him, "are you not Oderisi,
　the honor of Gubbio and honor of that art
　　which is called 'illumination' in Paris?"　　　　*81*

"Brother," he said, "the pages smile more brightly
　when Franco Bolognese puts his brush to them.
　　The honor is all his now, mine only in part.　　*84*
I certainly wouldn't have been so courteous
　while I was alive, for I had in my heart
　　an intense desire to be ever the best.　　　　　*87*
It is for such pride that we pay our debt here,
　and I would not be here yet, if I had not
　　turned to God while I still had power to sin.　　*90*
And, O, the vanity of human powers!
　How briefly lasts the crowning green wreath,
　　unless it is followed by an age wholly crass.　　*93*
Cimabue thought that as a painter
　he held the field, but now all cry for Giotto,
　　and so the other's fame now grows dim.　　　　*96*

Così ha tolto l'uno a l'altro Guido
  la gloria de la lingua; e forse è nato
99   chi l'uno e l'altro caccerà del nido.
Non è il mondan romore altro ch'un fiato
  di vento, ch'or vien quinci e or vien quindi,
102   e muta nome perché muta lato.
Che voce avrai tu più, se vecchia scindi
  da te la carne, che se fossi morto
105   anzi che tu lasciassi il 'pappo' e 'l 'dindi,'
pria che passin mill' anni? ch'è più corto
  spazio a l'etterno, ch'un muover di ciglia
108   al cerchio che più tardi in cielo è torto.
Colui che del cammin sì poco piglia
  dinanzi a me, Toscana sonò tutta;
111   e ora a pena in Siena sen pispiglia,
ond' era sire quando fu distrutta
  la rabbia fiorentina, che superba
114   fu a quel tempo sì com' ora è putta.
La vostra nominanza è color d'erba,
  che viene e va, e quei la discolora
117   per cui ella esce de la terra acerba."

E io a lui: "Tuo vero dir m'incora
  bona umiltà, e gran tumor m'appiani;
120   ma chi è quei di cui tu parlavi ora?"
"Quelli è," rispuose, "Provenzan Salvani;
  ed è qui perché fu presuntüoso
123   a recar Siena tutta a le sue mani.
Ito è così e va, sanza riposo,
  poi che morì; cotal moneta rende
126   a sodisfar chi è di là troppo oso."

E io: "Se quello spirito ch'attende,
  pria che si penta, l'orlo de la vita,
129   qua giù dimora e qua sù non ascende,
se buona orazïon lui non aita,
  prima che passi tempo quanto visse,
132   come fu la venuta lui largita?"

So too has one Guido taken from the other
  the glory of our tongue; and perhaps one is born
    who will chase one or the other out of the nest.   *99*
Worldly fame is no more than a gust of wind
  that blows now from one quarter, now from another,
    changing its name as it changes direction.   *102*
What greater fame will you have in a thousand years
  if you part from your body when it is old
    than if you had died when you were still lisping   *105*
'Pappo' and 'dindi'? Compared to eternity
  a thousand years is shorter than the blink of an eye
    is to one revolution of heaven's slowest sphere.   *108*
That person barely moving in front of me
  was once renowned throughout Tuscany.
    Now even Siena hardly whispers his name.   *111*
He was the lord there when they destroyed
  the rabid menace of Florence, a city
    as proud then as she is now a whore.   *114*
Your reputation is the color of grass,
  which comes and goes, faded by the same sun
    that makes it spring up green from the earth."   *117*

"Your true words instill humility," I said,
  "deep in my heart, and eases its swelling.
    But who is he of whom you spoke just now?"   *120*
"That," he replied, "is Provenzan Salvani,
  and he is here because he presumed
    to take all of Siena into his grasp.   *123*
He has gone like this, and goes on without rest,
  ever since he died; such coin whoever
    is too bold back there pays in recompense here."   *126*

Then I said, "If a spirit who waits
  until the end of his life before he repents
    must stay down below and not come up here   *129*
Until as much time has passed as he lived on earth,
  unless he is helped by holy prayers,
    how was he allowed to come up here?"   *132*

"Quando vivea più glorïoso," disse,
  "liberamente nel Campo di Siena,
135   ogne vergogna diposta, s'affisse;
e lì, per trar l'amico suo di pena,
  ch'e' sostenea ne la prigion di Carlo,
138   si condusse a tremar per ogne vena.
Più non dirò, e scuro so che parlo;
  ma poco tempo andrà, che ' tuoi vicini
141   faranno sì che tu potrai chiosarlo.
Quest' opera li tolse quei confini."

"When he was living at the height of his fame,"
he said, "he took his stand of his own free will
　　in Siena's square, putting aside all shame;   *135*
And there to deliver his friend from the pain
　that he was suffering in Charles' prison
　　he made himself tremble in every vein.   *138*
I will speak no more; I know my words may be
　obscure now, but your neighbors down there
　　will soon enough help you to understand me.   *141*
What he did then saved him from confinement here."

Canto XII

HAVING WALKED ALONG WITH THE *burdened souls of the proud, Dante and Virgil leave them and continue along the terrace. Virgil tells Dante to look down at the ground under their feet, which the pilgrim sees is carved with stories showing examples of Pride. The flagstones depict stories drawn from classical mythology, history, and the Old Testament. After the travelers have continued on for some distance as the day progresses, they come to the angel who watches over this terrace. In response to Dante's reverence,*

Di pari, come buoi che vanno a giogo,
  m'andava io con quell' anima carca,
3   fin che 'l sofferse il dolce pedagogo.
Ma quando disse: "Lascia lui e varca;
  ché qui è buono con l'ali e coi remi,
6   quantunque può, ciascun pinger sua barca";
dritto sì come andar vuolsi rife'mi
  con la persona, avvegna che i pensieri
9   mi rimanessero e chinati e scemi.
Io m'era mosso, e seguia volontieri
  del mio maestro i passi, e amendue
12   già mostravam com' eravam leggeri;
ed el mi disse: "Volgi li occhi in giùe:
  buon ti sarà, per tranquillar la via,
15   veder lo letto de le piante tue."

Come, perché di lor memoria sia,
  sovra i sepolti le tombe terragne
18   portan segnato quel ch'elli eran pria,
onde lì molte volte si ripiagne
  per la puntura de la rimembranza,
21   che solo a' pïi dà de le calcagne;

*the angel invites them to proceed upward through ascending steps carved
into the mountain. The travelers hear the first Beatitude being sung. Dante
realizes he is walking with a new lightness. Virgil points out that one
of the seven Ps that had been carved into his forehead at the gateway of
Purgatory has been erased. Dante confirms the fact by putting his hand to
his forehead.*

Side by side, as oxen go beneath a yoke,
   that laden soul and I went on together
     for as long as my dear tutor permitted.   *3*
But when he said, "Leave him and journey on,
   for each one here should speed his own ship
     as much as he is able with sail and oar,"   *6*
I straightened up my body and walked again
   as a person should, even though my thoughts
     remained bowed down and shrunken within.   *9*
I had started out and was gladly following
   the steps of my master, and both of us now
     showed by our stride how light we were.   *12*
Then he said to me, "Cast down your eyes.
   It will be good for you and calm you on your way
     to look at the bed on which you plant your feet."   *15*

Just as stones set in a church's floor
   above the buried dead bear images
     that memorialize what they were in life   *18*
And oftentimes make folk weep for them
   with pangs of mournful remembrance
     that only spur devout and faithful hearts,   *21*

sì vid' io lì, ma di miglior sembianza
secondo l'artificio, figurato
24   quanto per via di fuor del monte avanza.

Vedea colui che fu nobil creato
più ch'altra creatura, giù dal cielo
27   folgoreggiando scender, da l'un lato.
Vedëa Brïareo fitto dal telo
celestïal giacer, da l'altra parte,
30   grave a la terra per lo mortal gelo.
Vedea Timbreo, vedea Pallade e Marte,
armati ancora, intorno al padre loro,
33   mirar le membra d'i Giganti sparte.
Vedea Nembròt a piè del gran lavoro
quasi smarrito, e riguardar le genti
36   che 'n Sennaàr con lui superbi fuoro.

O Nïobè, con che occhi dolenti
vedea io te segnata in su la strada,
39   tra sette e sette tuoi figliuoli spenti!
O Saùl, come in su la propria spada
quivi parevi morto in Gelboè,
42   che poi non sentì pioggia né rugiada!
O folle Aragne, sì vedea io te
già mezza ragna, trista in su li stracci
45   de l'opera che mal per te si fé.
O Roboàm, già non par che minacci
quivi 'l tuo segno; ma pien di spavento
48   nel porta un carro, sanza ch'altri il cacci.

Mostrava ancor lo duro pavimento
come Almeon a sua madre fé caro
51   parer lo sventurato addornamento.
Mostrava come i figli si gittaro
sovra Sennacherìb dentro dal tempio,
54   e come, morto lui, quivi il lasciaro.
Mostrava la ruina e 'l crudo scempio
che fé Tamiri, quando disse a Ciro:
57   "Sangue sitisti, e io di sangue t'empio."

So too I saw sculpted the entire ledge
  that juts out as a path on that mountainside,
    but with greater art and verisimilitude. *24*

I saw on one side the one who was created
  nobler than any other creature falling
    down from heaven like a bolt of lightning. *27*
I saw on the other side Briareus
  transfixed by the celestial lightning bolt
    lie heavy on the earth in the chill of death. *30*
I saw Apollo, I saw Pallas, and Mars,
  still in arms, surrounding their father,
    gazing in wonder at the Giants' scattered limbs. *33*
I saw Nimrod at his gigantic tower's base
  as if perplexed and, looking at him,
    the people of Shinar, who shared his pride. *36*

Ah, Niobe, I saw you sculpted
  on that roadway, your eyes filled with grief,
    among your seven sons and seven daughters dead. *39*
Ah, Saul, how you looked there, by your own sword
  dead in Gilboa, whose mountains thereafter
    never felt rain, or even dew! *42*
Ah, reckless Arachne, I saw you there
  already half-spider, wretched upon
    the threads you spun to your own destruction. *45*
Ah, Rehoboam, your image seems
  frightened rather than menacing now, drawn
    off in a chariot with none in pursuit. *48*

Now was shown, on that hard floor, how Alcmaeon
  made that accursed necklace seem
    more expensive than his mother had thought. *51*
Now was shown how Sennacherib's sons
  attacked their father inside the temple
    and how they left his dead body there. *54*
Now was shown the mayhem and the slaughter
  Tomyris wrought when she said to Cyrus,
    "You thirsted for blood; now have your fill." *57*

Mostrava come in rotta si fuggiro
li Assiri, poi che fu morto Oloferne,
60   e anche le reliquie del martiro.
Vedeva Troia in cenere e in caverne;
o Ilïón, come te basso e vile
63   mostrava il segno che lì si discerne!

Qual di pennel fu maestro o di stile
che ritraesse l'ombre e ' tratti ch'ivi
66   mirar farieno uno ingegno sottile?
Morti li morti e i vivi parean vivi:
non vide mei di me chi vide il vero,
69   quant' io calcai, fin che chinato givi.
Or superbite, e via col viso altero,
figliuoli d'Eva, e non chinate il volto
72   sì che veggiate il vostro mal sentero!

Più era già per noi del monte vòlto
e del cammin del sole assai più speso
75   che non stimava l'animo non sciolto,
quando colui che sempre innanzi atteso
andava, cominciò: "Drizza la testa;
78   non è più tempo di gir sì sospeso.
Vedi colà un angel che s'appresta
per venir verso noi; vedi che torna
81   dal servigio del dì l'ancella sesta.
Di reverenza il viso e li atti addorna,
sì che i diletti lo 'nvïarci in suso;
84   pensa che questo dì mai non raggiorna!"
Io era ben del suo ammonir uso
pur di non perder tempo, sì che 'n quella
87   materia non potea parlarmi chiuso.

A noi venìa la creatura bella,
biancovestito e ne la faccia quale
90   par tremolando mattutina stella.
Le braccia aperse, e indi aperse l'ale;
disse: "Venite: qui son presso i gradi,
93   e agevolemente omai si sale.

Now was shown how the Assyrians fled
  after the murder of Holofernes,
    and also the grisly remains of that slaughter.   *60*
Now I saw Troy in ashes and ruins.
  Ah, Ilion, just how low you were brought
    was shown in the carving that could be seen there!   *63*

What master has there been of brush and pen
  who could have drawn and shaded these figures
    that would astonish the subtlest genius?   *66*
The dead seemed dead and the living seemed living.
  An eyewitness of the events upon which I walked,
    head bent down, saw them no better than I.   *69*
Be haughty then, and turn the other way,
  you sons of Eve; don't bend your faces down
    to see the evil path that you are on!   *72*

We had by now circled more of the mountain,
  and the sun had sped along more of its track
    than my preoccupied mind had estimated,   *75*
When he who always looked down the road
  began to speak, saying, "Raise your head!
    There's no more time for walking around entranced.   *78*
See the angel over there preparing
  to come to us, and see the sixth Hour
    returning from her handmaiden's service.   *81*
Adorn your face and bearing with reverence
  so he will be pleased to send us upward.
    Consider that this day will never dawn again!"   *84*
By now I was so used to his admonitions
  not to waste any time, that in this matter
    his speech could not be opaque to me.   *87*

The beautiful creature came toward us.
  He was clothed in white, and in his face
    was a light that shimmered like the morning star.   *90*
He opened his arms, and then opening his wings
  he said, "Come, the steps are close by,
    and from here on the climb up is easy.   *93*

A questo invito vegnon molto radi:
　o gente umana, per volar sù nata,
96　　　perché a poco vento così cadi?"
Menocci ove la roccia era tagliata;
　quivi mi batté l'ali per la fronte;
99　　　poi mi promise sicura l'andata.

Come a man destra, per salire al monte
　dove siede la chiesa che soggioga
102　　　la ben guidata sopra Rubaconte,
si rompe del montar l'ardita foga
　per le scalee che si fero ad etade
105　　　ch'era sicuro il quaderno e la doga;
così s'allenta la ripa che cade
　quivi ben ratta da l'altro girone;
108　　　ma quinci e quindi l'alta pietra rade.

Noi volgendo ivi le nostre persone,
　"*Beati pauperes spiritu!*" voci
111　　　cantaron sì, che nol diria sermone.
Ahi quanto son diverse quelle foci
　da l'infernali! ché quivi per canti
114　　　s'entra, e là giù per lamenti feroci.
Già montavam su per li scaglion santi,
　ed esser mi parea troppo più lieve
117　　　che per lo pian non mi parea davanti.
Ond' io: "Maestro, dì, qual cosa greve
　levata s'è da me, che nulla quasi
120　　　per me fatica, andando, si riceve?"
Rispuose: "Quando i P che son rimasi
　ancor nel volto tuo presso che stinti,
123　　　saranno, com' è l'un, del tutto rasi,
fier li tuoi piè dal buon voler sì vinti,
　che non pur non fatica sentiranno,
126　　　ma fia diletto loro esser sù pinti."

Allor fec' io come color che vanno
　con cosa in capo non da lor saputa,
129　　　se non che ' cenni altrui sospecciar fanno;

Very few answer this invitation.
 O race of man, born to soar on high,
  why do you fall down so in a little wind?"   *96*
He brought us where the rock was cleft;
 there he beat his wings across my forehead
  and promised it was safe for me to go.   *99*

Just as to the right of the church that sits
 above the Rubaconte and dominates
  the justly governed city below   *102*
The steep ascent is made easier to climb
 by a set of stairs that were constructed
  in an age of trustworthy weights and measures,   *105*
So too here the bank that falls sharply away
 from the circle above is made more gentle
  except that here and there the steep rock scrapes close. *108*

As we turned our ourselves in that direction
 we heard "*Beati pauperes spiritu*" sung
  by voices no words could ever describe.   *111*
Ah, how different were these passageways
 from those in Hell: here song ushered one in,
  while down there one entered to howling laments.   *114*
As we were ascending those holy stairs,
 it seemed to me that I was far lighter
  than I was before even on level ground;   *117*
And so I asked, "Tell me, Master, what weight
 has been lifted from me that now I feel
  almost no fatigue as I make my way up?"   *120*
He answered, "When the rest of the Ps
 that are left on your brow (though almost effaced)
  shall be completely erased, as one has been,   *123*
Your feet shall be so aligned with good will,
 that not only shall they not feel any fatigue,
  but they shall delight in being urged upward."   *126*

Then I was like someone who does not know
 he's been going around with something on his head
  but suspects as much from signs others show,   *129*

per che la mano ad accertar s'aiuta,
  e cerca e truova e quello officio adempie
132   che non si può fornir per la veduta;
e con le dita de la destra scempie
  trovai pur sei le lettere che 'ncise
135   quel da le chiavi a me sovra le tempie:
a che guardando, il mio duca sorrise.

And so feels around up there to make sure, and
  what he never could have found out with his eyes
    he ascertains by using his hand.   *132*
So too, spreading my fingers across my brow,
  I felt that of the letters inscribed thereon
    by him with keys, only six remained now.   *135*
And my leader smiled at this as he looked on.

CANTO XIII

DANTE AND VIRGIL HAVE COME *to the mountain's second terrace.*
Unlike the terrace of Pride, it is empty of decoration and made of dark-
colored rock. Virgil turns to the sun in praise to guide the travelers in the
right direction. Having walked some way, the travelers hear voices flying
through the air. These voices describe exempla of generosity, the virtue
opposite to the vice of Envy, which is curbed on this terrace. The travelers
then see the shades undergoing penance. They sit grouped together like

Noi eravamo al sommo de la scala,
    dove secondamente si risega
3   lo monte che salendo altrui dismala.
Ivi così una cornice lega
    dintorno il poggio, come la primaia;
6   se non che l'arco suo più tosto piega.
Ombra non lì è né segno che si paia:
    parsi la ripa e parsi la via schietta
9   col livido color de la petraia.

"Se qui per dimandar gente s'aspetta,"
    ragionava il poeta, "io temo forse
12   che troppo avrà d'indugio nostra eletta."
Poi fisamente al sole li occhi porse;
    fece del destro lato a muover centro,
15   e la sinistra parte di sé torse.
"O dolce lume a cui fidanza i' entro
    per lo novo cammin, tu ne conduci,"
18   dicea, "come condur si vuol quinc' entro.
Tu scaldi il mondo, tu sovr' esso luci;
    s'altra ragione in contrario non ponta,
21   esser dien sempre li tuoi raggi duci."

beggars, their eyelids sewn together with wire. Dante is upset by the sight
and made uncomfortable that he can see without being seen. Virgil allows
Dante to speak to the souls and the pilgrim makes a courteous address to
the group, asking whether any of the souls hail from Italy. The soul of the
Sienese Sapìa responds and recounts her story to Dante. Dante tells Sapìa
that he is still alive, and she asks for his prayers on his return.

Now we were standing at the top of the stairs
  where for the second time there is a cutback
    into the mountain that rids us of sin.   *3*
There another ledge carves round the slope
  just as the first does, except that its arc
    bends around more sharply upon itself.   *6*
No images are there to be seen,
  only the embankment and the bare road
    whose surface is the livid color of stone.   *9*

"If we wait here for someone we can ask,"
  reasoned the poet, "I am afraid
    our decision will entail too much delay."   *12*
Then he riveted his eyes upon the sun,
  and, making a pivot of his right side,
    he swung his left side around it.   *15*
"O sweet light," he said, "trusting in whom
  I set out upon this strange new road,
    give us the guidance that is needed here.   *18*
You warm the world as you shed light upon it.
  If no other reason urges us otherwise,
    your rays must forever be our guide."   *21*

Quanto di qua per un migliaio si conta,
     tanto di là eravam noi già iti,
24   con poco tempo, per la voglia pronta;
e verso noi volar furon sentiti,
     non però visti, spiriti parlando
27   a la mensa d'amor cortesi inviti.

La prima voce che passò volando
     "*Vinum non habent*" altamente disse,
30   e dietro a noi l'andò reïterando.
E prima che del tutto non si udisse
     per allungarsi, un'altra "I' sono Oreste"
33   passò gridando, e anco non s'affisse.
"Oh!" diss' io, "padre, che voci son queste?"
     E com' io domandai, ecco la terza
36   dicendo: "Amate da cui male aveste."
E 'l buon maestro: "Questo cinghio sferza
     la colpa de la invidia, e però sono
39   tratte d'amor le corde de la ferza.
Lo fren vuol esser del contrario suono;
     credo che l'udirai, per mio avviso,
42   prima che giunghi al passo del perdono.
Ma ficca li occhi per l'aere ben fiso,
     e vedrai gente innanzi a noi sedersi,
45   e ciascun è lungo la grotta assiso."

Allora più che prima li occhi apersi;
     guarda'mi innanzi, e vidi ombre con manti
48   al color de la pietra non diversi.
E poi che fummo un poco più avanti,
     udia gridar: "Maria, òra per noi":
51   gridar "Michele" e "Pietro" e "Tutti santi."
Non credo che per terra vada ancoi
     omo sì duro, che non fosse punto
54   per compassion di quel ch'i' vidi poi;
ché, quando fui sì presso di lor giunto,
     che li atti loro a me venivan certi,
57   per li occhi fui di grave dolor munto.

We had already gone what would be counted
  as a mile down here—and we did it
    in good time, through our ready will—   24
When we heard spirits flying toward us,
  not visible, but speaking courteous
    invitations to the table of love.   27

The first voice that flew by us called out,
  "*Vinum non habent,*" in a loud voice,
    and called out again after it had passed.   30
Before that voice was out of hearing range
  off in the distance, another came by, crying
    "I am Orestes," and it too did not stay.   33
"O father," I asked, "what are these voices?"
  And as I was asking a third voice came by,
    saying, "Love those by whom you were wronged."   36
And the good master said, "This circle scourges
  the sin of envy, and for that reason
    the cords of the whip are drawn from love.   39
The reins must sound an opposite note,
  which you will hear, as I believe,
    before you come to the pass of pardon.   42
But steady your vision now through the air
  and you will see people straight ahead of us,
    each of them seated along the rock wall."   45

I opened my eyes then wider than before
  and, looking ahead, could see shades who wore
    cloaks whose color blended in with the stone.   48
When we had gone a little farther on,
  I heard them cry, "Pray for us, Mary,"
    then "Michael," and "Peter," and then "All Saints."   51
I do not believe there walks on earth today
  a man so hard that he would not have been
    pierced with compassion for the next thing I saw,   54
For when I had come up close enough
  to see just what these spirits were doing,
    my eyes grew milky with overwhelming grief.   57

Di vil ciliccio mi parean coperti,
  e l'un sofferia l'altro con la spalla,
60   e tutti da la ripa eran sofferti.
Così li ciechi a cui la roba falla,
  stanno a' perdoni a chieder lor bisogna,
63   e l'uno il capo sopra l'altro avvalla,
perché 'n altrui pietà tosto si pogna,
  non pur per lo sonar de le parole,
66   ma per la vista che non meno agogna.
E come a li orbi non approda il sole,
  così a l'ombre quivi, ond' io parlo ora,
69   luce del ciel di sé largir non vole;
ché a tutti un fil di ferro i cigli fóra
  e cusce sì, come a sparvier selvaggio
72   si fa però che queto non dimora.

A me pareva, andando, fare oltraggio,
  veggendo altrui, non essendo veduto:
75   per ch'io mi volsi al mio consiglio saggio.
Ben sapev' ei che volea dir lo muto;
  e però non attese mia dimanda,
78   ma disse: "Parla, e sie breve e arguto."
Virgilio mi venìa da quella banda
  de la cornice onde cader si puote,
81   perché da nulla sponda s'inghirlanda;
da l'altra parte m'eran le divote
  ombre, che per l'orribile costura
84   premevan sì, che bagnavan le gote.
Volsimi a loro e: "O gente sicura,"
  incominciai, "di veder l'alto lume
87   che 'l disio vostro solo ha in sua cura,
se tosto grazia resolva le schiume
  di vostra coscïenza sì che chiaro
90   per essa scenda de la mente il fiume,
ditemi, ché mi fia grazioso e caro,
  s'anima è qui tra voi che sia latina;
93   e forse lei sarà buon s'i' l'apparo."

They seemed to be covered with coarse haircloth;
  each supported another with his shoulder,
    and all of them were propped against the bank. 60
Just so the blind who lack for everything
  take their place at church doors to beg for their needs,
    and one of them rests his head on another, 63
So that pity might be more quickly aroused,
  not only by the sound of their words
    but by the plight of their appearance as well. 66
And as the sun does not benefit the blind,
  so to these shades of whom I now speak
    the light of heaven denies its largesse, 69
For an iron wire pierces their eyelids
  and sews them shut, just as is done
    to tame a wild falcon that will not stay still. 72

As I went on it seemed disrespectful
  for me to see them without being seen,
    and so I turned to my sage counsel. 75
He knew very well what my silence meant
  and therefore did not wait for me to ask,
    but said, "Speak, but be brief and to the point." 78
Virgil was walking along beside me
  on the edge of the terrace, where one might fall,
    for there was no barrier enclosing it. 81
On my other side were the pious shades,
  forcing out through those hideous seams
    so many tears that their cheeks were awash. 84
I turned to them and, "O people assured,"
  I began, "of seeing the exalted light
    that is the sole object of your desire, 87
So may grace soon dissolve the scum
  that obscures your conscience and so allow
    the stream of your mind to flow pure and clear, 90
Tell me, for I would be dearly grateful,
  if there are among you any Italian souls.
    It might also profit them for me to know." 93

"O frate mio, ciascuna è cittadina
  d'una vera città; ma tu vuo' dire
96   che vivesse in Italia peregrina."
Questo mi parve per risposta udire
  più innanzi alquanto che là dov' io stava,
99   ond' io mi feci ancor più là sentire.
Tra l'altre vidi un'ombra ch'aspettava
  in vista; e se volesse alcun dir "Come?"
102   lo mento a guisa d'orbo in sù levava.
"Spirto," diss' io, "che per salir ti dome,
  se tu se' quelli che mi rispondesti,
105   fammiti conto o per luogo o per nome."

"Io fui sanese," rispuose, "e con questi
  altri rimendo qui la vita ria,
108   lagrimando a colui che sé ne presti.
Savia non fui, avvegna che Sapìa
  fossi chiamata, e fui de li altrui danni
111   più lieta assai che di ventura mia.
E perché tu non creda ch'io t'inganni,
  odi s'i' fui, com' io ti dico, folle,
114   già discendendo l'arco d'i miei anni.
Eran li cittadin miei presso a Colle
  in campo giunti co' loro avversari,
117   e io pregava Iddio di quel ch'e' volle.
Rotti fuor quivi e vòlti ne li amari
  passi di fuga; e veggendo la caccia,
120   letizia presi a tutte altre dispari,
tanto ch'io volsi in sù l'ardita faccia,
  gridando a Dio: 'Omai più non ti temo!'
123   come fé 'l merlo per poca bonaccia.
Pace volli con Dio in su lo stremo
  de la mia vita; e ancor non sarebbe
126   lo mio dover per penitenza scemo,
se ciò non fosse, ch'a memoria m'ebbe
  Pier Pettinaio in sue sante orazioni,
129   a cui di me per caritate increbbe.

"O my brother, we are all citizens
  of the one true city. You mean to ask
    who lived in Italy while still a pilgrim."   *96*
It seemed to me that I heard this in answer
  farther along from where I was standing,
    so I made myself heard by moving closer.   *99*
Among the shades I saw one with a look
  of expectation; and if you asked me how,
    it was raising its chin the way the blind do.   *102*
"Spirit," I said, "who tame yourself to ascend,
  if you are the one who answered me,
    make yourself known by your city or your name."   *105*

"I was from Siena," the shade replied,
  "and with these others I mend my sinful life,
    weeping to Him that he show Himself to us.   *108*
Wise I was not, though my name, Sapìa,
  might mean so, and I rejoiced much more
    at another's loss than at my own good fortune.   *111*
And lest you believe that I am fooling you,
  listen as I tell you how foolish I was
    when my life's arc had already bent downward.   *114*
My townsmen were in the field near Colle
  engaged in battle, and I prayed that God
    would do what in fact he had already willed.   *117*
When they were defeated and had now turned
  their bitter steps back, I watched the rout
    with such excessive happiness in my heart   *120*
That I turned my presumptuous face to heaven
  and cried out to God, 'Now I fear you no more,'
    like the blackbird after a spell of good weather.   *123*
I made peace with God in the final hour
  of my life, and my penitence here
    would not yet have reduced my debt   *126*
If that Peter who sold weavers' combs
  had not, out of grief and charity,
    remembered me in his holy prayers.   *129*

Ma tu chi se,' che nostre condizioni
vai dimandando, e porti li occhi sciolti,
132   sì com' io credo, e spirando ragioni?"

"Li occhi," diss' io, "mi fieno ancor qui tolti,
ma picciol tempo, ché poca è l'offesa
135   fatta per esser con invidia vòlti.
Troppa è più la paura ond' è sospesa
l'anima mia del tormento di sotto,
138   che già lo 'ncarco di là giù mi pesa."

Ed ella a me: "Chi t'ha dunque condotto
qua sù tra noi, se giù ritornar credi?"
141   E io: "Costui ch'è meco e non fa motto.
E vivo sono; e però mi richiedi,
spirito eletto, se tu vuo' ch'i' mova
144   di là per te ancor li mortai piedi."
"Oh, questa è a udir sì cosa nuova,"
rispuose, "che gran segno è che Dio t'ami;
147   però col priego tuo talor mi giova.
E cheggioti, per quel che tu più brami,
se mai calchi la terra di Toscana,
150   che a' miei propinqui tu ben mi rinfami.
Tu li vedrai tra quella gente vana
che spera in Talamone, e perderagli
153   più di speranza ch'a trovar la Diana;
ma più vi perderanno li ammiragli."

But who are you, going around asking
   about our condition, with your eyes not sewn,
      as I believe, and using breath to speak?"   *132*

"My eyes," I answered, "will be taken from me here,
   but for a short time only, for their offense
      is minor when it comes to looks of envy.   *135*
Greater is the fear—and it fills my soul—
   of the torments on the terrace just below.
      Their heavy load already weighs me down."   *138*

Then she said to me, "Then who has led you up here
   among us, if you believe you will return below?"
      I answered, "This one with me, who is silent;   *141*
And I am alive. Therefore just ask me,
   spirit elect, if you want me to move
      my mortal feet on your behalf down below."   *144*
"Oh, this is such a strange thing to hear,"
   she answered, "a great sign of God's love for you.
      Therefore help me sometime by saying a prayer.   *147*
And I beg you by whatever you hold most dear,
   if you ever tread the soil of Tuscany,
      restore my name among my people there.   *150*
You will see them among the vain folk who dream
   of Talamone's harbor, and will despair more
      than if they searched for the Diana's stream.   *153*
But the admirals will lose most on that shore."

CANTO XIV

THE CANTO OPENS WITH A *conversation between two as yet unidentified souls on the terrace of Envy, who wonder over Dante's identity. One of the souls inquires who the pilgrim is and where he is from. Dante responds with a veiled description of the Arno valley that leads the questioning soul to embark on a long critique of those who live along that river. Dante then asks for the names of the two souls; they are Guido del Duca and Rinieri*

"Chi è costui che 'l nostro monte cerchia
      prima che morte li abbia dato il volo,
3   e apre li occhi a sua voglia e coverchia?"
"Non so chi sia, ma so ch'e' non è solo;
      domandal tu che più li t'avvicini,
6   e dolcemente, sì che parli, acco'lo."

Così due spirti, l'uno a l'altro chini,
      ragionavan di me ivi a man dritta;
9   poi fer li visi, per dirmi, supini;
e disse l'uno: "O anima che fitta
      nel corpo ancora inver' lo ciel ten vai,
12   per carità ne consola e ne ditta
onde vieni e chi se'; ché tu ne fai
      tanto maravigliar de la tua grazia,
15   quanto vuol cosa che non fu più mai."

E io: "Per mezza Toscana si spazia
      un fiumicel che nasce in Falterona,
18   e cento miglia di corso nol sazia.
Di sovr' esso rech' io questa persona:
      dirvi ch'i' sia, saria parlare indarno,
21   ché 'l nome mio ancor molto non suona."

da Calboli. Guido del Duca continues his criticism of corrupt Italians and the degradation of noble families. Dante and Virgil at last leave the souls and continue on their way. As they walk they hear exempla of Envy and Dante is afraid. Virgil explains the voices and criticizes humankind for the earthbound obsessions that turn its eyes from Heaven.

"Who is this person circling our mountain
   before he has been given wings by death,
      and who opens and shuts his eyes at will?"   *3*
"I don't know who he is, but he's not alone.
   Why don't you ask him, since you are closer?
      And greet him courteously, so he will answer."   *6*

Thus two spirits, bending toward each other,
   were talking about me off to my right;
      then they turned their faces up to speak to me,   *9*
One of them saying, "O soul still embodied
   as you make your way to Heaven, indulge us
      for charity's sake and let us know   *12*
Where you are from and who you are,
   for the grace granted you astonishes us,
      as something will that has never yet happened." *15*

And I answered, "Through the middle of Tuscany
   winds a stream that rises in Falterona;
      a hundred-mile course does not quench its thirst. *18*
From along its banks I bring this bodily form.
   It would be useless to tell you who I am,
      for my name as yet does not resound."   *21*

"Se ben lo 'ntendimento tuo accarno
    con lo 'ntelletto," allora mi rispuose
24   quei che diceva pria, "tu parli d'Arno."
E l'altro disse lui: "Perché nascose
    questi il vocabol di quella riviera,
27   pur com' om fa de l'orribili cose?"

E l'ombra che di ciò domandata era,
    si sdebitò così: "Non so; ma degno
30   ben è che 'l nome di tal valle pèra;
ché dal principio suo, ov' è sì pregno
    l'alpestro monte ond' è tronco Peloro,
33   che 'n pochi luoghi passa oltra quel segno,
infin là 've si rende per ristoro
    di quel che 'l ciel de la marina asciuga,
36   ond' hanno i fiumi ciò che va con loro,
vertù così per nimica si fuga
    da tutti come biscia, o per sventura
39   del luogo, o per mal uso che li fruga:
ond' hanno sì mutata lor natura
    li abitator de la misera valle,
42   che par che Circe li avesse in pastura.
Tra brutti porci, più degni di galle
    che d'altro cibo fatto in uman uso,
45   dirizza prima il suo povero calle.
Botoli trova poi, venendo giuso,
    ringhiosi più che non chiede lor possa,
48   e da lor disdegnosa torce il muso.
Vassi caggendo; e quant' ella più 'ngrossa,
    tanto più trova di can farsi lupi
51   la maladetta e sventurata fossa.
Discesa poi per più pelaghi cupi,
    trova le volpi sì piene di froda,
54   che non temono ingegno che le occùpi.
Né lascerò di dir perch' altri m'oda;
    e buon sarà costui, s'ancor s'ammenta
57   di ciò che vero spirto mi disnoda.

"If my mind has correctly grasped the import
  of what you are saying," answered the one
    who had spoken first, "you mean the Arno."   *24*
And the other one asked him, "Why did he hide
  the name of that river, just as a person
    might hide the name of some terrible thing?"   *27*

Then the shade who was asked this question
  replied, "I do not know, but it is right
    that the name of such a river should perish.   *30*
For from its source, where the alpine range
  from which Pelorus was broken off, rises
    to such a height that few places surpass it,   *33*
Down to where it surrenders its waters,
  restoring what the sky draws up from the sea
    to replenish the source of rivers again—   *36*
All along its banks people flee from virtue
  as if it were a snake. Either some evil
    in the place drives them, or their own bad habits,   *39*
But the inhabitants of that miserable valley
  are so altered in their nature, it is as though
    Circe herself was the one who fed them.   *42*
Among wild hogs, more fit to feed on acorns
  than any food grown for human use,
    the feeble stream of that river first flows;   *45*
Then as it descends the water encounters
  curs whose snarls are worse than their bite
    and turns its snout from them in disdain;   *48*
It goes on falling, and the wider its flood,
  the more the accursed and ill-fated ditch
    finds that the dogs have turned into wolves;   *51*
Then, having fallen through many deep gorges,
  it comes upon foxes so full of fraud
    they have no fear they could ever be trapped.   *54*
Nor will I hold back because another hears me.
  It would be well for him to keep in mind
    what the true Spirit has disclosed to me.   *57*

Io veggio tuo nepote che diventa
cacciator di quei lupi in su la riva
60   del fiero fiume, e tutti li sgomenta.
Vende la carne loro essendo viva;
poscia li ancide come antica belva;
63   molti di vita e sé di pregio priva.
Sanguinoso esce de la trista selva;
lasciala tal, che di qui a mille anni
66   ne lo stato primaio non si rinselva."

Com' a l'annunzio di dogliosi danni
si turba il viso di colui ch'ascolta,
69   da qual che parte il periglio l'assanni,
così vid' io l'altr' anima, che volta
stava a udir, turbarsi e farsi trista,
72   poi ch'ebbe la parola a sé raccolta.
Lo dir de l'una e de l'altra la vista
mi fer voglioso di saper lor nomi,
75   e dimanda ne fei con prieghi mista;

Per che lo spirto che di pria parlòmi
ricominciò: "Tu vuo' ch'io mi deduca
78   nel fare a te ciò che tu far non vuo'mi.
Ma da che Dio in te vuol che traluca
tanto sua grazia, non ti sarò scarso;
81   però sappi ch'io fui Guido del Duca.
Fu il sangue mio d'invidia sì rïarso,
che se veduto avesse uom farsi lieto,
84   visto m'avresti di livore sparso.
Di mia semente cotal paglia mieto;
o gente umana, perché poni 'l core
87   là 'v' è mestier di consorte divieto?
Questi è Rinier; questi è 'l pregio e l'onore
de la casa da Calboli, ove nullo
90   fatto s'è reda poi del suo valore.
E non pur lo suo sangue è fatto brullo,
tra 'l Po e 'l monte e la marina e 'l Reno,
93   del ben richesto al vero e al trastullo;

I see your nephew, who will become a hunter
  and strike terror in the hearts of the wolves
    that live on the banks of that savage stream.   *60*
He sells their flesh while it is still alive,
  then slaughters them like some ancient beast,
    robbing many of life and himself of honor.   *63*
Blood-smeared will he come out of that dismal wood
  leaving it such that not in a thousand years
    will it ever grow back to its primeval state."   *66*

Like someone who hears a prediction
  of grievous ills and has a troubled look
    no matter from where the danger threatens.   *69*
So did I see the other soul, who had turned
  to listen, became troubled and gloomy
    when he had taken in all that was said.   *72*
The words of the one and the other's expression
  made me want to know their names, and so,
    with words of entreaty, I asked them.   *75*

The spirit that had spoken to me before
  began again, "You would have me bring myself
    to do for you what you will not do for me;   *78*
But since God wills that so much of His grace
  shine forth through you, I will not stint you.
    Know then that I was Guido del Duca.   *81*
My blood boiled with so much envy
  that if ever I saw a man become glad
    you would have seen my complexion turn livid.   *84*
Of my sowing, such straw do I reap.
  O human race, why do you set your hearts
    on what must be excluded from sharing?   *87*
This is Rinieri here, the pride and honor
  of the house of Calboli, where no one since
    has made himself an heir to his valor.   *90*
And it is not only his blood, between the Po
  and the mountains, between the Reno and the sea,
    that has lacked virtue for daily and courtly life,   *93*

ché dentro a questi termini è ripieno
di venenosi sterpi, sì che tardi
96   per coltivare omai verrebber meno.
Ov' è 'l buon Lizio e Arrigo Mainardi?
Pier Traversaro e Guido di Carpigna?
99   Oh Romagnuoli tornati in bastardi!
Quando in Bologna un Fabbro si ralligna?
quando in Faenza un Bernardin di Fosco,
102   verga gentil di picciola gramigna?
Non ti maravigliar s'io piango, Tosco,
quando rimembro, con Guido da Prata,
105   Ugolin d'Azzo che vivette nosco,
Federigo Tignoso e sua brigata,
la casa Traversara e li Anastagi
108   (e l'una gente e l'altra è diretata),
le donne e ' cavalier, li affanni e li agi
che ne 'nvogliava amore e cortesia
111   là dove i cuor son fatti sì malvagi.
O Bretinoro, ché non fuggi via,
poi che gita se n'è la tua famiglia
114   e molta gente per non esser ria?
Ben fa Bagnacaval, che non rifiglia;
e mal fa Castrocaro, e peggio Conio,
117   che di figliar tai conti più s'impiglia.
Ben faranno i Pagan, da che 'l demonio
lor sen girà; ma non però che puro
120   già mai rimagna d'essi testimonio.
O Ugolin de' Fantolin, sicuro
è 'l nome tuo, da che più non s'aspetta
123   chi far lo possa, tralignando, scuro.
Ma va via, Tosco, omai; ch'or mi diletta
troppo di pianger più che di parlare,
126   sì m'ha nostra ragion la mente stretta."

Noi sapavam che quell' anime care
ci sentivano andar; però, tacendo,
129   facëan noi del cammin confidare.

For all of the land within these boundaries
  is so choked with toxic weeds, that it is too late now
    for proper cultivation to root them out.   *96*
Where is the good Lizio, Arrigo Mainardi,
  Pier Traversaro, and Guido di Carpigna?
    O people of Romagna, turned into bastards!   *99*
When, in Bologna, will there be another Fabbro?
  When, in Faenza, a Bernadin di Fosco,
    noble scion of a humble plant?   *102*
Do not wonder, Tuscan, if I shed tears
  when I recall, with Guido da Prata,
    Ugolin d'Azzo, who lived among us,   *105*
Federigo Tignoso and his companions,
  the houses of the Traversaro and Anastagi—
    both families now without any heirs—   *108*
The ladies and knights, the labors and leisures
  that love and courtesy encouraged in us
    where hearts now have become so depraved.   *111*
O town of Bretinoro, why do you not disappear,
  now that your best family, and many others too,
    has left you to avoid degeneracy?   *114*
Bagnacavallo does well to have sons no more,
  but Castrocaro does badly, and Conio worse,
    continuing to breed such counts as they do.   *117*
The Pagani will do well when the Demon
  at last takes his leave, but not so well
    that the legacy they leave will be unsullied.   *120*
O Ugolin de' Fantolin, your name
  is secure, since no more sons are forthcoming
    to darken it with their depravity.   *123*
But now be on your way, Tuscan,
  for I would rather weep now than talk,
    our conversation has so distressed my mind."   *126*

We knew that those dear spirits heard us
  as we moved on; and so their silence
    made us confident of our direction.   *129*

      Poi fummo fatti soli procedendo,
        folgore parve quando l'aere fende,
132   voce che giunse di contra dicendo:
      "Anciderammi qualunque m'apprende";
        e fuggì come tuon che si dilegua,
135   se sùbito la nuvola scoscende.
      Come da lei l'udir nostro ebbe triegua,
        ed ecco l'altra con sì gran fracasso,
138   che somigliò tonar che tosto segua:
      "Io sono Aglauro che divenni sasso";
        e allor, per ristrignermi al poeta,
141   in destro feci, e non innanzi, il passo.

      Già era l'aura d'ogne parte queta;
        ed el mi disse: "Quel fu 'l duro camo
144   che dovria l'uom tener dentro a sua meta.
      Ma voi prendete l'esca, sì che l'amo
        de l'antico avversaro a sé vi tira;
147   e però poco val freno o richiamo.
      Chiamavi 'l cielo e 'ntorno vi si gira,
        mostrandovi le sue bellezze etterne,
150   e l'occhio vostro pur a terra mira;
      onde vi batte chi tutto discerne."

As we two took our solitary way,
  a voice like lightning when it splits the air
    came crashing down upon us, saying,   *132*
"Whoever apprehends me will slay me,"
  and then fled away like rolling thunder
    that fades out after its cloud is cleft.   *135*
No sooner had our ears some relief from this
  when there came the boom of another voice,
    as loud as a sudden thunderclap: *138*
"I am Aglauros, who was turned to stone."
  At this, to draw closer to the Poet,
    I stepped to the right instead of forward.   *141*

The air was quiet all around us now,
  and he said to me, "That was the hard bit
    that should hold humankind within its bounds.   *144*
But you take the baited hook, and when
  the ancient adversary reels you in,
    neither curb nor lure are of any help then.   *147*
The heavens call to you as they wheel around,
  showing to you their splendors eternal,
    but your eyes are only fixed on the ground,   *150*
And so you are stricken by the One who sees all."

Canto XV

THE CANTO OPENS WITH A *description of time indicating that it is now three hours before sunset on Mount Purgatory. The beams of the descending sun strike the pilgrim in the face, making it difficult for him to see. The blinding light of the sun soon intermingles with a new light, which we find is emanating from the angel who presides over the exit of the terrace of Envy and who invites the travelers to continue their ascension. There follows*

Quanto tra l'ultimar de l'ora terza
  e 'l principio del dì par de la spera
3   che sempre a guisa di fanciullo scherza,
tanto pareva già inver' la sera
  essere al sol del suo corso rimaso;
6   vespero là, e qui mezza notte era.
E i raggi ne ferien per mezzo 'l naso,
  perché per noi girato era sì 'l monte,
9   che già dritti andavamo inver' l'occaso,
quand' io senti' a me gravar la fronte
  a lo splendore assai più che di prima,
12   e stupor m'eran le cose non conte;
ond' io levai le mani inver' la cima
  de le mie ciglia, e fecimi 'l solecchio,
15   che del soverchio visibile lima.

Come quando da l'acqua o da lo specchio
  salta lo raggio a l'opposita parte,
18   salendo su per lo modo parecchio
a quel che scende, e tanto si diparte
  dal cader de la pietra in igual tratta,
21   sì come mostra esperïenza e arte;
così mi parve da luce rifratta
  quivi dinanzi a me esser percosso;
24   per che a fuggir la mia vista fu ratta.

a central discourse on the nature of divine love that demonstrates both the extent and limitations of Virgil's rational powers. Dante is then caught up in trance-like visions that show three exempla of the virtue of Mildness that counteract the Anger that is purged on the terrace to come. At the close of the visions, Virgil demonstrates his insight into the pilgrim's mind. The canto ends as the travelers approach a dark impenetrable cloud of smoke.

As much sky as between the third hour's end
  and the dawn of day is shown by that sphere
    that is always in motion like a child at play,   *3*
Was how much now appeared to be left
  of the sun's course as it moved toward dusk:
    it was evening there and here it was midnight.   *6*
The beams now struck us full in the face,
  for we had circled the mountain to such an extent
    that we were heading straight into the sunset,   *9*
When I felt my brow weighed down by the splendor
  far more than it had been before,
    and I was dazed by something unknown;   *12*
So I cupped my hands above my eyebrows
  and made for myself the kind of shade
    that takes the edge off excessive glare.   *15*

As when a beam of light bounces off water,
  or from a mirror, in another direction,
    rising from the surface at the same angle   *18*
As it entered, and at an equal distance
  from the line made by a falling stone—
    as scientific experiments show—   *21*
So it seemed to me that I was struck by light
  reflected from something in front of me
    and from which my eyes instantly recoiled.   *24*

"Che è quel, dolce padre, a che non posso
   schermar lo viso tanto che mi vaglia,"
27   diss' io, "e pare inver' noi esser mosso?"
"Non ti maravigliar s'ancor t'abbaglia
   la famiglia del cielo," a me rispuose:
30   "messo è che viene ad invitar ch'om saglia.
Tosto sarà ch'a veder queste cose
   non ti fia grave, ma fieti diletto
33   quanto natura a sentir ti dispuose."
Poi giunti fummo a l'angel benedetto,
   con lieta voce disse: "Intrate quinci
36   ad un scaleo vie men che li altri eretto."

Noi montavam, già partiti di linci,
   e "*Beati misericordes!*" fue
39   cantato retro, e "Godi tu che vinci!"
Lo mio maestro e io soli amendue
   suso andavamo; e io pensai, andando,
42   prode acquistar ne le parole sue;
e dirizza'mi a lui sì dimandando:
   "Che volse dir lo spirto di Romagna,
45   e 'divieto' e 'consorte' menzionando?"

Per ch'elli a me: "Di sua maggior magagna
   conosce il danno; e però non s'ammiri
48   se ne riprende perché men si piagna.
Perché s'appuntano i vostri disiri
   dove per compagnia parte si scema,
51   invidia move il mantaco a' sospiri.
Ma se l'amor de la spera supprema
   torcesse in suso il disiderio vostro,
54   non vi sarebbe al petto quella tema;
ché, per quanti si dice più lì 'nostro,'
   tanto possiede più di ben ciascuno,
57   e più di caritate arde in quel chiostro."

"Io son d'esser contento più digiuno,"
   diss' io, "che se mi fosse pria taciuto,
60   e più di dubbio ne la mente aduno.

"What is that, sweet father," I asked,
    "that I cannot screen my eyes from well enough
        and seems to be moving in our direction?"   27
"Do not be amazed that the family of Heaven
    still dazzles you," he said. "This is the messenger
        who has come to invite you to the ascent.   30
Soon it will no longer be hard for you
    to look upon them, but as great a delight
        as Nature has fashioned you to feel."   33
When we had reached the blessed angel,
    he said in a joyful voice, "Enter here
        to mount a stairway less steep than the others."   36

We had left that place and were on our way up.
    "Beati misericordes" was being sung behind,
        along with "Rejoice you who overcome."   39
My master and I, we two alone,
    were making the ascent, and thinking
        to profit from his words as we went along,   42
I turned to him and asked, "What did he mean,
    the spirit from Romagna, when he mentioned
        'exclusion' and spoke of 'sharing'?"   45

He said in response, "He knows the damage
    his worst fault can do; it is no wonder then
        if he reproves it, that it be less regretted.   48
Because your desires are directed
    where sharing them reduces your portion,
        Envy fans your sighs with her bellows.   51
But if love of the highest sphere
    turned your desire up toward Heaven
        the fear of loss would not be in your heart.   54
For there, the more there are who say 'ours,'
    the more of the good each one possesses,
        and the more charity burns in that cloister."   57

"I hunger more now to be satisfied,"
    I said, "than if I had kept silent before,
        and in my mind I assemble more doubt.   60

Com' esser puote ch'un ben, distributo
    in più posseditor, faccia più ricchi
63   di sé che se da pochi è posseduto?"

Ed elli a me: "Però che tu rificchi
    la mente pur a le cose terrene,
66   di vera luce tenebre dispicchi.
Quello infinito e ineffabil bene
    che là sù è, così corre ad amore
69   com' a lucido corpo raggio vene.
Tanto si dà quanto trova d'ardore;
    sì che, quantunque carità si stende,
72   cresce sovr' essa l'etterno valore.
E quanta gente più là sù s'intende,
    più v'è da bene amare, e più vi s'ama,
75   e come specchio l'uno a l'altro rende.
E se la mia ragion non ti disfama,
    vedrai Beatrice, ed ella pienamente
78   ti torrà questa e ciascun' altra brama.
Procaccia pur che tosto sieno spente,
    come son già le due, le cinque piaghe,
81   che si richiudon per esser dolente."

Com' io voleva dicer "Tu m'appaghe,"
    vidimi giunto in su l'altro girone,
84   sì che tacer mi fer le luci vaghe.
Ivi mi parve in una visïone
    estatica di sùbito esser tratto,
87   e vedere in un tempio più persone;
e una donna, in su l'entrar, con atto
    dolce di madre dicer: "Figliuol mio,
90   perché hai tu così verso noi fatto?
Ecco, dolenti, lo tuo padre e io
    ti cercavamo." E come qui si tacque,
93   ciò che pareva prima, dispario.

Indi m'apparve un'altra con quell' acque
    giù per le gote che 'l dolor distilla
96   quando di gran dispetto in altrui nacque,

How can it be that a good distributed
   to more possessors can enrich more people
      than if it were possessed by only a few?"   *63*

"Because you still set your mind on earthly things,"
   my master explained to me, "you only pluck
      strands of darkness from a light that is true.   *66*
That infinite and ineffable Good
   that is there above courses to love
      as a ray of light races to a bright body.   *69*
The more ardor it finds the more of itself it gives,
   so that however far love extends itself
      the more the Eternal Good increases upon it.   *72*
And the more souls above who love each other,
   the more there are to love and the more love there is,
      and these two reflect each other like mirrors.   *75*
And if my discourse does not appease your hunger,
   you will see Beatrice, and she will completely
      satisfy this and all your other desires.   *78*
Just continue your efforts to have erased,
   as two already have been, the five wounds
      that are healed by the very pain they cause."   *81*

I was about to say, "You've satisfied me,"
   when I saw that I had reached the next circle,
      and my wandering eyes kept me from speaking.   *84*
At once I seemed to be caught up in a trance
   on the terrace there, an ecstatic vision
      of a number of people in a temple,   *87*
And a lady there, about to enter,
   with the tender look of a mother saying,
      "My son, why have you done this to us?   *90*
Behold, your father and I have sought you
   sorrowing." And as she fell silent,
      all that had been there disappeared.   *93*

Then there appeared to me another woman,
   whose cheeks were wet with tears distilled by grief
      born of resentment against another,   *96*

e dir: "Se tu se' sire de la villa
    del cui nome ne' dèi fu tanta lite,
99   e onde ogne scïenza disfavilla,
vendica te di quelle braccia ardite
    ch'abbracciar nostra figlia, o Pisistràto."
102   E 'l segnor mi parea, benigno e mite,
risponder lei con viso temperato:
    "Che farem noi a chi mal ne disira,
105   se quei che ci ama è per noi condannato?"

Poi vidi genti accese in foco d'ira
    con pietre un giovinetto ancider, forte
108   gridando a sé pur: "Martira, martira!"
E lui vedea chinarsi, per la morte
    che l'aggravava già, inver' la terra,
111   ma de li occhi facea sempre al ciel porte,
orando a l'alto Sire, in tanta guerra,
    che perdonasse a' suoi persecutori,
114   con quello aspetto che pietà diserra.

Quando l'anima mia tornò di fori
    a le cose che son fuor di lei vere,
117   io riconobbi i miei non falsi errori.
Lo duca mio, che mi potea vedere
    far sì com' om che dal sonno si slega,
120   disse: "Che hai che non ti puoi tenere,
ma se' venuto più che mezza lega
    velando li occhi e con le gambe avvolte,
123   a guisa di cui vino o sonno piega?"
"O dolce padre mio, se tu m'ascolte,
    io ti dirò," diss' io, "ciò che m'apparve
126   quando le gambe mi furon sì tolte."
Ed ei: "Se tu avessi cento larve
    sovra la faccia, non mi sarian chiuse
129   le tue cogitazion, quantunque parve.
Ciò che vedesti fu perché non scuse
    d'aprir lo core a l'acque de la pace
132   che da l'etterno fonte son diffuse.

And she was saying, "If you rule the city
  whose name was contested among the gods
    and glitters with every form of knowledge,   *99*
Take vengeance upon those insolent arms
  that embraced our daughter, O Pisistratus!"
    And her lord, gentle and mild, seemed to me   *102*
To answer her with a temperate air,
  "What will we do to those who wish us ill
    if we condemn those who love us?"   *105*

Then I saw a crowd on fire with anger
  stoning a youth to death, and crying out
    loudly to each other, "Kill him, kill him!"   *108*
And I saw him sink to the ground, for death
  already lay heavy upon him, but
    he still turned his eyes toward heaven   *111*
And, though so fiercely assailed, prayed to the Lord,
  with a look on his face that elicits pity,
    to pardon those who persecuted him.   *114*

When my mind returned to the normal world
  and the things that are real outside of it
    I recognized my not untrue errors.   *117*
My leader, who could see me acting like
  someone who is trying to shake off sleep,
    said, "What's wrong? Why can't you stand straight?   *120*
You've staggered along for more than half a mile,
  covering your eyes, just like someone
    who is half-asleep or has had too much wine."   *123*
"O my sweet father," I said, "if you will listen,
  I will tell you about the visions I had
    while my legs were taken out from under me."   *126*
And he answered me, "Even if you wore
  a hundred masks upon your face, your thoughts
    would not be hidden from me, however slight.   *129*
You were shown these visions so you would not refuse
  to open your heart to the waters of peace
    that pour forth from the eternal fountain.   *132*

Non dimandai 'Che hai?' per quel che face
chi guarda pur con l'occhio che non vede,
135   quando disanimato il corpo giace;
ma dimandai per darti forza al piede:
così frugar conviensi i pigri, lenti
138   ad usar lor vigilia quando riede."

Noi andavam per lo vespero, attenti
oltre quanto potean li occhi allungarsi
141   contra i raggi serotini e lucenti.
Ed ecco a poco a poco un fummo farsi
verso di noi come la notte oscuro;
144   né da quello era loco da cansarsi.
Questo ne tolse li occhi e l'aere puro.

I did not ask you, 'What's wrong?' as someone
  who looks only with eyes that do not see
    when the person's body lies unconscious.   *135*
No, I asked in order to give strength to your feet;
  the sluggish must be prodded, slow as they are
    to use their wakefulness when it returns."   *138*

And so through the evening we journeyed on,
  straining our eyes as far as we could see
    against the last bright gleams of the setting sun,   *141*
When we saw coming toward us gradually
  a smoke that was as murky as night.
    There was no way to escape, nowhere to flee,   *144*
And it robbed us of the pure air and our sight.

CANTO XVI

DANTE AND VIRGIL ENTER THE *cloud of darkness that appeared at the end of the previous canto. Dante holds Virgil's shoulder in order not to lose him. They hear the voices of the wrathful praying and singing the "Agnus Dei." One of the invisible souls addresses them, asking to know who Dante is. Dante explains that he is still alive and asks the soul's identity.*

Buio d'inferno e di notte privata
   d'ogne pianeto, sotto pover cielo,
3   quant' esser può di nuvol tenebrata,
non fece al viso mio sì grosso velo
   come quel fummo ch'ivi ci coperse,
6   né a sentir di così aspro pelo,
che l'occhio stare aperto non sofferse;
   onde la scorta mia saputa e fida
9   mi s'accostò e l'omero m'offerse.
Sì come cieco va dietro a sua guida
   per non smarrirsi e per non dar di cozzo
12   in cosa che 'l molesti, o forse ancida,
m'andava io per l'aere amaro e sozzo,
   ascoltando il mio duca che diceva
15   pur: "Guarda che da me tu non sia mozzo."

Io sentia voci, e ciascuna pareva
   pregar per pace e per misericordia
18   l'Agnel di Dio che le peccata leva.
Pur "Agnus Dei" eran le loro essordia;
   una parola in tutte era e un modo,
21   sì che parea tra esse ogne concordia.
"Quei sono spirti, maestro, ch'i' odo?"
   diss' io. Ed elli a me: "Tu vero apprendi,
24   e d'iracundia van solvendo il nodo."

The soul is that of Marco Lombardo, whom Dante then asks to explain why the world has fallen into such corruption. Marco Lombardo begins an extended discourse that considers human free will, the need for laws, and the corruption brought about by the lack of imperial power.

Darkness of hell, or of a night bereft
   of every star, beneath a barren sky
      utterly obscured with shadowy clouds,   *3*
Had never so thickly veiled my sight
   as that smoke that enveloped us there—
      or had been so harsh and palpable   *6*
That it wouldn't let us keep our eyes open;
   and therefore my wise and trusted escort
      came to my side and offered me his shoulder.   *9*
Just as a blind man walks behind his guide
   so he won't get lost or knock against
      something that might harm or even kill him,   *12*
So did I go through that foul, bitter air
   listening to my leader, who was saying,
      "Make sure you do not get cut off from me."   *15*

I heard voices, and each of them seemed
   to be praying for peace and for mercy
      from the Lamb of God who takes away our sins.   *18*
Indeed, they all began with "Agnus Dei"
   and sang the words with one voice on pitch
      so that they seemed to be in perfect accord.   *21*
I asked, "Master, are these spirits I hear?"
   And he answered, "You sense the truth,
      and here they untie the knot of wrathfulness."   *24*

"Or tu chi se' che 'l nostro fummo fendi,
  e di noi parli pur come se tue
27   partissi ancor lo tempo per calendi?"
Così per una voce detto fue;
  onde 'l maestro mio disse: "Rispondi,
30   e domanda se quinci si va sùe."
E io: "O creatura che ti mondi
  per tornar bella a colui che ti fece,
33   maraviglia udirai, se mi secondi."
"Io ti seguiterò quanto mi lece,"
  rispuose; "e se veder fummo non lascia,
36   l'udir ci terrà giunti in quella vece."
Allora incominciai: "Con quella fascia
  che la morte dissolve men vo suso,
39   e venni qui per l'infernale ambascia.
E se Dio m'ha in sua grazia rinchiuso,
  tanto che vuol ch'i' veggia la sua corte
42   per modo tutto fuor del moderno uso,
non mi celar chi fosti anzi la morte,
  ma dilmi, e dimmi s'i' vo bene al varco;
45   e tue parole fier le nostre scorte."

"Lombardo fui, e fu' chiamato Marco;
  del mondo seppi, e quel valore amai
48   al quale ha or ciascun disteso l'arco.
Per montar sù dirittamente vai."
  Così rispuose, e soggiunse: "I' ti prego
51   che per me prieghi quando sù sarai."
E io a lui: "Per fede mi ti lego
  di far ciò che mi chiedi; ma io scoppio
54   dentro ad un dubbio, s'io non me ne spiego.
Prima era scempio, e ora è fatto doppio
  ne la sentenza tua, che mi fa certo
57   qui, e altrove, quello ov' io l'accoppio.
Lo mondo è ben così tutto diserto
  d'ogne virtute, come tu mi sone,
60   e di malizia gravido e coverto;

"And who are you who cut through our smoke
  and speak of us as though, even here,
    you measured time by a calendar's days?"   *27*
This had been said by one of the voices,
  and then my master told me, "Answer him,
    and ask if the road goes up from here."   *30*
And so I said, "O creature cleansing yourself
  to return in beauty to the One who made you,
    you will hear a wonder if you follow me."   *33*
"I will follow as far as permitted,"
  he replied, "and if the smoke blocks our sight,
    hearing will keep us together instead."   *36*
And so I began, "Wearing the swaddling clothes
  that death unwinds I make my way upward,
    and I have come here through the anguish of Hell.   *39*
And since God has enclosed me in such grace
  that he wills that I see His court, in a way
    wholly beyond all modern custom,   *42*
Do not hide from me what you were before death,
  but tell it to me, and tell me if I am headed
    toward the passage up. Your words will guide us."   *45*

"I was a Lombard called Marco by name,
  a man of the world who loved that valor
    at which today all aim with unstrung bows.   *48*
You are on the right path to make the ascent."
  So he answered, and then added, "I pray you,
    please pray for me when you are above."   *51*
I said to him, "You have my promise
  to do as you ask. But I will burst with the doubt
    I have inside unless I free myself of it,   *54*
A single doubt at first, but it has been doubled
  by what you just said, which confirms for me
    sentiments I have also elsewhere heard.   *57*
The world is very much a desert
  barren of every virtue, as you tell me,
    and overgrown with the malice it bears.   *60*

ma priego che m'addite la cagione,
   sì ch'i' la veggia e ch'i' la mostri altrui;
63   ché nel cielo uno, e un qua giù la pone."

Alto sospir, che duolo strinse in "uhi!"
   mise fuor prima; e poi cominciò: "Frate,
66   lo mondo è cieco, e tu vien ben da lui.
Voi che vivete ogne cagion recate
   pur suso al cielo, pur come se tutto
69   movesse seco di necessitate.
Se così fosse, in voi fora distrutto
   libero arbitrio, e non fora giustizia
72   per ben letizia, e per male aver lutto.
Lo cielo i vostri movimenti inizia;
   non dico tutti, ma, posto ch'i' 'l dica,
75   lume v'è dato a bene e a malizia,
e libero voler; che, se fatica
   ne le prime battaglie col ciel dura,
78   poi vince tutto, se ben si notrica.
A maggior forza e a miglior natura
   liberi soggiacete; e quella cria
81   la mente in voi, che 'l ciel non ha in sua cura.
Però, se 'l mondo presente disvia,
   in voi è la cagione, in voi si cheggia;
84   e io te ne sarò or vera spia.
Esce di mano a lui che la vagheggia
   prima che sia, a guisa di fanciulla
87   che piangendo e ridendo pargoleggia,
l'anima semplicetta che sa nulla,
   salvo che, mossa da lieto fattore,
90   volontier torna a ciò che la trastulla.
Di picciol bene in pria sente sapore;
   quivi s'inganna, e dietro ad esso corre,
93   se guida o fren non torce suo amore.
Onde convenne legge per fren porre;
   convenne rege aver, che discernesse
96   de la vera cittade almen la torre.

But I pray you, point out to me the reason,
  so I may see it and show it to others,
    for some blame the heavens, and some the earth."   *63*

At first he sighed deeply, a sigh that grief
  wrung into "O me." Then he began, "Brother,
    the world is blind, and, yes, you come from it.   *66*
You who are still alive assign each cause
  only to the heavens, as if they drew
    everything with them by necessity.   *69*
If that were so, your free will would be destroyed,
  and it would not be just to have joy
    for goodness, or feel grief for evil.   *72*
Yes, the heavens initiate your actions—
  I don't say all of them, but even if I did,
    you've still received light to see good and evil,   *75*
And you still have free will, which, though it may tire
  when it first battles the heavens, will later
    overcome all if it is properly nourished.   *78*
You, free, are subject to a greater power
  and a better nature, which creates within you
    the mind that is not in the heavens' charge.   *81*
And so, if the world around you goes astray
  the cause is in you, in you let it be sought.
    I will now be your true informant in this.   *84*
From the hands of the Creator, who loves it
  before it exists, the soul comes forth
    like a child at play, now weeping now laughing.   *87*
The simple little soul, which knows nothing
  except that, coming from a joyous Maker,
    it turns eagerly to whatever delights it.   *90*
When it tastes the savor of some trivial good
  it turns with eagerness to what delights it
    if it is not guided or its love reined in.   *93*
And so laws had to be imposed as a curb,
  and a ruler was needed who could discern
    at least the tower of the one true city.   *96*

Le leggi son, ma chi pon mano ad esse?
   Nullo, però che 'l pastor che procede,
99   rugumar può, ma non ha l'unghie fesse;
per che la gente, che sua guida vede
   pur a quel ben fedire ond' ella è ghiotta,
102   di quel si pasce, e più oltre non chiede.
Ben puoi veder che la mala condotta
   è la cagion che 'l mondo ha fatto reo,
105   e non natura che 'n voi sia corrotta.
Soleva Roma, che 'l buon mondo feo,
   due soli aver, che l'una e l'altra strada
108   facean vedere, e del mondo e di Deo.
L'un l'altro ha spento; ed è giunta la spada
   col pasturale, e l'un con l'altro insieme
111   per viva forza mal convien che vada;
però che, giunti, l'un l'altro non teme:
   se non mi credi, pon mente a la spiga,
114   ch'ogn' erba si conosce per lo seme.
In sul paese ch'Adice e Po riga,
   solea valore e cortesia trovarsi,
117   prima che Federigo avesse briga;
or può sicuramente indi passarsi
   per qualunque lasciasse, per vergogna
120   di ragionar coi buoni o d'appressarsi.
Ben v'èn tre vecchi ancora in cui rampogna
   l'antica età la nova, e par lor tardo
123   che Dio a miglior vita li ripogna:
Currado da Palazzo e 'l buon Gherardo
   e Guido da Castel, che mei si noma,
126   francescamente, il semplice Lombardo.
Dì oggimai che la Chiesa di Roma,
   per confondere in sé due reggimenti,
129   cade nel fango, e sé brutta e la soma."

"O Marco mio," diss' io, "bene argomenti;
   e or discerno perché dal retaggio
132   li figli di Levì furono essenti.

And laws there are, but who takes them in hand?
  No one, because the shepherd in charge
    may ruminate, but does not have cleft hooves.   *99*
The people, therefore, who see their leader lunge
  only at the goods for which they themselves lust,
    graze only on that and seek no further.   *102*
So you can plainly see that poor guidance
  has made the world wicked, and it is not
    your own nature that has become corrupt.   *105*
Rome, which made the world good, once had two suns,
  each illuminating a different road,
    the road of the world and the road of God.   *108*
One has extinguished the other, and the sword
  is now joined to the crook, and these two,
    forced to go together, can only go badly,   *111*
For, being joined, they do not fear each other.
  If you don't believe me, look at an ear of grain,
    for every plant is known by its seed.   *114*
In the land watered by the Adige and Po
  valor and courtesy were once to be found,
    before Frederick met with opposition.   *117*
Now it could safely be crossed by a person
  who wanted out of shame to avoid
    speaking with or meeting any good man.   *120*
Well, there are three good men still in whom
  the ancient age rebukes the new, waiting
    for God to take them to a better world: *123*
Currado del Palazzo and the good Gherardo
  and Guido da Castel, who is better named,
    as he is by the French, the honest Lombard.   *126*
From now on say that the Church of Rome,
  by confounding in herself two governments,
    falls in the mire, fouling her burden and herself."   *129*

"O Marco mine," I said, "you reason well;
  and now I see why the sons of Levi
    were excluded from the inheritance.   *132*

Ma qual Gherardo è quel che tu per saggio
di' ch'è rimaso de la gente spenta,
135   in rimprovèro del secol selvaggio?"
"O tuo parlar m'inganna, o el mi tenta,"
rispuose a me; "ché, parlandomi tosco,
138   par che del buon Gherardo nulla senta.
Per altro sopranome io nol conosco,
s'io nol togliessi da sua figlia Gaia.
141   Dio sia con voi, ché più non vegno vosco.
Vedi l'albor che per lo fummo raia
già biancheggiare, e me convien partirmi
144   (l'angelo è ivi) prima ch'io li paia."
Così tornò, e più non volle udirmi.

But who is this Gherardo, whom you say
    remains as one of the vanished people
        in reproach of the present barbarous age?"   135
"Either your words deceive me," responded Marco,
    "or you are testing me, for you, speaking Tuscan,
        seem not to have heard of the good Gherardo.   138
I know him by no other added name,
    unless I would take it from his daughter, Gaia.
        May God be with you, for I can come   141
No farther with you. You can already see
    gleaming through the smoke a brightening pallor.
        The angel is there, and must not spy me."   144
So he turned back and would hear me no more.

Canto XVII

Dante and Virgil emerge from *the smoke of the terrace of Anger. Dante is immediately overcome by a wave of visions that fill his imagination. These are the examples of Anger. A bright light striking his face awakens Dante from his visions. The angel of the terrace calls the travelers to ascend, his face hidden in his own brightness. As the travelers mount the stair, a further P is removed from the pilgrim's forehead and a*

Ricorditi, lettor, se mai ne l'alpe
   ti colse nebbia per la qual vedessi
3   non altrimenti che per pelle talpe,
come, quando i vapori umidi e spessi
   a diradar cominciansi, la spera
6   del sol debilemente entra per essi;
e fia la tua imagine leggera
   in giugnere a veder com' io rividi
9   lo sole in pria, che già nel corcar era.
Sì, pareggiando i miei co' passi fidi
   del mio maestro, usci' fuor di tal nube
12   ai raggi morti già ne' bassi lidi.

O imaginativa che ne rube
   talvolta sì di fuor, ch'om non s'accorge
15   perché dintorno suonin mille tube,
chi move te, se 'l senso non ti porge?
   Moveti lume che nel ciel s'informa,
18   per sé o per voler che giù lo scorge.
De l'empiezza di lei che mutò forma
   ne l'uccel ch'a cantar più si diletta,
21   ne l'imagine mia apparve l'orma;

*Beatitude is sung. As night approaches, Dante feels his physical strength
giving way. Dante asks Virgil what sin is purged on the terrace on which
they now stand. Virgil responds with an extended discourse on the nature of
love between creature and Creator and the characteristics of the seven capital
vices in one of the* Commedia's *most important passages of philosophical
poetry.*

Recall, Reader, if ever in the mountains
 a fog has shrouded you and you could not see
   except as moles do, through the pores of your skin,   *3*
How when the thick, moist mist begins at last
 to evaporate, the disk of the sun
   feebly penetrates the curtain of haze,   *6*
And you will be able to imagine at once
 how I saw the reappearance of the sun,
   which by now was very close to setting.   *9*
So, matching mine to my master's trusted steps,
 I came forth from such a fog to the rays
   that were already dead on the shores below.   *12*

O Imagination, that sweeps us away
 so completely from the outside world
   that we would not hear a thousand trumpets,   *15*
Who moves you when our senses are idle?
 A light moves you, either formed in Heaven,
   of itself, or by desire that discerns it from below.   *18*
I imagined I saw the impious deed
 of that woman who was transformed
   into the bird that most delights in song;   *21*

e qui fu la mia mente sì ristretta
dentro da sé, che di fuor non venìa
24   cosa che fosse allor da lei ricetta.
Poi piovve dentro a l'alta fantasia
un crucifisso, dispettoso e fero
27   ne la sua vista, e cotal si moria;
intorno ad esso era il grande Assüero,
Estèr sua sposa e 'l giusto Mardoceo,
30   che fu al dire e al far così intero.
E come questa imagine rompeo
sé per sé stessa, a guisa d'una bulla
33   cui manca l'acqua sotto qual si feo,
surse in mia visïone una fanciulla
piangendo forte, e dicea: "O regina,
36   perché per ira hai voluto esser nulla?
Ancisa t'hai per non perder Lavina;
or m'hai perduta! Io son essa che lutto,
39   madre, a la tua pria ch'a l'altrui ruina."

Come si frange il sonno ove di butto
nova luce percuote il viso chiuso,
42   che fratto guizza pria che muoia tutto;
così l'imaginar mio cadde giuso
tosto che lume il volto mi percosse,
45   maggior assai che quel ch'è in nostro uso.
I' mi volgea per veder ov' io fosse,
quando una voce disse "Qui si monta,"
48   che da ogne altro intento mi rimosse;
e fece la mia voglia tanto pronta
di riguardar chi era che parlava,
51   che mai non posa, se non si raffronta.
Ma come al sol che nostra vista grava
e per soverchio sua figura vela,
54   così la mia virtù quivi mancava.

"Questo è divino spirito, che ne la
via da ir sù ne drizza sanza prego,
57   e col suo lume sé medesmo cela.

And my mind was so restrained by this image,
  so self-contained, that it received nothing
    that came to it from the outside world.   *24*
Then rained down into my high fantasy
  the image of one crucified, scornful
    and fierce in his mien, and so when dying.   *27*
About him stood the grand Ahasuerus
  and his wife, Esther, and the just Mordecai,
    who was in word and deed beyond reproach.   *30*
When this image burst, spontaneously,
  as a bubble does when the water
    of which it is made suddenly gives way,   *33*
There rose up in my vision a young maiden
  weeping and wailing aloud, "O Queen,
    why through anger have you annulled yourself?   *36*
You have killed yourself so that you would not lose
  Lavinia, now you have lost me, and I mourn
    your ruin, Mother, before another's has happened."   *39*

As sleep is shattered when light abruptly
  strikes our closed eyes, and although shattered
    still shimmers a little before it all dies away,   *42*
So too my imagination dropped away
  as soon as a light struck my face, far brighter
    than any light we are used to seeing.   *45*
I was turning around to see where I was
  when a voice said, "Here is the way up,"
    removing from me every other intent   *48*
And giving my desire to see
  who the speaker was the sort of eagerness
    that never rests until it sees face to face.   *51*
But just as the sun overwhelms our sight
  and veils its form by its very excess,
    so too was my strength now failing me.   *54*

"This is a divine spirit directing us
  toward the ascent without our asking.
    He conceals his form within his own light.   *57*

Sì fa con noi, come l'uom si fa sego;
   ché quale aspetta prego e l'uopo vede,
60   malignamente già si mette al nego.
Or accordiamo a tanto invito il piede;
   procacciam di salir pria che s'abbui,
63   ché poi non si poria, se 'l dì non riede."

Così disse il mio duca, e io con lui
   volgemmo i nostri passi ad una scala;
66   e tosto ch'io al primo grado fui,
senti'mi presso quasi un muover d'ala
   e ventarmi nel viso e dir: "Beati
69   pacifici, che son sanz' ira mala!"
Già eran sovra noi tanto levati
   li ultimi raggi che la notte segue,
72   che le stelle apparivan da più lati.
"O virtù mia, perché sì ti dilegue?"
   fra me stesso dicea, ché mi sentiva
75   la possa de le gambe posta in triegue.

Noi eravam dove più non saliva
   la scala sù, ed eravamo affissi,
78   pur come nave ch'a la piaggia arriva.
E io attesi un poco, s'io udissi
   alcuna cosa nel novo girone;
81   poi mi volsi al maestro mio, e dissi:
"Dolce mio padre, dì, quale offensione
   si purga qui nel giro dove semo?
84   Se i piè si stanno, non stea tuo sermone."
Ed elli a me: "L'amor del bene, scemo
   del suo dover, quiritta si ristora;
87   qui si ribatte il mal tardato remo.
Ma perché più aperto intendi ancora,
   volgi la mente a me, e prenderai
90   alcun buon frutto di nostra dimora."
"Né creator né creatura mai,"
   cominciò el, "figliuol, fu sanza amore,
93   o naturale o d'animo; e tu 'l sai.

He treats us as we would treat ourselves;
   for whoever sees the need but waits to be asked
      already tends toward unkind denial.   *60*
Now let's match our steps to this invitation
   and try to ascend before it grows dark,
      or we will have to wait until daylight returns."   *63*

So said my leader, and then he and I
   turned our footsteps to mount a stairway;
      no sooner was I on the first step   *66*
Than I felt a moving wing fan the air
   and brush my face, and I heard
      "*Beati pacifici*, who are without wrath."   *69*
Twilight's last rays were already so high
   on the mountainside above, that the stars
      were coming out in many parts of the sky.   *72*
"O my strength, why are you melting away?"
   I said to myself, for I felt that my legs
      had no strength left and had given up the fight.   *75*

We were now where the stairway climbed no more
   and there we came to a halt, like a ship
      that stands at rest when it has reached the shore.   *78*
I listened a while to see if I could hear
   any sound coming from the new circle,
      and then I turned to my master and said,   *81*
"Tell me, sweet father, what sin is purged
   here in the circle where we are standing?
      Our feet may be stayed, but do not stay your speech."   *84*
And he said to me, "In this circle is restored
   the love of good that was less than it should be;
      here the idled oar is plied once again.   *87*
But so that you may understand more clearly,
   turn your mind toward me, and you will gather
      some good fruit or other from our delay."   *90*
And he went on, "Neither Creator nor creature
   was ever without love, either natural
      or of the mind, and this you already know.   *93*

Lo naturale è sempre sanza errore,
   ma l'altro puote errar per malo obietto
96   o per troppo o per poco di vigore.
Mentre ch'elli è nel primo ben diretto,
   e ne' secondi sé stesso misura,
99   esser non può cagion di mal diletto;
ma quando al mal si torce, o con più cura
   o con men che non dee corre nel bene,
102   contra 'l fattore adovra sua fattura.
Quinci comprender puoi ch'esser convene
   amor sementa in voi d'ogne virtute
105   e d'ogne operazion che merta pene.
Or, perché mai non può da la salute
   amor del suo subietto volger viso,
108   da l'odio proprio son le cose tute;
e perché intender non si può diviso,
   e per sé stante, alcuno esser dal primo,
111   da quello odiare ogne effetto è deciso.
Resta, se dividendo bene stimo,
   che 'l mal che s'ama è del prossimo; ed esso
114   amor nasce in tre modi in vostro limo.
È chi, per esser suo vicin soppresso,
   spera eccellenza, e sol per questo brama
117   ch'el sia di sua grandezza in basso messo;
è chi podere, grazia, onore e fama
   teme di perder perch' altri sormonti,
120   onde s'attrista sì che 'l contrario ama;
ed è chi per ingiuria par ch'aonti,
   sì che si fa de la vendetta ghiotto,
123   e tal convien che 'l male altrui impronti.
Questo triforme amor qua giù di sotto
   si piange: or vo' che tu de l'altro intende,
126   che corre al ben con ordine corrotto.
Ciascun confusamente un bene apprende
   nel qual si queti l'animo, e disira;
129   per che di giugner lui ciascun contende.
Se lento amore a lui veder vi tira
   o a lui acquistar, questa cornice,
132   dopo giusto penter, ve ne martira.

Natural love is always inerrant,
  but the other may err through an evil object
    or through having too much or too little vigor.   *96*
While it is directed toward the Primal Good
  and observes due measure with secondary goods,
    it cannot be the cause of sinful pleasure.   *99*
But when it is twisted toward evil, or runs
  with too much zeal, or too little, toward good,
    the creature works against its own Creator.   *102*
And so you can see that love must be
  the seed of every virtue within you
    and of every act that deserves punishment.   *105*
Now, since love can never turn its sight
  from its subject's well-being, all things
    are secure from ever hating themselves;   *108*
And since no being can be thought of as severed
  from the First, and as standing on its own,
    no being can possibly ever hate Him.   *111*
Therefore, if I distinguish correctly,
  the evil we love must be our neighbor's,
    and it is born in three ways in your mortal clay.   *114*
There is he who hopes to excel
  by his neighbor's fall from greatness
    and desires his fall for just this reason.   *117*
There is he who fears to lose power, favor,
  honor, and fame by another's exaltation
    and is so grieved by it that he loves the contrary.   *120*
And there is he who seems so outraged
  by injury that he lusts for vengeance
    and so needs to contrive another's hurt.   *123*
This threefold love is lamented down below.
  Now I would have you hear of the other,
    which strives for the good in undue measure.   *126*
Everyone dimly apprehends a good
  where the mind may find rest. Desiring it,
    everyone tries to attain that good.   *129*
If it is a sluggish love that draws you
  to see and attain it, this terrace here
    torments you for it, after due repentance.   *132*

Altro ben è che non fa l'uom felice;
  non è felicità, non è la buona
135   essenza, d'ogne ben frutto e radice.
L'amor ch'ad esso troppo s'abbandona,
  di sovr' a noi si piange per tre cerchi;
138   ma come tripartito si ragiona,
taccíolo, acció che tu per te ne cerchi."

And there is another good, one that does not
  make man happy, for it is not the essence
    of every good, its source and its fruit.   *135*
Love that gives itself to this with abandon
  is wept for in the three circles above,
    but the nature of its threefold division,   *138*
So you may seek it yourself, I will not speak of."

CANTO XVIII

VIRGIL PAUSES IN HIS DISCOURSE *to see if Dante has understood and, perceiving a continued doubt in his pupil, encourages him to say what is on his mind. Dante asks him to explain love. Virgil continues at length his philosophical discourse on the nature of love and free will. By the time Virgil has finished his explanation the moon is rising and Dante is beginning to feel drowsy. There suddenly breaks upon the scene a great*

Posto avea fine al suo ragionamento
l'alto dottore, e attento guardava
3   ne la mia vista s'io parea contento;
e io, cui nova sete ancor frugava,
di fuor tacea, e dentro dicea:"Forse
6   lo troppo dimandar ch'io fo li grava."
Ma quel padre verace, che s'accorse
del timido voler che non s'apriva,
9   parlando, di parlare ardir mi porse.
Ond' io:"Maestro, il mio veder s'avviva
sì nel tuo lume, ch'io discerno chiaro
12   quanto la tua ragion parta o descriva.
Però ti prego, dolce padre caro,
che mi dimostri amore, a cui reduci
15   ogne buono operare e 'l suo contraro."

"Drizza," disse,"ver' me l'agute luci
de lo 'ntelletto, e fieti manifesto
18   'error de' ciechi che si fanno duci.
L'animo, ch'è creato ad amar presto,
ad ogne cosa è mobile che piace,
21   tosto che dal piacere in atto è desto.
Vostra apprensiva da esser verace
tragge intenzione, e dentro a voi la spiega,
24   sì che l'animo ad essa volger face;

*crowd of people, running. These are the slothful who call out exempla of
zeal. Virgil asks the souls to show them the way to ascend, and one of them
replies. This is the abbot of San Zeno. After he has run off, two further
souls appear who are calling out examples of Sloth. The canto ends with
Dante's thoughts wandering as he falls into sleep.*

After the exalted teacher had finished
  his lecture to me, he gazed intently
    at my face to see if I was satisfied.   *3*
I was thirsty for more, and though outwardly
  I said not a word, inside I was saying,
    "Maybe I'm annoying him with my questions."   *6*
But, dear father that he was, he was aware
  of my undeclared and timid desire
    and spoke to give me courage to speak.   *9*
And so I said, "Master, my vision becomes
  so keen in your light that I clearly see
    each distinction you make, and all you describe. *12*
Therefore, sweet father dear, I beg you,
  explain to me love, to which you reduce
    every good action and its opposite."   *15*

"Direct upon me," he said, "the sharp eyes
  of your intellect, and you will soon see
    the folly of the blind leading the blind.   *18*
The mind, which is created ready to love,
  moves toward anything that pleases it
    as soon as that pleasure wakes it to act.   *21*
Your perception draws from real objects an image
  and unfolds it within you in such a way
    that your mind turns its attention there,   *24*

e se, rivolto, inver' di lei si piega,
   quel piegare è amor, quell' è natura
27   che per piacer di novo in voi si lega.
Poi, come 'l foco movesi in altura
   per la sua forma ch'è nata a salire
30   là dove più in sua matera dura,
così l'animo preso entra in disire,
   ch'è moto spiritale, e mai non posa
33   fin che la cosa amata il fa gioire.
Or ti puote apparer quant' è nascosa
   la veritate a la gente ch'avvera
36   ciascun amore in sé laudabil cosa;
però che forse appar la sua matera
   sempre esser buona, ma non ciascun segno
39   è buono, ancor che buona sia la cera."

"Le tue parole e 'l mio seguace ingegno,"
   rispuos' io lui, "m'hanno amor discoverto,
42   ma ciò m'ha fatto di dubbiar più pregno;
ché, s'amore è di fuori a noi offerto
   e l'anima non va con altro piede,
45   se dritta o torta va, non è suo merto."

Ed elli a me: "Quanto ragion qui vede,
   dir ti poss' io; da indi in là t'aspetta
48   pur a Beatrice, ch'è opra di fede.
Ogne forma sustanzïal, che setta
   è da matera ed è con lei unita,
51   specifica vertute ha in sé colletta,
la qual sanza operar non è sentita,
   né si dimostra mai che per effetto,
54   come per verdi fronde in pianta vita.
Però, là onde vegna lo 'ntelletto
   de le prime notizie, omo non sape,
57   e de' primi appetibili l'affetto,
che sono in voi sì come studio in ape
   di far lo mele; e questa prima voglia
60   merto di lode o di biasmo non cape.

And if the mind, so turned, inclines toward it,
  that inclination is love, and it is nature,
    bound up anew in you through pleasure.   *27*
Then, as fire, which is born to ascend,
  moves upward in its very essence
    to survive in its natural element,   *30*
Just so the captive mind attains its desire,
  a movement of the spirit that never rests
    until it enjoys the thing that it loves.   *33*
Now you can see how hidden is the truth
  from people who insist that every love
    is worthy of praise in and of itself,   *36*
Perhaps because in its substance love
  always seems good. But not every seal
    is as good as the wax used for the imprint."   *39*

"Your words and my wit in following them,"
  I said, "have revealed the nature of love to me,
    but that has filled me with even more doubt.   *42*
For if love is offered from outside of us,
  and if the soul moves on no other foot,
    it has no merit in going straight or crooked."   *45*

Then he said, "As far as reason can see here,
  I can tell you. Beyond that you must look
    to Beatrice, for it has to do with faith.   *48*
Every substantial form that is distinct
  from matter and yet united with it
    contains its own distinctive power,   *51*
One not perceived except in action
  nor ever shown except by its effect,
    as green leaves show the life of a plant.   *54*
Therefore, no one knows where the intellect
  gets its first principles, or its affection
    for primordial objects of desire.   *57*
They are in you as zeal for making honey
  is present in bees, and this primal will
    does not admit of either praise or blame.   *60*

Or perché a questa ogn' altra si raccoglia,
innata v'è la virtù che consiglia,
63   e de l'assenso de' tener la soglia.
Quest' è 'l principio là onde si piglia
ragion di meritare in voi, secondo
66   che buoni e rei amori accoglie e viglia.
Color che ragionando andaro al fondo,
s'accorser d'esta innata libertate;
69   però moralità lasciaro al mondo.
Onde, poniam che di necessitate
surga ogne amor che dentro a voi s'accende,
72   di ritenerlo è in voi la podestate.
La nobile virtù Beatrice intende
per lo libero arbitrio, e però guarda
75   che l'abbi a mente, s'a parlar ten prende."

La luna, quasi a mezza notte tarda,
facea le stelle a noi parer più rade,
78   fatta com' un secchion che tuttor arda;
e correa contro 'l ciel per quelle strade
che 'l sole infiamma allor che quel da Roma
81   tra ' Sardi e ' Corsi il vede quando cade.
E quell' ombra gentil per cui si noma
Pietola più che villa mantoana,
84   del mio carcar diposta avea la soma;
per ch'io, che la ragione aperta e piana
sovra le mie quistioni avea ricolta,
87   stava com' om che sonnolento vana.
Ma questa sonnolenza mi fu tolta
subitamente da gente che dopo
90   le nostre spalle a noi era già volta.
E quale Ismeno già vide e Asopo
lungo di sè di notte furia e calca,
93   pur che i Teban di Bacco avesser uopo,
cotal per quel giron suo passo falca,
per quel ch'io vidi di color, venendo,
96   cui buon volere e giusto amor cavalca.

Now so that every other will conforms to this,
  there is innate in you a sense of judgment
    that must hold the threshold of assent.   *63*
This is the principle that justifies merit
  for what you do, according to how
    it garners and winnows good and evil loves.   *66*
Those who reasoned this through to the root observed
  this inborn free will, and they were the ones
    who left to the world a system of ethics.   *69*
So even supposing that every love
  is kindled in you through necessity,
    the power to restrain it is still within you.   *72*
Beatrice understands this noble virtue
  as free will; therefore you should have it in mind
    if ever she should speak of it to you."   *75*

The moon, rising just before midnight
  like a glowing copper pitcher, made the stars
    seem fewer to us than they had earlier,   *78*
And it moved through the sky along the course
  that the sun inflames when the Romans see it
    setting between Sardinia and Corsica.   *81*
That noble shade through whom Pietola
  is more renowned than any Mantuan town
    had laid down the load I had placed on him,   *84*
So that I, having reaped his lucid answers
  to the questions I had posed, was left
    to vague, drifting thoughts in my drowsiness.   *87*
But that drowsiness was lifted from me
  all of a sudden by a crowd of people
    who had come round to us from behind our backs.   *90*
And just as the Ismenus and Asopus saw
  a furious crowd along their banks at night
    whenever the Thebans would summon Bacchus,   *93*
So too these souls, from what I saw of them,
  rounding the circle's bend and coming on
    with Right Will and Just Love riding them.   *96*

Tosto fur sovr' a noi, perché correndo
si movea tutta quella turba magna;
99   e due dinanzi gridavan piangendo:
"Maria corse con fretta a la montagna;
e Cesare, per soggiogare Ilerda,
102   punse Marsilia e poi corse in Ispagna."
"Ratto, ratto, che 'l tempo non si perda
per poco amor," gridavan li altri appresso,
105   "che studio di ben far grazia rinverda."

"O gente in cui fervore aguto adesso
ricompie forse negligenza e indugio
108   da voi per tepidezza in ben far messo,
questi che vive, e certo i' non vi bugio,
vuole andar sù, pur che 'l sol ne riluca;
111   però ne dite ond' è presso il pertugio."

Parole furon queste del mio duca;
e un di quelli spirti disse: "Vieni
114   di retro a noi, e troverai la buca.
Noi siam di voglia a muoverci sì pieni,
che restar non potem; però perdona,
117   se villania nostra giustizia tieni.
Io fui abate in San Zeno a Verona
sotto lo 'mperio del buon Barbarossa,
120   di cui dolente ancor Milan ragiona.
E tale ha già l'un piè dentro la fossa,
che tosto piangerà quel monastero,
123   e tristo fia d'avere avuta possa;
perché suo figlio, mal del corpo intero,
e de la mente peggio, e che mal nacque,
126   ha posto in loco di suo pastor vero."

Io non so se più disse o s'ei si tacque,
tant' era già di là da noi trascorso;
129   ma questo intesi, e ritener mi piacque.
E quei che m'era ad ogne uopo soccorso
disse: "Volgiti qua: vedine due
132   venir dando a l'accidïa di morso."

They were upon us in no time, the whole throng
  all moving together in one mass sprint,
    and two in the front shouting through their tears,   *99*
"Mary ran in great haste to the mountains"
  and "Caesar, to subdue Lerida,
    feinted at Marseilles and then ran on to Spain."   *102*
"Faster, faster, so that no time be lost
  through little love," cried the others behind them,
    "and so that zeal to act may renew God's grace!"   *105*

"O souls in whom keen fervor now perhaps
  makes up for the negligence and delay
    in doing good that your lukewarmness caused,   *108*
This man here, who is alive—and I do not lie—
  would like to ascend as soon as it is light,
    so tell us where the opening is at hand."   *111*

These were the words of my leader,
  and one of the spirits responded, "Come
    behind us and you will find the gap.   *114*
We are so filled with desire to move
  that we cannot stay, so pardon us
    if our penance seems to be rudeness to you.   *117*
I was abbot of San Zeno in Verona
  under the rule of the good Barbarossa,
    of whom Milan still speaks with sorrow.   *120*
And there is one with one foot in the grave
  who will soon lament that monastery
    and grieve that he ever had power there,   *123*
Because his son, crippled in his body,
  worse in his mind, and born to woe,
    he has put there in place of its lawful pastor."   *126*

I do not know whether he said more
  or if he was silent, he'd run so far ahead,
    but this much I heard and was pleased to retain.   *129*
Then he who was my constant salvation
  said to me, "Turn around so you can see
    two of them coming and giving a bite to sloth."   *132*

Di retro a tutti dicean: "Prima fue
  morta la gente a cui il mar s'aperse,
135   che vedesse Iordan le rede sue.
E quella che l'affanno non sofferse
  fino a la fine col figlio d'Anchise,
138   sé stessa a vita sanza gloria offerse."

Poi quando fuor da noi tanto divise
  quell' ombre, che veder più non potiersi,
141   novo pensiero dentro a me si mise,
del qual più altri nacquero e diversi;
  e tanto d'uno in altro vaneggiai,
144   che li occhi per vaghezza ricopersi,
e 'l pensamento in sogno trasmutai.

At the rear of the pack these two were saying,
  "The people for whom the Red Sea opened
    were dead before Jordan saw its heirs;   *135*
And those who did not maintain their effort
  all the way to the end with Anchises' son
    made for themselves a life without glory."   *138*

When those shades had left us so far behind
  that they could no longer be kept in sight
    a new thought took form within my mind,   *141*
And this to a number of others gave rise,
  so that, roaming from one to another theme
    in my mental wandering, I closed my eyes   *144*
And transmuted my musing into a dream.

Canto XIX

IT IS NIGHT ON THE *mountain and the sleeping Dante falls into a dream of a Siren. He is awoken by Virgil, who urges him to continue the journey. As Dante walks on, still preoccupied by his dream, the travelers encounter the angel of the terrace, who invites them to ascend. In response to Dante's continuing preoccupation, Virgil gives a brief interpretation of his dream and instructs him to turn his attention to the path ahead. When the*

Ne l'ora che non può 'l calor dïurno
   intepidar più 'l freddo de la luna,
3   vinto da terra, e talor da Saturno
—quando i geomanti lor Maggior Fortuna
   veggiono in orïente, innanzi a l'alba,
6   surger per via che poco le sta bruna—,
mi venne in sogno una femmina balba,
   ne li occhi guercia, e sovra i piè distorta,
9   con le man monche, e di colore scialba.
Io la mirava; e come 'l sol conforta
   le fredde membra che la notte aggrava,
12   così lo sguardo mio le facea scorta
la lingua, e poscia tutta la drizzava
   in poco d'ora, e lo smarrito volto,
15   com' amor vuol, così le colorava.
Poi ch'ell' avea 'l parlar così disciolto,
   cominciava a cantar sì, che con pena
18   da lei avrei mio intento rivolto.
"Io son," cantava, "io son dolce serena,
   che ' marinari in mezzo mar dismago;
21   tanto son di piacere a sentir piena!
Io volsi Ulisse del suo cammin vago
   al canto mio; e qual meco s'ausa,
24   rado sen parte; sì tutto l'appago!"

travelers arrive at the next terrace they see figures lying facedown upon the ground. These are the souls paying penance for the vice of Avarice. Dante converses with one of the souls, who indirectly identifies himself as Pope Adrian V. Dante respectfully kneels before the soul but is ordered to rise since earthly distinctions disappear and all are equal in Purgatory. Adrian describes his late conversion from the vice of Avarice.

At the hour when the heat of the day,
   overcome by Earth, and at times by Saturn,
      can no longer warm the cold of the moon,   *3*
When the geomancers see their Fortuna Major
   rise in the East before the break of dawn
      along a path that does not stay dark for long,   *6*
There came to me in a dream a woman,
   stammering and squint-eyed, crooked on her feet,
      with maimed hands and of sallow complexion.   *9*
I gazed at her, and just as the sun
   comforts cold limbs that the night has numbed,
      so too my gaze affected that woman,   *12*
Restoring her speech, making her stand
   straight and tall, and giving her wasted face
      the coloring that is required for love.   *15*
With her tongue untied, this woman began
   to sing in such a way that I
      could hardly turn my attention from her,   *18*
"I am," she sang, "the sweet Siren who
   leads mariners astray far out at sea,
      so enchanting it is to hear my song.   *21*
I lured Ulysses off course, so eager was he
   for my song. Whoever hears it rarely departs,
      so completely do I satisfy him."   *24*

Ancor non era sua bocca richiusa,
  quand' una donna apparve santa e presta
27   lunghesso me per far colei confusa.
"O Virgilio, Virgilio, chi è questa?"
  fieramente dicea; ed el venìa
30   con li occhi fitti pur in quella onesta.
L'altra prendea, e dinanzi l'apria
  fendendo i drappi, e mostravami 'l ventre;
33   quel mi svegliò col puzzo che n'uscia.
Io mossi li occhi, e 'l buon maestro: "Almen tre
  voci t'ho messe!" dicea, "Surgi e vieni;
36   troviam l'aperta per la qual tu entre."

Sù mi levai, e tutti eran già pieni
  de l'alto dì i giron del sacro monte,
39   e andavam col sol novo a le reni.
Seguendo lui, portava la mia fronte
  come colui che l'ha di pensier carca,
42   che fa di sé un mezzo arco di ponte;
quand' io udi' "Venite; qui si varca"
  parlare in modo soave e benigno,
45   qual non si sente in questa mortal marca.
Con l'ali aperte, che parean di cigno,
  volseci in sù colui che sì parlonne
48   tra due pareti del duro macigno.
Mosse le penne poi e ventilonne,
  "*Qui lugent*" affermando esser beati,
51   ch'avran di consolar l'anime donne.

"Che hai che pur inver' la terra guati?"
  la guida mia incominciò a dirmi,
54   poco amendue da l'angel sormontati.
E io: "Con tanta sospeccion fa irmi
  novella visïon ch'a sé mi piega,
57   sì ch'io non posso dal pensar partirmi."
"Vedesti," disse, "quell'antica strega
  che sola sovr' a noi omai si piagne;
60   vedesti come l'uom da lei si slega.

Her lips were not yet closed when a lady,
  holy and alert, appeared beside me
    to cast the woman into confusion.   27
"O Virgil, Virgil, who is this?"
  she scolded him, and he came forward
    with his eyes fixed on the respectable one.   30
He seized the other and laid her bare in front,
  rending her clothes to show me her belly,
    and the stench that came from it awakened me.   33
I turned my eyes, and my good master said,
  "I have called you at least three times. Arise,
    and let's find the opening where you can enter."   36

I did rise. All the sacred mountain's circles
  were already filled with the high day.
    We went on with the new sun behind us,   39
Virgil in the lead, my brow lowered
  like one who is burdened with heavy thoughts
    and bends over like half of a bridge's arch,   42
When I heard, "Come, here is the pass,"
  spoken in a gentle and kindly tone
    that is not heard in this mortal region.   45
With open wings that seemed like a swan's
  the angel who had spoken turned us upward
    between the two walls of solid granite,   48
Then moved his feathers so as to fan us,
  declaring that those who mourn—*qui lugent*—
    are blessed, for their souls shall be comforted.   51

"Why do you keep staring at the ground?
  What's wrong?" my guide asked me when we had climbed,
    the two of us, above the angel below.   54
"A strange vision I just had," I answered him,
  "has affected me with such apprehension
    that I cannot get it out of my mind."   57
"You have seen," he said, "that ancient witch
  who is the sole cause of lament above us,
    and you have seen how man is freed from her.   60

Bastiti, e batti a terra le calcagne;
 li occhi rivolgi al logoro che gira
63 lo rege etterno con le rote magne."

Quale 'l falcon, che prima a' pié si mira,
 indi si volge al grido e si protende
66 per lo disio del pasto che là il tira,
tal mi fec' io; e tal, quanto si fende
 la roccia per dar via a chi va suso,
69 n'andai infin dove 'l cerchiar si prende.
Com' io nel quinto giro fui dischiuso,
 vidi gente per esso che piangea,
72 giacendo a terra tutta volta in giuso.
"*Adhaesit pavimento anima mea*"
 sentia dir lor con sì alti sospiri,
75 che la parola a pena s'intendea.

"O eletti di Dio, li cui soffriri
 e giustizia e speranza fa men duri,
78 drizzate noi verso li alti saliri."
"Se voi venite dal giacer sicuri,
 e volete trovar la via più tosto,
81 le vostre destre sien sempre di fori."
Così pregò 'l poeta, e sì risposto
 poco dinanzi a noi ne fu; per ch'io
84 nel parlare avvisai l'altro nascosto,
e volsi li occhi a li occhi al segnor mio:
 ond' elli m'assentì con lieto cenno
87 ciò che chiedea la vista del disio.
Poi ch'io potei di me fare a mio senno,
 trassimi sovra quella creatura
90 le cui parole pria notar mi fenno,
dicendo: "Spirto in cui pianger matura
 quel sanza 'l quale a Dio tornar non pòssi,
93 sosta un poco per me tua maggior cura.
Chi fosti e perché vòlti avete i dossi
 al sù, mi dì, e se vuo' ch'io t'impetri
96 cosa di là ond' io vivendo mossi."

Let that be enough, and just tread the ground
  with your eyes turned to the lure that is spun
    in the mighty spheres by the eternal King."   *63*

And like the falcon that first looks down
  then turns up and stretches out toward the cry,
    hungering for the food that draws him on,   *66*
So too was I, ascending the cleft
  in the rocky stairs until I arrived
    at the next level where the circling resumed.   *69*
When I stepped onto the fifth gyre
  I saw people on it who wept and lamented
    as they lay prostrate, facedown on the ground.   *72*
"*Adhaesit pavimento anima mea*,"
  I heard them saying, with sighs so deep
    that their words could hardly be understood.   *75*

"O elect of God, whose suffering
  is lightened by both justice and hope,
    direct us toward the ascent on high."   *78*
"If you come without having to lie face down
  and would like to find the way most quickly,
    keep your right side ever toward the outer rim."   *81*
The poet asked this, and the answer came
  from a little farther ahead, the voice
    enabling me to find the face that was hidden.   *84*
I turned my eyes on the eyes of my master,
  and he in turn gave a glad sign of assent
    to what my look of desire requested.   *87*
And when I could do what I wished, I went
  to stand over that soul whose words before
    had made me notice him, saying,   *90*
"Spirit in whom weeping ripens that state
  without which there is no returning to God,
    suspend for me your greater care for a while.   *93*
Tell me who you were, and why your backs are upward,
  and if you would have me ask for anything
    from the place where I, a living man, set out."   *96*

Ed elli a me: "Perché i nostri diretri
  rivolga il cielo a sé, saprai; ma prima
99   *scias quod ego fui successor Petri.*
Intra Sïestri e Chiaveri s'adima
  una fiumana bella, e del suo nome
102   lo titol del mio sangue fa sua cima.
Un mese e poco più prova' io come
  pesa il gran manto a chi dal fango il guarda,
105   che piuma sembran tutte l'altre some.
La mia conversïone, omè!, fu tarda;
  ma, come fatto fui roman pastore,
108   così scopersi la vita bugiarda.
Vidi che lì non s'acquetava il core,
  né più salir potiesi in quella vita;
111   per che di questa in me s'accese amore.
Fino a quel punto misera e partita
  da Dio anima fui, del tutto avara;
114   or, come vedi, qui ne son punita.
Quel ch'avarizia fa, qui si dichiara
  in purgazion de l'anime converse;
117   e nulla pena il monte ha più amara.
Sì come l'occhio nostro non s'aderse
  in alto, fisso a le cose terrene,
120   così giustizia qui a terra il merse.
Come avarizia spense a ciascun bene
  lo nostro amore, onde operar perdési,
123   così giustizia qui stretti ne tene,
ne' piedi e ne le man legati e presi;
  e quanto fia piacer del giusto Sire,
126   tanto staremo immobili e distesi."

Io m'era inginocchiato e volea dire;
  ma com' io cominciai ed el s'accorse,
129   solo ascoltando, del mio reverire,
"Qual cagion," disse, "in giù così ti torse?"
  E io a lui: "Per vostra dignitate
132   mia coscïenza dritto mi rimorse."

He answered me, "Why Heaven keeps our backs
  turned to itself, that you shall know, but first,
    scias quod ego fui successor Petri. 99
Between Sestri and Chiavari descends
  a beautiful stream, and its name, Lavagna,
    forms the crest of my family's title. 102
For scarcely a month I felt how the great mantle
  weighs him down who would keep it unmuddied;
    all other burdens seem light as a feather. 105
My conversion—ah me!—was late in coming,
  but when I was made the Shepherd of Rome
    I found out how lying and false life is. 108
I saw that the heart is not at rest there,
  nor in that life could one rise any higher,
    and so the love of this one was kindled in me. 111
Up to that time I had been a wretched soul,
  parted from God and wholly avaricious.
    Now, as you see, I am punished here for it. 114
What avarice does is made clear here
  in the purging of the down-turned souls,
    and the mountain has no penalty more bitter. 117
Just as our eyes, fixed on earthly things,
  were never lifted on high, so justice here
    has plunged our eyes down to the earth. 120
Just as avarice extinguished our love
  of all that is good, so that our works were lost,
    so justice holds and constrains us here, 123
Bound hand and foot, and captive for as long
  as the just Lord pleases, so long shall we
    lie here stretched out and motionless." 126

I had knelt, and wanted to speak,
  but when I began, and he became aware
    of my reverence by the sound alone, 129
"Why," he asked, "have you bent down like this?"
  "Because of your rank," I answered him,
    "my conscience would not let me stay standing." 132

"Drizza le gambe, lèvati sù, frate!"
    rispuose; "non errar: conservo sono
135   teco e con li altri ad una podestate.
Se mai quel santo evangelico suono
    che dice 'Neque nubent' intendesti,
138   ben puoi veder perch' io così ragiono.
Vattene omai: non vo' che più t'arresti;
    ché la tua stanza mio pianger disagia,
141   col qual maturo ciò che tu dicesti.
Nepote ho io di là c'ha nome Alagia,
    buona da sé, pur che la nostra casa
144   non faccia lei per essempro malvagia;
e questa sola di là m'è rimasa."

"Straighten your legs, and rise up, brother!"
  he replied. "Make no mistake. I am a servant,
    along with you and the others, of one Power.   *135*
If you have ever understood the words
  '*neque nubent*' in the Holy Gospel,
    you will understand why I have spoken thus.   *138*
Now go your way; I would have you stay no more,
  for that would only hinder my weeping,
    which ripens that which you spoke of before.   *141*
I have a niece down below, Alagia by name,
  good in herself, unless she becomes aware
    of what our house can teach her of shame.   *144*
She is all that I have left back there."

Canto XX

Dante unwillingly moves away from *the soul of Pope Adrian V and continues his journey along the terrace of Avarice. The prostrate bodies of the penitent souls so fill the pavement that the travelers are forced to stay close to the rock face. The poet bemoans the power of Avarice. As the travelers advance, they hear the voice of one soul calling out the exempla of liberality. Dante speaks to the soul, inquiring about his identity and why he is the only one speaking. The soul introduces himself as Hugh Capet,*

Contra miglior voler voler mal pugna;
  onde contra 'l piacer mio, per piacerli,
3   trassi de l'acqua non sazia la spugna.
Mossimi; e 'l duca mio si mosse per li
  luoghi spediti pur lungo la roccia,
6   come si va per muro stretto a' merli;
ché la gente che fonde a goccia a goccia
  per li occhi il mal che tutto 'l mondo occupa,
9   da l'altra parte in fuor troppo s'approccia.
Maladetta sie tu, antica lupa,
  che più che tutte l'altre bestie hai preda
12   per la tua fame sanza fine cupa!
O ciel, nel cui girar par che si creda
  le condizion di qua giù trasmutarsi,
15   quando verrà per cui questa disceda?

Noi andavam con passi lenti e scarsi,
  e io attento a l'ombre, ch'i' sentia
18   pietosamente piangere e lagnarsi;
e per ventura udi' "Dolce Maria!"
  dinanzi a noi chiamar così nel pianto
21   come fa donna che in parturir sia;

founder of the French Capetian dynasty. His extended monologue describes
the crimes of that dynasty, which had Avarice as their root cause. The latter
part of his speech describes examples of Avarice. At the close of Hugh's
speech the travelers continue their progress but are interrupted by a violent
earthquake that shakes the whole mountain. Following it, the travelers keep
walking, but Dante is filled with perplexity.

Our will fights poorly against a better will;
  and so, against my wishes but granting his,
    I drew the sponge from the water unsoaked.   *3*
I moved on, as my leader made his way
  through the clear area along the rock's face
    as one walks on a rampart, close to the wall,   *6*
For the people from whose eyes, drop by drop,
  the evil melts that fills the whole world
    occupied the outermost part of the ledge.   *9*
A curse upon you, wolf of the ages,
  who take more prey than any other beast
    to satisfy your bottomless appetite!   *12*
O skies above, whose wheels are believed
  to alter the state of things here below,
    when will he come from whom the wolf shall flee?   *15*

We picked our way with steps scant and slow,
  my attention upon those shades as I listened
    to their piteous weeping and lamentation,   *18*
When I happened to hear, up ahead of us,
  someone call out tearfully, "O sweet Mary,"
    just as a woman in labor might do,   *21*

e seguitar: "Povera fosti tanto,
   quanto veder si può per quello ospizio
24   dove sponesti il tuo portato santo."
Seguentemente intesi: "O buon Fabrizio,
   con povertà volesti anzi virtute
27   che gran ricchezza posseder con vizio."
Queste parole m'eran sì piaciute,
   ch'io mi trassi oltre per aver contezza
30   di quello spirto onde parean venute.

Esso parlava ancor de la larghezza
   che fece Niccolò a le pulcelle,
33   per condurre ad onor lor giovinezza.
"O anima che tanto ben favelle,
   dimmi chi fosti," dissi, "e perché sola
36   tu queste degne lode rinovelle.
Non fia sanza mercé la tua parola,
   s'io ritorno a compiér lo cammin corto
39   di quella vita ch'al termine vola."
Ed elli: "Io ti dirò, non per conforto
   ch'io attenda di là, ma perché tanta
42   grazia in te luce prima che sie morto.
Io fui radice de la mala pianta
   che la terra cristiana tutta aduggia,
45   sì che buon frutto rado se ne schianta.
Ma se Doagio, Lilla, Guanto e Bruggia
   potesser, tosto ne saria vendetta;
48   e io la cheggio a lui che tutto giuggia.
Chiamato fui di là Ugo Ciappetta;
   di me son nati i Filippi e i Luigi
51   per cui novellamente è Francia retta.
Figliuol fu' io d'un beccaio di Parigi:
   quando li regi antichi venner meno
54   tutti, fuor ch'un renduto in panni bigi,
trova'mi stretto ne le mani il freno
   del governo del regno, e tanta possa
57   di nuovo acquisto, e sì d'amici pieno,

And then go on to say, "How poor you were
  can be seen by the nature of the inn
    where you set down the holy burden you bore."   *24*
And after that I heard, "O good Fabricius,
  you chose to be poor and virtuous
    over possessing great wealth in wickedness."   *27*
These words were so pleasing to me
  that I pressed forward to meet the spirit
    by whom they apparently had been spoken.   *30*

Then he spoke again, now of the dowries
  bestowed by Nicholas upon the maidens
    in order to guide their tender years to honor.   *33*
"O soul, who speak of so much goodness," I said.
  "tell me who you were, and why you alone
    refresh these deeds so worthy of praise.   *36*
Your words shall not go unrewarded
  if I return to finish my brief journey
    in that life which flies on to its conclusion."   *39*
And he said, "I will tell you, not for any aid
  I expect from there, but for the immense grace
    that shines forth in you before you are dead.   *42*
I was the root of the evil tree
  that cast its shadow over all Christian lands,
    preventing good fruit from being gathered there.   *45*
If Douai, Lille, Ghent, and Bruges only
  had the power, there would soon be vengeance,
    and for this I implore Him who judges all.   *48*
On earth I was known as Hugh Capet;
  of me were born the men called Philip and Louis,
    by whom of late France has been ruled.   *51*
I was the son of a Parisian butcher.
  When the old line of kings had dwindled away,
    except for one in a monk's grey robes,   *54*
I found the reins of royal government
  tight in my hands, with so much power
    from my new possessions and so many friends   *57*

ch'a la corona vedova promossa
la testa di mio figlio fu, dal quale
60   cominciar di costor le sacrate ossa.
Mentre che la gran dota provenzale
al sangue mio non tolse la vergogna,
63   poco valea, ma pur non facea male.
Lì cominciò con forza e con menzogna
la sua rapina; e poscia, per ammenda,
66   Pontì e Normandia prese e Guascogna.
Carlo venne in Italia e, per ammenda,
vittima fé di Curradino; e poi
69   ripinse al ciel Tommaso, per ammenda.
Tempo vegg' io, non molto dopo ancoi,
che tragge un altro Carlo fuor di Francia,
72   per far conoscer meglio e sé e ' suoi.
Sanz' arme n'esce e solo con la lancia
con la qual giostrò Giuda, e quella ponta
75   sì, ch'a Fiorenza fa scoppiar la pancia.
Quindi non terra, ma peccato e onta
guadagnerà, per sé tanto più grave,
78   quanto più lieve simil danno conta.
L'altro, che già uscì preso di nave,
veggio vender sua figlia e patteggiarne
81   come fanno i corsar de l'altre schiave.
O avarizia, che puoi tu più farne,
poscia c'ha' il mio sangue a te sì tratto,
84   che non si cura de la propria carne?
Perché men paia il mal futuro e 'l fatto,
veggio in Alagna intrar lo fiordaliso,
87   e nel vicario suo Cristo esser catto.
Veggiolo un'altra volta esser deriso;
veggio rinovellar l'aceto e 'l fiele,
90   e tra vivi ladroni esser anciso.
Veggio il novo Pilato sì crudele,
che ciò nol sazia, ma sanza decreto
93   portar nel Tempio le cupide vele.
O Segnor mio, quando sarò io lieto
a veder la vendetta che, nascosa,
96   fa dolce l'ira tua nel tuo secreto?

That the widowed crown settled upon
  the head of my son, whose progeny became
    generations of consecrated bones.   *60*
As long as the great dowry of Provence
  had not stripped my house of a sense of shame,
    it counted for little, but at least did no harm.   *63*
But when, by force and fraud, its pillage began,
  my heirs afterward took, as their amends,
    Ponthieu, Normandy, and Gascony.   *66*
Charles came into Italy, and, to make amends,
  made Conradin a victim, and then
    drove Thomas to Heaven to make further amends.   *69*
I see a time, not very long from now,
  that brings another Charles away from France,
    to make both himself and his kin better known.   *72*
He comes forth alone, bearing no arms
  except the lance that Judas used, and thrusts it
    in such a way to burst Florence's paunch.   *75*
From this he will acquire not land
  but sin and shame, so much the heavier for him
    the lighter he considers such a wrong.   *78*
The other Charles, who disembarked his ship
  a prisoner, I see selling his daughter,
    haggling like a pirate over a female slave.   *81*
O Avarice, what greater harm can you do me,
  since my race is so attached to you
    it has no care for its own flesh and blood?   *84*
So past and future evil may seem less,
  I see the fleur-de-lys enter Alagni
    and in His Vicar imprison Christ.   *87*
I see Him mocked a second time,
  I see the vinegar and gall renewed
    and Him slain between two living thieves.   *90*
I see this new Pilate is so cruel
  that this does not sate him, see his greedy sails
    set without sanction against the Temple.   *93*
O my Lord, when shall I rejoice
  to see the vengeance, still concealed
    in your secret mind, that makes sweet your wrath?   *96*

Ciò ch'io dicea di quell' unica sposa
de lo Spirito Santo e che ti fece
99   verso me volger per alcuna chiosa,
tanto è risposto a tutte nostre prece
quanto 'l dì dura; ma com' el s'annotta,
102   contrario suon prendemo in quella vece.
Noi repetiam Pigmalïon allotta,
cui traditore e ladro e paricida
105   fece la voglia sua de l'oro ghiotta;
e la miseria de l'avaro Mida,
che seguì a la sua dimanda gorda,
108   per la qual sempre convien che si rida.
Del folle Acàn ciascun poi si ricorda,
come furò le spoglie, sì che l'ira
111   di Iosüè qui par ch'ancor lo morda.
Indi accusiam col marito Saffira;
lodiam i calci ch'ebbe Elïodoro;
114   e in infamia tutto 'l monte gira
Polinestòr ch'ancise Polidoro;
ultimamente ci si grida: 'Crasso,
117   dilci, che 'l sai: di che sapore è l'oro?'
Talor parla l'uno alto e l'altro basso,
secondo l'affezion ch'ad ir ci sprona
120   ora a maggiore e ora a minor passo:
però al ben che 'l dì ci si ragiona,
dianzi non era io sol; ma qui da presso
123   non alzava la voce altra persona."

Noi eravam partiti già da esso,
e brigavam di soverchiar la strada
126   tanto quanto al poder n'era permesso,
quand' io senti', come cosa che cada,
tremar lo monte; onde mi prese un gelo
129   qual prender suol colui ch'a morte vada.
Certo non si scoteo sì forte Delo,
pria che Latona in lei facesse 'l nido
132   a parturir li due occhi del cielo.

What I said about the one and only bride
  of the Holy Spirit, and what made you
    turn to me for an explanation,   *99*
Is the response in all our prayers
  as long as it is day, but when night falls
    we take up another refrain in its place.   *102*
Then we call Pygmalion to mind,
  whose insatiable appetite for gold
    made him a traitor, a parricide, and thief;   *105*
And the misery of avaricious Midas,
  a consequence of his greedy request
    and forever a cause for ridicule.   *108*
Each then remembers how the foolish Achan
  stole the spoils, so that Joshua's wrath
    seems to sting him here all over again.   *111*
Then we accuse Sapphira and her husband,
  and praise the trampling of Heliodorus;
    and the whole mountain rings the disgrace   *114*
Of Polymestor, who killed Polydorus.
  Last is the cry, 'Tell us, Crassus,
    since you know, what does gold taste like?'   *117*
Sometimes one speaks loud, and another low,
  according to the zeal that spurs our speech,
    now with greater, now with lesser force.   *120*
So, in speaking of good as we do by day,
  I was not alone just now; it was just that
    no one else happened to raise his voice nearby." *123*

We had already taken our leave of him
  and were striving to progress along the road
    as fast as our powers permitted us,   *126*
When I felt, as if it were something falling,
  the whole mountain tremble, at which a chill
    took hold of me as it does someone dying.   *129*
Delos was not shaken so violently
  before Latona made her nest on the island
    to give birth to her twins, the two eyes of Heaven. *132*

Poi cominciò da tutte parti un grido
tal, che 'l maestro inverso me si feo,
135   dicendo: "Non dubbiar, mentr' io ti guido."
"*Glorïa in excelsis*" tutti "*Deo*"
dicean, per quel ch'io da' vicin compresi,
138   onde intender lo grido si poteo.
No' istavamo immobili e sospesi
come i pastor che prima udir quel canto,
141   fin che 'l tremar cessò ed el compiési.
Poi ripigliammo nostro cammin santo,
guardando l'ombre che giacean per terra,
144   tornate già in su l'usato pianto.
Nulla ignoranza mai con tanta guerra
mi fé desideroso di sapere,
147   se la memoria mia in ciò non erra,
quanta pareami allor, pensando, avere;
né per la fretta dimandare er' oso,
150   né per me lì potea cosa vedere:
così m'andava timido e pensoso.

Then there rose up such a cry all around us
  that my master drew closer to me and said,
    "Have no fear while I am your guide."   *135*
"Gloria in excelsis Deo," all were saying,
  as far as I could tell by what I heard
    from those nearby, whom I could understand.   *138*
We stood there motionless, breath suspended,
  like the shepherds who first heard the angels' song,
    until the quake had finally ended.   *141*
Then we set out on our sacred path once more,
  looking at the shades that lay on the ground,
    weeping again now as they had before.   *144*
Never had perplexity driven me
  to such a strong desire to know—
    if I am not deceived by memory—   *147*
As I struggled with then. I did not dare
  ask my master, since we could not delay,
    nor could I find on my own an answer there.   *150*
So, timid and pensive, I went on my way.

CANTO XXI

As Dante and Virgil continue *their journey along the terrace of Avarice, an unidentified shade appears to them and enters into conversation. The shade asks them about their status in Purgatory and Virgil explains that the pilgrim is still alive. Virgil then asks the soul to explain the cause of the earthquake. The soul explains the nature of Mount Purgatory, revealing that the cause of the earthquake was not natural but was a response to his liberation from penance. Virgil then asks the soul*

La sete natural che mai non sazia
    se non con l'acqua onde la femminetta
3   samaritana domandò la grazia,
mi travagliava, e pungeami la fretta
    per la 'mpacciata via dietro al mio duca,
6   e condoleami a la giusta vendetta.
Ed ecco, sì come ne scrive Luca
    che Cristo apparve a' due ch'erano in via,
9   già surto fuor de la sepulcral buca,
ci apparve un'ombra, e dietro a noi venìa,
    dal piè guardando la turba che giace;
12   né ci addemmo di lei, sì parlò pria,
dicendo: "O frati miei, Dio vi dea pace."
    Noi ci volgemmo sùbiti, e Virgilio
15   rendéli 'l cenno ch'a ciò si conface.
Poi cominciò: "Nel beato concilio
    ti ponga in pace la verace corte
18   che me rilega ne l'etterno essilio."
"Come!" diss' elli, e parte andavam forte:
    "se voi siete ombre che Dio sù non degni,
21   chi v'ha per la sua scala tanto scorte?"
E 'l dottor mio: "Se tu riguardi a' segni
    che questi porta e che l'angel profila,
24   ben vedrai che coi buon convien ch'e' regni.

to identify himself. The soul is that of the Roman poet Statius. Statius,
unaware of Virgil's identity, says that the Aeneid *was his greatest source of*
inspiration and warmly praises its writer. Dante, in spite of Virgil's silent
warning, is unable to restrain his pleasure on hearing his master praised
and smiles at Statius' words. To prevent further confusion, Virgil allows the
pilgrim to reveal his identity to Statius, at which Statius falls in reverence at
Virgil's feet.

The natural thirst that is never quenched
   save with the water the poor Samaritan woman
      asked to be given, the water of grace,   *3*
Was tormenting me, and our haste was urging me
   along the crowded way behind my leader,
      and I was grieving at the just retribution,   *6*
When, look! just as we read in Luke that Christ,
   newly risen from the sepulchral cave,
      appeared to two wayfarers on the road,   *9*
A shade appeared to us. He came up from behind
   while we kept our eyes on the crowd at our feet,
      and we were not aware of him until he spoke,   *12*
Saying, "O my brothers, may God give you peace."
   We wheeled around, and Virgil responded
      with a gesture that fit the situation,   *15*
And then continued, "May the true court
   that relegates me to exile eternal
      bring you in peace to the blessed assembly."   *18*
"How can this be?" he said, as we hurried on.
   "If you are shades that God does not deem worthy,
      who has brought you so far up His stairs?"   *21*
And my teacher said, "If you look at the marks
   that this man bears, traced on him by the angel,
      you will clearly see he is to reign with the good.   *24*

Ma perché lei che dì e notte fila
  non li avea tratta ancora la conocchia
27   che Cloto impone a ciascuno e compila,
l'anima sua, ch'è tua e mia serocchia,
  venendo sù, non potea venir sola,
30   però ch'al nostro modo non adocchia.
Ond' io fui tratto fuor de l'ampia gola
  d'inferno per mostrarli, e mosterrolli
33   oltre, quanto 'l potrà menar mia scola.
Ma dimmi, se tu sai, perché tai crolli
  diè dianzi 'l monte, e perché tutto ad una
36   parve gridare infino a' suoi piè molli."

Sì mi diè, dimandando, per la cruna
  del mio disio, che pur con la speranza
39   si fece la mia sete men digiuna.
Quei cominciò: "Cosa non è che sanza
  ordine senta la religïone
42   de la montagna, o che sia fuor d'usanza.
Libero è qui da ogne alterazione:
  di quel che 'l ciel da sé in sé riceve
45   esser ci puote, e non d'altro, cagione.
Per che non pioggia, non grando, non neve,
  non rugiada, non brina più sù cade
48   che la scaletta di tre gradi breve;
nuvole spesse non paion né rade,
  né coruscar, né figlia di Taumante,
51   che di là cangia sovente contrade;
secco vapor non surge più avante
  ch'al sommo d'i tre gradi ch'io parlai,
54   dov' ha 'l vicario di Pietro le piante.
Trema forse più giù poco o assai;
  ma per vento che 'n terra si nasconda,
57   non so come, qua sù non tremò mai.
Tremaci quando alcuna anima monda
  sentesi, sì che surga o che si mova
60   per salir sù; e tal grido seconda.

But since she who spins thread by day and by night
　　had not yet drawn off for him from the weight of wool
　　　　that Clotho amasses for each one of us,   27
His soul, which is sister to yours and mine,
　　could not make the ascent all on its own,
　　　　because it does not see as you and I do.   30
And so I was brought forth from Hell's gaping jaws
　　to show him the way, which I will do,
　　　　as far as one from my school can lead him.   33
But tell me, if you can, why the whole mountain
　　trembled so strongly just now, and why all on it
　　　　seemed to shout at once, down to its sea-girt base."   36

In asking this he threaded the needle
　　of my desire, and through sheer expectation
　　　　my thirst for knowledge became less acute.   39
And the shade responded, "There is nothing
　　that the holy order of the mountain suffers
　　　　that is without rule or outside its custom.   42
This place is free from all alteration.
　　Only that which Heaven receives
　　　　into and from itself may operate here.   45
Neither rain, therefore, nor hail nor snow,
　　nor dew nor frost, falls any higher
　　　　than the short stairway of three little steps.   48
Clouds dense nor thin do not appear here,
　　nor lightning flashes, nor Thaumas' daughter,
　　　　whose rainbow shifts so often below.   51
Nor does the earth's dry vapor rise beyond
　　the highest of the three steps of which I spoke,
　　　　where the Vicar of Peter has his feet.   54
It trembles lower down perhaps, little or much,
　　but never trembles up here from wind ensconced
　　　　in the bowels of the earth, I know not how.   57
It trembles here when some soul feels itself
　　pure enough to rise, to move above on high,
　　　　and that is followed by such a shout.   60

De la mondizia sol voler fa prova,
  che, tutto libero a mutar convento,
63   l'alma sorprende, e di voler le giova.
Prima vuol ben, ma non lascia il talento
  che divina giustizia, contra voglia,
66   come fu al peccar, pone al tormento.
E io, che son giaciùto a questa doglia
  cinquecent' anni e più, pur mo sentii
69   libera volontà di miglior soglia:
però sentisti il tremoto e li pii
  spiriti per lo monte render lode
72   a quel Segnor, che tosto sù li 'nvii."

Così ne disse; e però ch'el si gode
  tanto del ber quant' è grande la sete,
75   non saprei dir quant' el mi fece prode.
E 'l savio duca: "Omai veggio la rete
  che qui vi 'mpiglia e come si scalappia,
78   perché ci trema e di che congaudete.
Ora chi fosti, piacciati ch'io sappia,
  e perché tanti secoli giaciuto
81   qui se,' ne le parole tue mi cappia."

"Nel tempo che 'l buon Tito, con l'aiuto
  del sommo rege, vendicò le fóra
84   ond' uscì 'l sangue per Giuda venduto,
col nome che più dura e più onora
  era io di là," rispuose quello spirto,
87   "famoso assai, ma non con fede ancora.
Tanto fu dolce mio vocale spirto,
  che, tolosano, a sé mi trasse Roma,
90   dove mertai le tempie ornar di mirto.
Stazio la gente ancor di là mi noma:
  cantai di Tebe, e poi del grande Achille;
93   ma caddi in via con la seconda soma.
Al mio ardor fuor seme le faville,
  che mi scaldar, de la divina fiamma
96   onde sono allumati più di mille;

The will alone gives proof of its purity,
  when, wholly free to change its cloister,
    it surprises the soul and empowers it to will.   *63*
It wills before, indeed, but is thwarted by desire,
  which Divine Justice sets, counter to the will,
    toward punishment as once it was toward sin.   *66*
And I, who have lain in this torment
  five hundred years and more, only just now felt
    free volition for a better threshold.   *69*
Therefore you felt the temblor, and you heard
  the pious spirits throughout the mountain
    praise our Lord. Soon may he send them above!"   *72*

Thus the shade. And as we enjoy the drink more
  the thirstier we are, I could not begin
    to tell you how much he profited me.   *75*
Then my wise leader said, "Now I see the net
  that enmeshes you here, and how it is untangled,
    why the mountain trembles, and why you rejoice.   *78*
And now may it please you to let me know
  who you were in life; and why you have lain here
    so many centuries let me learn from your words."   *81*

"In the time when the good Titus," the shade replied,
  "aided by the King most high, avenged the wounds
    from which issued the blood that Judas sold,   *84*
I was famous enough in that other world
  with the name of poet, which lasts longest
    and honors most, but was not yet of the faith.   *87*
So sweet was my poetic voice that Rome
  drew me to herself from Toulouse and deemed me
    worthy to have my brows adorned with myrtle.   *90*
The people over there still call me Statius,
  I sang of Thebes and then of great Achilles,
    but I fell on the way with my second burden.   *93*
The seeds of my poetic fire were the sparks
  from the divine flame that warmed my spirit
    and have kindled more than a thousand others: *96*

de l'Eneïda dico, la qual mamma
  fummi, e fummi nutrice, poetando:
99   sanz' essa non fermai peso di dramma.
E per esser vivuto di là quando
  visse Virgilio, assentirei un sole
102   più che non deggio al mio uscir di bando."

Volser Virgilio a me queste parole
  con viso che, tacendo, disse 'Taci';
105   ma non può tutto la virtù che vuole;
ché riso e pianto son tanto seguaci
  a la passion di che ciascun si spicca,
108   che men seguon voler ne' più veraci.
Io pur sorrisi come l'uom ch'ammicca;
  per che l'ombra si tacque, e riguardommi
111   ne li occhi ove 'l sembiante più si ficca;
e "Se tanto labore in bene assommi,"
  disse, "perché la tua faccia testeso
114   un lampeggiar di riso dimostrommi?"
Or son io d'una parte e d'altra preso:
  l'una mi fa tacer, l'altra scongiura
117   ch'io dica; ond' io sospiro, e sono inteso
dal mio maestro, e "Non aver paura,"
  mi dice, "di parlar; ma parla e digli
120   quel ch'e' dimanda con cotanta cura."

Ond' io: "Forse che tu ti maravigli,
  antico spirto, del rider ch'io fei;
123   ma più d'ammirazion vo' che ti pigli.
Questi che guida in alto li occhi miei,
  è quel Virgilio dal qual tu togliesti
126   forte a cantar de li uomini e d'i dèi.
Se cagion altra al mio rider credesti,
  lasciala per non vera, ed esser credi
129   quelle parole che di lui dicesti."
Già s'inchinava ad abbracciar li piedi
  al mio dottor, ma el li disse: "Frate,
132   non far, ché tu se' ombra e ombra vedi."

I mean the *Aeneid*, which in poetry
  was my mother as well as my nurse
    and without which I would have little weight.   99
To have lived in that world when Virgil lived
  I would serve one more year than what I owe
    before my coming forth from banishment."   102

These words turned Virgil toward me with a look
  that, silent itself, said, "Be silent."
    But willpower cannot do all that it wills,   105
For smiles and tears follow so closely
  the emotion from which each of these springs,
    that in the most honest they least follow the will.   108
I only smiled, but it was a meaningful smile.
  The shade was silent and looked into my eyes,
    where one's expression is most definite,   111
And, "So may your great labor end in good,"
  he asked, "why did your face a moment ago
    light up and show me the flash of a smile?"   114
I was caught in the middle. On one side
  I was made to keep silent, and on the other
    conjured to speak. I sighed, and was understood   117
By my master, who said to me, "Do not fear
  to speak. Go ahead and explain to him
    what he is asking with such great concern."   120

And so I said, "Perhaps you are wondering,
  ancient spirit, why I am smiling;
    but I would have you seized with more wonder.   123
This person who directs my eyes on high
  is that Virgil from whom you derived
    the power to sing of gods and men.   126
If you thought there was any other reason
  for my smile, dismiss it as untrue and believe
    it was the very words that you spoke of him."   129
Already he was bending down to touch
  my teacher's feet, but he said to him, "No,
    brother, for you are a shade, and I too am such.   132

Ed ei surgendo: "Or puoi la quantitate
comprender de l'amor ch'a te mi scalda,
135   quand' io dismento nostra vanitate,
trattando l'ombre come cosa salda."

And, rising, he said, "Now you may well know
  how much warmth the love I have for you brings
    when I forget our emptiness so   *135*
And treat mere shades as if they were solid things."

Canto XXII

THE TRAVELERS HAVE ALREADY PASSED *the angel of the terrace of Avarice and ascended to the sixth terrace. Virgil expresses his affection for Statius and asks how he came to spend so long on the terrace of the avaricious. Statius tells him that his vice was not Avarice but its opposite, Prodigality, a similar straying from the golden mean of moderation. Virgil then asks how Statius came to be a Christian. Statius replies that it was*

Già era l'angel dietro a noi rimaso,
　　　l'angel che n'avea vòlti al sesto giro,
3　　　　　avendomi dal viso un colpo raso;
e quei c'hanno a giustizia lor disiro
　　　detto n'avea beati, e le sue voci
6　　　　　con *sitiunt*, sanz' altro, ciò forniro.
E io più lieve che per l'altre foci
　　　m'andava, sì che sanz' alcun labore
9　　　　　seguiva in sù li spiriti veloci;
quando Virgilio incominciò: "Amore,
　　　acceso di virtù, sempre altro accese,
12　　　　　pur che la fiamma sua paresse fore;
onde da l'ora che tra noi discese
　　　nel limbo de lo 'nferno Giovenale,
15　　　　　che la tua affezion mi fé palese,
mia benvoglienza inverso te fu quale
　　　più strinse mai di non vista persona,
18　　　　　sì ch'or mi parran corte queste scale.
Ma dimmi, e come amico mi perdona
　　　se troppa sicurtà m'allarga il freno,
21　　　　　e come amico omai meco ragiona:
come poté trovar dentro al tuo seno
　　　loco avarizia, tra cotanto senno
24　　　　　di quanto per tua cura fosti pieno?"

Virgil's own writing that first attracted him to the Christian message and that he then practiced Christianity in secret. Statius then inquires after other great classical writers and figures and Virgil reveals that they all, like himself, are to be found in Limbo. The trio of travelers continues its progress around the terrace and eventually comes to a beautiful and fragrant tree. Coming from it are voices intoning the exempla of restraint.

The angel who had steered us to the sixth circle
  was now left behind, having erased
    another incision from my forehead,   3
And having said that those who thirst for justice
  are blessed, going as far as *sitiunt*
    without completing the rest of the words.   6
I moved on more lightly than I had before
  at the other entrances, so that now
    I was following the swift spirits up with ease,   9
When Virgil began, "A love kindled by virtue
  has always kindled another love,
    provided only that its flame could be seen.   12
From the time, therefore, when Juvenal came down
  into Hell's Limbo and our company there
    and made your affection known to me,   15
My good will toward you has been as great
  as any ever felt for someone unseen,
    so that these stairs will seem short to me now.   18
But tell me, and as a friend forgive me
  if through presumption I relax my reins,
    and as a friend speak with me now—   21
How could avarice ever find room
  in your breast, amid all the wisdom
    that you nourished there with such great care?"   24

Queste parole Stazio mover fenno
un poco a riso pria; poscia rispuose:
27   "Ogne tuo dir d'amor m'è caro cenno.
Veramente più volte appaion cose
che danno a dubitar falsa matera
30   per le vere ragion che son nascose.
La tua dimanda tuo creder m'avvera
esser ch'i' fossi avaro in l'altra vita,
33   forse per quella cerchia dov' io era.
Or sappi ch'avarizia fu partita
troppo da me, e questa dismisura
36   migliaia di lunari hanno punita.
E se non fosse ch'io drizzai mia cura,
quand' io intesi là dove tu chiame,
39   crucciato quasi a l'umana natura:
'Per che non reggi tu, o sacra fame
de l'oro, l'appetito de' mortali?'
42   voltando sentirei le giostre grame.
Allor m'accorsi che troppo aprir l'ali
potean le mani a spendere, e pente'mi
45   così di quel come de li altri mali.
Quanti risurgeran coi crini scemi
per ignoranza, che di questa pecca
48   toglie 'l penter vivendo e ne li stremi!
E sappie che la colpa che rimbecca
per dritta opposizione alcun peccato,
51   con esso insieme qui suo verde secca;
però, s'io son tra quella gente stato
che piange l'avarizia, per purgarmi,
54   per lo contrario suo m'è incontrato."

"Or quando tu cantasti le crude armi
de la doppia trestizia di Giocasta,"
57   disse 'l cantor de' buccolici carmi,
"per quello che Cliò teco lì tasta,
non par che ti facesse ancor fedele
60   la fede, sanza qual ben far non basta.

These words brought a little smile to Statius' lips,
  and then he responded, "Your every word
    is to me a precious token of love;   27
But, truly, things do often appear
  to offer false material for doubt
    because the true reasons for them are concealed.   30
Your question convinces me that you think,
  perhaps because of the circle where I was,
    that I was avaricious in that other life.   33
Know now that avarice was too far
  distant from me, and that this lack of measure
    many thousands of lunations have punished;   36
And if I had not redirected my will,
  giving heed to the lines in which you exclaim,
    as if in a rage against human nature,   39
'To what do you not drive the appetite
  of mortal men, O accursed hunger for gold?'
    I would be rolling stones now at the grim jousts.   42
It was then I saw that our hands can open
  their wings too wide in spending money,
    and I repented that as well as other sins.   45
How many will rise again with hair shorn
  through ignorance, which blocks repentance
    of this sin, both in life and at the last hour!   48
Know this too: a fault that rebuts any sin
  by being in direct opposition to it
    dries up here its own rank verdure as well.   51
Therefore if I, to purge my own sin
  have been among those who bewail their avarice
    it is because I fell into its opposite."   54

And Virgil, the singer of bucolic songs,
  now said, "So when you sang of the bloody war
    between the two sons of mournful Jocasta,   57
It does not seem, from how Clio touched you then,
  that the faith without which all good works
    are done in vain had as yet made you faithful.   60

Se così è, qual sole o quai candele
  ti stenebraron sì, che tu drizzasti
63   poscia di retro al pescator le vele?"

Ed elli a lui: "Tu prima m'invïasti
  verso Parnaso a ber ne le sue grotte,
66   e prima appresso Dio m'alluminasti.
Facesti come quei che va di notte,
  che porta il lume dietro e sé non giova,
69   ma dopo sé fa le persone dotte,
quando dicesti: 'Secol si rinova;
  torna giustizia e primo tempo umano,
72   e progenïe scende da ciel nova.'
Per te poeta fui, per te cristiano:
  ma perché veggi mei ciò ch'io disegno,
75   a colorare stenderò la mano.
Già era 'l mondo tutto quanto pregno
  de la vera credenza, seminata
78   per li messaggi de l'etterno regno;
e la parola tua sopra toccata
  si consonava a' nuovi predicanti;
81   ond' io a visitarli presi usata.
Vennermi poi parendo tanto santi,
  che, quando Domizian li perseguette,
84   sanza mio lagrimar non fur lor pianti;
e mentre che di là per me si stette,
  io li sovvenni, e i lor dritti costumi
87   fer dispregiare a me tutte altre sette.
E pria ch'io conducessi i Greci a' fiumi
  di Tebe poetando, ebb' io battesmo;
90   ma per paura chiuso cristian fu'mi,
lungamente mostrando paganesmo;
  e questa tepidezza il quarto cerchio
93   cerchiar mi fé più che 'l quarto centesmo.
Tu dunque, che levato hai il coperchio
  che m'ascondeva quanto bene io dico,
96   mentre che del salire avem soverchio,

If that is true, then what sun or what candles
  dispelled your darkness, so that thereafter
    you trimmed your sails to follow the Fisherman?"   *63*

And Statius answered, "It was you who first
  sent me to drink from Parnassus' grottoes,
    and you who first lit my way to God.   *66*
You were like one who goes by night, carrying
  a lamp on his back. It does him no good
    but teaches all those who follow behind: *69*
You were like that when you said, 'Time is reborn;
  Justice returns with the first age of man,
    and a new race descends from the sky.'   *72*
I was a poet through you, through you a Christian.
  But so you may better see what I am sketching,
    I will set my hand to fill in the colors.   *75*
The entire world was already pregnant
  with the true faith, inseminated
    by the envoys of the eternal kingdom;   *78*
And the words of yours I have just touched upon
  accorded so well with the new preachers
    that I made it a practice to visit them.   *81*
They came to seem to me so holy
  that when Domitian began his persecution
    their weeping was not without my tears.   *84*
While I remained there, in that world,
  I gave them comfort, and their righteousness
    made me despise every other sect,   *87*
And before my verse had led the Greeks
  to the rivers of Thebes, I was baptized,
    but stayed a closet Christian out of fear,   *90*
Long pretending to be a pagan; and,
  because I was lukewarm, I had to circle
    the fourth ring more than four hundred years.   *93*
You, then, who lifted the veil
  that hid from me the great good of which I speak,
    tell me, while we still have time in this ascent,   *96*

dimmi dov' è Terrenzio nostro antico,
   Cecilio e Plauto e Varro, se lo sai:
99   dimmi se son dannati, e in qual vico."

"Costoro e Persio e io e altri assai,"
   rispuose il duca mio, "siam con quel Greco
102   che le Muse lattar più ch'altri mai,
nel primo cinghio del carcere cieco;
   spesse fiate ragioniam del monte
105   che sempre ha le nutrice nostre seco.
Euripide v'è nosco e Antifonte,
   Simonide, Agatone e altri piùe
108   Greci che già di lauro ornar la fronte.
Quivi si veggion de le genti tue
   Antigone, Deïfile e Argia,
111   e Ismene sì trista come fue.
Védeisi quella che mostrò Langia;
   èvvi la figlia di Tiresia, e Teti,
114   e con le suore sue Deïdamia."

Tacevansi ambedue già li poeti,
   di novo attenti a riguardar dintorno,
117   liberi da saliri e da pareti;
e già le quattro ancelle eran del giorno
   rimase a dietro, e la quinta era al temo,
120   drizzando pur in sù l'ardente corno,
quando il mio duca: "Io credo ch'a lo stremo
   le destre spalle volger ne convegna,
123   girando il monte come far solemo."
Così l'usanza fu lì nostra insegna,
   e prendemmo la via con men sospetto
126   per l'assentir di quell' anima degna.
Elli givan dinanzi, e io soletto
   di retro, e ascoltava i lor sermoni,
129   ch'a poetar mi davano intelletto.

Ma tosto ruppe le dolci ragioni
   un alber che trovammo in mezza strada,
132   con pomi a odorar soavi e buoni;

Where is our ancient Terence, our Caecilius,
　our Plautus and Varro? Tell me if you know
　　if they are damned, and if so, in what place?"   99

"All those, Persius, I, and many more,"
　my leader replied, "are with that Greek
　　the Muses suckled more than any other   102
In the first circle of the dark prison.
　We often talk about that sacred mountain
　　where those who nursed us dwell forever.   105
Euripides is with us there, and Antiphon,
　Simonides, Agathon, and many others,
　　Greeks whose brows laurel once adorned.   108
Of your characters there may be seen
　Antigone, Deiphyle, Argia,
　　and Ismene, still despondent as ever.   111
She that revealed Langia may also be seen,
　as well as Tiresias' daughter, and Thetis,
　　and Deidamia with her sisters."   114

Both of the poets were silent now,
　intent again on looking all around
　　without the constraint of stairs and walls.   117
Already four handmaidens of the day
　were left behind, and the fifth was guiding
　　the gleaming shaft of the chariot higher,   120
When my leader said, "I think we should turn
　our right shoulders to the outer edge
　　and circle the mountain as we are accustomed."   123
And so habit became our teacher there,
　and we made our way with less uncertainty
　　with the assent of that other worthy soul.   126
They went ahead and I followed behind,
　alone, but listening to what they said,
　　which helped me understand the poet's art.   129

But soon their pleasant talk was interrupted
　by a tree we found in the middle of the path
　　with fruit that was sweet and good to smell.   132

e come abete in alto si digrada
di ramo in ramo, così quello in giuso,
135   cred' io, perché persona sù non vada.
Dal lato onde 'l cammin nostro era chiuso,
cadea de l'alta roccia un liquor chiaro
138   e si spandeva per le foglie suso.
Li due poeti a l'alber s'appressaro;
e una voce per entro le fronde
141   gridò: "Di questo cibo avrete caro."
Poi disse: "Più pensava Maria onde
fosser le nozze orrevoli e intere,
144   ch'a la sua bocca, ch'or per voi risponde.
E le Romane antiche, per lor bere,
contente furon d'acqua; e Danïello
147   dispregiò cibo e acquistò savere.
Lo secol primo, quant' oro fu bello,
fé savorose con fame le ghiande,
150   e nettare con sete ogne ruscello.
Mele e locuste furon le vivande
che nodriro il Batista nel diserto;
153   per ch'elli è glorïoso e tanto grande
quanto per lo Vangelio v'è aperto."

And, unlike a fir tree whose branches taper
  up to its top, this tree tapered downward,
    to prevent, I believe, anyone from climbing.   *135*
On the side where our progress was obstructed
  clear water fell from the high rock above
    and sprinkled itself upon the upper leaves.   *138*
As the two poets approached the tree
  a voice called out from among its boughs,
    "Of this food you shall have a scarcity."   *141*
And then it said, "Mary gave more thought
  to the propriety of the wedding feast
    than the mouth with which she prays for you.   *144*
The ancient Roman matrons were content
  with water for their drink; and Daniel scorned
    feasting in favor of wisdom's increment.   *147*
In the Golden Age, hunger made acorns seem
  a delicious food, and thirst itself
    made nectar flow in every brook and stream.   *150*
Honey and locusts were all the Baptist ate
  to nourish himself in the barren waste,
    and for this he is as glorious and great   *153*
As revealed to you by the Evangelist."

CANTO XXIII

AS THE TRAVELERS CONTINUE THEIR *journey they encounter a large group of singing souls. The souls are horribly disfigured by famine, and Dante wonders how they come to be so wasted. The pilgrim is then recognized by one of the souls, whom he recognizes in turn only by the sound of his voice, his face being so disfigured. This is the soul of Forese Donati. Forese explains the penance of the souls on the terrace of Gluttony.*

Mentre che li occhi per la fronda verde
  ficcava ïo sì come far suole
3   chi dietro a li uccellin sua vita perde,
lo più che padre mi dicea: "Figliuole,
  vienne oramai, ché 'l tempo che n'è imposto
6   più utilmente compartir si vuole."
Io volsi 'l viso, e 'l passo non men tosto,
  appresso i savi, che parlavan sìe,
9   che l'andar mi facean di nullo costo.
Ed ecco piangere e cantar s'udìe
  "*Labïa mëa, Domine*" per modo
12   tal, che diletto e doglia parturìe.
"O dolce padre, che è quel ch'i' odo?"
  comincia' io; ed elli: "Ombre che vanno
15   forse di lor dover solvendo il nodo."

Sì come i peregrin pensosi fanno,
  giugnendo per cammin gente non nota,
18   che si volgono ad essa e non restanno,
così di retro a noi, più tosto mota,
  venendo e trapassando ci ammirava
21   d'anime turba tacita e devota.
Ne li occhi era ciascuna oscura e cava,
  palida ne la faccia, e tanto scema
24   che da l'ossa la pelle s'informava.

Dante asks Forese how he has managed to ascend so quickly up Mount Purgatory and Forese attributes this to the prayers of his virtuous wife. He then inveighs against the brazen women of contemporary Florence and the decline of the city. At Forese's insistence, Dante explains how he himself comes to be on the mountain.

While I was peering through the green foliage,
　just as those men do who waste their lives
　　hunting little birds, the shade who was more　　　　3
Than a father to me said, "Come along now,
　my son, for the time allotted to us
　　should be assigned to a better use."　　　　　　　　6
I turned my face, and my steps no less quickly,
　to follow the sages, whose conversation
　　made the journey cost nothing for me,　　　　　　9
When suddenly we heard a mournful song,
　"*Labia mea, Domine*," chanted in tones
　　that brought forth both delight and grief at once.　　12
"O sweet father," I asked, "what is that I hear?"
　"Shades," he answered, "who perhaps go their way
　　loosening the knot of the debt that they owe."　　15

Just as pilgrims who are absorbed in thought
　will overtake strangers along the road
　　and turn toward them without halting their steps,　　18
So, coming up behind us at a faster pace
　and passing us by, a silent and devout
　　company of souls looked in wonder at us.　　　　21
The eyes of each of them were dark and sunken,
　their faces sallow, and their flesh so wasted
　　that their skin took its shape from the bones beneath.　　24

Non credo che così a buccia strema
　Erisittone fosse fatto secco,
27　　per digiunar, quando più n'ebbe tema.
Io dicea fra me stesso pensando: "Ecco
　la gente che perdé Ierusalemme,
30　　quando Maria nel figlio diè di becco!"
Parean l'occhiaie anella sanza gemme:
　chi nel viso de li uomini legge "omo"
33　　ben avria quivi conosciuta l'emme.
Chi crederebbe che l'odor d'un pomo
　sì governasse, generando brama,
36　　e quel d'un'acqua, non sappiendo como?
Già era in ammirar che sì li affama,
　per la cagione ancor non manifesta
39　　di lor magrezza e di lor trista squama,
ed ecco del profondo de la testa
　volse a me li occhi un'ombra e guardò fiso;
42　　poi gridò forte: "Qual grazia m'è questa?"
Mai non l'avrei riconosciuto al viso;
　ma ne la voce sua mi fu palese
45　　ciò che l'aspetto in sé avea conquiso.
Questa favilla tutta mi raccese
　mia conoscenza a la cangiata labbia,
48　　e ravvisai la faccia di Forese.

"Deh, non contendere a l'asciutta scabbia
　che mi scolora," pregava, "la pelle,
51　　né a difetto di carne ch'io abbia;
ma dimmi il ver di te, dì chi son quelle
　due anime che là ti fanno scorta;
54　　non rimaner che tu non mi favelle!"
"La faccia tua, ch'io lagrimai già morta,
　mi dà di pianger mo non minor doglia,"
57　　rispuos' io lui, "veggendola sì torta.
Però mi dì, per Dio, che sì vi sfoglia;
　non mi far dir mentr' io mi maraviglio,
60　　ché mal può dir chi è pien d'altra voglia."

I do not believe that Erysichthon himself
   had withered so much to skin and bones
      even when he was most crazed with hunger.   27
As I thought on it, I said to myself,
   "Behold the people who lost Jerusalem
      when Mary began to peck at her son."   30
Their eye sockets were rings without gems.
   Those who read "OMO" in the face of man
      would easily here have made out the "M."   33
Who would believe, if he did not know how,
   that the smell of fruit, or of water, could have
      such an effect through the craving it caused?   36
I was wondering what could make them so famished,
   for I did not yet know what made them shriveled
      and why their skin was so wretched and scaly,   39
When all of a sudden, from the depths of his skull
   a shade turned his eyes upon me and stared,
      crying aloud, "What grace is mine now?"   42
I would never have recognized him by sight,
   but his voice made perfectly plain to me
      what his countenance had completely effaced;   45
And this spark rekindled in me
   my knowledge of his altered features,
      and I saw again the face of Forese.   48

"Ah, don't take any notice of the dry scabs
   that discolor my skin," he begged me,
      "nor the lack of meat on my bones,   51
But tell me the truth about yourself,
   and tell me about those two souls there
      who escort you. Please don't delay. Speak to me!"   54
"Your face, which I wept for when you died,"
   I answered him, "makes me weep no less
      when I see it so disfigured now.   57
So in God's name tell me, what has withered you?
   Don't ask me to speak while I am astonished.
      No one speaks well when he'd rather be silent."   60

Ed elli a me: "De l'etterno consiglio
cade vertù ne l'acqua e ne la pianta
63   rimasa dietro ond' io sì m'assottiglio.
Tutta esta gente che piangendo canta
per seguitar la gola oltra misura,
66   in fame e 'n sete qui si rifà santa.
Di bere e di mangiar n'accende cura
l'odor ch'esce del pomo e de lo sprazzo
69   che si distende su per sua verdura.
E non pur una volta, questo spazzo
girando, si rinfresca nostra pena:
72   io dico pena, e dovria dir sollazzo,
ché quella voglia a li alberi ci mena
che menò Cristo lieto a dire 'Elì,'
75   quando ne liberò con la sua vena."

E io a lui: "Forese, da quel dì
nel qual mutasti mondo a miglior vita,
78   cinqu' anni non son vòlti infino a qui.
Se prima fu la possa in te finita
di peccar più, che sovvenisse l'ora
81   del buon dolor ch'a Dio ne rimarita,
come se' tu qua sù venuto ancora?
Io ti credea trovar là giù di sotto,
84   dove tempo per tempo si ristora."

Ond' elli a me: "Sì tosto m'ha condotto
a ber lo dolce assenzo d'i martìri
87   la Nella mia con suo pianger dirotto.
Con suoi prieghi devoti e con sospiri
tratto m'ha de la costa ove s'aspetta,
90   e liberato m'ha de li altri giri.
Tanto è a Dio più cara e più diletta
la vedovella mia, che molto amai,
93   quanto in bene operare è più soletta;
ché la Barbagia di Sardigna assai
ne le femmine sue più è pudica
96   che la Barbagia dov' io la lasciai.

And he said to me, "From the eternal Will
  a power falls on the tree and the water
    there behind us. That is what makes me thin.   *63*
All of these people who weep while they chant
  followed their appetites beyond due measure
    and regain holiness here in hunger and thirst.   *66*
Our craving to eat and drink is kindled
  by the fragrance that issues from the fruit
    and the water sprinkled upon the branches,   *69*
And not once only, as we circle this floor,
  is our pain refreshed. I say our pain,
    but I really ought to say our solace,   *72*
For the same desire leads us to the trees
  as led Christ to say, '*Eli*' gladly
    when he made us free with blood from his veins."   *75*

I responded, "Forese, from that day
  when you exchanged the world for a better life,
    not five years have passed up until now.   *78*
If your power to keep on sinning ended
  just at the hour of the good sorrow
    that marries our souls again to God,   *81*
How did you get up here already?
  I thought I might find you down below,
    where time must be repaid with time."   *84*

And he replied, "I have been brought so quickly
  to drink the sweet wormwood of these torments
    by my Nella with her flood of tears.   *87*
With her devoted prayers and with her sighs
  she drew me from the slope where one must wait
    and freed me also from the other circles.   *90*
My dear widow whom I loved so well
  is all the more precious and beloved of God
    the more alone she is in the good works she does.   *93*
For the Barbagia of Sardinia
  is much more modest in its women
    than is the Barbagia where I left her.   *96*

O dolce frate, che vuo' tu ch'io dica?
  Tempo futuro m'è già nel cospetto,
99   cui non sarà quest' ora molto antica,
nel qual sarà in pergamo interdetto
  a le sfacciate donne fiorentine
102   l'andar mostrando con le poppe il petto.
Quai barbare fuor mai, quai saracine,
  cui bisognasse, per farle ir coperte,
105   o spiritali o altre discipline?
Ma se le svergognate fosser certe
  di quel che 'l ciel veloce loro ammanna,
108   già per urlare avrian le bocche aperte;
ché, se l'antiveder qui non m'inganna,
  prima fien triste che le guance impeli
111   colui che mo si consola con nanna.
Deh, frate, or fa che più non mi ti celi!
  vedi che non pur io, ma questa gente
114   tutta rimira là dove 'l sol veli."

Per ch'io a lui: "Se tu riduci a mente
  qual fosti meco, e qual io teco fui,
117   ancor fia grave il memorar presente.
Di quella vita mi volse costui
  che mi va innanzi, l'altr' ier, quando tonda
120   vi si mostrò la suora di colui,"
e 'l sol mostrai; "costui per la profonda
  notte menato m'ha d'i veri morti
123   con questa vera carne che 'l seconda.
Indi m'han tratto sù li suoi conforti,
  salendo e rigirando la montagna
126   che drizza voi che 'l mondo fece torti.
Tanto dice di farmi sua compagna
  che io sarò là dove fia Beatrice;
129   quivi convien che sanza lui rimagna.
Virgilio è questi che così mi dice,"
  e addita'lo; "e quest' altro è quell' ombra
132   per cuï scosse dianzi ogne pendice
lo vostro regno, che da sé lo sgombra."

O sweet brother, what do you want me to say?
  Already in my vision is a future time
    before this hour shall be very old,   *99*
When it will be forbidden from the pulpit
  that the brazen-faced Florentine ladies
    go around bare-breasted flaunting their nipples.   *102*
What barbarous women, what Saracens,
  have ever needed spiritual instruction,
    or other rules, to make them dress decently?   *105*
But if these shameless women were assured
  of what swift Heaven is preparing for them,
    their mouths would already be open to howl.   *108*
For if our foresight here does not deceive me
  they will be sorry before he who now
    is consoled by lullabies first has a beard.   *111*
Ah, brother, now no longer hide from me.
  You see how not only I but all those here
    are gazing there where your form blocks the sun."   *114*

To which I responded, "If you call to mind
  what you were with me and I was with you,
    that memory would still be painful now.   *117*
He who goes before me turned me aside
  from that life just the other day, when the sister
    of that one"—I pointed to the sun—   *120*
"Shone full back there. It is he who led me
  through the deep night of the truly dead
    in my flesh and blood body that follows him.   *123*
His encouragement has drawn me up from there,
  climbing and circling the rings of the mountain
    that makes you straight whom the world has bent.   *126*
He promises that he will stay at my side
  until I come to where Beatrice will be;
    thereafter without him I must abide.   *129*
Virgil it is who says this to me,"
  and I pointed to him. "The other shade
    is the one your realm just now set free   *132*
During the rumbling the whole mountain made."

Canto XXIV

DANTE, FORESE, VIRGIL, AND STATIUS *continue their journey around the terrace of Gluttony. Dante inquires after Forese's sister Piccarda and finds that she is already in Heaven. Forese identifies some of the other penitent gluttons. Dante engages one of them, Bonagiunta of Lucca, in conversation. They discuss the sweet new style of poetry for which Dante became noted and its authenticity in comparison with Bonagiunta's own*

Né 'l dir l'andar, né l'andar lui più lento
facea, ma ragionando andavam forte,
3   sì come nave pinta da buon vento;
e l'ombre, che parean cose rimorte,
per le fosse de li occhi ammirazione
6   traean di me, di mio vivere accorte.
E io, continüando al mio sermone,
dissi: "Ella sen va sù forse più tarda
9   che non farebbe, per altrui cagione.
Ma dimmi, se tu sai, dov' è Piccarda;
dimmi s'io veggio da notar persona
12   tra questa gente che sì mi riguarda."
"La mia sorella, che tra bella e buona
non so qual fosse più, trïunfa lieta
15   ne l'alto Olimpo già di sua corona."
Sì disse prima; e poi: "Qui non si vieta
di nominar ciascun, da ch'è sì munta
18   nostra sembianza via per la dïeta.
Questi," e mostrò col dito, "è Bonagiunta,
Bonagiunta da Lucca; e quella faccia
21   di là da lui più che l'altre trapunta
ebbe la Santa Chiesa in le sue braccia:
dal Torso fu, e purga per digiuno
24   l'anguille di Bolsena e la vernaccia."

*verse. Forese inquires of Dante when they will meet again and predicts the
downfall of his own brother, Corso Donati, before moving off to continue
his penance. Dante and his two companions come to a second tree, around
which the starving souls are gathered. From the tree issue examples of
Gluttony. Continuing their walk, they come to the angel of the terrace and
are released with a Beatitude.*

Walking did not slow our talk, nor did talking
  slow us down, as conversing we moved on
    like ships propelled by a favoring wind.   *3*
The shades, that seemed like things twice dead,
  shot me looks of amazement from their hollow eyes
    when it dawned on them that I was still alive.   *6*
And, continuing where I had left off, I said,
  "Perhaps he climbs more slowly than he would
    if he were not keeping pace with someone else.   *9*
But tell me, if you know, where Piccarda is.
  And tell me if I'm seeing anyone of note
    among these people who are staring at me."   *12*
"I cannot say whether my sister was more
  virtuous than she was beautiful. Triumphant now,
    she rejoices in her crown on high Olympus."   *15*
He said this first, and then he went on,
  "It is not forbidden for us to use names here,
    since our features are sucked dry by fasting.   *18*
That one," and he pointed, "is Bonagiunta,
  Bonagiunta of Lucca; and just behind him,
    the face more cracked and withered than the rest,   *21*
Is one who held the Holy Church in his arms.
  He was from Tours, and now by fasting purges
    eels from Bolsena stewed in white wine."   *24*

Molti altri mi nomò ad uno ad uno;
e del nomar parean tutti contenti,
27   sì ch'io però non vidi un atto bruno.
Vidi per fame a vòto usar li denti
Ubaldin da la Pila e Bonifazio
30   che pasturò col rocco molte genti.
Vidi messer Marchese, ch'ebbe spazio
già di bere a Forlì con men secchezza,
33   e sì fu tal, che non si sentì sazio.
Ma come fa chi guarda e poi s'apprezza
più d'un che d'altro, fei a quel da Lucca,
36   che più parea di me aver contezza.
El mormorava; e non so che "Gentucca"
sentiv' io là, ov' el sentia la piaga
39   de la giustizia che sì li pilucca.
"O anima," diss' io, "che par sì vaga
di parlar meco, fa sì ch'io t'intenda,
42   e te e me col tuo parlare appaga."
"Femmina è nata, e non porta ancor benda,"
cominciò el, "che ti farà piacere
45   la mia città, come ch'om la riprenda.
Tu te n'andrai con questo antivedere:
se nel mio mormorar prendesti errore,
48   dichiareranti ancor le cose vere.
Ma dì s'i' veggio qui colui che fore
trasse le nove rime, cominciando
51   'Donne ch'avete intelletto d'amore.'"
E io a lui: "I' mi son un che, quando
Amor mi spira, noto, e a quel modo
54   ch'e' ditta dentro vo significando."
"O frate, issa vegg' io," diss' elli, "il nodo
che 'l Notaro e Guittone e me ritenne
57   di qua dal dolce stil novo ch'i' odo!
Io veggio ben come le vostre penne
di retro al dittator sen vanno strette,
60   che de le nostre certo non avvenne;
e qual più a gradire oltre si mette,
non vede più da l'uno a l'altro stilo";
63   e, quasi contentato, si tacette.

He named many others for me, one by one,
  and each of them seemed content to be named:
    I did not see among them a single dark look.   *27*
I saw, chewing on fresh air in his hunger,
  Ubaldino dalla Pila, and Boniface,
    who with his crozier shepherded many.   *30*
I saw Messer Marchese, who whiled away time
  drinking in Forli, not that he was thirsty,
    but was the sort who could never feel sated.   *33*
But, as we notice one more than another,
  so too did I with the shade from Lucca,
    who seemed to want to know more about me.   *36*
He was muttering, and something like "Gentucca"
  was all that carried to my ears from his mouth,
    where he most felt the justice that plucks at them.   *39*
"O soul," I said, "who seem so eager
  to speak with me, speak in a way
    I can understand, and so satisfy us both."   *42*
"A woman is born and does not yet wear the veil,"
  the soul began, "who will make my city
    pleasing to you, however men revile it.   *45*
You will go from here with this prophecy;
  if you have misunderstood my murmuring,
    the real events will make it clear to you yet.   *48*
But tell me if I see before me the one
  who brought out the new verses that begin,
    '*Ladies who have intelligence of love*'?"   *51*
And I said to him, "I am one who, when Love
  inspires me, takes note, and what he dictates
    deep within me, I then go and express."   *54*
"O brother," he said, "now I see the knot
  that kept the Notary, and Guittone, and me
    tied off from the sweet new style that I hear.   *57*
How well I see that your pens follow
  very closely the dictates of Love,
    which certainly did not happen with ours,   *60*
And whoever looks into this more closely
  will see no other difference between the two styles."
    And then, as if satisfied, he said no more.   *63*

Come li augei che vernan lungo 'l Nilo,
  alcuna volta in aere fanno schiera,
66   poi volan più a fretta e vanno in filo,
così tutta la gente che lì era,
  volgendo 'l viso, raffrettò suo passo,
69   e per magrezza e per voler leggera.
E come l'uom che di trottare è lasso,
  lascia andar li compagni, e sì passeggia
72   fin che si sfoghi l'affollar del casso,
sì lasciò trapassar la santa greggia
  Forese, e dietro meco sen veniva,
75   dicendo: "Quando fia ch'io ti riveggia?"
"Non so," rispuos' io lui, "quant' io mi viva;
  ma già non fïa il tornar mio tantosto,
78   ch'io non sia col voler prima a la riva;
però che 'l loco u' fui a viver posto,
  di giorno in giorno più di ben si spolpa,
81   e a trista ruina par disposto."

"Or va," diss' el; "che quei che più n'ha colpa,
  vegg' ïo a coda d'una bestia tratto
84   inver' la valle ove mai non si scolpa.
La bestia ad ogne passo va più ratto,
  crescendo sempre, fin ch'ella il percuote,
87   e lascia il corpo vilmente disfatto.
Non hanno molto a volger quelle ruote,"
  e drizzò li occhi al ciel, "che ti fia chiaro
90   ciò che 'l mio dir più dichiarar non puote.
Tu ti rimani omai; ché 'l tempo è caro
  in questo regno, sì ch'io perdo troppo
93   venendo teco sì a paro a paro."

Qual esce alcuna volta di gualoppo
  lo cavalier di schiera che cavalchi,
96   e va per farsi onor del primo intoppo,
tal si partì da noi con maggior valchi;
  e io rimasi in via con esso i due
99   che fuor del mondo sì gran maliscalchi.

As birds that winter along the Nile
  sometimes flock together high in the air
    and then flying faster string out in a line,   66
So all of the people who were gathered there
  turned away from us and picked up their pace,
    light as they were and lean through desire.   69
And just as a runner who is exhausted
  lets his companions go ahead, while he walks
    until his chest stops heaving and panting,   72
So did Forese let the holy flock pass
  and walked with me behind them. And he asked,
    "How long will it be till I see you again?"   75
"I do not know," I said, "how long I will live,
  but my return to this shore could not come so soon
    that in my mind I will not be here already.   78
For the place where I was put to live
  is stripped of good more and more each day
    and seems disposed to perdition."   81

"Yes," he said, "and the one who is most to blame
  I see dragged behind the tail of a beast
    down to the valley of no absolution.   84
The beast goes faster with every step it takes,
  always faster, until it smashes him down
    and leaves his body horribly dismembered.   87
These wheels do not have long to turn"—and he
  looked up at the sky—"before what my words
    have not made clear becomes clear to you.   90
Now you must stay behind, for time is so dear
  in this domain, that I lose too much
    by going with you and matching your pace."   93

As a horseman will sometimes gallop off
  from a troop of riders in order to have
    the honor of the first encounter,   96
So too did he, lengthening his stride,
  pull away from us, and I stayed with those two
    who were such great leaders of the world.   99

E quando innanzi a noi intrato fue,
  che li occhi miei si fero a lui seguaci,
102   come la mente a le parole sue,
parvermi i rami gravidi e vivaci
  d'un altro pomo, e non molto lontani
105   per esser pur allora vòlto in laci.
Vidi gente sott' esso alzar le mani
  e gridar non so che verso le fronde,
108   quasi bramosi fantolini e vani
che pregano, e 'l pregato non risponde,
  ma, per fare esser ben la voglia acuta,
111   tien alto lor disio e nol nasconde.
Poi si partì sì come ricreduta;
  e noi venimmo al grande arbore adesso,
114   che tanti prieghi e lagrime rifiuta.
"Trapassate oltre sanza farvi presso:
  legno è più sù che fu morso da Eva,
117   e questa pianta si levò da esso."

Sì tra le frasche non so chi diceva;
  per che Virgilio e Stazio e io, ristretti,
120   oltre andavam dal lato che si leva.
"Ricordivi," dicea, "d'i maladetti
  nei nuvoli formati, che, satolli,
123   Tesëo combatter co' doppi petti;
e de li Ebrei ch'al ber si mostrar molli,
  per che no i volle Gedeon compagni,
126   quando inver' Madïan discese i colli."
Sì accostati a l'un d'i due vivagni
  passammo, udendo colpe de la gola
129   seguite già da miseri guadagni.
Poi, rallargati per la strada sola,
  ben mille passi e più ci portar oltre,
132   contemplando ciascun sanza parola.
"Che andate pensando sì voi sol tre?"
  sùbita voce disse; ond' io mi scossi
135   come fan bestie spaventate e poltre.

When Forese had gone so far ahead
  that I could only follow him with my eyes,
    just as my mind still followed his words,   *102*
Another tree appeared before me,
  its branches green and laden with fruit,
    not far off, for I had just turned there.   *105*
I saw a crowd beneath it lifting their hands
  and calling—I don't know what—up to the leaves,
    like little children, eager and foolish,   *108*
Who beg someone who does not respond,
  and, to make their longing even more keen,
    holds up what they beg for and does not hide it.   *111*
Then they left, as if they had a change of heart,
  and we came up to the lofty tree
    that refuses so many prayers and tears.   *114*
"Pass on, without approaching any closer.
  The tree from which Eve ate is higher above,
    and this is an offshoot of that higher tree."   *117*

I do not know who spoke from among the leaves.
  Virgil, Statius, and I, drawing together,
    moved on beside the face of the cliff.   *120*
"Remember," the voice said now, "those accursed,
  cloud-born creatures, with twiform chests, who
    fought with Theseus when they were drunk with wine;   *123*
And those Hebrews whose thirst showed they were soft,
  so that Gideon would not take them with him
    when he stormed down from the hills against Midian."   *126*
And so, keeping close to one edge of the path,
  on we went, hearing of gluttonous sinners
    who had long since collected their wretched wages.   *129*
Then, spread out now along the empty way,
  we pressed on a thousand paces or more,
    each of us lost in wordless reflection,   *132*
When a voice suddenly asked, "What are you thinking
  as you walk along, you solitary three?"
    This startled me as if I were a timid beast.   *135*

Drizzai la testa per veder chi fossi;
  e già mai non si videro in fornace
138   vetri o metalli sì lucenti e rossi,
com' io vidi un che dicea: "S'a voi piace
  montare in sù, qui si convien dar volta;
141   quinci si va chi vuole andar per pace."

L'aspetto suo m'avea la vista tolta;
  per ch'io mi volsi dietro a' miei dottori,
144   com' om che va secondo ch'elli ascolta.
E quale, annunziatrice de li albori,
  l'aura di maggio movesi e olezza,
147   tutta impregnata da l'erba e da' fiori;
tal mi senti' un vento dar per mezza
  la fronte, e ben senti' mover la piuma,
150   che fé sentir d'ambrosïa l'orezza.
E senti' dir: "Beati cui alluma
  tanto di grazia, che l'amor del gusto
153   nel petto lor troppo disir non fuma,
esurïendo sempre quanto è giusto!"

I lifted my head to see who it was.
  Never was glass or metal in a furnace
    seen to be so red-hot and glowing   *138*
As the one I saw, who said, "If you wish
  to mount higher, this is where you turn;
    this is the road for those who seek peace."   *141*

His visage had taken away my sight,
  so I turned and walked behind my teachers,
    like a man who goes guided only by sound.   *144*
And as the breeze of May that heralds dawn
  exudes a fragrance as it begins to blow,
    suffused with the scent of grass and flowers,   *147*
Just such a wind I felt full on my brow,
  and I was aware of an ambrosial bouquet
    wafted upon me by his feathers now.   *150*
And I heard the angel's words: "Blessed are they
  whom grace so illumines that their appetite
    fills them not with desire that leads them astray, *153*
But with hunger always for what is right."

Canto XXV

DANTE, VIRGIL, AND STATIUS CLIMB *the narrow staircase leading to the final terrace of Purgatory. Dante is filled with desire to ask a question and his hesitancy to do so is overcome by Virgil's encouragement. The pilgrim wants to know how the souls of the gluttonous, who have no need of food, can become so emaciated with hunger. Virgil gives a preliminary response but leaves the main explanation to Statius. Statius gives a long and detailed*

Ora era onde 'l salir non volea storpio;
   ché 'l sole avëa il cerchio di merigge
3   lasciato al Tauro e la notte a lo Scorpio:
per che, come fa l'uom che non s'affigge
   ma vassi a la via sua, che che li appaia,
6   se di bisogno stimolo il trafigge,
così intrammo noi per la callaia,
   uno innanzi altro prendendo la scala
9   che per artezza i salitor dispaia.
E quale il cicognin che leva l'ala
   per voglia di volare, e non s'attenta
12   d'abbandonar lo nido, e giù la cala;
tal era io con voglia accesa e spenta
   di dimandar, venendo infino a l'atto
15   che fa colui ch'a dicer s'argomenta.
Non lasciò, per l'andar che fosse ratto,
   lo dolce padre mio, ma disse: "Scocca
18   l'arco del dir, che 'nfino al ferro hai tratto."

Allor sicuramente apri' la bocca
   e cominciai: "Come si può far magro
21   là dove l'uopo di nodrir non tocca?"

account of the generation of human beings, the Creation by God of the individual human soul, and the nature of the soul-body after death. Toward the canto's close the three travelers reach the terrace of the lustful, where they see a great wall of flame with souls moving around inside it. The exempla of chastity emerge spoken from the flames.

There was no time now to delay on the climb,
 for Taurus had reached the day's meridian
  and the night's was occupied by Scorpio. 3
Therefore, like those who do not stop and stare
 but hurry on their way no matter what appears,
  pricked by the goad of necessity, 6
We made our way up through the gap,
 one after the other ascending the stairs
  whose narrowness precludes climbing in pairs. 9
And like the little stork that lifts its wing
 because it wants to fly, but then doesn't dare
  to leave the nest and so drops it again, 12
So too was I, with a desire to ask
 kindled and quenched, going only as far
  as beginning to open my mouth to speak. 15
My sweet father, in spite of our rapid pace,
 did not neglect to say, "Shoot the bow of speech
  that you have drawn all the way to the iron." 18

Then I opened my mouth with some confidence
 and asked, "How can these spirits grow lean
  when they have no need of nourishment?" 21

"Se t'ammentassi come Meleagro
si consumò al consumar d'un stizzo,
24   non fora," disse, "a te questo sì agro;
e se pensassi come, al vostro guizzo,
guizza dentro a lo specchio vostra image,
27   ciò che par duro ti parrebbe vizzo.
Ma perché dentro a tuo voler t'adage,
ecco qui Stazio; e io lui chiamo e prego
30   che sia or sanator de le tue piage."

"Se la veduta etterna li dislego,"
rispuose Stazio, "là dove tu sie,
33   discolpi me non potert' io far nego."
Poi cominciò: "Se le parole mie,
figlio, la mente tua guarda e riceve,
36   lume ti fiero al come che tu die.
Sangue perfetto, che poi non si beve
da l'assetate vene, e si rimane
39   quasi alimento che di mensa leve,
prende nel core a tutte membra umane
virtute informativa, come quello
42   ch'a farsi quelle per le vene vane.
Ancor digesto, scende ov' è più bello
tacer che dire; e quindi poscia geme
45   sovr' altrui sangue in natural vasello.
Ivi s'accoglie l'uno e l'altro insieme,
l'un disposto a patire, e l'altro a fare
48   per lo perfetto loco onde si preme;
e, giunto lui, comincia ad operare
coagulando prima, e poi avviva
51   ciò che per sua matera fé constare.
Anima fatta la virtute attiva
qual d'una pianta, in tanto differente,
54   che questa è in via e quella è già a riva,
tanto ovra poi, che già si move e sente,
come spungo marino; e indi imprende
57   ad organar le posse ond' è semente.

"If you call to mind how Meleager," he said,
  "was consumed when a firebrand was consumed,
    this question would not be so hard for you;					*24*
And if you consider how, when you squirm,
  your image in the mirror also squirms,
    what was hard before would now seem easy.					*27*
But so that your desire can be laid to rest,
  here is Statius, and I call upon him
    to be your doctor and heal your wound."					*30*

"If I explain to him the eternal view,"
  Statius replied, "when you are present,
    my excuse is that I cannot deny you."					*33*
Then he began. "My son, if your mind observes
  and receives my words, they will enlighten you
    as to the 'how' of what you are asking.					*36*
The perfect blood, which is never drunk
  by the thirsty veins and remains as surplus
    like food that one removes from the table,					*39*
Acquires in the heart the power to inform
  all the body's members, like the blood in the veins
    that flows through them to become those members.					*42*
Digested again, it descends to the parts
  not politely mentioned, and from there it drips
    upon another's blood in a natural vessel.					*45*
There the one and the other are mingled,
  the one disposed to be passive, the other active
    because of the perfection of its origin;					*48*
And, joined with the former, the latter begins
  to operate, coagulating first and then giving life
    to what it has formed as its material.					*51*
The active virtue having become a soul,
  like that of a plant—but with the difference
    that this is in process and that is complete—					*54*
Functions now in that it moves and feels
  like a sea sponge; then it starts to form organs
    for the powers of which it is itself the seed.					*57*

Or si spiega, figliuolo, or si distende
　la virtù ch'è dal cor del generante,
60　　dove natura a tutte membra intende.
Ma come d'animal divegna fante,
　non vedi tu ancor: quest' è tal punto,
63　　che più savio di te fé già errante,
sì che per sua dottrina fé disgiunto
　da l'anima il possibile intelletto,
66　　perché da lui non vide organo assunto.

Apri a la verità che viene il petto;
　e sappi che, sì tosto come al feto
69　　'articular del cerebro è perfetto,
lo motor primo a lui si volge lieto
　sovra tant' arte di natura, e spira
72　　spirito novo, di vertù repleto,
che ciò che trova attivo quivi, tira
　in sua sustanzia, e fassi un'alma sola,
75　　che vive e sente e sé in sé rigira.
E perché meno ammiri la parola,
　guarda il calor del sole che si fa vino,
78　　giunto a l'omor che de la vite cola.

Quando Làchesis non ha più del lino,
　solvesi da la carne, e in virtute
81　　ne porta seco e l'umano e 'l divino:
l'altre potenze tutte quante mute;
　memoria, intelligenza e volontade
84　　in atto molto più che prima agute.
Sanza restarsi, per sé stessa cade
　mirabilmente a l'una de le rive;
87　　quivi conosce prima le sue strade.
Tosto che loco lì la circunscrive,
　la virtù formativa raggia intorno
90　　così e quanto ne le membra vive.
E come l'aere, quand' è ben pïorno,
　per l'altrui raggio che 'n sé si reflette,
93　　di diversi color diventa addorno;

Now, my son, the power that is in the heart
  of the begetter both expands and distends,
    as Nature makes room for all of the members.   *60*
But you do not yet see how it becomes
  a human from an animal, a point
    that has caused minds wiser than yours to err,   *63*
So that in his teaching he separated
  the soul from the potential intellect,
    because he saw no organ that has assumed it.   *66*

"Open your heart to the truth that is coming
  and know that as soon as in the fetus
    the articulation of the brain is complete,   *69*
The Prime Mover turns to it in joy
  at such a work of art of Nature, and breathes
    a new spirit into it, replete with virtue,   *72*
Which then absorbs what is active there
  into its substance and makes one single soul
    that lives and feels and revolves in itself.   *75*
And so that my words will surprise you less,
  look at the sun's heat, which becomes wine
    when combined with juice that oozes from grapes.   *78*

"And when Lachesis has run out of thread,
  the soul is loosed from the flesh and, virtually,
    carries with it the human and divine.   *81*
The other faculties all become mute,
  but memory, will, and intellect
    when in action become more acute;   *84*
And, without delay, the soul of itself falls
  wondrously to one of the two shores.
    Here it first knows what lies ahead for it.   *87*
Then, as soon as it is circumscribed by space,
  its formative virtue radiates out,
    in shape and bulk like the once-living members.   *90*
And just as the air, when it is very moist,
  becomes adorned with various colors
    by another's rays reflected within it,   *93*

così l'aere vicin quivi si mette
e in quella forma ch'è in lui suggella
96   virtüalmente l'alma che ristette;
e simigliante poi a la fiammella
che segue il foco là 'vunque si muta,
99   segue lo spirto sua forma novella.
Però che quindi ha poscia sua paruta,
è chiamata ombra; e quindi organa poi
102   ciascun sentire infino a la veduta.
Quindi parliamo e quindi ridiam noi;
quindi facciam le lagrime e ' sospiri
105   che per lo monte aver sentiti puoi.
Secondo che ci affliggono i disiri
e li altri affetti, l'ombra si figura;
108   e quest' è la cagion di che tu miri."

E già venuto a l'ultima tortura
s'era per noi, e vòlto a la man destra,
111   ed eravamo attenti ad altra cura.
Quivi la ripa fiamma in fuor balestra,
e la cornice spira fiato in suso
114   che la reflette e via da lei sequestra;
ond' ir ne convenia dal lato schiuso
ad uno ad uno; e io temëa 'l foco
117   quinci, e quindi temeva cader giuso.
Lo duca mio dicea: "Per questo loco
si vuol tenere a li occhi stretto il freno,
120   però ch'errar potrebbesi per poco."

"Summae Deus clementïae" nel seno
al grande ardore allora udi' cantando,
123   che di volger mi fé caler non meno;
e vidi spirti per la fiamma andando;
per ch'io guardava a loro e a' miei passi
126   compartendo la vista a quando a quando.
Appresso il fine ch'a quell' inno fassi,
gridavano alto: "Virum non cognosco";
129   indi ricominciavan l'inno bassi.

So the neighboring air shapes itself too
  in the form virtually imprinted upon it
    by the soul that has stopped and settled there.   *96*
Then, just as a single tongue of flame
  follows the fire wherever it moves,
    the spirit is followed by its new form.   *99*
And because it has the semblance of a body
  it is called a shade, and forms from the air
    the sense organs, up to and including sight.   *102*
This is how we are able to speak and laugh,
  this is the source of our tears and sighs
    that you may have heard around the mountain.   *105*
In response to the stimulus of desires
  and other feelings the shade takes its form.
    This is the cause of what made you marvel."   *108*

By now we had come to the final twist
  and, turning to the right, immediately had
    other concerns that demanded attention.   *111*
Here the bank shoots forth flames, and the terrace
  exhales an upward blast that bends them aside,
    creating a path sequestered from their heat.   *114*
So we had to walk on that open side
  in single file; I feared the fire on one hand,
    and on the other that I might well fall off.   *117*
My leader said, "You have to keep a tight rein
  on your eyes along here. This is a place
    where it wouldn't take much to make a false step."   *120*

"*Summae Deus clementiae*" I then heard
  sung in the very heart of that burning,
    which drew my attention no less than my steps;   *123*
And I saw spirits going through the flames,
  which caused me to look both at them and my feet,
    switching my gaze from one to the other.   *126*
After the final verse of that hymn,
  they cried aloud, "*Virum non cognosco,*"
    and then sang it once more in a lower voice.   *129*

Finitolo, anco gridavano: "Al bosco
si tenne Diana, ed Elice caccionne
132   che di Venere avea sentito il tòsco."

Indi al cantar tornavano; indi donne
gridavano e mariti che fuor casti
135   come virtute e matrimonio imponne.
E questo modo credo che lor basti
per tutto il tempo che 'l foco li abbruscia:
138   con tal cura conviene e con tai pasti
che la piaga da sezzo si ricuscia.

When the hymn was finished, they cried again,
  "Diana kept to the woods and drove out
    Callisto, who was tainted by Venus."   *132*

Then they resumed their song, shouting in the fire
  names of wives and husbands chaste and pure,
    as virtue and matrimony both require.   *135*
And all the while that these souls endure
  the fire's burning, this is all that they do;
    this is the treatment and diet that cure   *138*
Their wounds at last and heal them anew.

Canto XXVI

As the travelers continue their *precarious progress along the edge of the terrace of the lustful, the sun casts Dante's shadow onto the flames. The souls within the wall of fire, intrigued by this, come to ask who he is. Before Dante answers he is distracted by the appearance of another group of souls coming toward those by whom he had been questioned. The two groups hurriedly exchange brief chaste kisses before the groups separate, each*

Mentre che sì per l'orlo, uno innanzi altro,
   ce n'andavamo, e spesso il buon maestro
3   diceami: "Guarda: giovi ch'io ti scaltro";
feriami il sole in su l'omero destro,
   che già, raggiando, tutto l'occidente
6   mutava in bianco aspetto di cilestro;
e io facea con l'ombra più rovente
   parer la fiamma; e pur a tanto indizio
9   vidi molt' ombre, andando, poner mente.
Questa fu la cagion che diede inizio
   loro a parlar di me; e cominciarsi
12   a dir: "Colui non par corpo fittizio";
poi verso me, quanto potëan farsi,
   certi si fero, sempre con riguardo
15   di non uscir dove non fosser arsi.

"O tu che vai, non per esser più tardo,
   ma forse reverente, a li altri dopo,
18   rispondi a me che 'n sete e 'n foco ardo.
Né solo a me la tua risposta è uopo;
   ché tutti questi n'hanno maggior sete
21   che d'acqua fredda Indo o Etïopo.
Dinne com' è che fai di te parete
   al sol, pur come tu non fossi ancora
24   di morte intrato dentro da la rete."

calling out examples of Lust. Dante then turns back to the questioning
group and explains his presence in Purgatory. His interlocutor explains the
examples and introduces himself as the poet Guido Guinizelli. Guinizelli
also points out the poet Arnaut Daniel, who then speaks to Dante in his
native Occitan.

While we three were edging along the brink,
  one after another, with my good master
    often saying, "Watch out where I'm pointing,"   *3*
The sun was beating on my right shoulder,
  for its spreading rays were now transforming
    the whole face of the West from azure to white.   *6*
My shadow was making the flames appear
  more glowing red, and I saw many shades
    notice this slight sign as they went on by.   *9*
It was this that first caused them to speak of me,
  and they began to say, one to the other,
    "That one's body does not seem to be airy."   *12*
Then a few of the spirits came toward me
  as far as they could, always being careful
    not to come out where they would not be burned.   *15*

"O you who go behind the others, not
  out of slowness, but out of reverence perhaps,
    answer me who burn in thirst and fire.   *18*
Nor for me alone is your answer needed,
  for all these others thirst for it more
    than Indian or Ethiopian thirsts for cold water.   *21*
Tell us how you make a wall of yourself
  to block off the sun, just as if you had not
    yet been enmeshed in the net of death."   *24*

Sì mi parlava un d'essi; e io mi fora
  già manifesto, s'io non fossi atteso
27   ad altra novità ch'apparve allora;
ché per lo mezzo del cammino acceso
  venne gente col viso incontro a questa,
30   la qual mi fece a rimirar sospeso.
Lì veggio d'ogne parte farsi presta
  ciascun' ombra e basciarsi una con una
33   sanza restar, contente a brieve festa;
così per entro loro schiera bruna
  s'ammusa l'una con l'altra formica,
36   forse a spïar lor via e lor fortuna.

Tosto che parton l'accoglienza amica,
  prima che 'l primo passo lì trascorra,
39   sopragridar ciascuna s'affatica:
la nova gente: "Soddoma e Gomorra";
  e l'altra: "Ne la vacca entra Pasife,
42   perché 'l torello a sua lussuria corra."
Poi, come grue ch'a le montagne Rife
  volasser parte, e parte inver' l'arene,
45   queste del gel, quelle del sole schife,
l'una gente sen va, l'altra sen vene;
  e tornan, lagrimando, a' primi canti
48   e al gridar che più lor si convene;
e raccostansi a me, come davanti,
  essi medesmi che m'avean pregato,
51   attenti ad ascoltar ne' lor sembianti.

Io, che due volte avea visto lor grato,
  incominciai: "O anime sicure
54   d'aver, quando che sia, di pace stato,
non son rimase acerbe né mature
  le membra mie di là, ma son qui meco
57   col sangue suo e con le sue giunture.
Quinci sù vo per non esser più cieco;
  donna è di sopra che m'acquista grazia,
60   per che 'l mortal per vostro mondo reco.

One of them said this to me, and I would have
  made myself known, had I not been intent
    on another strange thing that then appeared.   *27*
For down the middle of that burning road
  more souls were coming from the opposite direction,
    and this made me pause and gaze at them.   *30*
I saw all of the shades on both sides hurrying
  to exchange kisses, one after another
    without pause, content with just this brief greeting.   *33*
In much the same way, within their dark swarm
  one ant will rub its head against another's,
    perhaps to espy its route and its fortune.   *36*

As soon as they finish the friendly greeting
  and before going on another step,
    each of them tries to outcry the others,   *39*
The newcomers shouting, "Sodom and Gomorrah,"
  and the others, "Pasiphae enters the cow,
    so that the bull might run to her lust."   *42*
Then, like cranes that might fly, some of them north
  to the Riphaean mountains, others to the sands,
    these shy of the frost, those of the sun,   *45*
One company of souls comes on, and the other
  passes by, and then they return to their chants
    weeping, and to the cry that befits them most.   *48*
Then the same group that had first beseeched me
  drew near to me again, and from the looks
    on their faces, were eager to listen.   *51*

Having twice now seen what they desired,
  I began, "O souls, certain of attaining,
    whenever it may be, a state of peace,   *54*
My limbs have not remained over there,
  either green or ripe, but are here with me,
    complete with all their blood and their joints.   *57*
I go up from here to be blind no longer.
  A lady is above who has won me grace,
    by which I bring through your world my mortal part.   *60*

Ma se la vostra maggior voglia sazia
   tosto divegna, sì che 'l ciel v'alberghi
63   ch'è pien d'amore e più ampio si spazia,
ditemi, acciò ch'ancor carte ne verghi,
   chi siete voi, e chi è quella turba
66   che se ne va di retro a' vostri terghi."

Non altrimenti stupido si turba
   lo montanaro, e rimirando ammuta,
69   quando rozzo e salvatico s'inurba,
che ciascun' ombra fece in sua paruta;
   ma poi che furon di stupore scarche,
72   lo qual ne li alti cuor tosto s'attuta,
"Beato te, che de le nostre marche,"
   ricominciò colei che pria m'inchiese,
75   "per morir meglio, esperïenza imbarche!
La gente che non vien con noi, offese
   di ciò per che già Cesar, trïunfando,
78   'Regina' contra sé chiamar s'intese:
però si parton 'Soddoma' gridando,
   rimproverando a sé com' hai udito,
81   e aiutan l'arsura vergognando.
Nostro peccato fu ermafrodito;
   ma perché non servammo umana legge,
84   seguendo come bestie l'appetito,
in obbrobrio di noi, per noi si legge,
   quando partinci, il nome di colei
87   che s'imbestiò ne le 'mbestiate schegge.
Or sai nostri atti e di che fummo rei:
   se forse a nome vuo' saper chi semo,
90   tempo non è di dire, e non saprei.
Farotti ben di me volere scemo:
   son Guido Guinizzelli, e già mi purgo
93   per ben dolermi prima ch'a lo stremo."

Quali ne la tristizia di Ligurgo
   si fer due figli a riveder la madre,
96   tal mi fec' io, ma non a tanto insurgo,

But, so may your greatest aspiration soon
  be satisfied, and you abide in the Heaven
    that is full of love and is most spacious, 63
Tell me, so that I may yet rule it on pages,
  who you are, and what is that throng
    that is going away now at your rear?" 66

A mountain man is no more astonished
  nor looks around more perplexed and dumbfounded
    when he comes from the backwoods into a city 69
Than was each of these shades, to judge by their looks.
  But when they shrugged off their astonishment,
    which in lofty hearts does not take much time, 72
"Blessed are you," began again the one
  who had first questioned me, "who to die better
    acquire experience of our regions. 75
The souls who do not come with us committed
  the sin that Caesar was once taunted with
    when someone called out 'Queen' in his Triumph. 78
And so they go off crying, "Sodom,"
  reproving themselves, just as you heard,
    and help the burning with their sense of shame. 81
Our sin was that of heterosexuals,
  but because we did not observe human law,
    following appetite like beasts instead, 84
We revile ourselves, when we part from the others,
  by saying the name of the woman who
    bestialized herself in the beast-shaped wood. 87
Now you know the deeds of which we were guilty.
  If you wanted to know each of our names,
    there is no time to tell them, nor would I know, 90
But I will tell you my name. I am
  Guido Guinizzelli, and I purge myself already
    because of my repentance well before I died." 93

As in the presence of Lycurgus' grim rage
  Hypsipyle's sons felt when they saw her again,
    so did I feel, but I did not rush in as they did 96

quand' io odo nomar sé stesso il padre
   mio e de li altri miei miglior che mai
99   rime d'amore usar dolci e leggiadre;
e sanza udire e dir pensoso andai
   lunga fïata rimirando lui,
102   né, per lo foco, in là più m'appressai.
Poi che di riguardar pasciuto fui,
   tutto m'offersi pronto al suo servigio
105   con l'affermar che fa credere altrui.

Ed elli a me: "Tu lasci tal vestigio,
   per quel ch'i' odo, in me, e tanto chiaro,
108   che Letè nol può tòrre né far bigio.
Ma se le tue parole or ver giuraro,
   dimmi che è cagion per che dimostri
111   nel dire e nel guardar d'avermi caro."
E io a lui: "Li dolci detti vostri,
   che, quanto durerà l'uso moderno,
114   faranno cari ancora i loro incostri."
"O frate," disse, "questi ch'io ti cerno
   col dito," e additò un spirto innanzi,
117   "fu miglior fabbro del parlar materno.
Versi d'amore e prose di romanzi
   soverchiò tutti; e lascia dir li stolti
120   che quel di Lemosì credon ch'avanzi.
A voce più ch'al ver drizzan li volti,
   e così ferman sua oppinïone
123   prima ch'arte o ragion per lor s'ascolti.
Così fer molti antichi di Guittone,
   di grido in grido pur lui dando pregio,
126   fin che l'ha vinto il ver con più persone.
Or se tu hai sì ampio privilegio,
   che licito ti sia l'andare al chiostro
129   nel quale è Cristo abate del collegio,
falli per me un dir d'un paternostro,
   quanto bisogna a noi di questo mondo,
132   dove poter peccar non è più nostro."

When I heard my father, and the father
  of others better than me in writing sweet
    and gracious love poems, identify himself.   *99*
No, I only pondered long and gazed at him
  without hearing or speaking, and did not
    draw near to him, because of the fire.   *102*
When I had fed my fill of looking at him,
  I offered myself to be at his service,
    with the kind of oath that makes others believe.   *105*

Then he said to me, "What I hear from you
  leaves traces in me so deep and so clear
    that Lethe cannot erase or dim them.   *108*
But if your words just now swore to the truth,
  tell me for what reason you show yourself
    in speech and looks to hold me so dear."   *111*
And I answered, "It is your sweet verses,
  which, as long as modern use shall last,
    will make dear the ink with which they are written."   *114*
"O, my brother," he said, "that one over there,"
  and he pointed to a spirit ahead of us,
    "was the better craftsman of our mother tongue.   *117*
Love poets and writers of prose romance—
  he surpassed them all; and let the fools talk
    who think the troubadour of Limoges is better.   *120*
They hold rumor in higher regard than truth,
  and they become settled in their opinion
    before consulting with art or reason.   *123*
Many of our fathers did the same with Guittone,
  taking up the cry to award him the prize,
    until with most people the truth prevailed.   *126*
Now, since you have such ample privilege
  that you are permitted to go to the cloister
    where Christ is the abbot of the college,   *129*
Say a paternoster there for me,
  or as much of one as is needed here,
    where we no longer have the power to sin."   *132*

Poi, forse per dar luogo altrui secondo
che presso avea, disparve per lo foco,
135   come per l'acqua il pesce andando al fondo.

Io mi fei al mostrato innanzi un poco,
e dissi ch'al suo nome il mio disire
138   apparecchiava grazïoso loco.
El cominciò liberamente a dire:
    "*Tan m'abellis vostre cortes deman,*
141   *qu'ieu no me puesc ni voill a vos cobrire.*
Ieu sui Arnaut, que plor e vau cantan;
    consiros vei la passada folor,
144   *e vei jausen lo joi qu'esper, denan.*
Ara vos prec, per aquella valor
    que vos guida al som de l'escalina,
147   *sovenha vos a temps de ma dolor!*"
Poi s'ascose nel foco che li affina.

Then, perhaps to make room for one behind,
  he vanished into the flames like a fish
    that goes through the water down to the bottom.   *135*

I moved a little closer to the spirit
  whom he had pointed out, and said that my heart
    was preparing a grateful place for his name,   *138*
And he began to speak to me graciously:
  "Your courteous request pleases me so
    I neither can nor would hide myself from you.   *141*
I am Arnaut, who weep and sing as I go,
  viewing my former folly with sorrow
    and rejoicing to see the joy I will know.   *144*
And now I pray you, by the power
  that guides you to the top of the stair,
    remember my pain upon a fit hour."   *147*
Then he hid in the fire that refines them there.

Canto XXVII

THE TRAVELERS COME TO THE angel of the terrace of Lust, who pronounces a Beatitude. He informs the travelers that they too must pass through the wall of flames in order to continue their journey. Dante is terrified and Virgil must persuade him to go on. It is only at the mention of Beatrice that the pilgrim agrees to continue. Dante, Virgil, and Statius walk through the burning flames following the sound of voices singing on

Sì come quando i primi raggi vibra
  là dove il suo fattor lo sangue sparse,
3   cadendo Ibero sotto l'alta Libra,
e l'onde in Gange da nona rïarse,
  sì stava il sole; onde 'l giorno sen giva,
6   come l'angel di Dio lieto ci apparse.
Fuor de la fiamma stava in su la riva,
  e cantava *"Beati mundo corde!"*
9   in voce assai più che la nostra viva.
Poscia "Più non si va, se pria non morde,
  anime sante, il foco: intrate in esso,
12   e al cantar di là non siate sorde,"
ci disse come noi li fummo presso;
  per ch'io divenni tal, quando lo 'ntesi,
15   qual è colui che ne la fossa è messo.
In su le man commesse mi protesi,
  guardando il foco e imaginando forte
18   umani corpi già veduti accesi.
Volsersi verso me le buone scorte;
  e Virgilio mi disse: "Figliuol mio,
21   qui può esser tormento, ma non morte.
Ricorditi, ricorditi! E se io
  sovresso Gerïon ti guidai salvo,
24   che farò ora presso più a Dio?

the other side. Emerging from the flames, Dante and his guides continue onward as the sun sets, finally stopping when night has fallen. Dante falls asleep and dreams of a vision of Leah and Rachel. He awakens at dawn. Virgil addresses the pilgrim, telling him that he has nothing more to teach him and proclaiming Dante's freedom.

As when it strikes with its dawning rays
  the place where its Maker shed His blood
    while the Ebro falls beneath the zenith Scales,   *3*
And the Ganges' waters are scorched by noon,
  so stood the sun. And so day was departing
    when the blissful angel of God appeared.   *6*
He stood on the bank outside the flames
  and was singing, "*Beati mundo corde*"
    in a voice that was more alive than ours.   *9*
Then, "There is no going farther, holy souls,
  if the fire does not bite you. Enter it,
    and do not be deaf to the chanting beyond,"   *12*
He said to us when we were near to him,
  and when I heard it I became like someone
    who is about to be put into the pit.   *15*
I bent forward over my clasped hands, staring
  into the fire and vividly imagining
    human bodies I had once seen burned.   *18*
My noble escorts both turned to me,
  and Virgil explained, "My son, there may be
    torment here, but there is not death.   *21*
Remember, remember! And if I
  guided you safely on Geryon's back,
    what shall I do now, closer to God?   *24*

Credi per certo che se dentro a l'alvo
di questa fiamma stessi ben mille anni,
27   non ti potrebbe far d'un capel calvo.
E se tu forse credi ch'io t'inganni,
fatti ver' lei, e fatti far credenza
30   con le tue mani al lembo d'i tuoi panni.
Pon giù omai, pon giù ogne temenza;
volgiti in qua e vieni: entra sicuro!"
33   E io pur fermo e contra cosci̇enza.
Quando mi vide star pur fermo e duro,
turbato un poco disse: "Or vedi, figlio:
36   tra Bëatrice e te è questo muro."

Come al nome di Tisbe aperse il ciglio
Piramo in su la morte, e riguardolla,
39   allor che 'l gelso diventò vermiglio;
così, la mia durezza fatta solla,
mi volsi al savio duca, udendo il nome
42   che ne la mente sempre mi rampolla.
Ond' ei crollò la fronte e disse: "Come!
volenci star di qua?" indi sorrise
45   come al fanciul si fa ch'è vinto al pome.
Poi dentro al foco innanzi mi si mise,
pregando Stazio che venisse retro,
48   che pria per lunga strada ci divise.

Sì com' fui dentro, in un bogliente vetro
gittato mi sarei per rinfrescarmi,
51   tant' era ivi lo 'ncendio sanza metro.
Lo dolce padre mio, per confortarmi,
pur di Beatrice ragionando andava,
54   dicendo: "Li occhi suoi già veder parmi."
Guidavaci una voce che cantava
di là; e noi, attenti pur a lei,
57   venimmo fuor là ove si montava.

"*Venite, benedicti Patris mei,*"
sonò dentro a un lume che lì era,
60   tal che mi vinse e guardar nol potei.

You can be sure that even if you stayed
  a thousand years in the belly of this flame
    you would not lose a single hair on your head.   *27*
And if you think that I am deceiving you,
  go up to it and test it for yourself
    holding out the hem of your robe in your hands.   *30*
Now put aside all your fear, turn this way
  and walk right in there with confidence."
    And I, against my conscience, would not budge.   *33*
When he saw me stand there obstinately
  he said, a little annoyed, "Now look here, son,
    between Beatrice and you there is this wall."   *36*

As Pyramus, dying, opened his eyes
  when he heard Thisbe's name and looked at her,
    that time when the mulberry first became red,   *39*
So too, my stubbornness melting away,
  I turned to my wise leader when I heard the name
    that wells up continuously in my mind.   *42*
He shook his head at this and said, "Well?
  Do want to stay on this side?" And he smiled,
    as if at a child won over with an apple.   *45*
Then he went into the fire ahead of me,
  asking Statius, who had been between us
    for a long way now, to bring up the rear.   *48*

As soon as I was in I would have thrown myself
  into molten glass to cool myself down,
    so beyond all measure was the burning there.   *51*
My sweet father, to comfort and encourage me,
  went on talking about Beatrice, saying,
    "I think I can see her eyes already."   *54*
Guiding us was a voice that chanted
  from the other side; and, concentrating
    on it, we came out where the ascent began.   *57*

"*Venite, benedicti Patris mei,*"
  sounded from within a light that was there,
    so overwhelming I could not bear to observe it.   *60*

"Lo sol sen va," soggiunse, "e vien la sera;
  non v'arrestate, ma studiate il passo,
63   mentre che l'occidente non si annera."
Dritta salia la via per entro 'l sasso
  verso tal parte ch'io toglieva i raggi
66   dinanzi a me del sol ch'era già basso.
E di pochi scaglion levammo i saggi,
  che 'l sol corcar, per l'ombra che si spense,
69   sentimmo dietro e io e li miei saggi.
E pria che 'n tutte le sue parti immense
  fosse orizzonte fatto d'uno aspetto,
72   e notte avesse tutte sue dispense,
ciascun di noi d'un grado fece letto;
  ché la natura del monte ci affranse
75   la possa del salir più e 'l diletto.
Quali si stanno ruminando manse
  le capre, state rapide e proterve
78   sovra le cime avante che sien pranse,
tacite a l'ombra, mentre che 'l sol ferve,
  guardate dal pastor, che 'n su la verga
81   poggiato s'è e lor di posa serve;
e quale il mandrïan che fori alberga,
  lungo il peculio suo queto pernotta,
84   guardando perché fiera non lo sperga;
tali eravamo tutti e tre allotta,
  io come capra, ed ei come pastori,
87   fasciati quinci e quindi d'alta grotta.
Poco parer potea lì del di fori;
  ma, per quel poco, vedea io le stelle
90   di lor solere e più chiare e maggiori.
Sì ruminando e sì mirando in quelle,
  mi prese il sonno; il sonno che sovente,
93   anzi che 'l fatto sia, sa le novelle.

Ne l'ora, credo, che de l'orïente
  prima raggiò nel monte Citerea,
96   che di foco d'amor par sempre ardente,

"The sun is setting," it added, "and evening comes;
  do not stop, but quicken your pace
    before the western horizon blackens."   *63*
The way led straight up into the rock
  at such an angle that my back intercepted
    the rays of the sun, which was now quite low,   *66*
And we had managed only a few of the steps
  when I and my sages saw my shadow fade out,
    whereby we knew that the sun had set behind us.   *69*
Then, before the immense and varied expanse
  of the horizon had all turned the same shade,
    and night held sway in all her dominions,   *72*
Each of us took a stair as his bed,
  for the mountain's nature dispossessed us
    of the power and the will to climb anymore.   *75*
As goats become quiet when they ruminate
  after being frisky and headlong
    up in the mountains before they feed,   *78*
Standing silent in the shade on a summer day
  and guarded by a herdsman, who leans
    on his staff as he tends to their rest;   *81*
And as a shepherd, who lives in the open,
  passes the night beside his quiet flock
    and watches so a beast will not scatter it—   *84*
Such were the three of us during that night,
  I as a goat and they as shepherds,
    hemmed in on both sides by high walls of rock.   *87*
Little could be seen outside those walls,
  but through that little I saw the stars,
    larger and brighter than they usually are.   *90*
As I was ruminating and gazing at them
  sleep overtook me, sleep that often
    knows the news before the event.   *93*

At the hour, I think, when Cytherea,
  who always seems glowing with the fire of love,
    first shone on the eastern flank of the mountain,   *96*

giovane e bella in sogno mi parea
  donna vedere andar per una landa
99   cogliendo fiori; e cantando dicea:
"Sappia qualunque il mio nome dimanda
  ch'i' mi son Lia, e vo movendo intorno
102   le belle mani a farmi una ghirlanda.
Per piacermi a lo specchio, qui m'addorno;
  ma mia suora Rachel mai non si smaga
105   dal suo miraglio, e siede tutto giorno.
Ell' è d'i suoi belli occhi veder vaga
  com' io de l'addornarmi con le mani;
108   lei lo vedere, e me l'ovrare appaga."

E già per li splendori antelucani,
  che tanto a' pellegrin surgon più grati,
111   quanto, tornando, albergan men lontani,
le tenebre fuggian da tutti lati,
  e 'l sonno mio con esse; ond' io leva'mi,
114   veggendo i gran maestri già levati.

"Quel dolce pome che per tanti rami
  cercando va la cura de' mortali,
117   oggi porrà in pace le tue fami."
Virgilio inverso me queste cotali
  parole usò; e mai non furo strenne
120   che fosser di piacere a queste iguali.
Tanto voler sopra voler mi venne
  de l'esser sù, ch'ad ogne passo poi
123   al volo mi sentia crescer le penne.
Come la scala tutta sotto noi
  fu corsa e fummo in su 'l grado superno,
126   in me ficcò Virgilio li occhi suoi,

e disse: "Il temporal foco e l'etterno
  veduto hai, figlio; e se' venuto in parte
129   dov' io per me più oltre non discerno.
Tratto t'ho qui con ingegno e con arte;
  lo tuo piacere omai prendi per duce;
132   fuor se' de l'erte vie, fuor se' de l'arte.

I seemed to see in a dream a lady
  young and beautiful, going through a meadow
    gathering flowers and singing these words: *99*
"If anyone asks my name, let him know
  that I am Leah and I go about weaving
    my fair hands around to make me a garland.   *102*
I adorn myself here so that my reflection
  will please me, but my sister Rachel never leaves
    her mirror, sitting before it all day long.   *105*
She is as eager to gaze at her own fair eyes
  as I am to adorn myself with my hands.
    She sees, and I do, and we are both satisfied."   *108*

And now the splendors of the early dawn
  that become more welcome to the pilgrim soul
    the nearer he lodges to his home   *111*
Were putting to flight the shadows all around
  and my sleep along with them. Up I rose,
    seeing the great masters already risen.   *114*

"The sweet fruit that mortals desire
  and search for through so many branches
    today will lay your cravings to rest."   *117*
Virgil addressed me with words of this sort,
  and never have there been any gifts
    that could give pleasure equal to these.   *120*
Desire upon desire to ascend
  so overwhelmed me that with every stride
    I felt that I was growing wings for flight.   *123*
When the stairs had all run out beneath us
  and we were standing on the topmost step,
    Virgil fixed his eyes on me and said,   *126*

"The temporal fire and the eternal
  you have seen, my son, and now you have come
    where on my own I can see no farther.   *129*
I have brought you here by my wits and skill.
  Take your own pleasure as your guide now.
    You are free of the steep way, free of the narrow.   *132*

Vedi lo sol che 'n fronte ti riluce;
   vedi l'erbette, i fiori e li arbuscelli
135   che qui la terra sol da sé produce.
Mentre che vegnan lieti li occhi belli
   che, lagrimando, a te venir mi fenno,
138   seder ti puoi e puoi andar tra elli.
Non aspettar mio dir più né mio cenno;
   libero, dritto e sano è tuo arbitrio,
141   e fallo fora non fare a suo senno:
per ch'io te sovra te corono e mitrio."

Look at the sun shining on your brow,
  look at the new grass, the flowers and trees
    that the earth produces here on its own.   *135*
You may wander among them or sit in their shade
  until the beautiful eyes come rejoicing,
    the eyes that weeping made me come to your aid.   *138*
Expect no further word or sign from me.
  Your will is free now, whole, and true;
    not to follow its lead would now be folly.   *141*
Sovereign of yourself I crown and miter you."

Canto XXVIII

Dante and his guides enter *the Earthly Paradise, which is filled with lush foliage, delicate scents, and gentle breezes. They come to a river of clear water on the other side of which walks a young lady, singing and collecting flowers. Dante courteously addresses her, asking her to draw near so that he might hear her song. She does so, moving slowly toward him until, at the water's edge, she lifts her eyes to him. The lady then explains*

Vago già di cercar dentro e dintorno
  la divina foresta spessa e viva,
3   ch'a li occhi temperava il novo giorno,
sanza più aspettar, lasciai la riva,
  prendendo la campagna lento lento
6   su per lo suol che d'ogne parte auliva.
Un'aura dolce, sanza mutamento
  avere in sé, mi feria per la fronte
9   non di più colpo che soave vento;
per cui le fronde, tremolando, pronte
  tutte quante piegavano a la parte
12   u' la prim' ombra gitta il santo monte;
non però dal loro esser dritto sparte
  tanto, che li augelletti per le cime
15   lasciasser d'operare ogne lor arte;
ma con piena letizia l'ore prime,
  cantando, ricevieno intra le foglie,
18   che tenevan bordone a le sue rime,
tal qual di ramo in ramo si raccoglie
  per la pineta in su 'l lito di Chiassi,
21   quand' Ëolo scilocco fuor discioglie.

Già m'avean trasportato i lenti passi
  dentro a la selva antica tanto, ch'io
24   non potea rivedere ond' io mi 'ntrassi;

the nature of the place in which the travelers find themselves. This is the Earthly Paradise granted to Adam and Eve, which is not affected by terrestrial weather but only by the motion of the celestial heavens. The lady explains the characteristics of the two rivers that flow through it, Lethe and Eunoe, and finally describes the Paradise as that touched on by ancient poets when they described the Golden Age of humankind.

Eager now to search the environs
  of the divine forest, lush and green,
    that tempered the new day to my vision,   *3*
I left the bank without any delay,
  traversing ever so slowly the landscape
    whose very soil exuded fragrance.   *6*
A sweet breeze that was never variable
  in itself was striking my forehead
    with no more force than a gentle wind,   *9*
And in it all the fluttering boughs
  bent easily down toward the quarter where
    the holy mountain casts its first shadow,   *12*
Yet were not deflected downward so far
  that the little birds in the canopy
    neglected to practice all their arts,   *15*
But full of joy greeted the early hours
  with their songs, and the harboring leaves
    supported their rhymes with the kind of drone   *18*
That moves in crescendo from branch to branch
  in the pine forest on Chiassi's shore
    when Aeolus unleashes the Sirocco.   *21*

My slow steps had now transported me
  so deep into the ancient wood, that I
    could not see back where I had entered it,   *24*

ed ecco più andar mi tolse un rio,
    che 'nver' sinistra con sue picciole onde
27   piegava l'erba che 'n sua ripa uscìo.
Tutte l'acque che son di qua più monde,
    parrieno avere in sé mistura alcuna
30   verso di quella, che nulla nasconde,
avvegna che si mova bruna bruna
    sotto l'ombra perpetüa, che mai
33   raggiar non lascia sole ivi né luna.

Coi piè ristetti e con li occhi passai
    di là dal fiumicello, per mirare
36   la gran varïazion d'i freschi mai;
e là m'apparve, sì com' elli appare
    subitamente cosa che disvia
39   per maraviglia tutto altro pensare,
una donna soletta che si gia
    e cantando e scegliendo fior da fiore
42   ond' era pinta tutta la sua via.

"Deh, bella donna, che a' raggi d'amore
    ti scaldi, s'i' vo' credere a' sembianti
45   che soglion esser testimon del core,
vegnati in voglia di trarreti avanti,"
    diss' io a lei, "verso questa rivera,
48   tanto ch'io possa intender che tu canti.
Tu mi fai rimembrar dove e qual era
    Proserpina nel tempo che perdette
51   la madre lei, ed ella primavera."

Come si volge, con le piante strette
    a terra e intra sé, donna che balli,
54   e piede innanzi piede a pena mette,
volsesi in su i vermigli e in su i gialli
    fioretti verso me, non altrimenti
57   che vergine che li occhi onesti avvalli;
e fece i prieghi miei esser contenti,
    sì appressando sé, che 'l dolce suono
60   veniva a me co' suoi intendimenti.

When all further progress was halted by a stream
  whose little waves were bending leftward
    the blades of grass that grew on its banks.
The purest waters that we know on earth
  would seem to have some defilement in them
    compared to that water, which conceals nothing,
Although it flows dark and darker
  under the perpetual shade, which never allows
    the rays of the sun or moonbeams to enter.

My feet stayed on one side, but with my eyes
  I passed to the rivulet's other side
    to view the profusion of flowering boughs,
And then there appeared to me—the way a thing
  will suddenly appear and through its wonder
    drive every other thought away—
There appeared a lady, all alone, singing
  as she went along picking choice flowers
    from the many with which her path was painted.

"Ah, beautiful lady," I said, "who warm yourself
  in the rays of Love, to judge by your looks,
    which often testify to the heart within,
May it be your pleasure to come forward,
  up to this stream, close enough that I
    might be able to understand your song.
You make me remember where and what
  Proserpina was when her mother lost her,
    and she herself lost the season of spring."

As a dancer turns, keeping her feet
  close to the ground and to each other,
    hardly setting foot before foot,
She turned toward me upon the vermilion
  and yellow petals, no differently than
    a virgin who lowers her modest eyes,
And thus gave satisfaction to my prayer,
  drawing so close that her voice's sweet sound
    reached my ears with all its meaning intact.

27

30

33

36

39

42

45

48

51

54

57

60

Tosto che fu là dove l'erbe sono
   bagnate già da l'onde del bel fiume,
63   di levar li occhi suoi mi fece dono.
Non credo che splendesse tanto lume
   sotto le ciglia a Venere, trafitta
66   dal figlio fuor di tutto suo costume.
Ella ridea da l'altra riva dritta,
   trattando più color con le sue mani,
69   che l'alta terra sanza seme gitta.
Tre passi ci facea il fiume lontani;
   ma Elesponto, là 've passò Serse,
72   ancora freno a tutti orgogli umani,
più odio da Leandro non sofferse
   per mareggiare intra Sesto e Abido,
75   che quel da me perch' allor non s'aperse.

"Voi siete nuovi, e forse perch' io rido,"
   cominciò ella, "in questo luogo eletto
78   a l'umana natura per suo nido,
maravigliando tienvi alcun sospetto;
   ma luce rende il salmo *Delectasti*,
81   che puote disnebbiar vostro intelletto.
E tu che se' dinanzi e mi pregasti,
   dì s'altro vuoli udir; ch'i' venni presta
84   ad ogne tua question tanto che basti."

"L'acqua," diss' io, "e 'l suon de la foresta
   impugnan dentro a me novella fede
87   di cosa ch'io udi' contraria a questa."

Ond' ella: "Io dicerò come procede
   per sua cagion ciò ch'ammirar ti face,
90   e purgherò la nebbia che ti fiede.
Lo sommo Ben, che solo esso a sé piace,
   fé l'uom buono e a bene, e questo loco
93   diede per arr' a lui d'etterna pace.
Per sua difalta qui dimorò poco;
   per sua difalta in pianto e in affanno
96   cambiò onesto riso e dolce gioco.

As soon as she had come to where the grass
  was just bathed by the ripples of the lovely stream,
    she made me the gift of lifting her eyes.   *63*
I do not believe that such a light shone
  under Venus' eyelids when she was pierced
    unintentionally by an arrow of her son.   *66*
She was smiling from the opposite bank
  as she stood there weaving the riot of colors
    that high land spins off without any seed.   *69*
The stream kept us three paces apart,
  but the Hellespont, where Xerxes crossed it—
    forever a curb on all human pride—   *72*
Was no more hated by Leander
  for the surge between Sestos and Abydos
    than by me then because it did not part.   *75*

"You are newcomers, and perhaps you wonder,"
  she began, "why I am smiling in this place
    chosen as the nest of the human race.   *78*
Perhaps you marvel and are in doubt.
  But the psalm *Delectasti* sheds some light
    that may uncloud your intellects.   *81*
And you there in front, who entreated me,
  say if you would hear more, for I have come
    ready to answer all of your questions."   *84*

"The water," I said, "and the forest's sound
  are at odds with a recent belief of mine
    in something I heard contrary to this."   *87*

Then she began, "I will tell you how
  what makes you wonder proceeds from its cause,
    and I will dispel the fog that afflicts you.   *90*
The highest Good, who alone pleases Himself
  made man good and to do good, and gave him this place
    as a pledge of eternal peace to come.   *93*
Through his own fault his stay here was short;
  through his own fault he exchanged honest smiles
    and good cheer for hard labor and tears.   *96*

Perché 'l turbar che sotto da sé fanno
l'essalazion de l'acqua e de la terra,
99 che quanto posson dietro al calor vanno,
a l'uomo non facesse alcuna guerra,
questo monte salìo verso 'l ciel tanto,
102 e libero n'è d'indi ove si serra.
Or perché in circuito tutto quanto
l'aere si volge con la prima volta,
105 se non li è rotto il cerchio d'alcun canto,
in questa altezza ch'è tutta disciolta
ne l'aere vivo, tal moto percuote,
108 e fa sonar la selva perch' è folta;
e la percossa pianta tanto puote,
che de la sua virtute l'aura impregna
111 e quella poi, girando, intorno scuote;
e l'altra terra, secondo ch'è degna
per sé e per suo ciel, concepe e figlia
114 di diverse virtù diverse legna.
Non parrebbe di là poi maraviglia,
udito questo, quando alcuna pianta
117 sanza seme palese vi s'appiglia.
E saper dei che la campagna santa
dove tu se,' d'ogne semenza è piena,
120 e frutto ha in sé che di là non si schianta.
L'acqua che vedi non surge di vena
che ristori vapor che gel converta,
123 come fiume ch'acquista e perde lena;
ma esce di fontana salda e certa,
che tanto dal voler di Dio riprende,
126 quant' ella versa da due parti aperta.
Da questa parte con virtù discende
che toglie altrui memoria del peccato;
129 da l'altra d'ogne ben fatto la rende.
Quinci Letè; così da l'altro lato
Eünoè si chiama, e non adopra
132 se quinci e quindi pria non è gustato:
a tutti altri sapori esto è di sopra.
E avvegna ch'assai possa esser sazia
135 la sete tua perch' io più non ti scuopra,

So that the disturbances caused below
  by the exhalations of the land and sea
    (that follow heat as far as they can)   *99*
Might not trouble man, this mountain
  rose high toward Heaven and stands clear of them
    from the point where Purgatory's gate is locked.   *102*
Now, because all air revolves in a circuit
  along with the universe's primal circling,
    if its revolution is nowhere interrupted,   *105*
That great motion strikes this mountain's height,
  which stands free in pure air, and causes the forest,
    dense as it is, to reverberate with sound.   *108*
And when a plant is struck in this way
  it impregnates the wind with its potency,
    which then scatters it as it whirls around,   *111*
And the rest of the earth, depending upon
  its own aptitude and that of its climate,
    brings forth varied growth from diverse virtues.   *114*
It should not, therefore, be a marvel on earth,
  at least once this is heard, if a plant takes root
    in a place where there is no visible seed.   *117*
You should also know that the holy plain
  where you are now is full of every seed,
    and has fruit that cannot be picked down there.   *120*
The water you see does not spring from a vein
  restored by vapor that has been condensed by cold,
    like a stream that acquires and loses force,   *123*
But issues from a fountain constant and sure
  that by the will of God regains as much
    as it releases into both of its channels.   *126*
On this side it descends with the power
  to take away the memory of sin; on that side
    it restores the memory of every good deed.   *129*
Here it is called Lethe, and on the other side,
  Eunoe; and it does not work if not tasted
    first on this side and then on the other.   *132*
Its savor surpasses all other sweetness.
  And although your thirst might be satisfied
    even if I disclosed nothing more to you,   *135*

darotti un corollario ancor per grazia;
   né credo che 'l mio dir ti sia men caro,
138   se oltre promession teco si spazia.
Quelli ch'anticamente poetaro
   l'età de l'oro e suo stato felice,
141   forse in Parnaso esto loco sognaro.
Qui fu innocente l'umana radice;
   qui primavera sempre e ogne frutto;
144   nettare è questo di che ciascun dice."

Io mi rivolsi 'n dietro allora tutto
   a' miei poeti, e vidi che con riso
147   udito avëan l'ultimo costrutto;
poi a la bella donna torna' il viso.

In grace I will give you a corollary,
  and I do not think my speech will be less welcome
    if it extends beyond what I promised you.   *138*
The ancient poets who sang of the Age
  of Gold and its blessed existence
    perhaps dreamed in Parnassus of this place.   *141*
Here mankind had its innocent root;
  here it is always spring; here is the nectar
    of which all speak; here is every fruit."   *144*

At that I turned around a short while
  to face my poets, and saw that they had been
    listening to these final words with a smile.   *147*
Then I turned back to the fair lady again.

Canto XXIX

DANTE CONTINUES TO WALK BESIDE *the stream as the lady walks on the opposite bank, until they come to face the east. A bright light suddenly fills the forest, a light that does not dim, and a melody fills the air. The poet laments the fact that the pleasures of Eden have been denied to humanity since the Fall. Having invoked the Muses to aid him in his description,*

Cantando come donna innamorata,
  continüò col fin di sue parole:
3   *"Beati quorum tecta sunt peccata!"*
E come ninfe che si givan sole
  per le salvatiche ombre, disïando
6   qual di veder, qual di fuggir lo sole,
allor si mosse contra 'l fiume, andando
  su per la riva; e io pari di lei,
9   picciol passo con picciol seguitando.
Non eran cento tra ' suoi passi e ' miei,
  quando le ripe igualmente dier volta,
12   per modo ch'a levante mi rendei.

Né ancor fu così nostra via molta,
  quando la donna tutta a me si torse,
15   dicendo: "Frate mio, guarda e ascolta."
Ed ecco un lustro sùbito trascorse
  da tutte parti per la gran foresta,
18   tal che di balenar mi mise in forse.
Ma perché 'l balenar, come vien, resta,
  e quel, durando, più e più splendeva,
21   nel mio pensier dicea: "Che cosa è questa?"
E una melodia dolce correva
  per l'aere luminoso; onde buon zelo
24   mi fé riprender l'ardimento d'Eva,

the poet then recounts the appearance of seven lights that announce the arrival of a mysterious procession that emerges through the forest. The following extended religious drama represents the history of the revelation of divine truth through the books of the Old and New Testaments and the coming of Christ.

She went on singing like a lady in love,
  and at the end of her lyrics she continued,
    "*Beati quorum tecta sunt peccata!*"   *3*
And, like nymphs who used to walk alone
  through the forest's shade, this one desiring
    to see the sun, and that one to avoid it,   *6*
She went her way, moving upstream now
  along the bank, and keeping up with her
    I matched her little steps with mine.   *9*
We had not taken a hundred between us
  when the stream turned and doubled back on itself,
    so that I found myself facing the East again.   *12*

Nor had we gone far in that direction
  when the lady turned around to face me
    and said, "My brother, look now and listen!"   *15*
And then, ah, a sudden brightness
  shot through the great garden all around me,
    making me think it must have been lightning,   *18*
But since lightning ceases the moment it strikes
  and this, lasting, became more resplendent,
    I asked myself, "What can this be?"   *21*
And a sweet melody was running through
  the luminous air, so that righteous zeal
    made me reprove the boldness of Eve;   *24*

che là dove ubidia la terra e 'l cielo,
  femmina, sola e pur testé formata,
27   non sofferse di star sotto alcun velo;
sotto 'l qual se divota fosse stata,
  avrei quelle ineffabili delizie
30   sentite prima e più lunga fïata.
Mentr' io m'andava tra tante primizie
  de l'etterno piacer tutto sospeso,
33   e disïoso ancora a più letizie,
dinanzi a noi, tal quale un foco acceso,
  ci si fé l'aere sotto i verdi rami;
36   e 'l dolce suon per canti era già inteso.

O sacrosante Vergini, se fami,
  freddi o vigilie mai per voi soffersi,
39   cagion mi sprona ch'io mercé vi chiami.
Or convien che Elicona per me versi,
  e Uranìe m'aiuti col suo coro
42   forti cose a pensar mettere in versi.

Poco più oltre, sette alberi d'oro
  falsava nel parere il lungo tratto
45   del mezzo ch'era ancor tra noi e loro;
ma quand' i' fui sì presso di lor fatto,
  che l'obietto comun, che 'l senso inganna,
48   non perdea per distanza alcun suo atto,
la virtù ch'a ragion discorso ammanna,
  sì com' elli eran candelabri apprese,
51   e ne le voci del cantare "Osanna."
Di sopra fiammeggiava il bello arnese
  più chiaro assai che luna per sereno
54   di mezza notte nel suo mezzo mese.
Io mi rivolsi d'ammirazion pieno
  al buon Virgilio, ed esso mi rispuose
57   con vista carca di stupor non meno.
Indi rendei l'aspetto a l'alte cose
  che si movieno incontr' a noi sì tardi,
60   che foran vinte da novelle spose.

For, where Heaven and earth were obedient,
  she alone, a woman just now created,
    could not bear to remain under any veil,   27
Under which if she had been devout
  I would have enjoyed those ineffable delights
    much earlier and for a longer time.   30
While I made my way through so many firstfruits
  of eternal joy, in a state of wonder,
    and still desirous of even more joy,   33
The air in front of us under the green boughs
  became like a blazing fire to us,
    and the sweet sound now was heard as a song.   36

O Virgins most holy, if I have ever endured
  hunger, cold, or vigils for you,
    the occasion prompts me to claim my reward.   39
Now should Helicon pour out its waters through me,
  and Urania aid me with her choir
    to put into verse things hard to conceive.   42

A little farther on, seven trees of gold
  seemed to appear, an illusion created
    by the long distance that still intervened;   45
But when I came near enough to them
  that their features were no longer blurred by distance,
    and my senses were able to grasp them whole,   48
The faculty that prepares objects for reason
  made them out to be what they were, candlesticks,
    and the words of the chant to be "Hosanna."   51
The beautiful array flared from above,
  far brighter than the full moon that shines
    at mid-month in a clear midnight sky.   54
Filled with wonder, I turned around
  to my good Virgil, and he answered me
    with a look no less charged with amazement.   57
Then I turned my face to the high things again,
  which moved in our direction so slowly
    they would have been outpaced by new-wed brides.   60

La donna mi sgridò: "Perché pur ardi
　　sì ne l'affetto de le vive luci,
63　　　　e ciò che vien di retro a lor non guardi?"
Genti vid' io allor, come a lor duci,
　　venire appresso, vestite di bianco;
66　　　　e tal candor di qua già mai non fuci.
L'acqua imprendëa dal sinistro fianco,
　　e rendea me la mia sinistra costa,
69　　　　s'io riguardava in lei, come specchio anco.
Quand' io da la mia riva ebbi tal posta,
　　che solo il fiume mi facea distante,
72　　　　per veder meglio ai passi diedi sosta,
e vidi le fiammelle andar davante,
　　lasciando dietro a sé l'aere dipinto,
75　　　　e di tratti pennelli avean sembiante;
sì che lì sopra rimanea distinto
　　di sette liste, tutte in quei colori
78　　　　onde fa l'arco il Sole e Delia il cinto.
Questi ostendali in dietro eran maggiori
　　che la mia vista; e, quanto a mio avviso,
81　　　　diece passi distavan quei di fori.
Sotto così bel ciel com' io diviso,
　　ventiquattro seniori, a due a due,
84　　　　coronati venien di fiordaliso.
Tutti cantavan: "Benedicta tue
　　ne le figlie d'Adamo, e benedette
87　　　　sieno in etterno le bellezze tue!"

Poscia che i fiori e l'altre fresche erbette
　　a rimpetto di me da l'altra sponda
90　　　　libere fuor da quelle genti elette,
sì come luce luce in ciel seconda,
　　vennero appresso lor quattro animali,
93　　　　coronati ciascun di verde fronda.
Ognuno era pennuto di sei ali;
　　le penne piene d'occhi; e li occhi d'Argo,
96　　　　se fosser vivi, sarebber cotali.

The lady scolded me, "Why are you so set
  on the display of living lights
    and do not look at what comes behind them?"   *63*
Then I saw people all clothed in white,
  whiter than anything ever seen on earth,
    coming behind as if following the lights.   *66*
The water received my image on the left
  and reflected my left side to me whenever
    I glanced upon it, just like a mirror.   *69*
When I had reached a point on the bank
  where only the stream kept me from them,
    I halted my steps so that I could see better,   *72*
And I saw that as the flames advanced
  they left the air behind them painted,
    as if they were brushes drawn along by a hand,   *75*
So that the sky overhead was left streaked
  with seven bands in all of the colors
    the sun makes his bow of, and Delia her sash.   *78*
These banners receded into the distance
  farther than I could see, and to my eye
    the outermost were about ten paces apart.   *81*
Beneath a sky as beautiful as I describe
  came twenty-four elders, two by two,
    each of them wearing a crown of lilies.   *84*
All were chanting, "Blessed are you
  among the daughters of Adam,
    and blessed be your beauty forever."   *87*

When the flowers and other fresh foliage
  on the opposite bank across the stream
    were left without those chosen people,   *90*
There followed, as light in the heavens
  is followed by light, four living creatures,
    each of them crowned with verdant leaves.   *93*
And each of them had six feathered wings,
  wings full of eyes; the eyes of Argus,
    were he alive, would be like those.   *96*

A descriver lor forme più non spargo
rime, lettor; ch'altra spesa mi strigne,
99 tanto ch'a questa non posso esser largo;
ma leggi Ezechïel, che li dipigne
come li vide da la fredda parte
102 venir con vento e con nube e con igne;
e quali i troverai ne le sue carte,
tali eran quivi, salvo ch'a le penne
105 Giovanni è meco e da lui si diparte.

Lo spazio dentro a lor quattro contenne
un carro, in su due rote, trïunfale,
108 ch'al collo d'un grifon tirato venne.
Esso tendeva in sù l'una e l'altra ale
tra la mezzana e le tre e tre liste,
111 sì ch'a nulla, fendendo, facea male.
Tanto salivan che non eran viste;
le membra d'oro avea quant' era uccello,
114 e bianche l'altre, di vermiglio miste.
Non che Roma di carro così bello
rallegrasse Affricano, o vero Augusto,
117 ma quel del Sol saria pover con ello;
quel del Sol che, svïando, fu combusto
per l'orazion de la Terra devota,
120 quando fu Giove arcanamente giusto.
Tre donne in giro da la destra rota
venian danzando; l'una tanto rossa
123 ch'a pena fora dentro al foco nota;
l'altr' era come se le carni e l'ossa
fossero state di smeraldo fatte;
126 la terza parea neve testé mossa;
e or parëan da la bianca tratte,
or da la rossa; e dal canto di questa
129 l'altre toglien l'andare e tarde e ratte.
Da la sinistra quattro facean festa,
in porpore vestite, dietro al modo
132 d'una di lor ch'avea tre occhi in testa.

I cannot fling out more verses, reader,
  to describe their forms; pinched by other costs,
    I cannot afford to be lavish here.   *99*
But read Ezekiel, who depicts them
  just as he saw them, descending
    from the cold in wind, cloud, and fire,   *102*
And just as you will find them in his pages,
  such were they there, except that on the wings
    John is with me and disagrees with him.   *105*

The space defined by these four beasts contained
  a triumphal chariot that rolled on two wheels
    behind a griffin, to whose neck it was yoked.   *108*
The griffin's two uplifted wings straddled
  the middle band of light, with three on each side,
    so that he harmed no band by cutting through it, *111*
And the wings rose so high that they were lost to sight.
  Its body was golden where it was a bird,
    and the rest was white, with vermilion touches. *114*
Not only did Rome never gratify
  an Africanus or an Augustus
    with so splendid a chariot, but even the Sun *117*
Had not one so fine when it went off course
  and was consumed at the devout Earth's prayer
    to Jove, whose justice was mysterious.   *120*
Three ladies came dancing a circle dance
  at the right wheel, one of them so ruddy
    she would hardly have been noticed in a fire; *123*
Another was as if her flesh and bones
  were made of emerald; and the third
    was as white as new-fallen snow.   *126*
They seemed to be led now by the white one,
  now by the red, and from this one's song
    the others took their tempo, fast or slow.   *129*
By the left wheel four other ladies danced,
  clothed in purple, following the measure
    of one of them who had three eyes in her head. *132*

Appresso tutto il pertrattato nodo
vidi due vecchi in abito dispari,
135   ma pari in atto e onesto e sodo.
L'un si mostrava alcun de' famigliari
di quel sommo Ipocràte che natura
138   a li animali fé ch'ell' ha più cari;
mostrava l'altro la contraria cura
con una spada lucida e aguta,
141   tal che di qua dal rio mi fé paura.
Poi vidi quattro in umile paruta;
e di retro da tutti un vecchio solo
144   venir, dormendo, con la faccia arguta.

E questi sette col primaio stuolo
erano abitüati, ma di gigli
147   dintorno al capo non facëan brolo,
anzi di rose e d'altri fior vermigli;
giurato avria poco lontano aspetto
150   che tutti ardesser di sopra da' cigli.
E quando il carro a me fu a rimpetto,
un tuon s'udì, e quelle genti degne
153   parvero aver l'andar più interdetto,
fermandosi ivi con le prime insegne.

Behind the whole group I have just described
  I saw two old men, unlike in dress
    but alike in bearing, venerable and grave.   *135*
One of them clearly belonged to the clan
  of the great Hippocrates, whom Nature made
    for the creatures who are dearest to her.   *138*
The other showed a contrary concern,
  with a sword so bright and sharp that it made me
    quake with fear on the other side of the stream.   *141*
Then I saw four folk of humble aspect;
  and behind them all an old man coming
    all alone, asleep, and with shrewd features.   *144*

And these seven were like the first band,
  in their garments, but around their heads
    no lilies were woven into a garland,   *147*
But roses rather, and other flowers so red
  that one who viewed them from a little farther away
    would swear they were on fire above their brows.   *150*
When the chariot pulled up across the stream,
  thunder was heard, and that throng without fault,
    forbidden to advance farther, it would seem,   *153*
Behind their lead banners came to a halt.

Canto XXX

THE PROCESSION OF THE CHURCH *Triumphant comes to a halt and turns to face the chariot. Songs and cries of praise ring out from the group. A woman appears on the chariot clothed in white, green, and red. Dante, realizing who she must be, turns in excitement to Virgil, only to find that his guide has left him. The woman tells Dante to forestall his tears and*

Quando il settentrïon del primo cielo,
    che né occaso mai seppe né orto
3   né d'altra nebbia che di colpa velo,
e che faceva lì ciascun accorto
    di suo dover, come 'l più basso face
6   qual temon gira per venire a porto,
fermo s'affisse: la gente verace,
    venuta prima tra 'l grifone ed esso,
9   al carro volse sé come a sua pace;
e un di loro, quasi da ciel messo,
    "*Veni, sponsa, de Libano*" cantando
12   gridò tre volte, e tutti li altri appresso.

Quali i beati al novissimo bando
    surgeran presti ognun di sua caverna,
15   la revestita voce alleluiando,
cotali in su la divina basterna
    si levar cento, *ad vocem tanti senis*,
18   ministri e messaggier di vita etterna.
Tutti dicean: "*Benedictus qui venis!*"
    e fior gittando e di sopra e dintorno,
21   "*Manibus*, oh, *date lilïa plenis!*"

Io vidi già nel cominciar del giorno
    la parte orïental tutta rosata,
24   e l'altro ciel di bel sereno addorno;

288

finally identifies herself as Beatrice. Beatrice's harsh reception of Dante is tempered by the charitable singing of the angels, and the pilgrim is reduced to tears. Beatrice then describes Dante's descent into corruption and his straying from the right path, which she herself had set him upon.

When the Seven Stars of the first Heaven,
  that never knew either setting or rising
    nor veil of any cloud than that of sin   *3*
And that made each one there aware of his duty,
  just as the stars of the Bear lower down
    enable the helmsman to come into port—   6
When those stars had stopped still, the truthful people
  who had first come between them and the griffin
    turned to the chariot as to their peace.   9
And one of them, as if sent from Heaven,
  sang out thrice, "*Veni, sponsa de Libano*,"
    and then all the others joined in as well.   *12*

As the blessed at the last trumpet blast
  will rise at once, each from his tomb,
    singing Alleluia with reclothed voices,   *15*
So upon the divine chariot there rose,
  ad vocem tanti senis, a hundred
    ministers and messengers of life eternal.   *18*
All of them cried, "*Benedictus qui venis!*"
  and, scattering flowers up and around,
    "*Manibus, oh, date lilia plenis!*"   *21*

I have sometimes seen at the break of day
  the eastern horizon suffused with rose
    while the rest of the sky was bright and clear,   *24*

e la faccia del sol nascere ombrata,
  sì che per temperanza di vapori
27   l'occhio la sostenea lunga fïata:
così dentro una nuvola di fiori
  che da le mani angeliche saliva
30   e ricadeva in giù dentro e di fori,
sovra candido vel cinta d'uliva
  donna m'apparve, sotto verde manto
33   vestita di color di fiamma viva.
E lo spirito mio, che già cotanto
  tempo era stato ch'a la sua presenza
36   non era di stupor, tremando, affranto,
sanza de li occhi aver più conoscenza,
  per occulta virtù che da lei mosse,
39   d'antico amor sentì la gran potenza.
Tosto che ne la vista mi percosse
  l'alta virtù che già m'avea trafitto
42   prima ch'io fuor di püerizia fosse,
volsimi a la sinistra col respitto
  col quale il fantolin corre a la mamma
45   quando ha paura o quando elli è afflitto,
per dicere a Virgilio: "Men che dramma
  di sangue m'è rimaso che non tremi:
48   conosco i segni de l'antica fiamma."
Ma Virgilio n'avea lasciati scemi
  di sé, Virgilio dolcissimo patre,
51   Virgilio a cui per mia salute die'mi;
né quantunque perdeo l'antica matre,
  valse a le guance nette di rugiada,
54   che, lagrimando, non tornasser atre.

"Dante, perché Virgilio se ne vada,
  non pianger anco, non piangere ancora;
57   ché pianger ti conven per altra spada."

Quasi ammiraglio che in poppa e in prora
  viene a veder la gente che ministra
60   per li altri legni, e a ben far l'incora;

And the face of the sun rising through mist
  that tempered its brightness in such a way
    that the eye could sustain it for a long while.   *27*
So too within a cloud of flowers
  that rose from the hands of the angels and then
    fell down within and without the chariot,   *30*
There appeared to me, crowned in olive
  above a white veil, a lady mantled in green
    whose dress was the color of living flame;   *33*
And my spirit, which for so long a time
  had been trembling in awe of her presence
    but had not yet been completely overcome,   *36*
Now, not through further visual knowledge
  but an unseen virtue emanating from her,
    felt the great power of our early love.   *39*
And as soon as my eyes did feel the force
  of that transcendent virtue that had already
    pierced me before I was out of my boyhood,   *42*
I turned to my left with all of the trust
  of a little child who runs to his mama
    when he is scared or in some kind of distress,   *45*
To say to Virgil, "Not a drop of blood
  is left in my body that is not trembling:
    I recognize the signs of the ancient flame."   *48*
But Virgil had left us bereft of himself,
  Virgil, sweetest father, Virgil to whom
    I entrusted myself for my salvation;   *51*
Nor was all that our ancient mother lost
  enough to keep my dew-washed cheeks
    from turning dark again with tears.   *54*

"Dante, do not weep yet because Virgil
  has gone away; do not weep yet!
    There is another sword that will make you weep!"   *57*

Like an admiral who goes from stern to prow
  to see the men serving on the other ships
    and encourages them to do their best,   *60*

in su la sponda del carro sinistra,
  quando mi volsi al suon del nome mio,
63   che di necessità qui si registra,
vidi la donna che pria m'appario
  velata sotto l'angelica festa,
66   drizzar li occhi ver' me di qua dal rio.
Tutto che 'l vel che le scendea di testa,
  cerchiato de le fronde di Minerva,
69   non la lasciasse parer manifesta,
regalmente ne l'atto ancor proterva
  continüò come colui che dice
72   e 'l più caldo parlar dietro reserva:

"Guardaci ben! Ben son, ben son Beatrice.
  Come degnasti d'accedere al monte?
75   non sapei tu che qui è l'uom felice?"

Li occhi mi cadder giù nel chiaro fonte;
  ma veggendomi in esso, i trassi a l'erba,
78   tanta vergogna mi gravò la fronte.
Così la madre al figlio par superba,
  com' ella parve a me; perché d'amaro
81   sente il sapor de la pietade acerba.
Ella si tacque; e li angeli cantaro
  di sùbito "*In te, Domine, speravi*";
84   ma oltre "*pedes meos*" non passaro.
Sì come neve tra le vive travi
  per lo dosso d'Italia si congela,
87   soffiata e stretta da li venti schiavi,
poi, liquefatta, in sé stessa trapela,
  pur che la terra che perde ombra spiri,
90   sì che par foco fonder la candela;
così fui sanza lagrime e sospiri
  anzi 'l cantar di quei che notan sempre
93   dietro a le note de li etterni giri;
ma poi che 'ntesi ne le dolci tempre
  lor compatire a me, par che se detto
96   avesser: "Donna, perché sì lo stempre?"

So too on the left side of the chariot,
  when I turned there at the sound of my name,
    which of necessity is recorded here,   63
I saw the lady, who had first appeared to me
  shrouded by the angelic festival,
    direct her eyes to me across the stream.   66
Although the veil that fell from her head,
  encircled with Minerva's olive leaves,
    did not allow her to be seen distinctly,   69
She was royal in her mien and ever severe
  as she continued to speak, like someone
    who saves the hottest words till the end.   72

"Look at me well. I am indeed, I am indeed
  Beatrice! How did you dare to climb the mountain?
    Did you not know that man is happy here?"   75

My eyes fell down to the clear water, but,
  seeing myself there, I drew them back to the grass,
    so great was the shame that weighed on my brow.   78
She seemed as harsh to me as a mother
  might seem to her son, for stern pity
    has a savor that is bitter to taste.   81
Now she was silent, and the angels
  suddenly sang, "*In te, Domine, speravi,*"
    but did not continue beyond "*pedes meos.*"   84
Just as snow in the living timber
  along Italy's spine is blown, frozen,
    and compacted by Slavonic winds,   87
And then, liquefied, trickles through itself,
  provided Africa blows in some warm air,
    so that it seems like a candle melted by flame—   90
So was I without tears or sighs
  before the chants of those who sing forever
    in harmony with the eternal spheres.   93
But when I heard how in their sweet, tempered modes
  they took my side, just as if they had said,
    "Lady, why are you so sharp with him?"—   96

lo gel che m'era intorno al cor ristretto,
  spirito e acqua fessi, e con angoscia
99   de la bocca e de li occhi uscì del petto.

Ella, pur ferma in su la detta coscia
  del carro stando, a le sustanze pie
102   volse le sue parole così poscia:
"Voi vigilate ne l'etterno die,
  sì che notte né sonno a voi non fura
105   passo che faccia il secol per sue vie;
onde la mia risposta è con più cura
  che m'intenda colui che di là piagne,
108   perché sia colpa e duol d'una misura.
Non pur per ovra de le rote magne,
  che drizzan ciascun seme ad alcun fine
111   secondo che le stelle son compagne,
ma per larghezza di grazie divine,
  che sì alti vapori hanno a lor piova,
114   che nostre viste là non van vicine,
questi fu tal ne la sua vita nova
  virtüalmente, ch'ogne abito destro
117   fatto averebbe in lui mirabil prova.
Ma tanto più maligno e più silvestro
  si fa 'l terren col mal seme e non cólto,
120   quant' elli ha più di buon vigor terrestro.
Alcun tempo il sostenni col mio volto:
  mostrando li occhi giovanetti a lui,
123   meco il menava in dritta parte vòlto.
Sì tosto come in su la soglia fui
  di mia seconda etade e mutai vita,
126   questi si tolse a me, e diessi altrui.
Quando di carne a spirto era salita,
  e bellezza e virtù cresciuta m'era,
129   fu' io a lui men cara e men gradita;
e volse i passi suoi per via non vera,
  imagini di ben seguendo false,
132   che nulla promession rendono intera.

Then the ice that had cramped my heart
  became breath and water, and poured with anguish
    from my breast and through my mouth and eyes.   *99*

She remained motionless on the aforesaid side
  of the chariot, then addressed these words
    to those merciful, angelic beings: *102*
"You keep watch in the everlasting day,
  so that neither night nor slumber steals from you
    a single step the world makes on its way;   *105*
And so my answer is more concerned
  that he who weeps there may understand me,
    so that fault and grief may be of equal measure.   *108*
Not only by the work of the celestial wheels,
  which direct every seed to some purposed end
    in accordance with its accompanying stars,   *111*
But by the largesse of divine acts of grace,
  which have as their rain vapors so exalted
    that our vision does not begin to approach them,   *114*
Was this man so blessed in his youth, virtually
  so well endowed, that every sound disposition
    would have been marvelously borne out in him.   *117*
But the more the land has good and strong soil,
  the more it becomes wild and rank with weeds
    when uncultivated and poorly sown.   *120*
For a while I sustained him with the expression
  on my face, and my youthful eyes turned him
    toward the right goal and led him with me.   *123*
But when on the threshold of my second age
  I exchanged my life, this man deserted me
    and gave himself over to other causes.   *126*
When I had ascended from flesh to spirit,
  and beauty and virtue were enhanced in me,
    I was less dear and less welcome to him,   *129*
And he turned his steps along a path not true,
  pursuing false images of the good
    that never fulfill the promises they make.   *132*

Né l'impetrare ispirazion mi valse,
  con le quali e in sogno e altrimenti
135   lo rivocai: sì poco a lui ne calse!
Tanto giù cadde, che tutti argomenti
  a la salute sua eran già corti,
138   fuor che mostrarli le perdute genti.
Per questo visitai l'uscio d'i morti,
  e a colui che l'ha qua sù condotto,
141   li prieghi miei, piangendo, furon porti.
Alto fato di Dio sarebbe rotto,
  se Letè si passasse e tal vivanda
144   fosse gustata sanza alcuno scotto
di pentimento che lagrime spanda."

Nor did it avail me to obtain inspirations
  with which I called him back, both in dreams
    and otherwise, so little did they matter.   *135*
He fell so low that every device
  for his salvation was now deficient,
    except to show him the souls that were lost.   *138*
To this end I visited the mouth of Hell
  and went to him who has led him up here,
    offering my prayers, and weeping as well.   *141*
The high decree of God would be broken
  if Lethe were crossed and such a feast as appears
    were tasted without some kind of token   *144*
Of contrition that flows in a flood of tears."

Canto XXXI

In continuation of her speech *begun in canto XXX, Beatrice continues her berating of the pilgrim, demanding from him a confession of his past sins and inconsistency toward herself. In a choked voice, Dante admits his faults before bursting into tears under the relief of confession. Beatrice asks what drew Dante's love away from her, and Dante claims he was distracted by present pleasures. Beatrice commends his confession but goes on to explain how he should have remained faithful to her even after her earthly death. Beatrice continues her harsh criticism and orders the*

"O tu che se' di là dal fiume sacro,"
    volgendo suo parlare a me per punta,
3   che pur per taglio m'era paruto acro,
ricominciò, seguendo sanza cunta,
    "dì, dì se questo è vero: a tanta accusa
6   tua confession conviene esser congiunta."
Era la mia virtù tanto confusa,
    che la voce si mosse, e pria si spense
9   che da li organi suoi fosse dischiusa.
Poco sofferse; poi disse: "Che pense?
    Rispondi a me; ché le memorie triste
12   in te non sono ancor da l'acqua offense."
Confusione e paura insieme miste
    mi pinsero un tal "sì" fuor de la bocca,
15   al quale intender fuor mestier le viste.
Come balestro frange, quando scocca
    da troppa tesa, la sua corda e l'arco,
18   e con men foga l'asta il segno tocca,
sì scoppia' io sottesso grave carco,
    fuori sgorgando lagrime e sospiri,
21   e la voce allentò per lo suo varco.

pilgrim to raise his head and look at her. She stands, facing the griffin, even more beautiful than she had appeared in Dante's memory. Dante faints from remorse and grief. On awakening, he finds he is being pulled through the river Lethe by Matelda. She then leads Dante to the group of nymphs. Dante and his companions approach Beatrice, who still stands watching the griffin, whose two natures are reflected in her eyes. The nymphs call on Beatrice to turn her gaze upon the pilgrim.

"You on the other side of the sacred stream,"
  she said, turning on me the point of her words
    that had seemed sharp enough with just their edge,   *3*
And then went on to say without a pause,
  "Say it, say if this is true. Your confession
    must be joined to an accusation like this."   *6*
My faculties were so confounded
  that my voice started up but spent itself
    before it issued from my organs of speech.   *9*
She waited, and then said, "What are you thinking?
  Answer me. Your sinful memories
    have not yet been washed away by the water."   *12*
Confusion and fear mingled together
  forced from my mouth a kind of "yes,"
    but you had to read my lips to hear it.   *15*
As a crossbow will crack when it is cocked
  with too much tension on the cord and bow,
    so that the arrow strikes home with much less force,   *18*
So did I collapse beneath that heavy load,
  disgorging a flood of tears and sighs
    as my voice struggled to come from my throat.   *21*

Ond' ella a me: "Per entro i mie' disiri,
   che ti menavano ad amar lo bene
24   di là dal qual non è a che s'aspiri,
quai fossi attraversati o quai catene
   trovasti, per che del passare innanzi
27   dovessiti così spogliar la spene?
E quali agevolezze o quali avanzi
   ne la fronte de li altri si mostraro,
30   per che dovessi lor passeggiare anzi?"

Dopo la tratta d'un sospiro amaro,
   a pena ebbi la voce che rispuose,
33   e le labbra a fatica la formaro.
Piangendo dissi: "Le presenti cose
   col falso lor piacer volser miei passi,
36   tosto che 'l vostro viso si nascose."

Ed ella: "Se tacessi o se negassi
   ciò che confessi, non fora men nota
39   la colpa tua: da tal giudice sassi!
Ma quando scoppia de la propria gota
   l'accusa del peccato, in nostra corte
42   rivolge sé contra 'l taglio la rota.
Tuttavia, perché mo vergogna porte
   del tuo errore, e perché altra volta,
45   udendo le serene, sie più forte,
pon giù il seme del piangere e ascolta:
   sì udirai come in contraria parte
48   mover dovieti mia carne sepolta.
Mai non t'appresentò natura o arte
   piacer, quanto le belle membra in ch'io
51   rinchiusa fui, e che so' 'n terra sparte;
e se 'l sommo piacer sì ti fallio
   per la mia morte, qual cosa mortale
54   dovea poi trarre te nel suo disio?
Ben ti dovevi, per lo primo strale
   de le cose fallaci, levar suso
57   di retro a me che non era più tale.

At that she said, "Within your desire for me
  that was leading you to love the good
    beyond which there is nothing to aspire to,   24
What pitfalls did you find in your path,
  or what chains did you find that caused you
    to cast aside all hope of going on?   27
And what enticements or advantages
  did you find displayed on others' faces
    that you felt obliged to strut before them?"   30

After I had heaved a bitter sigh,
  I barely had the voice to make an answer
    and my lips labored to form the words.   33
In tears I said, "Whatever was before me,
  with its false pleasures, turned my steps aside
    the moment your face was hidden from me."   36

And she, "If you had been silent, or had denied
  what you have just confessed, your fault would be
    no less observed—so great is the Judge.   39
But when the accusation of the sin
  bursts from one's own mouth, in our court
    the grindstone turns back to blunt the sword's edge.   42
Still, that you may now bear shame for your error,
  and so that if on a future occasion
    you hear the sirens you may be stronger,   45
Set aside the seeds of tears and listen
  so you will hear how my buried flesh
    ought to have put you on an opposite path.   48
Never did nature or art present to you
  such pleasing beauty as the fair limbs
    that enclosed me then and are now scattered dust.   51
And if beauty so surpassing failed you
  at my death, what mortal thing on earth
    should then have captured your desire?   54
Indeed, at the very first arrow shot
  by deceitful things, you should have risen up
    and followed me, who was no longer of them.   57

Non ti dovea gravar le penne in giuso,
  ad aspettar più colpo, o pargoletta
60   o altra novità con sì breve uso.
Novo augelletto due o tre aspetta;
  ma dinanzi da li occhi d'i pennuti
63   rete si spiega indarno o si saetta."

Quali fanciulli, vergognando, muti
  con li occhi a terra stannosi, ascoltando
66   e sé riconoscendo e ripentuti,
tal mi stav' io; ed ella disse: "Quando
  per udir se' dolente, alza la barba,
69   e prenderai più doglia riguardando."

Con men di resistenza si dibarba
  robusto cerro, o vero al nostral vento
72   o vero a quel de la terra di Iarba,
ch'io non levai al suo comando il mento;
  e quando per la barba il viso chiese,
75   ben conobbi il velen de l'argomento.

E come la mia faccia si distese,
  posarsi quelle prime creature
78   da loro aspersïon l'occhio comprese;
e le mie luci, ancor poco sicure,
  vider Beatrice volta in su la fiera
81   ch'è sola una persona in due nature.
Sotto 'l suo velo e oltre la rivera
  vincer pariemi più sé stessa antica,
84   vincer che l'altre qui, quand' ella c'era.
Di penter sì mi punse ivi l'ortica,
  che di tutte altre cose qual mi torse
87   più nel suo amor, più mi si fé nemica.
Tanta riconoscenza il cor mi morse,
  ch'io caddi vinto; e quale allora femmi,
90   salsi colei che la cagion mi porse.

You should never have allowed some young thing
  or passing novelty to cause your wings to droop
    as you waited for another blow to land.   60
A fledgling might allow two or three attempts,
  but before the eyes of a full-fledged bird
    in vain is any net or arrow deployed."   63

As children who are ashamed stand mute
  with their eyes on the ground, listening,
    seeing what they have done and repenting,   66
Just so stood I. And then she said, "Grieved
  as you are now by what you hear, lift your beard,
    and what you see will bring you more grief."   69

Whether uprooted by our northern wind
  or a warm wind blowing from Iarbas' land,
    a sturdy oak puts up less resistance   72
Than I did when ordered to lift my chin.
  And when she said "beard" to ask for my face,
    I recognized the venom in her words.   75

When I finally did lift up my head,
  I saw that those primordial creatures
    had paused from scattering flowers about,   78
And my eyes, that were still a little blurry,
  made out Beatrice turning toward the beast
    that has two natures but is only one person.   81
Even beneath her veil and beyond the stream
  she surpassed her former self in beauty
    more than she had surpassed all others on earth.   84
The nettle of remorse stung me so much then
  that the more anything had ever lured me
    to its love, the more I hated that thing now.   87
My conscience gnawed so much at my heart
  that I fainted and fell. What happened to me then
    she who was the reason for it knows.   90

Poi, quando il cor virtù di fuor rendemmi,
  la donna ch'io avea trovata sola
93   sopra me vidi, e dicea: "Tiemmi, tiemmi!"
Tratto m'avea nel fiume infin la gola,
  e tirandosi me dietro sen giva
96   sovresso l'acqua lieve come scola.
Quando fui presso a la beata riva,
  "*Asperges me*" sì dolcemente udissi,
99   che nol so rimembrar, non ch'io lo scriva.
La bella donna ne le braccia aprissi;
  abbracciommi la testa e mi sommerse
102   ove convenne ch'io l'acqua inghiottissi.
Indi mi tolse, e bagnato m'offerse
  dentro a la danza de le quattro belle;
105   e ciascuna del braccio mi coperse.
"Noi siam qui ninfe e nel ciel siamo stelle;
  pria che Beatrice discendesse al mondo,
108   fummo ordinate a lei per sue ancelle.
Merrenti a li occhi suoi; ma nel giocondo
  lume ch'è dentro aguzzeranno i tuoi
111   le tre di là, che miran più profondo."
Così cantando cominciaro; e poi
  al petto del grifon seco menarmi,
114   ove Beatrice stava volta a noi.
Disser: "Fa che le viste non risparmi;
  posto t'avem dinanzi a li smeraldi
117   ond'Amor già ti trasse le sue armi."
Mille disiri più che fiamma caldi
  strinsermi li occhi a li occhi rilucenti,
120   che pur sopra 'l grifone stavan saldi.
Come in lo specchio il sol, non altrimenti
  la doppia fiera dentro vi raggiava,
123   or con altri, or con altri reggimenti.
Pensa, lettor, s'io mi maravigliava,
  quando vedea la cosa in sé star queta,
126   e ne l'idolo suo si trasmutava.

When my heart had restored my sense of the world,
  I saw above me the lady I had found alone,
    and she was saying, "Hold on to me, hold on!"   93
She had already brought me into the river
  up to my neck, and, pulling me behind her,
    was skimming the water as light as a shuttle.   96
When I was getting close to the blessed shore
  I heard "*Asperges me*" sung so sweetly
    I can't remember it, much less describe it.   99
The beautiful lady opened her arms
  and embracing my head dipped me under,
    where I could not help but swallow some water.   102
Then she drew me out and led me bathed
  into the dance of the four lovely ones,
    and each of them covered me with an arm.   105
"Here we are nymphs, and in Heaven stars.
  Before Beatrice descended to the world
    we were ordained to be her handmaids.   108
We will bring you to her eyes; but the three
  on the other side, who see more deeply,
    will sharpen your eyes with their joyous inner light."   111
Thus these four began singing, and then
  brought me up to the breast of the griffin
    where Beatrice stood turned toward us   114
And went on to say, "Do not withhold your gaze.
  We have placed before you the very emeralds
    from which Love once shot his arrows at you."   117
A thousand desires hotter than flame
  bound my eyes to those eyes that flashed light
    and still were fixed on the griffin alone.   120
Just as the sun shines forth from a mirror
  that twofold beast radiated from her eyes
    now one, and now another of its natures.   123
Consider, Reader, if I was astonished
  when I saw the thing stand still in itself
    while its image continually changed its form.   126

Mentre che piena di stupore e lieta
l'anima mia gustava di quel cibo
129   che, saziando di sé, di sé asseta,
sé dimostrando di più alto tribo
ne li atti, l'altre tre si fero avanti,
132   danzando al loro angelico caribo.
"Volgi, Beatrice, volgi li occhi santi,"
era la sua canzone, "al tuo fedele
135   che, per vederti, ha mossi passi tanti!
Per grazia fa noi grazia che disvele
a lui la bocca tua, sì che discerna
138   la seconda bellezza che tu cele."

O isplendor di viva luce etterna,
chi palido si fece sotto l'ombra
141   sì di Parnaso, o bevve in sua cisterna,
che non paresse aver la mente ingombra,
tentando a render te qual tu paresti
144   là dove armonizzando il ciel t'adombra,
quando ne l'aere aperto ti solvesti?

While my soul, full of amazement and joy,
  was tasting that food that both satisfies
    and stimulates hunger for itself,   *129*
The other three, whose bearing showed
  their higher order, now came forward
    dancing to the tune of angelic music.   *132*
"Turn, Beatrice," they sang, "turn your holy eyes
  upon your faithful one, for he has come far
    and traveled so many paces to see you.   *135*
For grace's sake do us the grace to unveil
  your mouth to him, that he may discern
    the deeper beauty that you conceal."   *138*

O splendor of living light eternal!
  Who has ever grown so pale in the shade
    of Parnassus, or drunk so deep from its well   *141*
That he would not be a study in frustration
  when trying to render you as you were then
    in your free and open self-revelation   *144*
Under the canopy of that harmonious Heaven?

CANTO XXXII

CONTINUING THE SCENE WITH WHICH *canto XXXI closed, the pilgrim's gaze remains fixed upon Beatrice's smile. The nymphs reproach him for his too-fixed attention. Following a moment of stunned blindness as his eyes adjust to other sights, the pilgrim sees the triumphal procession of the Church turning eastward and departing. The chariot drawn by the griffin moves off, and Dante, Statius, and Matelda follow it. The procession reaches a tall tree devoid of foliage. The griffin draws the chariot to the*

Tant' eran li occhi miei fissi e attenti
  a disbramarsi la decenne sete,
3   che li altri sensi m'eran tutti spenti.
Ed essi quinci e quindi avien parete
  di non caler—così lo santo riso
6   a sé traéli con l'antica rete!—;
quando per forza mi fu vòlto il viso
  ver' la sinistra mia da quelle dee,
9   perch' io udi' da loro un "Troppo fiso!"
e la disposizion ch'a veder èe
  ne li occhi pur testé dal sol percossi,
12   sanza la vista alquanto esser mi fée.
Ma poi ch'al poco il viso riformossi
  (e dico "al poco" per rispetto al molto
15   sensibile onde a forza mi rimossi),
vidi 'n sul braccio destro esser rivolto
  lo glorïoso essercito, e tornarsi
18   col sole e con le sette fiamme al volto.
Come sotto li scudi per salvarsi
  volgesi schiera, e sé gira col segno,
21   prima che possa tutta in sé mutarsi;
quella milizia del celeste regno
  che procedeva, tutta trapassonne
24   pria che piegasse il carro il primo legno.

*base of the tree and the tree bursts into leaf. The host then sings a hymn
that overcomes the pilgrim's senses, and he falls asleep. The pilgrim is
awakened by a bright light and by Matelda calling to him. Beatrice is now
sitting at the base of the tree surrounded by the seven nymphs and next
to the empty chariot. The group then witnesses a drama representing the
corruption of the Church.*

My eyes remained fixed on her, and so intent
  on satisfying a ten-year thirst
    that all my other senses were lost, 3
Enclosed on every side with walls
  of sheer indifference, as her sacred smile
    pulled them to herself with their net of old, 6
Until my gaze was forced to turn
  off to my left by those goddesses,
    whom I heard cry, "Too fixed a stare!" 9
At that moment it was as if my eyes
  had just been smitten by the sun,
    leaving me without vision for a while. 12
But when my eyes adjusted to lesser sights
  (and I say lesser only in comparison
    to the greater from which I was forced to turn) 15
I noticed that the glorious army
  had wheeled to its right and now faced east,
    with the seven candles and the sun before it. 18
Just as a squadron under uplifted shields
  turns to save itself, following its standards,
    before the entire force can reform its ranks, 21
So too the soldiers of the heavenly kingdom
  who were marching out front had all passed by
    before the chariot turned its leading yoke. 24

Indi a le rote si tornar le donne,
  e 'l grifon mosse il benedetto carco
27   sì, che però nulla penna crollonne.
La bella donna che mi trasse al varco
  e Stazio e io seguitavam la rota
30   che fé l'orbita sua con minore arco.
Sì passeggiando l'alta selva vòta,
  colpa di quella ch'al serpente crese,
33   temprava i passi un'angelica nota.
Forse in tre voli tanto spazio prese
  disfrenata saetta, quanto eramo
36   rimossi, quando Bëatrice scese.

Io senti' mormorare a tutti "Adamo";
  poi cerchiaro una pianta dispogliata
39   di foglie e d'altra fronda in ciascun ramo.
La coma sua, che tanto si dilata
  più quanto più è sù, fora da l'Indi
42   ne' boschi lor per altezza ammirata.

"Beato se', grifon, che non discindi
  col becco d'esto legno dolce al gusto,
45   poscia che mal si torce il ventre quindi."
Così dintorno a l'albero robusto
  gridaron li altri; e l'animal binato:
48   "Sì si conserva il seme d'ogne giusto."
E vòlto al temo ch'elli avea tirato,
  trasselo al piè de la vedova frasca,
51   e quel di lei a lei lasciò legato.
Come le nostre piante, quando casca
  giù la gran luce mischiata con quella
54   che raggia dietro a la celeste lasca,
turgide fansi, e poi si rinovella
  di suo color ciascuna, pria che 'l sole
57   giunga li suoi corsier sotto altra stella;
men che di rose e più che di vïole
  colore aprendo, s'innovò la pianta,
60   che prima avea le ramora sì sole.

Then the ladies returned to the chariot's wheels
  and the griffin drew its blessed burden
    without a single of his feathers being ruffled.   *27*
The fair lady who had pulled me through the ford
  and Statius and I were following the wheel
    that made a smaller arc as it turned,   *30*
And passing under the high limbs of a wood
  made void by fault of her who trusted the snake,
    we marched to the rhythm of angelic song.   *33*
We had gone perhaps three times as far
  as an arrow flies from the string of a bow
    when Beatrice stepped down from the chariot.   *36*

I heard everyone there murmuring, "Adam,"
  and then they circled a tree stripped of its leaves
    and everything else that grew on its branches,   *39*
Which spread more widely the higher the tree rose,
  and whose height would cause even an Indian
    in his native forest to gaze with wonder.   *42*

"Blessed are you, griffin, that your beak
  does not plunder this tree's fruit, sweet to taste
    but that wrenches the belly later with pain."   *45*
All the others around the mighty tree
  shouted these words, and the twin-natured beast
    replied, "So is the seed of justice preserved."   *48*
Turning to the yoke-pole that he had pulled
  he drew it to the foot of the widowed trunk
    and left it bound to that from which it had come.   *51*
As our plants, when the great cascade of light
  falls upon them, mingled with the rays
    of the constellation that follows Pisces,   *54*
Begin to swell, and then renew themselves,
  each with its own color, before the Sun
    hitches his coursers to other stars,   *57*
Just so, assuming a hue less red than rose
  yet deeper than violet, the tree whose branches
    had just been so bare now made itself new.   *60*

Io non lo 'ntesi, né qui non si canta
   l'inno che quella gente allor cantaro,
63   né la nota soffersi tutta quanta.
S'io potessi ritrar come assonnaro
   li occhi spietati udendo di Siringa,
66   li occhi a cui pur vegghiar costò sì caro;
come pintor che con essempro pinga,
   disegnerei com' io m'addormentai;
69   ma qual vuol sia che l'assonnar ben finga.
Però trascorro a quando mi svegliai,
   e dico ch'un splendor mi squarciò 'l velo
72   del sonno, e un chiamar: "Surgi: che fai?"
Quali a veder de' fioretti del melo
   che del suo pome li angeli fa ghiotti
75   e perpetüe nozze fa nel cielo,
Pietro e Giovanni e Iacopo condotti
   e vinti, ritornaro a la parola
78   da la qual furon maggior sonni rotti,
e videro scemata loro scuola
   così di Moïsè come d'Elia,
81   e al maestro suo cangiata stola;
tal torna' io, e vidi quella pia
   sovra me starsi che conducitrice
84   fu de' miei passi lungo 'l fiume pria.
E tutto in dubbio dissi: "Ov' è Beatrice?"
   Ond' ella: "Vedi lei sotto la fronda
87   nova sedere in su la sua radice.
Vedi la compagnia che la circonda:
   li altri dopo 'l grifon sen vanno suso
90   con più dolce canzone e più profonda."

E se più fu lo suo parlar diffuso,
   non so, però che già ne li occhi m'era
93   quella ch'ad altro intender m'avea chiuso.
Sola sedeasi in su la terra vera,
   come guardia lasciata lì del plaustro
96   che legar vidi a la biforme fera.

The hymn that the company chanted then
  I could not understand; it is not sung on earth,
    and I could not bear to hear the music through.   *63*
If I could describe how those pitiless eyes
  were lulled to sleep by the story of Syrinx,
    those eyes whose long vigil cost so dearly,   *66*
I would depict, as a painter working
  from a model might, how I nodded off.
    But good luck on portraying how you fall asleep.   *69*
I will pass on therefore to when I awoke
  and say that a brightness tore through sleep's veil,
    as did the call, "Arise; what are you doing?"   *72*
As, when brought to the blossoming apple tree
  that makes the angels hungry for its fruit
    and hosts perpetual marriage feasts in Heaven,   *75*
Peter, James, and John, overcome with fear,
  returned to themselves again at the word
    by which deeper slumbers than theirs were broken,   *78*
And saw their company's number diminished
  by Moses and Elijah, and saw too
    the transfiguration of their teacher—   *81*
Such did I become. And then I saw, standing
  above me, the same pious, kind lady
    who had guided my steps along the river;   *84*
And, all in doubt, I asked, "Where is Beatrice?"
  And she answered, "See her sitting on the root
    beneath the new blossoms of the tree,   *87*
And see the company that encircle her.
  The rest are ascending behind the griffin
    with song that is sweeter and more profound."   *90*

I do not know if she went on to say more,
  for now there appeared before my eyes
    she who had sequestered all my other thoughts.   *93*
She was sitting there alone on the bare ground,
  as if left behind to guard the chariot
    that I had seen the biform creature bind.   *96*

In cerchio le facevan di sé claustro
  le sette ninfe, con quei lumi in mano
99   che son sicuri d'Aquilone e d'Austro.

"Qui sarai tu poco tempo silvano;
  e sarai meco sanza fine cive
102   di quella Roma onde Cristo è romano.
Però, in pro del mondo che mal vive,
  al carro tieni or li occhi, e quel che vedi,
105   ritornato di là, fa che tu scrive."
Così Beatrice; e io, che tutto ai piedi
  d'i suoi comandamenti era divoto,
108   la mente e li occhi ov' ella volle diedi.

Non scese mai con sì veloce moto
  foco di spessa nube, quando piove
111   da quel confine che più va remoto,
com' io vidi calar l'uccel di Giove
  per l'alber giù, rompendo de la scorza,
114   non che d'i fiori e de le foglie nove;
e ferì 'l carro di tutta sua forza;
  ond' el piegò come nave in fortuna,
117   vinta da l'onda, or da poggia, or da orza.

Poscia vidi avventarsi ne la cuna
  del triünfal veiculo una volpe
120   che d'ogne pasto buon parea digiuna;
ma, riprendendo lei di laide colpe,
  la donna mia la volse in tanta futa
123   quanto sofferser l'ossa sanza polpe.

Poscia per indi ond' era pria venuta,
  l'aguglia vidi scender giù ne l'arca
126   del carro e lasciar lei di sé pennuta;
e qual esce di cuor che si rammarca,
  tal voce uscì del cielo e cotal disse:
129   "O navicella mia, com' mal se' carca!"

The seven nymphs formed a cloister around her
  and held up lights that would not be blown out
    even should Aquilo and Auster rage. *99*

"Here for a short time you will dwell in the woods
  and then forever be a citizen with me
    of that Rome where Christ Himself is Roman. *102*
And so, for the sake of the ailing world
  keep your eyes on the chariot, and what you see
    make sure you write down upon your return." *105*
Thus Beatrice. And I, in my devotion
  prostrate at the feet of her commands,
    gave my eyes and my mind to what she willed. *108*

Never has lightning descended so swiftly
  out of a cloudbank, plunging down
    from the remotest regions of the sky, *111*
As I saw Jove's bird, the eagle, swoop down
  and plummet through the tree, shredding its bark
    along with its blossoms and fresh, new leaves. *114*
It struck the chariot with all of its force,
  battering it like a ship in a storm
    driven by waves now leeward, now windward. *117*

Then I saw, leaping into the cradle
  of the triumphal vehicle, a vixen
    that seemed starved of proper nourishment, *120*
But, railing at its vile transgression,
  my lady drove the creature back
    as fast as its fleshless bones could carry it. *123*

Next, from where it had arrived before,
  I saw the eagle dive into the chariot's box
    and leave it feathered with its plumage. *126*
I heard then a voice that came from the sky
  but sounding like it came from a grieving heart:
    "O my little ship, how ill are you laden!" *129*

Poi parve a me che la terra s'aprisse
  tr'ambo le ruote, e vidi uscirne un drago
132   che per lo carro sù la coda fisse;
e come vespa che ritragge l'ago,
  a sé traendo la coda maligna,
135   trasse del fondo, e gissen vago vago.
Quel che rimase, come da gramigna
  vivace terra, da la piuma, offerta
138   forse con intenzion sana e benigna,
si ricoperse, e funne ricoperta
  e l'una e l'altra rota e 'l temo, in tanto
141   che più tiene un sospir la bocca aperta.

Trasformato così 'l dificio santo
  mise fuor teste per le parti sue,
144   tre sovra 'l temo e una in ciascun canto.
Le prime eran cornute come bue,
  ma le quattro un sol corno avean per fronte:
147   simile mostro visto ancor non fue.

Sicura, quasi rocca in alto monte,
  seder sovresso una puttana sciolta
150   m'apparve con le ciglia intorno pronte;
e come perché non li fosse tolta,
  vidi di costa a lei dritto un gigante;
153   e basciavansi insieme alcuna volta.
Ma perché l'occhio cupido e vagante
  a me rivolse, quel feroce drudo
156   la flagellò dal capo infin le piante;
poi, di sospetto pieno e d'ira crudo,
  disciolse il mostro, e trassel per la selva,
159   tanto che sol di lei mi fece scudo
a la puttana e a la nova belva.

Then it seemed to me the earth gaped open
  between the wheels, and I saw a dragon rise
    and stick his tail up through the chariot;   *132*
Then, as a wasp withdraws its sting, it drew back
  its poisonous tail, pulling out with it
    part of the floor before it slithered off.   *135*
What remained was again covered, as fertile soil
  is covered with weeds, but this time with plumage,
    offered perhaps with sincere, kind intent,   *138*
And both of the wheels and the chariot pole
  were completely covered over with feathers
    in less time than a sigh keeps the lips open.   *141*

Transformed in this way, the sacred edifice
  sprouted heads on all of its parts,
    three on the pole and one on each corner.   *144*
The first three heads were horned like oxen;
  but the others had single horns on their brows:
    such a monster has never been seen before.   *147*

Sitting on it, a disheveled whore,
  as secure as a fortress on a high mountain,
    was batting her eyes. I saw her there,   *150*
And saw a giant standing beside her,
  as if to prevent her being taken from him,
    and time and again they would kiss each other.   *153*
But because she turned her lustful, roving eye
  upon me, her savage lover mercilessly
    beat the harlot from head to foot.   *156*
Then, fierce with rage and full of jealousy,
  he pulled the monster from the tree and drew it
    so far off that the forest screened from me   *159*
Both the harlot and that bizarre, monstrous brute.

CANTO XXXIII

BEATRICE AND THE SEVEN NYMPHS *lament the corruption of the contemporary Church. Beatrice encourages the pilgrim to express his questions, but he points out that she already knows his thoughts and wishes. Beatrice presents an obscure and prophetic speech, interpreting the visionary events of canto XXXII. The pilgrim explains that he cannot understand her complex words; Beatrice replies that recognizing the deficiency of his*

"*Deus, venerunt gentes,*" alternando
or tre or quattro dolce salmodia,
3   le donne incominciaro, e lagrimando;
e Bëatrice, sospirosa e pia,
quelle ascoltava sì fatta, che poco
6   più a la croce si cambiò Maria.
Ma poi che l'altre vergini dier loco
a lei di dir, levata dritta in pè,
9   rispuose, colorata come foco:
"*Modicum, et non videbitis me;
et iterum, sorelle mie dilette,*
12   *modicum, et vos videbitis me.*"
Poi le si mise innanzi tutte e sette,
e dopo sé, solo accennando, mosse
15   me e la donna e 'l savio che ristette.
Così sen giva; e non credo che fosse
lo decimo suo passo in terra posto,
18   quando con li occhi li occhi mi percosse;
e con tranquillo aspetto "Vien più tosto,"
mi disse, "tanto che, s'io parlo teco,
21   ad ascoltarmi tu sie ben disposto."
Sì com' io fui, com' io dovëa, seco,
dissemi: "Frate, perché non t'attenti
24   a domandarmi omai venendo meco?"

own knowledge is an important part of his learning process. The pilgrim is
amazed that he has no memory of ever having strayed from his devotion
to Beatrice; the lady reminds him that he has drunk from the river Lethe,
which wipes out the memory of sin. The group comes to the river Eunoe,
and Dante is led through its waters again by Matelda. The pilgrim is now
prepared for his journey into the heavens.

"*Deus, venerunt gentes,*" alternating
  between three and four, the ladies began
    a sweet psalmody, and wept as they sang.   *3*
And Beatrice, sighing and full of pity,
  was listening to them, so deeply moved
    that Mary was little more so at the Cross.   *6*
But when these other virgins gave way
  for her to speak, she rose up on her feet
    and, colored like fire she responded,   *9*
"*Modicum et non videbitis me*;
  et iterum, my beloved sisters,"
    modicum et vos videbitis me."   *12*
Then she set all seven in front of her;
  and behind her, with a gesture, myself
    and the lady and the sage that remained.   *15*
Then she went on, and I don't believe
  she had taken her tenth step on the ground
    when with her eyes she struck my own   *18*
And said to me with a tranquil look,
  "Come more quickly, so that if I speak with you
    you will be well placed to listen to me."   *21*
As soon as I was with her, as was my duty,
  she said to me, "Brother, now that you are with me,
    why do you not try to ask me something?"   *24*

Come a color che troppo reverenti
dinanzi a suo maggior parlando sono,
27 che non traggon la voce viva ai denti,
avvenne a me, che sanza intero suono
incominciai: "Madonna, mia bisogna
30 voi conoscete, e ciò ch'ad essa è buono."
Ed ella a me: "Da tema e da vergogna
voglio che tu omai ti disviluppe,
33 sì che non parli più com' om che sogna.
Sappi che 'l vaso che 'l serpente ruppe,
fu e non è; ma chi n'ha colpa, creda
36 che vendetta di Dio non teme suppe.
Non sarà tutto tempo sanza reda
l'aguglia che lasciò le penne al carro,
39 per che divenne mostro e poscia preda;
ch'io veggio certamente, e però il narro,
a darne tempo già stelle propinque,
42 secure d'ogn' intoppo e d'ogne sbarro,
nel quale un cinquecento diece e cinque,
messo di Dio, anciderà la fuia
45 con quel gigante che con lei delinque.
E forse che la mia narrazion buia,
qual Temi e Sfinge, men ti persuade,
48 perch' a lor modo lo 'ntelletto attuia;
ma tosto fier li fatti le Naiade,
che solveranno questo enigma forte
51 sanza danno di pecore o di biade.
Tu nota; e sì come da me son porte,
così queste parole segna a' vivi
54 del viver ch'è un correre a la morte.
E aggi a mente, quando tu le scrivi,
di non celar qual hai vista la pianta
57 ch'è or due volte dirubata quivi.
Qualunque ruba quella o quella schianta,
con bestemmia di fatto offende a Dio,
60 che solo a l'uso suo la creò santa.

Just as someone with too much reverence
  speaks in the presence of his superiors
    but cannot quite drag his voice to his lips,   *27*
So was I then, and without fully formed words
  I began, "My lady, you know what I need
    and you know how best to fulfill it."   *30*
And she said to me, "I want you from now on
  to divest yourself of fear and shame
    so that you don't talk like a man in a dream.   *33*
Know that the vessel the serpent broke
  was and is not; and let the guilty party
    believe that God's vengeance fears no hindrance.   *36*
The eagle that feathered the chariot,
  whereby it became monstrous and then a prey,
    will not be forever without an heir;   *39*
For I see clearly and will therefore foretell
  that stars already near promise us a time
    safe from all delay and free of obstacles,   *42*
When a Five Hundred Ten and Five
  sent by God will slay the thievish woman
    and the giant who sins alongside her.   *45*
Perhaps my words, as dark as those of Themis
  or of the Sphinx, are less persuasive
    because, like theirs, they enshroud your mind.   *48*
But soon the facts will be the Naiads
  that will solve this difficult enigma,
    without the loss of flocks or ears of grain.   *51*
Take note of them; and make known these words,
  just as they come from me, to those
    who live the life that is a race to death.   *54*
And when you write them keep in mind
  not to conceal what you have seen of the tree
    that now has twice been plundered here.   *57*
Whoever robs that tree or does it harm
  offends God with an act of blasphemy,
    Who for His own purpose made it sacred.   *60*

Per morder quella, in pena e in disio
  cinquemilia anni e più l'anima prima
63   bramò colui che 'l morso in sé punio.
Dorme lo 'ngegno tuo, se non estima
  per singular cagione esser eccelsa
66   lei tanto e sì travolta ne la cima.
E se stati non fossero acqua d'Elsa
  li pensier vani intorno a la tua mente,
69   e 'l piacer loro un Piramo a la gelsa,
per tante circostanze solamente
  la giustizia di Dio, ne l'interdetto,
72   conosceresti a l'arbor moralmente.
Ma perch' io veggio te ne lo 'ntelletto
  fatto di pietra e, impetrato, tinto,
75   sì che t'abbaglia il lume del mio detto,
voglio anco, e se non scritto, almen dipinto,
  che 'l te ne porti dentro a te per quello
78   che si reca il bordon di palma cinto."

E io: "Sì come cera da suggello,
  che la figura impressa non trasmuta,
81   segnato è or da voi lo mio cervello.
Ma perché tanto sovra mia veduta
  vostra parola disïata vola,
84   che più la perde quanto più s'aiuta?"

"Perché conoschi," disse, "quella scuola
  c'hai seguitata, e veggi sua dottrina
87   come può seguitar la mia parola;
e veggi vostra via da la divina
  distar cotanto, quanto si discorda
90   da terra il ciel che più alto festina."
Ond' io rispuosi lei: "Non mi ricorda
  ch'i' stranïasse me già mai da voi,
93   né honne coscïenza che rimorda."
"E se tu ricordar non te ne puoi,"
  sorridendo rispuose, "or ti rammenta
96   come bevesti di Letè ancoi;

For having eaten of that tree the first soul pined
  in pain and longing five thousand years and more
    for Him who took upon Himself that bite.   63
Your wits are sleeping if you do not think
  there is a special reason why it stands so tall
    and why its canopy is upside down.   66
And if your thoughts had not, like Elsa's water,
  petrified your mind, and your delight in them
    not been like Pyramus staining the mulberry,   69
The events themselves would have shown you
  the moral nature of the justice of God
    in His interdiction of the tree.   72
But since I see that your mind indeed
  has turned to stone and been stained so dark
    that the light of my words only dazzles you,   75
I would like for you to bear them within you,
  if not written, at least depicted, just as
    a pilgrim returns with his palm-wreathed staff."   78

And I replied, "Just as wax under a seal
  does not alter the imprinted figure,
    so has my brain now been stamped by you.   81
But why is it that your long-desired words
  soar up so far beyond my sight
    that the harder I try the more I lose them?"   84

"So that you may understand," she said,
  "the school that you have followed,
    and see if its doctrine accords with my words,   87
And so that you may see that your way
  is as far from the divine as the highest heaven
    that spins the fastest is as far from earth."   90
To which I responded, "I do not remember
  ever estranging myself from you,
    nor does my conscience gnaw me for that."   93
"And if you are not able to remember that,"
  she answered with a smile, "do recall
    how you have drunk of Lethe today.   96

e se dal fummo foco s'argomenta,
  cotesta oblivïon chiaro conchiude
   99   colpa ne la tua voglia altrove attenta.
Veramente oramai saranno nude
  le mie parole, quanto converrassi
   102   quelle scovrire a la tua vista rude."

E più corusco e con più lenti passi
  teneva il sole il cerchio di merigge,
   105   che qua e là, come li aspetti, fassi,
quando s'affisser, sì come s'affigge
  chi va dinanzi a gente per iscorta
   108   se trova novitate o sue vestigge,
le sette donne al fin d'un'ombra smorta,
  qual sotto foglie verdi e rami nigri
   111   sovra suoi freddi rivi l'alpe porta.
Dinanzi ad esse Ëufratès e Tigri
  veder mi parve uscir d'una fontana,
   114   e, quasi amici, dipartirsi pigri.

"O luce, o gloria de la gente umana,
  che acqua è questa che qui si dispiega
   117   da un principio e sé da sé lontana?"
Per cotal priego detto mi fu: "Priega
  Matelda che 'l ti dica." E qui rispuose,
   120   come fa chi da colpa si dislega,
la bella donna: "Questo e altre cose
  dette li son per me; e son sicura
   123   che l'acqua di Letè non gliel nascose."
E Bëatrice: "Forse maggior cura,
  che spesse volte la memoria priva,
   126   fatt' ha la mente sua ne li occhi oscura.
Ma vedi Eünoè che là diriva:
  menalo ad esso, e come tu se' usa,
   129   la tramortita sua virtù ravviva."

Come anima gentil, che non fa scusa,
  ma fa sua voglia de la voglia altrui
   132   tosto che è per segno fuor dischiusa;

And if we think where there is smoke there is fire,
  then your forgetfulness provides clear proof
    that turning your will elsewhere was a sin.   *99*
But from now on my words will truly be
  as naked as is necessary
    to make them plain to your crude sight."   *102*

Burning more brightly and with slower steps,
  the sun now held the meridian circle,
    which shifts position from different vantage points,   *105*
When all of a sudden, just as a guide will stop
  in front of a group if he happens upon
    something strange or its vestiges,   *108*
The seven ladies stopped at the edge
  of a patch of pale shade, such as mountains cast
    over cold streams running beneath dark boughs.   *111*
In front of them it seemed to me I saw
  the Tigris and Euphrates pour from one spring
    and then part from each other slowly like friends.   *114*

"O light, O glory of the human race,
  what water is this here that gushes out
    from one source and then splits into two?"   *117*
She answered my question by saying, "Ask this
  of Matelda." And the beautiful lady,
    as if exculpating herself, responded,   *120*
"This and other things as well I have told him,
  and I am certain that Lethe's waters
    did not hide it from him." And Beatrice said,   *123*
"Perhaps it was some greater concern,
  which often diminishes the memory,
    that has shadowed over the eyes of his mind.   *126*
But see Eunoe that flows forth there.
  Bring him to it and, as you are accustomed,
    revive his enfeebled faculties."   *129*

As a gentle spirit that makes no excuse,
  but makes another's will its own
    just as soon as a signal is given,   *132*

così, poi che da essa preso fui,
   la bella donna mossesi, e a Stazio
135   donnescamente disse: "Vien con lui."

S'io avessi, lettor, più lungo spazio
   da scrivere, i' pur cantere' in parte
138   lo dolce ber che mai non m'avria sazio;
ma perché piene son tutte le carte
   ordite a questa cantica seconda,
141   non mi lascia più ir lo fren de l'arte.
Io ritornai da la santissima onda
   rifatto sì come piante novelle
144   rinovellate di novella fronda,
puro e disposto a salire a le stelle.

So, when she had taken me in hand,
  the beautiful lady said to Statius
    in a gracious manner, "Now come with him."   *135*

If, Reader, I had more space to deploy
  my writing, I would sing now, at least in part,
    of that sweet drink that could never cloy.   *138*
But since none of the sheets prepared from the start
  for this canticle still remain vacant,
    I am restrained by the curb of my art.   *141*
Like a tree that has been rejuvenated
  with fresh new leaves, those most sacred waters
    returned me now as if newly created,   *144*
Pure and made ready to ascend to the stars.

Notes

Canto I

1–3   *little boat of my native wit*   The poet's "wit" (*ingegno*) is a key point of tension throughout the *Commedia*: how can he balance his poetic and intellectual brilliance with the need to recognize his own human limitations in the face of God? The metaphor of the boat on the sea may recall Ulysses' fateful voyage (*Inf.* XXVI): the story of a man who overvalued his own *ingegno* and tried to pass beyond the limits allotted to human knowledge by sailing to Purgatory, only to be justly punished for his presumption. The metaphor of a boat journey to describe the *Commedia* itself will recur at the opening of the *Paradiso* (II.1–18).

4–6   *second kingdom*   We find here described in brief the purpose of this "second kingdom," Purgatory.

8–9   *O sacred Muses . . . Calliope*   Calliope is the Muse of epic poetry who is often evoked by the Roman authors who inspired Dante: Ovid (*Met.* V.338–39), Virgil (*Aen.* IX.525), and Horace (*Odes* III.4).

10–12   *the wretched daughters of Pierus*   Dante is referring here to the story told by Ovid (*Met.* V.294–678) of the daughters of King Pierus. The women challenged the Muses to a singing contest. Although they lost, they remained haughty and defiant and so, as a punishment, they were transformed by the gods into magpies. Other stories mentioned in the *Commedia* in which mortals unwisely challenge the gods to contests of skill are those of Arachne (*Inf.* XVII.14–18) and Marsyas (*Par.* I.19–22).

13–18   *sweet color*   The evocation of dawn here marks a striking change in mood from the darkness and hopelessness of Hell and is an important introduction to the theme of rebirth in this canto and *cantica*. The new beginning and feelings of rebirth that we associate with dawn are a forerunner of the spiritual rebirth that will take place in Purgatory. Furthermore, the cosmic details that the poet provides identify this dawn as Easter day 1300. Therefore, the resurrection that the canto describes is seen in the light of Christ's own Resurrection.

13   *sapphire*   An important symbolic stone in medieval thought signifying purity and freedom. Dante also later describes the Virgin Mary as a sapphire (*Par.* XXIII.101).

19   *the beautiful planet*   Venus. Dante refers to a belief in the power of the planets to influence human action.

21   *the Fishes*   The constellation of Pisces.

22–24   *I turned to the right*   In descending through Hell, passing through the center of the Earth and out on the other side, Dante and Virgil have arrived in the Southern Hemisphere, which Dante believed had remained uninhabited since Adam and Eve were expelled from the Garden of Eden. At this moment, Dante turns to face the south and sees stars that have not been seen by human beings since the Fall.

31   *an old man alone*   Although not named in this canto, this is Marcus Porcius Cato, a Roman statesman who committed suicide when the liberty of the Roman Republic was destroyed by civil war and replaced by the Empire. The paradox of why Dante, an enthusiastic advocate for imperial rule, should allot such honor to Cato as he does here has been a source of extensive scholarly discussion. Cato is repeatedly referred to by Dante in his different works as an example of Roman virtue and a defender of civil liberty and justice (*Conv.* IV.28.16; *Mon.* II.5.15–16).

37   *four most holy stars*   The four stars that Dante sees here are later identified as emblems of the four cardinal virtues: Justice, Prudence, Temperance, and Fortitude (*Purg.* XXIX.121–32, XXXI.106–9). That they shine so vividly here on Cato reiterates his importance as the representative of Roman moral virtue.

40–48   *Who are you*   The uniqueness of Dante's journey is highlighted here by Cato's questions. Cato mistakes the travelers for damned shades who have somehow and against divine law escaped from Hell. The questions provide a useful narrative excuse for Virgil to reiterate the reasons behind the pilgrim's journey.

49–51   *made me bow my head*   The development of humility is one of the great themes of the *Purgatorio*. The humble position that Virgil here makes Dante adopt is an important first step in the pilgrim's learning process. The reverential kneeling and bowed head are also an enactment of Church ritual, identifying Purgatory as a place governed by Christian laws.

52   *a lady*   We know from *Inf.* II that this lady is Beatrice.

61–68   *I was sent to his aid*   Virgil provides for Cato an account of the events that took place in the *Inferno* cantos I and II when he came to Dante's aid in order to act as his guide through Hell and now through Purgatory impelled by the wishes of Beatrice and assisted by divine aid.

71–75   *one who has given his life*   Virgil appeals to Cato to understand the pilgrim's thirst for liberty since the Roman had gone so far as to commit suicide in the name of freedom.

77–79   *Minos does not bind me*   Here Virgil refers to his own infernal home in Limbo that lies on the boundary of Hell and outside of Minos' jurisdiction.

79   *your Marcia*   Cato's wife whom he divorced in an act of stoicism but who later returns faithfully to him. Dante is drawing on Lucan's account of Cato and Marcia in the *Pharsalia* book II.

82   *your seven realms*   The first indication of the structure of Purgatory and an acknowledgement of Cato's authority over it.

80–93   *yours for her*   Virgil seeks to win Cato's favor by promising to take his greetings back to his once beloved wife Marcia, who now dwells in Limbo. Cato's refusal to be swayed by his earlier earthly attachments and his response instead to the will of the "Lady of Heaven" highlights the change in values that will govern this new realm. This is a strong contrast to the inhabitants of Hell who were so eager to dwell on their past earthly lives. In Purgatory it is God, not the world, who is the aim. The difference in insight between the unredeemed pagan Virgil and the enlightened Cato (who was released from Limbo in the Harrowing of Hell [*Inf.* IV.46–63]) is also revealed in this encounter.

88   *evil river*   The river Acheron, which passes through Hell.

102–5   *some reeds*   Cato's description of the reeds that grow around the shores of Purgatory is a further reminder of the lessons of humility on which this canto and *cantica* focus. The reed, flexible and unresisting to the will of the wind, is a positive symbol for this humility. That Dante must here gird himself with the reed is emblematic of the spiritual state he must now adopt.

121–29   *We came to a place*   Since the rejuvenating dawn imagery of its opening lines, this canto has been marked with an atmosphere of resurrection and rebirth. At this point the pilgrim too begins his own rebirth as the stains and tears of Hell are washed from his face. This ritualistic washing echoes the sacrament of baptism, which removes original sin and welcomes the new believer into the community of the Church.

134–36   *the humble sprout*   The reed that Virgil plucks to tie around Dante's waist, in another striking image of rebirth, immediately regrows in the same place.

Canto II

1–6   *The sun now had reached that horizon*   The canto opens with a complex description of sunrise over Purgatory. The explanation emphasizes the relation of Purgatory to Jerusalem that sits on the exact opposite side of the globe and shares its meridian. Night is imagined as another cosmic point that rises from the east (the direction of the Ganges) in the constellation of Libra (the scales) that disappears as night progresses.

7–9   *lovely Aurora*   The goddess of the dawn. Dante uses the personified Aurora to describe the dawn also in *Purg.* IX.1–6, IXX.1–6, and XXVII.109–14.

13–24   *I saw that light*   This detailed description of the approach of the heavenly boat piloted by an angel is a stunning account of the workings of the senses and perception. Evocations of speed, brilliance, and color all combine to vividly recreate the scene and build up expectation—what will this light turn out to be? The theme of the power and limitations of human sense perception recurs throughout the *Commedia* and is often used to carry a moral or theological message about the necessary limitations of human capacities in the face of the mysteries of God.

28–30   *Down on your knees*   As at the meeting with Cato, Virgil guides Dante to the correct reverential gestures due to the individual he is encountering. Virgil, although a pagan, demonstrates a surprising knowledge of the rules of Purgatory at this early stage.

29   *Angel of the Lord*   As Virgil tells him, this is the first of many angels that Dante will encounter during his ascent through Purgatory. They are the bringers of divine messages and the enactors of divine will.

31–42   *See how*   The description of the heavenly vessel and its angelic pilot is in stark and open contrast to the description of the infernal Charon, who ferries the souls across the river Styx and into Hell (*Inf.* III.82–120).

46   *In exitu Israël de Aegypto*   This is the opening line of Ps. 113, which describes the exodus of the enslaved Israelites as they left Egypt and journeyed to the Promised Land. The themes of freedom and deliverance that the psalm tells provide an important subtext to the arrival of these souls in Purgatory. They too have been freed by the Will of God from the enslavement of sin. Traditionally the psalm was sung on Easter Sunday—itself a reiteration of the sacrifice of the Passover and the liberation of the Israelites— the day on which these fictional events are in fact occurring. The story of the exodus is an extremely important intertext to the *Commedia* as a whole.

47–48   *They began to sing*   While Hell was a realm of discord and chaotic noise, Purgatory is characterized by communal singing. The harmonious singing of the souls reflects their newfound unity of purpose. Choral singing is also a reference to the liturgy of the Church. Liturgical rituals are a central structuring and narrative feature of the *Purgatorio*. The sign of the Cross with which the angel marks the souls as they leave the boat is another element of the liturgical scene.

55–56   *The Sun's arrows*   Dante uses a cosmic metaphor to indicate the time of day, the constellation Capricorn (the goat) being driven off the center of the sky by the pursuing arrows of the rising sun.

67–69   *the breaths I drew*   This is the first of several moments during the *Purgatorio* at which the fact that the pilgrim is still alive in his body is emphasized (see also III.18, III.88–99, V.4–6, V.25–36, XXVI.7–12). The wonder of the souls on realizing this reminds us of the strangeness and uniqueness of the experience Dante is describing.

71   *messenger who bears an olive branch*   It was still customary in Dante's day that a messenger bringing good news would carry an olive branch.

79–81   *Oh empty shades*   Dante fruitlessly attempts to embrace the insubstantial shade, emphasizing the corporeality of the pilgrim in contrast to the incorporeality of the souls. The scene is based on Virgil's *Aeneid* in which the Roman poet describes the meeting in the underworld of the Trojan hero Aeneas with his dead father Anchises (*Aen.* VI.792–94, II.700–702).

91   *Casella*   Little is known of the historical Casella although it is speculated that he was a singer and friend of Dante living in Florence. This encounter has provoked much scholarly consideration since it is the first of the encounters in the *Purgatorio* between Dante and friends from his own life.

91–92   *I make this journey*   The pleasing paradox expressed in these lines reminds us of the purpose of personal salvation that underlines the pilgrim's journey.

98–99   *For three months*   These lines are a subtle reference to the jubilee year that was established by Pope Boniface VIII in 1300. During this year all pilgrims who came to Rome and visited the basilicas of St Peter and St Paul were granted plenary indulgences that released them from the time they would otherwise have had to spend in Purgatory.

106   *new law*   Referring to the new law of love and forgiveness of sins that governs Purgatory in contrast to the old law of punishment and retribution that governed Hell. This is a further indication of the newness of this realm, another of the elements employed in these early cantos by which it is distinguished from Hell.

112   *Love that converses with me*   A canzone by Dante that is the focus of the *Convivio* book 3 and that was probably written in the 1290s. Dante in the *Convivio* interprets the poem as an allegorical praise of philosophy, although its status as a courtly love lyric and as a theological exploration has also been considered by later scholars.

115–18   *nothing touched our minds*   The effect of Casella's song upon his listeners contains within it a powerful comment on the state of the listening souls and the pilgrim himself. Despite being at the threshold of Purgatory, about to begin an ascent that will lead them to their ultimate desire, they are waylaid and distracted by earthly music. This continuing attachment to sensory beauty, although criticized by the irate Cato, is a touching acknowledgement of the pleasure of human art that draws the listening souls together. It also, however, emphasizes the continuing imperfection of the pilgrim and surrounding souls who can still be held back from God by earthly distraction.

119–23   *the venerable old man*   Cato's spirited entrance in which he berates the souls for their distraction and tardiness is a moment of comic drama touched with serious intent that breaks the meditative spell cast by Casella's song. He reminds both souls and reader of the true purpose of this journey: to shed the distractions of the world and attain God.

124   *Doves*   Dante makes frequent uses of metaphors drawn from the natural world to evoke the mood and details of his descriptions. Here the souls who had been intent upon Casella's song only to be driven off by Cato's rebuke are compared to intently feeding doves who are disturbed and take sudden flight. In this case they are driven on by "greater cares" to begin their purgation and move toward God.

Canto III

3   *justice sifts and searches*   Divine justice is at the heart of the redemptive scheme of Purgatory.

4–9   *my faithful companion*   Dante's praise of Virgil at the opening of the canto is striking in its loving sincerity. It is also significant, however, since it occurs at the beginning of a canto in which the roles of the two characters begin to shift. As the canto continues, the insight of the pagan Virgil is shown to be incomplete and insufficient and it is the pilgrim Dante who begins to take charge of his own journey.

14–15   *that hill most high*   This is our first real view of the mountain of Purgatory as its vast height becomes evident. All of a sudden we feel the real significance of the difficulty of the journey that faces the pilgrim as well as the clarity of his destination in "the heavens."

18   *the shadow*   Another instance in which the pilgrim's continuing corporeality is emphasized. The canto as a whole has as a major theme the significance of the body in the process of purgation. This will be further picked out in the discussion of the dead body of Virgil and the body of Manfred destroyed in battle.

19–21   *my shadow only*   A moment of great dramatic tension in which the pilgrim, seeing only one shadow on the ground before Virgil and himself, believes that his faithful guide has abandoned him. It is a moment that starkly reminds us that Dante and Virgil are not of the same state and cannot have the same destination. Virgil's eternal fate is decided while Dante's has yet to be written.

22–44   *Then Virgil my solace*   Virgil's long discourse begins by reassuring the pilgrim of his continuing presence but develops into a more profound and melancholy meditation on his own dead body, the nature of the souls in the afterlife, and the limits of human knowledge in understanding their condition. It closes with a warning not to seek beyond those limits for fear of sharing the lamentable fate of those in Limbo, who believed in the supremacy of human reason.

25–27   *It is evening*   Virgil died at Brindisi in southern Italy before his body was moved, under the orders of the Emperor Augustus, to Naples. The sharp contrast between the evening, which Virgil emphasizes as lying over his own body, and the new dawn, which has highlighted Dante's body as it stands at the foot of Purgatory, is a further instance of this canto's clear delineation of the characters' greatly differing states.

28–30   *If I cast no shadow*   Virgil asserts that the airy bodies of the souls are comparable in nature to the heavenly spheres that, despite being material, do not interrupt light. The enigma of the nature of the airy bodies is explored at different points throughout the *Purgatorio*, most notably in the discourse of Statius in canto XXV.

31–36   *The Power*   Although not named, this power (*virtù*) names the creative power of God. The re-creation of the souls after death and the purgation that they undergo is directly and mysteriously linked to God's will. At this point Virgil, a pagan, shows surprising insight into a central question of Christian doctrine, the nature of the Trinity (*One Substance in Three Persons*; see Augustine's *De Trinitate* for the foundational statement of the doctrine). The great mystery of how something can be both three and one at the same time is necessarily beyond human comprehension and, indeed, is supposed to remain that way (for biblical iterations of this idea, see Is. 55:8; Rom. 11:33).

37   *quia*   The term means "because." Virgil is advising humankind to consider things that lie within the limits of their own rational capacities without seeking to know the *why* of divine mysteries.

40–44   *you have seen*   Virgil reminds Dante of the souls he saw in Limbo, great and good individuals (*Aristotle, Plato*) who, Virgil tells us here, were brought to damnation by their inability to accept the limits of human reason by their desperate desire *to know*. The pathos of the scene is reinforced when we remember that Virgil, as a Limbo dweller, is here describing his own sad fate.

50   *Lerici and Turbia*   Two towns on the steep coastline of Liguria in northern Italy.

52–56   *Now who would know*   The usually knowledgeable Virgil is unsure of how to proceed up the mountain, and it is instead Dante who discerns the way to move forward. Although Dante's respectful tone toward Virgil is undiminished (he is still *master*), this moment marks a subtle change in their roles and levels of insight. The pagan Virgil will become increasingly unsure of how to proceed in this Christian realm, while the Christian Dante, by reason of his faith and baptism, has the potential to develop in this environment and grow in knowledge.

79–85   *As sheep*   The simile that describes this group of souls touchingly captures their new afterlife character. We find out that they are the souls of the excommunicate, who died separated from the community of the Church. Here, instead, they are compared to a flock of sheep, an image rich in biblical significance (see Ps. 22; Is. 40:11); the previously wayward, excommunicate souls are here united in humble timidity, patiently waiting to be let into the Christian community of Purgatory. The simile too, drawn in such lifelike detail from the natural world, is a reminder to focus on the tangible things of nature that lie within human understanding in contrast to the intangible reasoning of God.

88–99   *the light broken*   The second point in this canto at which the continuing presence of the pilgrim's body, revealed by his shadow, is brought to the fore. The strangeness of this is again dramatically emphasized by the surprised reaction of the souls.

103–45   *Manfred*   Natural son of the Holy Roman Emperor Frederick II of Hohenstaufen, Manfred lived 1232–1266. Manfred became regent of Italy and was later crowned king on the supposed death of the legitimate heir. When Manfred tried to secure imperial power in Italy he was excommunicated by the Pope. Manfred was killed in battle at Benevento on February 26, 1266. Manfred encouraged an intellectual and creative culture at his court. This, along with his political achievements, perhaps explains Dante's positive depiction of him here.

110–11   *Look now*   When Dante does not recognize Manfred—unsurprisingly since he would not have known him in life—Manfred identifies himself by encouraging the pilgrim to look at his wounds. Descriptions of Manfred's battle wounds were a feature of contemporary chronicles of the event, but the real impact of this scene comes from the implicit parallel Dante is making between Manfred and the risen Christ. After His Resurrection, Christ shows His wounds to His disciples as a means of verifying His identity (Lk. 24:40; Jn. 24:20). When we remember that the meeting between Dante and Manfred is taking place on Easter Sunday the parallel becomes even more striking. By comparing Manfred to Christ, Dante may be suggesting that his death too was a form of undeserved martyrdom.

112   *Empress Constance*   Wife of Henry VI of Hohenstaufen and mother of Frederick II, Constance appears in her own right as a blessed soul in *Par.* III.109–20.

119–23   *I delivered myself*   Contemporary reports also mention Manfred's deathbed conversion. By repeating this story in describing the salvation of Manfred, Dante is making a striking comparison between the authority and actions of the temporal Church and the ultimate justice and forgiveness of God. Although he was excommunicated by the Church, Manfred is saved because at the moment of his death he willingly gives himself up to the mercy of God and asks for forgiveness. The justice of God is presented as being beyond temporal authority and His mercy as being open to all who turn to receive it. Although Dante supports the authority of the Church, he is keenly aware of its corruption and fallibility.

Canto IV

1–12 *Whenever one of our senses* While this may seem a rather round-about way to express having lost track of time because he was caught up in an interesting conversation, Dante is here giving an Aristotelian account of the nature of the soul. According to Aristotle, the human soul is unitary and contains within itself the different faculties of sensation, desire, and reason. Because the soul is unitary, when it is focused intently on one thing—as Dante was focused on listening to Manfred—its other faculties (in this case, the sense of time passing) fall into the background. This is the first of several complex scientific and philosophical descriptions that mark this canto.

5 *erroneous view* This refers to Plato's view of the human soul as being three separate souls: the intellect, the animal soul, and the vegetative soul.

15 *full fifty degrees* The sun moves across the sky at around 15 degrees per hour, and so about three hours, twenty minutes have passed.

18 *Here is what you ask* The souls have led Dante and Virgil, as they requested in canto III, to a place where they can begin to ascend the mountain.

19–51 *A farmer thrusting a forkful of thorns* This passage initiates the difficult physical journey that the travelers must make up the mountain. Dante focuses upon the physical challenges of the climb, using metaphor and comparison to help his readers fully imagine its difficulties. We must remember, however, that Dante is describing not only a physical but also a moral journey. The physical experiences of the pilgrim are an integral part of his learning process. We are reminded of this at lines 27–30, where physical progress is directly linked to moral desire. The passage is also a touching presentation of the relationship of Dante and Virgil, the former exhausted and dragging himself up the mountain, the latter encouraging and pushing him onward.

25 *hike up to San Leo and down to Noli* San Leo, Noli, Bismontova, and Cacume are all Italian locations that are difficult to reach on foot, being located on high peaks or cliffs.

27–30 *here a man must fly* Desire is one of the great themes of the *Commedia*. Without it the pilgrim could not complete his journey. Here the motivating power of the pilgrim's desire is coupled with the guiding and motivating influence of Virgil, who, in his encouragement of the pilgrim, maintains his hope of attaining his desires and shows him the way toward them.

36–39   *Just keep climbing*   The pilgrim's question and Virgil's response might be seen as a small discussion on having faith. Neither Virgil nor the pilgrim knows exactly where they are going, only that they must go onward and upward, trusting that help will come to them. This exchange heightens the sense of difficulty and perseverance that this scene manifests. It is hard to resist a comparison to a tired child asking its parents, "Are we there yet?"

59   *the chariot of light*   The sun.

56–60   *was amazed*   The pilgrim is still in the process of fully comprehending his new position on the globe. Now that the sun is at its high point, he can see that it is in the north in relation to where he is now. Not having yet thought through the celestial logic of the Southern Hemisphere and its relation to the sun, he is surprised by this.

61–66   *the luminous orb*   Virgil dispels the pilgrim's surprise by explaining the logic of the sun's noonday position in the Southern Hemisphere in lyrical terms. To paraphrase, he explains that, if the sun were in the constellation of Gemini (which contains the stars Castor and Pollux) making the month late May or early June, from the travelers' current position in the Southern Hemisphere the sun would seem even farther north (toward the northern constellations of Ursa Major and Ursa Minor).

67–75   *picture both Zion and this mountain*   Virgil here reiterates the fact that the mountain of Purgatory is directly opposite Jerusalem (Zion) on the globe and shares its horizon.

72   *the road that Phaeton failed to drive*   The myth, recounted in Ovid's *Metamorphoses* (I.747–II.332), tells the story of Phaeton, son of the sun god Helios, who asked his father to allow him to drive the chariot of the sun as proof of his divine origins. Phaeton loses control of the chariot and burns a track across the sky (the Milky Way) and the Earth (the Sahara Desert). To prevent further destruction, Jupiter destroys Phaeton and the chariot with a thunderbolt. The road that Phaeton failed to drive is thus the correct daily course of the sun.

76–84   *never before have I seen as clearly*   Dante expands on Virgil's explanation and demonstrates his own understanding by explaining the position of the equator in relation to Mount Purgatory and Jerusalem.

88–96   *This mountain*   Virgil's explanation of the mountain is as much moral as it is geographical, describing the experience of climbing rather than answering the pilgrim's question on the distance to be climbed. The mountain to be climbed is one of spiritual improvement and the acquisition of moral virtue. The lower slopes are harder to climb, representing the difficulty of beginning on the path of virtue, while the higher slopes are increasingly easy as virtue is more solidly acquired.

98–135 *Belacqua* The travelers' encounter with Belacqua is one of the most gently humorous of the whole *Commedia*. The historical Belacqua was a musical instrument maker from Florence known to Dante and famous for his lethargic manner and witty tongue. Here, Dante recreates these earthly traits to create a scene that is both humorous and profound. Belacqua's sarcastic retorts (98–99, 114), which contrast with Virgil's serious tone, speak to the real physical exhaustion of the pilgrim that no doubt he feels in spite of Virgil's moral encouragement. Belacqua also mocks the pilgrim's ardent intellectual response to Virgil's explanation of the sun's position (119–20), making fun of the student's eagerness to please his master. Alongside Belacqua's mocking laziness, however, is the subtle pathos of his current position. Here we see the result of his terrestrial negligence, which condemns him to a long wait for the beginning of his penitence in Purgatory.

106–13 *One of them who seemed so weary* The physical lethargy of Belacqua is described in exquisite detail here so that even his tiny movements have weight to them.

123 *I am not grieved for you now* Although Belacqua must go through a period of waiting, his ultimate salvation is assured. Dante's words here perhaps imply an earlier fear that Belacqua might have been damned for his negligence to the circle of the neutrals in Hell (*Inf.* III).

130–32 *I delayed to the end* Belacqua is among the negligent late-repentant, those who put off turning to God until the very end of their lives. For this they are condemned to wait outside the gates of Purgatory for a time equal to their terrestrial lives.

133–35 *Unless I am aided by prayers* As we saw in the encounter with Manfred, the prayers of those still alive can have a significant effect on the length of time that souls must spend in Purgatory. The connection of Purgatory to the living world is explored throughout the *cantica*.

136–39 *But now the poet, not waiting for me* The leisurely interlude of Belacqua is cut short by Virgil, who is moving onward even as he calls to the pilgrim to come along.

Canto V

4–6 *Look at how the sun's rays* The real materiality of the pilgrim's body is again the focus of attention and introduces the importance of the body for this canto as a whole. Scenes of bodily violence and death and the use of the body as an expression of salvation characterize the canto's second half.

10–18 *Why is your mind so befuddled* Virgil's rebuke of Dante's distraction here is in keeping with the haste to progress that he showed at the end of the preceding canto. His focus of purpose and swiftness of movement are in direct contrast to the slow and dangerous negligence that the souls in this area of Purgatory demonstrate. In light of this, Virgil criticizes Dante not only for slowing down but for being distracted from his true purpose by the cares and interests of earthly life.

20–21 *turning a shade of red* Dante, affected by Virgil's rebuke, blushes for his mistake.

23 *Miserere* Probably penitential psalm 50, which was sung every day in the morning liturgical service of Lauds. This is another instance of the liturgical singing that characterizes Purgatory and that first appeared in canto II.

25–36 *When they came to realize that my body* A second even more intense moment in which the pilgrim's body is the focus of attention. This focus is heightened as the souls cut short their song to break into a gently comic "oh!" of surprise. Virgil, in explaining the situation to the souls, emphasizes the fact that Dante, as a still-living man, can take news of the souls back to Earth and there pray for them.

43–51 *Just keep on moving* Virgil again insists on continuing the journey in spite of the eagerness of the souls to talk with them. That the souls do not understand the travelers' haste (51) is perhaps a sign of their continued blindness to their own sin of negligence.

52–56 *We, all of us, met with violent deaths* This passage describes the state of these souls who, like those of canto IV, delayed their repentance until the very moment of their death. Unlike the earlier group, however, these souls all met violent deaths. The two groups are of very different character; the lethargy of Belacqua and his companions is contrasted with the activity and speed of this group of souls. Despite the violence and activity that marked their deaths, the idea of peace at the end of life is central to these souls, a peace that they could not find in life and could only find in (re) union with God. The immediacy of the relationship with God described by the souls is striking.

61–63   *by the very peace*   The peace that these souls found at the very moment of violent death is described by Dante as the compelling aim of his own journey.

64–84   *One of them began*   The first soul to tell his personal story to Dante in this canto is Jacopo del Cassero (c. 1260–1298). An ally of the Florentine Guelph party, Jacopo was chief magistrate of Rimini and Bologna and was murdered on his way to take up the same position in Milan. He was murdered on the orders of Azzo VIII of Este.

69   *between Romagna and Naples*   An area comprising Umbria, Lazio, and the Marche.

70–72   *Fano*   The town on the Adriatic course in which Jacopo was born. As his hometown, Jacopo hopes that its citizens will pray for his soul and thus decrease his time in Purgatory.

79–84   *If I had only fled toward La Mira*   Jacopo describes the tragic choice by which, in fleeing from his pursuers, he took the route over the treacherous marshes around Padua and became trapped in the reeds and mud. The slow-motion image as Jacopo watches his own blood pour onto the marshy ground is a moment of moving drama.

88–129   *I am Buonconte*   The second and most extended personal story of this canto is that of Buonconte da Montefeltro (1250–1289), a Ghibelline general and son of Guido da Montefeltro, whom Dante encountered in *Inf.* XXVII. The stories of father and son told by Dante are opposites. The political, scheming Guido allies himself with the corrupt Pope Boniface VIII, relying on papal absolution (as opposed to personal contrition) to remove his many sins. At the moment of death, however, his soul is taken down by the devil into Hell. In contrast his son Buonconte, a man of action, leaves off repenting until the very moment of his death. However, since his repentance is sincere, the devil loses the battle for his soul and Buonconte is saved.

92   *Campaldino*   The site of the battle in which Buonconte died. This battle was over the town of Arezzo and was a battle in which Dante himself fought on the side of the Guelphs. It is noteworthy that, although Buonconte fought on the opposite side, Dante allots him this place of honor.

98–99   *spilling blood*   While Jacopo dies in a slow pool of his own blood, Buonconte is described in midflight leaving a trail of blood behind him.

100–108   *At that point*   Dante picks out the dramatic moment of Buonconte's death and the argument between the angel and devil as a tale of hope for those still alive. This single moment of repentance, enacted through the naming of Mary and a single tear, is enough to save the contrite soul from damnation. The contrast to Guido da Montefeltro's death is again marked. While Guido had relied on the words of a corrupt churchman without really repenting, the honest repentance of his son needs no ecclesiastical intermediary.

118–26   *the pregnant air was turned into water*   The story of Buonconte's body swept along by the river echoes the story of Palinurus told in Virgil's *Aeneid* book VI.

127–28   *loosening the cross*   Buonconte's final act had been to form his own body into the shape of the Cross. The emphasis that this canto places on the body (the pilgrim's body, the dying bodies of Jacopo and Buonconte) is here recontextualized within the significance of Christian belief in the crucified and resurrected body of Christ. The human body can be the conduit through which salvation can come.

130–36   *I am la Pia*   The final soul to speak to Dante in this canto is that of a woman, whose exact historical identity is not certain, although she may be Pia dei Tolomei, who married Nello dei Pannocchieschi and was murdered by him in 1295. The only definite information we have is what she gives us herself; she was born in Siena and was killed in Maremma. Pia's speech is marked by a considerate courtesy toward Dante and a beautiful economy of speech that nevertheless conveys the gentle melancholy of her life.

Canto VI

1–12   *When a game of dice*   The extended opening metaphor by which the pilgrim Dante, surrounded by eager and supplicating souls, is compared to the winner of a dice game is extremely evocative. In a canto that is overtly concerned with the state of strife-ridden thirteenth-century Italy, it conjures up an image of contemporary street life.

13–24   *The Aretine was there*   An extended list of the souls found in this area of Purgatory. All are figures from Dante's contemporary Italy who met their deaths through political strife and clan warfare. This list presents a striking picture of the factionalism and violence of Italy at the time. Not all of the identifications are certain.

13–14   *The Aretine*   Benincasa da Laterina, a judge who was killed by the highwayman Ghino di Tacco.

15   *the one who drowned*   This may be Guccio dei Tarlati, who fled from the battle of Campaldino chased by or chasing his enemies.

16–18   *Federico Novello*   A member of the Conti Guidi family, Novello was killed helping one family against another. "The Pisan" may be the son of Marzucco da Scornigliano.

19   *Count Orso*   Orso was murdered by his cousin Alberto to avenge the death of Alberto's father.

19–24   *Pierre de la Brosse*   Chamberlain to Philip III of France, Pierre was hanged for having accused the queen, Mary of Brabant, of poisoning the king's son by his first wife. Dante's description here suggests that he believed Pierre to be innocent.

28–48   *O light of my mind*   Dante's important question to Virgil on the efficacy of prayer becomes a useful opportunity for the poet to consider the theoretical background to prayer and the difference between Virgil's pagan world and the redeemed world of Christianity.

29–42   *you deny in a certain passage*   Dante is referring to Virgil's *Aen.* VI.373–76. Here the hero Aeneas is told that the will of the gods cannot be changed by prayer. Virgil reconciles the tension Dante is feeling between belief in the authority of Virgil's text and the reality of the souls before his eyes by explaining that pagan prayers could have no efficacy because they were disconnected from God.

43–48   *But do not concern yourself*   One of several moments in the *Purgatorio* in which Virgil looks ahead to the coming of Beatrice, who will be able more fully to answer the pilgrim's theological doubts (see also XV.76–78, XVIII.46–48).

49–51   *let us pick up the pace*   The pilgrim's newfound energy and touching eagerness to reach Beatrice is an echo of the hope and inspiration that mention of her instilled in the fearful pilgrim of *Inf.* II.136–38.

52–57   *We will go on*   Virgil corrects the pilgrim's mistaken view that they might reach the mountain's summit before nightfall. The sun (*the one whose rays are hidden*) will reappear at least once before they attain their goal.

61–66   *But look at that soul*   The solitary stillness of this soul is in marked contrast to the rushing crowd that opened the canto. Commentators have compared this description to Lam. 3:28 ("he shall sit solitary and hold his peace") and Gen. 49:9 ("Resting you couched as a lion"). It is also reminiscent of the dignified and static souls of Dante's own Limbo.

70–74 *Sordello* The reticence of the solitary figure is entirely broken down when he learns that Virgil too originates from the area of Mantua. At this, he reveals himself to be Sordello. Sordello was a troubadour who, although Italian, composed poems in Occitan. In the *DVE* Dante criticizes Sordello for rejecting the poetic potential of his native Italian, a language that Dante himself champions. The poet's depiction of Sordello here, eager to embrace his fellow Mantuan, perhaps enacts an imagined humility and regret for his linguistic treachery. The loving meeting of the two Mantuans is also, however, an important counterpoint to the political strife and division of contemporary Italy that Dante goes on to criticize. This point is emphasized at lines 79–81.

76–151 *Ah, servile Italy* This extended and vitriolic passage is a long invective against the state of Dante's contemporary Italy. It is rhetorically rich and was instrumental in forming the idea of the Italian nation for later writers.

76–78 *house of whores* Dante's personification of corrupt Italy draws on biblical imagery from Lam. 1:1 and Is. 1:21.

88–90 *Justinian repaired the harness* The Roman emperor Justinian had ordered a thorough revision and clarification of Roman law. Dante uses the image of the harness, that which controls the willful horse, as a metaphor for law. The emperor is the one who should "ride" and "control" the wayward state, and thus Dante attributes the corruption of the state to the lack of an emperor.

97–105 *O German Albert* Albert of Hapsburg, the elected but uncrowned Holy Roman emperor. Dante criticizes Albert for abandoning the Empire and leaving it to descend into chaos and corruption. Dante singles out the greed of Albert and his father Rudolph as the cause of their negligence.

106–8 *Come see the Montecchi and Cappelletti* The Montecchi, Cappelletti, Monaldi, and Filippeschi are four families representing the divisive and divided Guelph and Ghibelline factions, whose internecine feuds were destroying Italy. The Montecchi and Filippeschi were Ghibelline families from Verona and Orvieto, respectively, while the Cappelletti and Monaldi were Guelphs from Cremona and Orvieto.

127–51 *My Florence* Dante reserves his bitterest criticism—in highly ironic terms—for his native city of Florence.

Canto VII

4–36   *I am Virgil*   The presentation that Virgil makes of himself in the
opening lines of this canto is one of the most extended and moving of the
entire poem. Although damned, he is damned for something that he could
do nothing about: being born before Christ. He, along with the other pa-
gans to be found in Limbo, was innocent of any specific sin, only lacking
the saving faith of Christianity. He is damned for what he *did not do*. Virgil
provides other accounts of his situation to the souls in Purgatory in *Purg.*
XXI.31–33 and XXII.100–15.

6   *my bones were interred by Octavian*   Virgil lived under the reign of the
Roman Emperor Augustus, also called Octavian.

14–15   *bending low*   Sordello, on hearing Virgil's identity, bends to em-
brace him around the knees in an attitude of reverence. A similar scene takes
place at the meeting between Virgil and the poet Statius in XXI.130–36.

16–17   *O glory of the Latins*   Sordello's address emphasizes the impor-
tance of Virgil in the development of the Latin language used for poetry.
Dante saw literary Latin as the model from which literature in his own
Florentine (and other vernaculars) could and should develop.

22   *the kingdom of woe*   Hell.

24   *Power from heaven moved me*   At several points in these early cantos,
Virgil reiterates the divine help that has enabled him to come to the pilgrim
Dante and guide him through the realms of the afterlife. He reminds us that
he is not an autonomous agent but is the tool and mouthpiece that is being
used to bring Dante to God.

28–30   *There is a place down there*   Virgil's concise description of Limbo
captures the essence of the scene described in *Inf.* IV but also puts a new
perspective on it. Limbo is characterized by sighing, by fruitless desire rather
than pain. However, while within the murky realm of Hell, Limbo is a place
of *light*, here, from the illuminated perspective of Purgatory, Virgil sees it
now as a place of darkness. In the context of the canto, this is a metaphorical
darkness of ignorance of faith.

31–33   *the innocent infants*   As well as the faithless pagans, Limbo is the
home of the unbaptized infants. The *human guilt* Virgil mentions is original
sin that the infants' untimely deaths prevented from being removed by the
waters of baptism. The image of the infants, clasped in the jaws of death,
is one of great pathos and contributes to the melancholy tone of Virgil's
speech as a whole.

35–36   *three holy virtues*   The three holy virtues are Faith, Hope, and Love, the central tenets of Christianity. The *other four* that Virgil mentions are Justice, Prudence, Temperance, and Fortitude. These latter were established in classical ethics, particularly in Aristotle's *Nicomachean Ethics*, and were thus "known" to Virgil and his fellow Limbo dwellers.

40–60   *We are not assigned a fixed place*   Sordello explains the rule of the mountain by which the souls are unable to ascend at night. The rule contains within it a very important message: without the guiding light of the sun (a symbol for the illumination of God) the human will is impotent and lost, unable to make any positive progress since its object is invisible. The *aimless wandering* that the souls can do at night is in contrast to the purposeful onward progress the souls must make during the sunlit hours.

61–136   *At that my lord said*   The extended description of the Valley of the Princes that occupies the second half of the canto draws heavily on Virgil's own description in the *Aeneid* book 6 of the Elysian Fields. It is also an echo of Dante's own Limbo, itself an echo of the pagan afterlife.

73–81   *Gold and fine silver*   The description of the Valley of the Princes bursts into the poem like a colorful rainbow. It is a rich and luxurious description that compares the flowers of the valley to the colors of gemstones and exotic natural dyes. Despite its beauty, however, it lacks the natural lushness and purity that will characterize the Earthly Paradise. We are still in a form of earthly court, peopled by princes and attached to material luxury.

83   *singing "Salve Regina"*   Another important instance of communal singing in *Purgatorio*. The *Salve Regina* (Hail, Queen) hymn was traditionally sung during the Compline (evening) service of the Church. This service is evoked in this scene. The hymn calls on the Virgin Mary to protect the faithful from the dangers of the night; a scene enacting these dangers and Mary's saving intervention will be played out in the next canto.

91–136   *The one sitting highest*   The final forty-five lines of the canto are dedicated to a description of the negligent princes who inhabit the valley. With this description, Dante gives a gentler picture of the problems that beset his contemporary Europe. While lacking the vitriolic fury of the end of canto VI, the description of the princes expresses the sadness of missed opportunities on the part of those who had the chance to make the world better. There is also a comic hint in these descriptions, focusing on the physical traits of the princes—particularly their noses!—and removing any grandeur that might be expected in such a regal group. Dante draws for his structure on a poem by Sordello himself that contains a descending hierarchical list beginning with an emperor and moving downward through the ranks. A central theme in Dante's list that is absent from Sordello's source poem is the degeneration of noble families in their offspring. The illustrious and honorable natures of fathers are described as being corrupted in their sons. A further striking feature is the pairing of the souls. Dante seats souls together who were in conflict during their lives, as if to show how togetherness in salvation transcends any earthly differences.

91–96   *Emperor Rudolph*   Rudolph I of Hapsburg (1212–1291) was elected Holy Roman Emperor in 1273 but did not go to Italy to be crowned. Dante criticizes Rudolph for having neglected his responsibilities and failed to resolve the political conflicts of Italy. His lack of engagement and initiative is repeated even in Purgatory as he sits apart, above the others, and does not join in their singing.

97–102   *Ottokar*   King Ottokar II of Bohemia (1253–1278), who contested Rudolph of Hapsburg's emperorship. Here instead the two figures sit together, communally lamenting their failure. The negative description of Ottokar's son Wenceslaus begins the theme of the degeneration of noble lines.

103–7   *The snub-nosed one*   Philip III, the Bold, king of France (1245–1285) beats his breast in a gesture of penitence. Philip failed to recapture Sicily—once part of France—from the Spanish and died of a fever after losing his fleet in a naval battle. The *lily* refers to the French royal coat of arms.

104–8   *the one who has a kindly look*   King Henry I of Navarre, the Fat.

109–11   *the plague of France*   Philip III and Henry I were the father and father-in-law, respectively, of Philip IV, the Fair, whom Dante harshly criticizes throughout the *Commedia* (see *Inf.* IXX.87; *Purg.* XX.85–93, XXXII.152–53; *Par.* IXX.118–20).

112   *That burly one*   Pedro (Peter) III of Aragon, who held Sicily against French reoccupation attempts. These attempts were carried out under the command of Charles of Anjou.

113   *the one with the very masculine nose*   Charles of Anjou, who, among many other titles, was king of Naples and Sicily 1266–1282.

115   *the youth who is sitting behind him*   It is most likely that this is the last-born son of Pedro III of Aragon, who never came to the throne.

119   *James and Frederick*   James was the second son of Pedro of Aragon and became king of Sicily in 1285. On his elder brother's death he became king of Aragon and transferred the kingship of Sicily to his younger brother Frederick. In spite of this, James went on to cede Sicily to Charles II of

Naples. Charles and James made war against Frederick but withdrew their troops in 1299 and Frederick was confirmed as king.

120   *the better heritage*   While inheriting their father's territorial possessions, Dante suggests that James and Frederick failed to inherit his nobility of spirit.

121–23   *Human worth*   Dante draws on the familiar image of the genealogical tree. Human worth, however, is not guaranteed because one comes from "good stock" but is on an individual basis and is only granted by the Will of God. Dante explores this question in *Conv.* IV.10–19.

124–29   *the large-nosed one*   Dante returns to considering Charles of Anjou and Peter of Aragon and the inferiority and corruption of their offspring. This complex passage, when unpicked, tells us that Charles II (the plant) was as inferior to Charles I as Charles I was to Peter II. The message is emphasized through the wives of the kings; Constance was the wife of Peter III, while Beatrice and Margaret were wives of Charles I.

130–32   *king of the simple life*   Henry III of England (reigned 1216–1272).

Canto VIII

1–6   *It was twilight*   The opening six lines of this canto are some of the most beautifully evocative of the entire poem. They explore the different emotions that the coming of night can bring about in those away from home. The sailor is filled with nostalgic longing for the loved ones he has left behind; the pilgrim is filled with melancholy for the delay night brings in his progress toward his sacred goal. The two scenes describe contrasting motions of desire, motions that underpin Dante's whole journey: the desire to return home and the desire to come to God.

8–18   *one of the souls who had risen up*   One of the many scenes in the *Purgatorio* that evokes the liturgical practices of the Church. This scene is influenced by the monastic practices of Dante's period. The solitary figure rises and turns to face the east, the direction of the rising sun toward which Church buildings were traditionally orientated. The souls together sing the traditional hymn of the Compline evening service, "Te lucis ante." The text of the hymn calls on God to protect the faithful from the temptations of the night that come in the form of sexual dreams. The fixed gaze and communal singing of the souls create an atmosphere of focused unity; we can imagine the group joined together by their fear of the coming night and their belief in the protection that will come to them.

19–21   *Sharpen well, reader, your eyes*   This enigmatic address to the reader (the first of seven in the *Purgatorio*: see IX.70–72, X.106–11, XVII.1–9, XXIX.97–105, XXXI.124–26, XXXIII.136–41) encourages us to look beneath the veil of the story Dante is telling and search for the meaning within. This does not mean, however, that the meaning is easy to find or even that it can be found. A central theme of this canto is the mystery of divine intervention and protection.

25–39   *I saw descending from above*   This canto contains a "sacred drama" that alternates with Dante's conversations with the souls. The first "act" describes the arrival of two angels. Their presence and flaming swords is reminiscent of the two angels who drove Adam and Eve out of the Garden of Eden after they had succumbed to temptation (Gen. 3:24). It is yet another element that compares this valley with the Garden of Eden. Open to different interpretations, the blunted swords that these angels hold, however, suggest that the danger in this valley is not a real threat; these souls, safe in Purgatory, are not in physical or spiritual danger.

28–29   *green as newborn leaves*   Green was traditionally the color of hope and is thus a fitting emphasis for the protection and hope of salvation that the angels bring to the souls in the valley.

31–33   *One of them alighted*   The angels land on either side of the valley, thus protectively enclosing the souls in the valley between them. They stand like sentries, guarding the space.

34–36   *their actual faces bedazzled my eyes*   Dante's second encounter with an angel in the *Purgatorio* is as overwhelming for his sight as was his first vision of the celestial boatman in canto II.

37   *Mary's bosom*   The *Salve Regina* antiphon that appeared in canto VII has already highlighted the significance of Mary's intervention for the souls in this area of Purgatory. We now find that it is she who sends the protecting angels to defend the souls threatened by the coming serpent. The expression "Mary's bosom" echoes "Abraham's bosom" mentioned in Lk. 16:22. That Mary is the ultimate guardian of the valley again sets this space apart from the Garden of Eden, the province of Eve.

53   *Noble Judge Nino*   Nino Visconti, grandson of Count Ugolino (*Inf.* XXXII–XXXIII). Nino was a judge who frequently visited Florence and thus possibly knew Dante personally as this passage seems to testify.

56–57   *How long is it*   Since darkness is falling the evidence that Dante is still alive, his shadow, is no longer visible. Nino therefore mistakes Dante for a shade like himself.

58–60   *I came this morning*   Dante for the first time in *Purgatorio* explains his own situation to a questioning soul. The *other life* referred to is life in Heaven.

66–69   *come see what God in his grace has willed*   The mysterious intervention of divine aid is a central theme of this canto as a whole. Here its relevance for the pilgrim's own journey is reiterated. Nino's words emphasize that the reason behind God's actions is forever mysterious to humanity but it is nonetheless a cause for absolute gratitude; its worth indeed lies in its mystery.

71–72   *tell my Giovanna*   Nino's only daughter. The importance of prayers from the pure hearted to aid the souls in Purgatory is reiterated.

73–81   *I do not think her mother has loved me*   Nino's melancholy reflection stems from the perceived fickleness of his wife Beatrice, who remarried soon after his death. Beatrice married Galeazzo Visconti of Milan, whose family crest was a viper. The cockerel was the crest of Nino's family.

85–93   *my famished eyes kept moving upward*   As night falls the stars become increasingly visible, and Dante notices that the four stars he had seen in the morning (I.22–25) have been replaced by three new stars. The four morning stars have been read as symbolizing the four cardinal virtues. The three stars that have replaced them symbolize the three theological virtues, Faith, Hope, and Love. The significance of this shift has been variously discussed by commentators. It may mark a shift from the active life of the daytime to the contemplative life of the night; or it perhaps signifies the historical replacement of the classical pagan era (and its moral ethics) with the new Christian era founded on grace.

95–108   *Behold our adversary*   The second act of the sacred drama that recommences here describes the arrival of the serpent in the valley. Dante's description emphasizes the sinister and sensual nature of the creature and overtly suggests an identification of this serpent with the one that tempted Eve, reiterating the connection between this valley and the Garden of Eden. In the valley, however, the snake is driven out by the protecting angels sent by the Virgin Mary. The corruption of Eden and Eve is thus replaced by the salvation of the valley through the favor of Mary.

104   *celestial raptors*   Like the "heavenly bird" (II.37) who carried the souls to the shores of Mount Purgatory, these angels are compared to birds, although here they are compared to the hunting hawks of medieval falconry.

109–20   *The shade who had drawn closer*   Currado belonged to the powerful Malaspina family that controlled territory between Lombardy and

Tuscany. The family was known for its uncommon solidarity in comparison to the violent factionalism rife in Italy as a whole.

112 *the lantern that leads you* While this lantern may certainly be interpreted as the guiding light of God's grace, it may equally refer to the pilgrim's guide, Virgil (for Virgil as lantern/light, see I.43, XXII.64–69).

113 *wax in your judgment and will* The malleability of human character and nature is a recurring trope of the *Purgatorio* and the *Paradiso*. Human nature, as it grows in humility and receptiveness to God, can be molded anew, receiving the imprint of the divine.

120 *I bore to my own the love that is purified here* Currado's words suggest an overattachment to his own family and property, an attachment that is now being replaced with a purer desire for God.

121–32 *I have never been there* The tone of praise that Dante adopts to describe the Malaspina family is in direct contrast to his vitriolic criticism of the rest of his contemporary Italy. He suggests that they, through both their family traditions (custom) and the individual quality of their members (nature), have remained uncorrupted by the bad governance under which Italy is struggling. Dante's praise of the Malaspinas has a very direct personal motive. On his exile from Florence, the Malaspinas became Dante's hosts and protectors for a time (as Currado's prophecy in lines 133–39 testifies).

133–39 *No, go on* Currado prophesies that Dante's high opinion of the Malaspina family will prove to be absolutely justified by forthcoming events. These events will be Dante's own exile from Florence and the subsequent welcome he received from the Malaspina family.

133–35 *not for a seventh time* In springtime the sun is in the constellation of Aries, the ram. Currado's words suggest that in less than seven years (before spring can return seven times) Dante's high opinion of the Malaspinas will be justified. The fictional date of the *Commedia* is 1300 and the historical Dante was sent into exile in 1302.

Canto IX

1–6 *The concubine of ancient Tithonus* This passage has generally been taken to refer to moonrise around 9:00 p.m. as seen from Mount Purgatory in the Southern Hemisphere. Tithonus was the husband of Aurora, goddess of the sunrise. His concubine would therefore be Aurora's opposite, moonrise. The rising moon is personified as a lover leaving her beloved's bed. The first half of this canto is replete with references to classical mythology, which are contrasted in the canto's second half by its overtly Christian set-ting and themes. This contrast marks one of several tensions that character-ize the canto as a whole and identify it as a canto of transition from one way of being to another.

5–6   *that frigid creature*   The constellation of Scorpio, which is visible in the eastern sky in the Southern Hemisphere at 9:00 p.m., just before moonrise.

7–9   *two of the steps*   Night rises between sunset and midnight, putting the time at this second step of the night at 9:00 p.m.

10–11   *I, who had something of Adam in me*   We are reminded that Dante is making this journey in his physical body (that *something of Adam*) and thus feels tiredness, unlike his shade companions. Unlike the preceding cantos, canto IX primarily focuses upon the pilgrim, his dream, and his entrance through the gates of Purgatory proper.

12   *the five of us*   Dante, Virgil, Sordello, Nino Visconti, and Currado Malaspina.

13–15   *the swallow*   Ovid's *Met.*VI.424–674 tells the story of the sisters Philomela and Procne. Philomela is raped by Procne's husband Tereus, who, to prevent her telling anyone, cuts out her tongue and imprisons her. To tell her story and reveal his wickedness, she weaves a tapestry depicting the event and sends it to her sister. To take revenge, Procne kills her son Itys and feeds him to the unsuspecting Tereus. On realizing what she has done, Tereus pursues both Procne and Philomela, but all three are transformed into birds. The women are transformed into a nightingale and a swallow, though sources differ as to which was which. Birds are a recurring trope of this canto.

16   *pilgrimage*   The subtlety of Dante's original Italian term *peregrina* cannot be fully conveyed in translation since it can (and here probably does) simultaneously mean "pilgrim," "wanderer," and "falcon."

20   *a golden eagle*   Dante's sleeping mind, which was already beginning to soar like a falcon, is visited by a dream of an eagle hovering above him. The eagle is a highly symbolic creature in Dante's thought. It recalls biblical prophets and saints (Ezekiel, St Paul, St John the Evangelist) and is at the same time the symbol of Roman imperial power. The descent of an eagle was also read as symbolizing the descent of divine power to Earth.

23–24   *Ganymede left his companions behind*   Ganymede was a beauti-ful boy with whom Zeus fell in love. In the guise of an eagle, Zeus de-scended to Earth, snatched up Ganymede, and took him to heaven to be the cupbearer of the gods. The spot from which *Ganymede left his companions* was Mount Ida. Later Christian interpretations read the story as an allegory of the ascent of the soul.

30–33   *snatch me up to the sphere of fire*   When we read on, we find that the images of Dante's dream are manifestations of the heat he feels from the rising sun. This does not, however, diminish the great drama of this moment and Dante's physical terror. As happens throughout this canto, however, threatened physical danger is revealed to hold beneath it a positive explanation or result. In the first instance of this, Dante is snatched up to the fiery sphere by the eagle; medieval bestiary, however, drawing from biblical sources (Ps. 102:5; Deut. 32:10–11; Is. 40:31) believed that eagles were burned and renewed when they flew close to the sun, regaining their youth. Dante's dream suggests the spiritual renewal through physical suffering that is to begin in the second half of the canto.

34–39   *In just the same way as Achilles*   These lines derive from the *Achilleid* (247–50) by the Roman poet Statius, which tells the story of the Greek hero Achilles. The moment referred to here describes when the child Achilles is taken away from his tutor the centaur Chiron to protect him from the forthcoming war that the Greeks will wage at Troy.

43   *Only my Comfort*   The souls that met in the Valley of the Princes have been left behind, but Virgil continues at Dante's side.

46   *Have no fear*   Virgil's words are laden with biblical resonance, recalling the *nolite timere* uttered by angels and by Christ in reference to Christ's Nativity and Resurrection and during Revelation (Lk. 2:10, 24:35; Matt. 28:5; Apoc. 1:17).

52–63   *when your soul was slumbering*   Virgil interprets the dream from which Dante has awoken terrified and pale. The physical threat that the dream contained is revealed to have an entirely different and positive source. Dante has been visited by St Lucy (who we found in *Inf.* II.100 had already acted on his behalf), who, wanting to speed and ease his journey, has carried his sleeping body to the gates of Purgatory. The intervention of Lucy (whose name is related to *lux*, "light") symbolizes the unmerited and unexpected aid that divine grace brings to humankind. Lucy's gentle and tender intervention, juxtaposed with the violence of the dream eagle, establishes a further contrast between the classical past and the Christian present.

70–72   *Reader, you surely see*   Dante adopts his own image of being carried aloft by the soaring eagle/St Lucy to describe the ascending tone and theme that his poem will now assume.

78–84 *a warder* As with the angels Dante has seen in Purgatory so far, the angel guarding the gate is too resplendent for him to look at. The shining sword recalls the angel who guards the Garden of Eden (Gen. 3:24). The sword is also a traditional attribute of St Paul.

85–93 *Say from there* Not for the first time, Dante must account for his presence to a guardian of a realm in order to have access (Minos *Inf.* V.19–20, Chiron *Inf.* XXII.63, Cato *Purg.* I.40–48). As in the encounter with Cato, Virgil testifies to the divine aid with which Dante travels and thus persuades the guardian to allow the pilgrim to enter.

94–102 *The first step* The symbolism of the three steps of the gate of Purgatory has given rise to much scholarly discussion. A widely accepted interpretation reads the steps as symbolic of the stages of the sacrament of confession; the white step that reflects the viewers to themselves is conviction of sin and oral confession, the second is contrition (being broken open), and the third is the act of penance symbolized in sacrificial blood. There is also deep Christological resonance to the imagery; the second step is broken into the form of a cross like the body of Christ broken at the Crucifixion, while the third step is like an open flowing vein, grotesque yet pulsing with vitality and new life.

108–11 *Beg him humbly* The angel appears here as a priest-like figure to whom Dante must show reverence. The ritual of kneeling and beating the breast in contrition also recalls the act of confession.

112–14 *Seven Ps* Despite the hanging threat of the sword, the wounds that Dante receives are lightly given and ultimately positive. The seven Ps represent the seven capital vices that Dante will purge during his ascent up the mountain. The "P" may stand for *peccatum* (sin), *plaga* (wound), or *penitentia* (penitence), all of which have a similar meaning in this context.

115–16 *Ashes* While his face is resplendent, the angel is clothed in garments that emphasize humility and mourning.

117–29 *two keys* The two keys of gold and silver that the angel holds are those that Christ gave to St Peter (Matt. 16:19), the keys to Heaven. The *one which is more precious*, the gold, has been interpreted as the temporal power of the Church to forgive sins; the one that needs *more skill* to turn is the intimate discretion of the individual human heart.

131–32 *I admonish you* The trope of the danger of looking back is found in both classical mythology (the story of Orpheus and Eurydice) and the Bible (the story of Lot's wife; Gen. 19:26).

133–38   *that sacred door*   The canto creates a buildup to this moment as we see in detail the stages of the pilgrim's approach to the door. When it finally opens, it is an overwhelming aural experience. Dante uses a scene from Lucan's *Pharsalia* III.153–68 in which Julius Caesar breaks into the treasury of Rome (found at the foot of the Tarpeian Rock and guarded by Lucius Caecilius Metellus) to express the moment.

139–45   *I turned aside*   The final lines of the canto focus upon the sensory confusion the pilgrim experiences at this point. The overwhelming sound of the gate is mingled with the sound of singing that both is and is not audible. The hymn "Te Deum laudamus" (We Praise You, God) was traditionally sung when novices first entered a monastic order.

Canto X

2–3   *souls with evil loves*   Dante argues throughout the *Commedia* that misdirected and misused love is the basis of sin. Excessive love of self, love of the failure of others, and excessive love of material things are all the instincts behind sin. The poet expresses this through contrasting images of crooked and straight—we remember the "straight path" that the pilgrim had turned aside from at the opening of *Inf.* I.3.

5–6   *if I had turned back*   In the previous canto, the angel admonished Dante to resist the urge to look behind him, a trope familiar from classical and biblical stories.

7–9   *We were climbing*   This evocative passage that describes the travelers' climb through the fissure of rock introduces the theme of sensory confusion that recurs throughout this canto. We cannot truly tell whether the rock is solid or moving. What we read is not so much an objective description but a description of the *experience* of the climb. The significance of personal experience and perception is central to the canto as a whole.

16   *that needle's eye*   Dante draws this image from Matt. 19:24: "It is easier for a camel to pass through the eye of a needle than for a rich man to enter the kingdom of Heaven."

29–99   *I saw that the face of the encircling cliff*   This is the travelers' first encounter with the exempla of virtue that they will meet on every terrace. These exempla are always drawn from the same three sources: the Old Testament, the New Testament, and the classical past. This first group of images shows exempla of the virtue of humility, the opposite of the sin of Pride, which is purged on this terrace. Perhaps the most striking feature of these exempla is the visible presence of the divine hand that made them. The carvings are superlative, blurring the line between art and reality. Dante's senses, and the senses of the reader herself, are in a state of confused perception throughout the canto—is what we see real or not? The contrast of the eternal art of God and the transient art of man will be an important theme for the terrace as a whole over the next two cantos.

31–33 *not only Polyclitus but Nature herself* The quality of the carvings is superior not only to those of Polyclitus, one of the most renowned sculptors of the classical world, but to the work of nature herself. By these comparisons, Dante highlights the superlative quality of God's art.

34–45 *The angel who came to earth* The first exemplum shows the Annunciation when the angel Gabriel came to Earth to tell Mary that she had been chosen to give birth to the son of God. This moment was read as a crowning example of humility, as the Virgin willingly and humbly submits to the Will of God in spite of the responsibility and sadness that will follow. The Annunciation is recounted in Lk. 1:26–38.

35–36 *the peace that had been wept* The Annunciation and the birth of Christ ultimately make possible Christ's Crucifixion, which will enable humankind to be redeemed after the long years following the Fall of man and his exile from Heaven.

39–45 *not at all like silent language* Dante emphasizes the verisimilitude of the divine carvings by questioning how they are perceived. The visible images are not static and are not silent but are living before the viewer. But it is precisely the viewer's perception of them that brings them to life; in the imagination and senses of the viewer, the scenes take on a reality. Dante is here making a very important point about the nature of the biblical message and the moral messages that follow it. The latter are only given value by the living reality that recreates them. In emphasizing the visibility of invisible speech, Dante is also drawing on the visual arts that would have surrounded him in medieval Italy, where we find many images of the Annunciation that include within them the text of the story, often as "speech bubbles" coming from the mouths of the characters.

40 *Ave . . . Ecce ancilla Dei* The opening and closing Latin phrases of the encounter of Gabriel and Mary: *Ave*, the respectful salutation and Mary's humble "Behold the handmaid of the Lord."

55–69 *Carved into the marble there were the oxen* The second carved exemplum depicts the moment at which King David joyfully humbles himself by dancing before the Ark of the Covenant. Michal, his wife, looks down with disdain. The event is recounted in 2 Sam. 6:13–16. The theme of sensory confusion in the face of the exquisite carvings is again highlighted in the "discord between eyes and nose" aroused by the "sculpted incense smoke."

73–93   *the crowning glory of a Roman prince*   The final exemplum shows a story from the life of the Roman Emperor, Trajan, recounted in several medieval texts, including the *Golden Legend* of Jacobus de Voragine (1230–1298) and works by Gregory the Great. When about to set off on a military campaign, Trajan is waylaid by a widow demanding justice for her murdered son. The widow overcomes Trajan's initial reluctance by reminding him that it is for his own good actions that he will be judged. Dante here refers to the popular legend that Pope Gregory was so impressed by the story of Trajan that he prayed for his salvation so fervently that God restored Trajan to life long enough for him to accept Christ and be saved.

93   *Justice wills it, and compassion holds me here*   Trajan exemplifies the two defining characteristics of God's treatment of humanity: justice and mercy.

94–99   *The One who never sees anything new*   Dante contrasts here the eternity of God, the One to whom nothing is new, with the limited vision of the living man, who has never seen the like of these carvings before. This contrast, which highlights the wonderful creativity of God, is a source of delight to the pilgrim.

100–139   *Here come a great crowd*   The canto's final passage is a highly constructed narrative drama that plays on the theme of sensory confusion that runs throughout the canto. The group that approaches the travelers are those who are to be purged of the sin of Pride. Pride was considered the root of all sins and therefore the most serious. Rather than immediately showing the suffering sinners, however, Dante delays the impact of the terrible vision he will ultimately present, thus intensifying the drama.

106–11   *But, reader*   Dante's third address to the reader in the *Purgatorio* is a dramatic pause that both strengthens the reader for what is to come and intensifies our expectation of the horrible suffering we are about to see.

115–20   *The nature of their torment*   At last the group of sinners becomes visible. To purge the sin of Pride, the sinners carry great rocks on their backs that bend them toward the ground. This symbolizes the contrast to Pride in which one individual looks down on others, believing himself better than those around him.

121–29 *O vainglorious Christians* The poet steps out of the narrative to denounce the proud. He declares that those who are proud have mistaken the real potential of human existence, by which humankind, created by God, has the ability to ascend to God. Paradoxically, however, this ascension takes place by a recognition of one's smallness, one's createdness. Dante uses the trope of metamorphosis, the transformation of the caterpillar into the butterfly, to describe the transformed and ascending soul.

130 *corbel* Corbels are a common feature of Romanesque and Gothic architecture. They are carved crouching human figures placed at the top of columns so they appear to be bearing the weight of the ceiling on their shoulders.

Canto XI

1–24 *Our Father* Dante writes an expanded version of the Lord's Prayer (Matt. 6:9–13), the prayer that Christ taught to the apostles (Augustine provided the most influential discussion of the prayer in the Middle Ages in *De Sermone Domini* II.15–39). Dante's paraphrasing of the prayer reflects his own theological and philosophical vision, focusing on the divine aid that is essential to salvation, the role of human and divine will, and the power of prayer. Bursting in at the canto's opening, the prayer at first has no individual identified speaker. Only after its conclusion do we find that it was a communally voiced prayer spoken by the penitent souls themselves. That the prideful join together in reciting the prayer that identifies all humankind as children of the same God (*Our Father*) is an important reinforcement of the lessons of humility that they are learning.

2–3 *circumscribed only by the greater love* Dante is addressing the theological question posed by the suggestion that God is in Heaven and thus, somehow, limited. In a paraphrase that engages directly with the vision of a universe founded on and sustained by love, Dante makes love the only element that can be said to be quantifiable about God; He loves those things he created first—the upper heavens and the angels—most.

4–6 *Praised be Thy name* The three persons of the Trinity are referred to in this passage: Name, Power, and Breath, Father, Son, and Holy Spirit.

15 *go backward in this wilderness* The terrace of the prideful is also described in X.20–21 as a desert. This recalls the desert through which the Israelites wandered as told in Exodus and evoked in *Purg.* II.46 by the singing souls arriving in Purgatory. Here again, Purgatory is compared to that

period of penitential waiting that God imposed before the Israelites could enter the Promised Land.

19–24   *This final prayer*   The prayer closes with a direct appeal to God to help those still alive on Earth. Although commentators disagree over which part of the larger prayer lines 22–24 refer to, it is most likely lines 19–21. Dante differs from the theology of his period in suggesting that souls in Purgatory are able to aid the living with prayer; however, in doing so he is perfectly adapting to the narrative he has created that seeks to bridge the afterlife and the temporal life of his readers. In his poem, Dante imagines a voice for the silent dead; he fulfills a common wish of humanity that they not be forgotten by those who have died before them. In doing so, he manifests a *community* between the living and the dead that was already imagined by Christian theology.

26–27   *in our dreams*   The nightmare of being crushed and suffocated by a giant rock.

30   *purging away the dark mist*   In *Purg.* X.121–22 Pride is described as weakening our true clear vision of the world.

31–36   *If good is always said of us*   These six lines of extra-narrative comment reiterate the value of prayers by the virtuous living in aiding the souls in Purgatory.

37   *justice and pity*   As in X.91–93, justice and mercy are highlighted as the two principles by which God deals with humanity.

43–44   *burdened with the flesh of Adam*   A reiteration of the pilgrim's corporeality (previously described in reference to Adam at *Purg.* IX.10), these lines also connect that corporeality with the burden carried by the souls of the proud. Dante's mortality manifests the punishment for Adam's original sin of Pride.

58–72   *I was Italian*   The soul who first speaks to the travelers is that of Omberto Aldobrandesco, the son of a powerful and renowned family in northern Tuscany. The Aldobrandeschi allied with the Papacy against the cities of northern Italy (principally Siena), which supported the Emperor Frederick II. Omberto was most likely assassinated by the Sienese at Campagnatico in 1259. Omberto appears here as an example of one who took excessive pride in his family name and birth. His false modesty in mentioning his illustrious father, Guglielmo, is a sign that he still has a long way to go in his penance.

63   *our common mother*   This is Eve. Just as the canto opens with reference to a common Father, the lesson of humility and unity that humanity's shared origins should bring about is reiterated here.

78   *I walked hunched over in their company*   The pilgrim adopts the same position as the souls who walk bowed down by their burden. He too is enacting a penance for Pride.

79–81   *are you not Oderisi*   The pilgrim identifies the soul who called to him as Oderisi of Gubbio, a manuscript illuminator who was active in the second half of the thirteenth century.

82–108   *Brother*   Oderisi's speech addresses the transience of earthly fame in the particular sphere of artistic achievement. He lists several artists and writers from the late thirteenth century, each of whom has been superseded by another. The theme of the transience of human success is drawn from Eccl. 1:4–11. The choice of artists as exemplifying the transience of human achievement is significant when we consider the emphasis given to the beauty and perfection of the divine art that the travelers see on the terrace of the proud.

94–99   *Cimabue thought that as a painter*   Dante selects artists and writers who exemplify the best of their art but who are nevertheless superseded by those who come after them. Cimabue (c. 1240–1302) is followed and bettered by Giotto (c. 1266–1337); the two Guidos to whom Dante refers are usually identified with Guido Guinizelli and Guido Cavalcanti. The final ambiguous reference to the new "bird" who will chase these poets from their place of prominence is taken to refer to Dante himself. Although Dante appears to be praising himself, he is simultaneously including himself in the list of artists who will necessarily be superseded.

105–6   *pappo and dindi*   Dante recreates baby talk here (the words for "food" and "money") to indicate the period of early childhood.

109–42   *That person barely moving*   The final passage of the canto is dedicated to a description by Oderisi of Provenzan Salvani (c. 1220–1269). Salvani was from Siena and became a dictatorial ruler of the city. After the battle of Montaperti in which the Sienese beat the Florentines, Salvani advocated razing the city of Florence to the ground. He was later captured and executed by the Florentines. Salvani represents Pride in political power and, indirectly, the Pride of cities themselves.

133–42   *When he was living*   Oderisi describes an act of humility on the part of Provenzan Salvani that has reduced his time in Purgatory. Early commentators tell us that Salvani, in order to raise the ransom on a friend who had been captured by Charles of Anjou at the battle of Tagliacozzo, went begging through the streets dressed in sackcloth.

140–41   *your neighbors down there*   Oderisi makes an oblique reference to the humiliation that Dante himself will soon have to suffer when he is sent into exile. He too will have to beg for aid.

Canto XII

1   *beneath a yoke*   The image of the yoke makes frequent appearance in the Bible, referring both to enslavement and guilt but also to the positive weight and responsibility of accepting God (see, e.g., Lam. 1:14; Matt. 11:28–30).

7–9   *I straightened up my body*   Dante, like the souls of the proud, has been walking bent low to the ground. Here, although he now stands up straight, he retains in his mind the lessons of humility that were inscribed upon his bent body.

16–21   *Just as stones*   Dante compares the carved flagstones that pave this section of the terrace to the carved tombstones that could be found in the floors of the medieval churches of Florence. Many are still visible today, in the Church of Santa Croce for example.

25–63   *I saw*   Dante dedicates thirty-eight lines to describing the images of Pride carved into the flagstones. This highly constructed and literary passage is made up of succinct and virtuoso descriptions of events from the Bible, classical mythology, and history. Commentators have pointed out that, in the original Italian, an acrostic is visible in the opening words of the twelve *terzine*; four *terzine* begin with *vedea* (I saw), four with *O*, and four with *mostrava* (showed). These spell out *VOM* [*UOM*], "man."

25–27   *the one who was created*   Lucifer, the most beautiful of the angels created by God, who rebelled against him and was cast out of Heaven. Dante describes his own vision of Lucifer (Satan) in *Inf.* XXXIV.28–60.

28–33   *Briareus*   One of the giants from classical mythology, who rebelled against the Olympian gods and was defeated. The victorious gods, Apollo, Pallas, and Mars, are listed along with implicit reference to their father Zeus. The event is narrated in *Met.* I.151–62 and *Theb.* II.595–601.

34–36   *Nimrod*   A figure from Gen. 10:9–10, 11:1–9, Nimrod constructed the Tower of Babel in Shinar. God punished Nimrod's Pride by making him and his people speak different languages, unintelligible to each other. Dante encounters Nimrod himself in *Inf.* XXXI.46–81.

37–39 *Niobe* A further figure whose story appears in *Met*. VI.142–312, Niobe boasted that because she had seven sons and seven daughters she was superior to the goddess Latona, who was mother of only Apollo and Diana. As punishment, Latona ordered Apollo and Diana to kill Niobe's children. Niobe herself becomes a stone, weeping tears.

40–42 *Saul* Saul (I Sam. 31:1–6) was the first king of Israel. He killed himself following defeat at the battle of Gilboa during which three of his sons were killed. The reference to rain and dew is drawn from 2 Sam. 1:21, in which King David curses Gilboa.

43–45 *Arachne* Arachne challenged the goddess Athene to a weaving contest. The goddess, threatened and affronted by Arachne's skill and presumption, transformed her into a spider (*Met*.VI.1–145).

46–48 *Rehoboam* Son of Solomon and king of Israel, Rehoboam refused to lower the taxes his father had imposed. In response, his people revolted and executed his general, at which Rehoboam fled.

49–51 *Alcmaeon* Alcmaeon murdered his mother, who had been bribed with a necklace into betraying his father. The story appears in Statius' *Theb*. II.265–305 and IV.187–212 and is referred to again by Dante in *Inf*. II.32–36 and *Par*. IV.103–5.

52–54 *Sennacherib* King of Assyria who led a campaign against Israel and was defeated. He was then murdered by his sons (see 2 Kings 18:13–37, 19:1–37).

55–57 *Tomyris* and *Cyrus* Tomyris was queen of the Cythians and Cyrus the Great was founder of the Persian Empire. Cyrus murdered Tomyris' son, whom he had held hostage. It was said that, when Tomyris later captured Cyrus in battle, she had him decapitated and his head thrown into a vat filled with blood, the event that Dante obliquely refers to here.

58–60 *Holofernes* The Assyrian general, beheaded by the Jewish widow Judith whom he had intended to seduce (see the apocryphal Book of Judith 8–14).

61–63 *Troy* The fall of the city of Troy, destroyed by the Greeks, is described in *Aeneid* book 2 and *Met*. XV.422–35.

64–60 *What master has there been* The perfection and verisimilitude of divinely created art is reiterated as it was in canto X, thus continuing the comparison present throughout these cantos of the fleeting works of human beings and the eternal works of God.

70–72   *Be haughty then*   In this ironic exhortation, Dante again equates bodily posture (*turn, bend down*) with moral state.

76–83   *he who always looked down the road*   The ever-present and vigilant Virgil guides the pilgrim through the final acts of penance on this terrace, telling him when to stop his meditations and how to appear with reverence before the angel.

80–81   *the sixth Hour*   An indication of time, drawing on the figurative tradition of personified Hours.

88–90   *The beautiful creature*   The first angel that the travelers encounter within the gates of Purgatory. Dante is able to tolerate the brightness of this *beautiful creature*, although he could not tolerate that of the previous angels. Angels in the Gospels appear dressed in white only after the Resurrection (Matt. 28:2–3; Mk. 16:5; Lk. 24:4; Jn. 20:2); white is also the color worn by the blessed in the Apocalypse (6:11, 7:9, 15:10, 19:14). These changes mark a new stage in the pilgrim's journey, suggesting he has already made significant spiritual progress.

91   *He opened his arms*   The angel's physical invitation to the travelers is a gesture that imitates the all-embracing welcome and forgiveness that God gives (see III.122–23).

95–96   *O race of man*   The image of flight and ascent echoes the narrator's lament of canto X.121–30.

98–135   *there he batted my forehead*   Although the traveler does not yet realize it, the first of the seven Ps inscribed on his forehead has now been removed.

100–105   *Just to the right of the church*   Dante evokes an image from his historical Florence to describe a steep ascent eased by steps. The church referred to is San Miniato al Monte, which sits on a hill high above the city. The bridge across the river that leads to it was originally called Rubaconte and was later renamed Ponte alle Grazie. The *age of trustworthy weights and measures* refers to a famous scandal of 1283 in which a member of the Chiaramonte family of Florence sold salt using dishonest measures and was later punished for his fraud.

110   *Beati pauperes spiritu*   The first of the Beatitudes, one of which will accompany Dante each time he ascends from one terrace to another and that mark the removal of a vice. The Beatitudes come from the Sermon on the Mount (Matt. 5:3–12). The text of this first Beatitude reads, "Blessed are the poor in spirit for theirs is the kingdom of Heaven" and traditionally refers to the virtue of humility.

112–14   *Ah, how different*   A reminder of the radically different characters of Purgatory and Hell. Hell was marked by discord, chaos, and pain; Purgatory, instead, is the realm of community, hope, and song.

115–26   *I was far lighter*   The physical lightness that the pilgrim feels as he climbs upward is a manifestation of the spiritual lightness brought about by the removal of a vice. The effect is most evident with the removal of Pride, considered the root of all vice. Since this vice has now been removed, the others are also *almost effaced*.

127–36   *Then I was like someone*   The canto closes with a gently comic image as the pilgrim, disbelieving Virgil's words, touches his own forehead just to make sure that one of the Ps has really gone. The patient Virgil smiles at his pupil's wonder and success.

Canto XIII

4–6   *There another ledge*   The travelers have climbed to the mountain's second terrace, which, being higher up, encircles a narrower part of the mount.

7–9   *No shaded figures*   Unlike the terrace of Pride, this terrace is totally without visual ornament and is only distinguished by the dark, livid color of the rock. This dark purplish or bluish color was considered the color of Envy (*livor* in Latin means both "livid" and "envy"). As so often happens in the *Commedia*, the physical surroundings manifest the sin, vice, or blessed state of the sinner within them.

16–21   *O sweet light*   The warm and guiding sun that Virgil praises here is analogous to the guiding light and warming love of God. The relevance of this short passage is not only significant to this moment, therefore, but to the canto and the *cantica* as a whole. As we will see, the penance described in this canto is a loss of sight. God's love is ever present, however, even while the souls cannot yet see it.

25–33   *we heard spirits*   The exempla of this terrace are presented in the form of disembodied voices flying through the air. The significance of this will not become apparent until we know the penance that the souls are undergoing (they are deprived of sight and therefore their instruction must be aural). The *table of love* to which the voices invite the listeners is a veiled reference to the sacrament of the Eucharist, the table at which the believer joins with the body and blood of Christ. Most importantly, Love is the virtue that stands opposite Envy. Love, as the greatest virtue (1 Cor. 13:13; John 3:16; 1 John 4:16), finds its greatest exemplum in Christ's sacrifice.

28–29   *Vinum non habent*   The words the Virgin Mary spoke to Christ at the wedding at Cana in Galilee, told in Jn. 2:1–12. Jesus and Mary attended a wedding party at which the wine ran out. After Mary told Jesus "*Vinum non habent*" (they have no wine), he transformed the water in six water jars into wine. This was Jesus' first miracle and was interpreted as representing Christ's coming and his sacred marriage to the Church.

32–33   *I am Orestes*   The second exemplum refers to the story of Orestes told in Cicero's *De Amicitia* and *De Finibus*. Orestes, son of Agamemnon, and his friend Pylades were taken prisoner by Tauris. Tauris wanted to kill Orestes but did not know him by sight. In order to protect each other, both Orestes and Pylades claimed to be Orestes. The story was taken as a great example of the love between friends.

36   *Love those by whom you are wronged*   From Jesus' Sermon on the Mount, told in Matt. 5:43–45: "Love your enemy, do good to them that hate you and pray for those that persecute and calumniate you."

37–42   *This circle scourges the sin of envy*   Virgil informs Dante of the vice that is being purged on this terrace, Envy. Love is identified as the virtue opposed to Envy. Virgil draws his metaphor from the training of horses (whip, reins), a metaphor that has already been used in reference to wayward Italy in canto VI.88–99.

46–72   *I opened my eyes*   As on the terrace of Pride, Dante constructs a measured buildup to a full vision of the suffering souls of this terrace. The souls are at first difficult to see, seated on the ground wearing cloaks the same color as the rock of the terrace. They are depicted as beggars, calling out for aid to the saints. Dante further builds the pathos of the scene, describing his own grief at the sight his readers have not yet seen. Finally the souls appear, like blind beggars, their eyelids sewn together with iron wires. The Italian *invidia* (envy) means "without sight" and helps us better understand the nature of Envy, as an inability to see others as oneself. In spite of the gruesome penance, the passage is filled with positive undertones. The souls sit supporting each other, overcoming the malicious divisions that the vice of Envy had instilled in them. As in the penance of the proud, spiritual lessons are manifested in physical actions. In calling on the compassion of others, they are enacting the opposite to Envy. The wild falcon to which they are later compared is ultimately a positive image, since falcons were trained in order to work in greater harmony with their master and thus attain greater nobility and discipline. Once this training was complete, they could fly free and work with the directions of their master.

50–51   *Pray for us, Mary*   Although much more abbreviated than the Lord's Prayer uttered by the proud, the souls of the envious utter invocations from the traditional litany of the saints.

58   *coarse haircloth*   The garment traditionally worn by those undergoing penance or those in mourning (see Lam. 2:10; Gen. 37:34; 4 Kgs. 6:30; Jdt. 4:8; Ps. 68:12; Matt. 11:21).

85–93   *O people assured*   Dante's courteous address expresses the goal toward which these souls are moving and gives voice to the hope that must lead them on. He identifies their physical blindness with the spiritual blindness of Envy, which afflicts them. Dante's words directly echo lines 82–84, which describe the weeping of the souls, their tears seeping through the wounds of their blinded eyes. In his address these tears are subtly transformed into cleansing streams, the agents of grace, which wash away vice and ultimately open the eyes to God.

94–96   *O my brother*   Sapìa's correction of the pilgrim is a sign of her own spiritual development; she is learning to see community where she had previously reveled in division. It also expresses, however, a central lesson of Purgatory as a whole. The one true city is the city of God, and temporal life should be seen as a pilgrimage journeying toward it. This recognition can become easily obscured in the divisions (national, familial, personal) that characterize temporal life.

102   *tame yourself to ascend*   A reiteration of the image of the spiritual flight resulting from penance that the earlier metaphor of the wild falcon introduced.

106–29   *I was from Siena*   The soul of Sapìa, a member of the Salvani family of Siena and aunt of Provenzan Salvani, who was described in XI.121–38. Sapìa tells how, in her maturity, she watched a battle at Colle between her own townsmen of Siena and the Florentines. She wished for the defeat of the Sienese and, on getting her wish, describes how she presumptuously cried to God that she no longer need fear Him.

109   *Sapìa*   Sapìa is derived from the Latin *savio*, "to be wise."

110–11   *I rejoiced much more*   Sapìa's description encapsulates a central feature of Dante's conception of Envy. It is not as simple as the desire for another's possessions; it is a reveling in the loss or unhappiness of others and an inability to appreciate one's own happiness. It is a malicious loathing that is directed both at others and at oneself.

Canto XIV

1–6 *Who is this person* This is the only point in the *Commedia* at which a dialogue between unidentified souls opens a canto. It is an effective and characterful moment that evokes the newfound interdependence of the envious souls who are casting off their vice and developing in courtesy and community.

16–21 *Through the middle of Tuscany* Dante makes an indirect response to the soul's question of who he is and where he is from. He downplays his own name and modestly denies any fame, instead focusing on his place of origin, the Arno valley (named by the questioning soul in line 24). The fact that Dante does not name the Arno directly facilitates the harsh criticism of the valley that will follow.

28–66 *And the shade who was asked* This is an extended, bitter criticism of the residents of the Arno valley. The poet uses animal imagery to evoke the corruption of the people and the degradation of their morality and humanity. The river itself is transformed into a beast with unquenchable thirst (18) and a snout (48).

31–36 *For from its source* Dante describes the water cycle of the river that begins at its source on Monte Falterona and descends to its mouth in the Mediterranean. These meteorological theories were explained by Aristotle in his *Meteorology* I and later by Aquinas in *In Meteorologiam Aristotelis commentarius* I.

31–32 *the alpine range from which Pelorus was broken off* Pelorus is a mountain in Sicily. It was originally thought that the Apennine mountain range extended the whole length of the Italian peninsula and into Sicily, which was originally attached to it. The island was believed to have been broken off from the mainland by an earthquake. This is described in Virgil's *Aen.* III.410–19.

37–38 *people free from virtue* These lines echo and contrast the fearful snake who appears in the Valley of the Princes in canto VIII.

40–42 *the inhabitants of that miserable valley* Dante here uses the story of Circe (see Homer's *Odyssey* and later the *Aeneid* and the *Metamorphoses*) to express the corruption of the humanity of those living along the Arno valley. Circe was a witch who transformed Odysseus' crew of sailors into pigs. Odysseus himself escapes but goes to bed with the seductive Circe. His crew is later released from the enchantment.

46–48 *the water encounters curs* A reference to the city crest of Arezzo, which shows a dog snarling at a boar and bears the Latin inscription "A cane non magno saepe tenetur aper" (a small dog often holds a boar at bay).

51 *the dogs have turned into wolves* The "dogs" of Arezzo have transformed into the "wolves" of Florence. Wolves are emblematic of Avarice and cupidity in the *Commedia* (*Inf.* I.49–51; *Purg.* XX.10–12).

53–54 *foxes so full of fraud* Referring to the crafty residents of Pisa.

55–57 *what the true Spirit has disclosed* The soul is claiming that his prophecy comes directly from the Holy Spirit. There is significant biblical precedent for this (see Jn. 16:13).

58–66 *I see your grandson* The individual referred to is Fulcieri, the nephew of Rinieri da Calboli, who enforced a tyrannical and violent regime in Florence. For contemporary accounts see Dino Compagni (II.30) and Villani (VIII.59).

77–84 *You would have me bring myself* The soul's gentle rebuke of Dante for having refused to reveal his name becomes an occasion for the soul to demonstrate his own generosity. The soul acts out of the new love he is acquiring and the recognition of Dante's privileged state. He identifies himself as Guido del Duca, a Ghibelline judge who presided in different cities in the Romagna and who died around 1250.

82–84 *My blood boiled* Dante describes what he and his contemporaries believed to be the physiological effects of Envy.

85 *Of my sowing* Evoking a well-known biblical image that appears in Prov. 22:8, Hos. 8:7, and Gal. 6:8.

88 *This is Rinieri* A Guelph from Romagna, Rinieri was active in the power struggles that took place throughout the territory in the second half of the thirteenth century. Rinieri and Guido del Duca, a Guelph and Ghibelline respectively, are here overcoming the political divisions that existed between their factions, becoming instead citizens of the "one true city."

88–123 *no one since has made himself an heir to his valor* Following Guido del Duca's acerbic criticism of the residents of the Arno valley, he now turns his invective against the Romagna, focusing on the degradation of family lines.

91–92 *between the Po* The Po and the Reno are the rivers that mark the historical boundaries of Romagna.

97–102   *Where is the good Lizio*   Guido del Duca lists a series of no-
table and worthy figures from Romagna's past. Significantly they are a mix
of Guelph and Ghibelline.

104–11   *When, in Bologna, will there be another Fabbro*   The list of praise-
worthy figures from Romagna's history continues, with a focus upon fami-
lies noted for their generosity and courtesy.

112–21   *O town of Bretinoro*   The invective continues with a further list
of towns and families who have fallen into corruption.

128   *their silence*   The silence of the souls heightens the drama of the
voices that suddenly break like lightning and thunder upon the scene.

131–32   *a voice like lightning*   As with the exempla of Love, the exempla
of Envy appear as disembodied voices streaking through the air.

133   *Whoever apprehends me will slay me*   The words spoken by Cain to
God when he is exiled for killing his brother, Abel. Cain killed his brother
out of envy for the superiority of Abel's offering to God, thus committing
the first murder (Gen. 4).

139   *I am Aglauros*   The story of Aglauros appears in *Met.* II.708–832.
The god Mercury was in love with Aglauros' sister and enlisted Aglauros'
help to win her. The goddess Minerva, in revenge for an earlier slight, or-
dered the goddess Envy to infect Aglauros. Aglauros then refused to let
Mercury enter her sister's chamber, saying she would never move from
before the locked door. As punishment for her challenge, Mercury turned
her to stone.

143–51   *That was the hard bit*   In the Italian, Virgil uses the plural *voi*,
suggesting that his critical speech that ends this canto is directed not at the
pilgrim but at humankind. Virgil uses three images of animal husbandry to
explore his point. First, the control that the *hard bit* of the exempla of Envy
exerts on humankind; second, the *baited hook* that the devil uses to tempt
mankind (the fish is a traditional image for the Christian soul); and third,
the *lure*, an image from falconry, which God uses to draw the soul toward
him. This last is followed by the image of flight and ascension that has al-
ready been used extensively in Purgatory to express the movement of the
soul toward God (see, e.g., Dante's dream in *Purg.* IX).

Canto XV

1–6 *As much sky* The elaborate temporal indicator that opens the canto tells us that it is now three hours before sunset on Mount Purgatory, the time at which the canonical hour of Vespers takes place. Since it is three hours before sunset in Purgatory (*there*) it must be three hours before sunrise in Jerusalem, which sits exactly opposite to Purgatory on the globe. Since Florence (*here*) is roughly 45 degrees west of Jerusalem, that means that it is midnight in Italy.

2–3 *that sphere* The sun, which according to Dante's cosmology is in constant motion, is compared to a child continually at play. The image of the child recurs throughout the *Purgatorio* and is used to suggest both the playful though unguided instinctual desires of the soul and the state of natural innocence that childhood represents.

7–33 *The beams now struck us* Light is one of the canto's most important images. In this passage the poet focuses on the physical light that overcomes the pilgrim's sight. At first this light comes from the sun, but it quickly intermingles with the overpowering light emanating from the angel who presides over the terrace. Following the blindness that characterizes the penance of the envious, this light breaks upon the darkness with both physical and spiritual force. It is not only visible light but the light of the enlightened mind. Virgil's coming speech (67–78), which explains the nature of divine love—which had been misunderstood by the envious—significantly employs light as the metaphor for that love.

10–15 *I felt my brow weighed down* The pilgrim is not yet able to stand the brightness of the light. This physical inability is a symbol of his continuing spiritual unreadiness to understand what is before him. The passage draws significantly on the Neoplatonic metaphysics of light.

16–21 *As when a beam of light* Dante describes a scientific phenomenon that had been established in Euclid's *Optics*. Light, striking a reflective surface at a certain angle, will be reflected from that surface in the opposite direction at the same angle in relation to the straight midpoint (*the line made by a falling stone*).

25–33 *What is that, sweet father* The pilgrim cannot yet readily identify the angel of the terrace, indicating his "blindness" to the celestial realities he is encountering. Virgil's final words suggest that Purgatory and the removal of vice is restoring humankind to an original nature in which it could perceive celestial beings: a prelapsarian clarity of vision that was both physical and moral. The welcoming invitation of the angel is a fitting contrast to the sin of Envy that this terrace has purged.

35–36   *a stairway less steep*   The ascent of the mountain becomes easier after the root vice of Pride and its close second Envy have been purged.

38–39   *Beati misericordes*   Unidentified voices sing the Beatitude that marks the soul's exit from the terrace of Envy. This is the fifth Beatitude from the Sermon on the Mount, "Blessed are the merciful, for they shall obtain mercy" (Matt. 5:7). The Beatitude ends, "Be glad and rejoice, for your reward is very great in heaven," which seems a likely source for the *Rejoice you that overcome*.

43–45   *What did he mean*   Dante's questions arises from Guido del Duca's words in XIV.85–87.

46–48   *He knows the damage*   Guido del Duca admitted Envy as his worst fault (XIV.85). His criticism of it is a redeeming act of charity, since it is intended to dissuade others from participating in the same vice.

49–81   *Because your desires are so directed*   The extended discourse on the nature of love on Earth and in Heaven is a vital preliminary to the central philosophical discourses that take place in cantos XVI–XVIII. The two sections of Virgil's speech explore the nature of love on Earth and love in Paradise.

49–50   *sharing them reduces your portion*   Virgil describes the earthly love of finite temporal good. He suggests that humanity is obsessed with material things, which, by virtue of their finite materiality, cannot be shared; what one person has another person *cannot have*. Thus Envy can take root.

51   *Envy fans your sighs*   The sense in the Italian original suggests that the *bellows* are the lungs filled with air and induced to sigh with Envy.

52–57   *But if love*   The finite nature of temporal goods is contrasted to the infinite love of Heaven. The more people among whom this good is shared, the greater it becomes.

61–66   *How can it be*   A further instance in this canto of the pilgrim's continuing lack of *vision*. He is still bound to the physical world and the limitations of materiality in which if one possesses another lacks. Virgil uses the significant metaphor of light and darkness to express the pilgrim's limited understanding. Obsession with material things has been considered one of the chief impediments to spiritual enlightenment; its significance was considered at length in Augustine's story of conversion in his *Confessions* book VII.

67–75   *That infinite and ineffable Good*   This is a stunning example of that philosophically informed verse that becomes ever more prevalent as the *Commedia* progresses. The Good of Heaven is divine love, which Virgil describes using the metaphor of light so central to this canto. Divine love runs to any other love it finds, thereby continually increasing its extent, just as a beam of light can continue infinitely reflecting off mirrored surfaces.

76–78   *And if my discourse does not appease*   In spite of Virgil's detailed and lucid explanation, he himself acknowledges its own incompleteness. Virgil, a pagan and the exemplum of human rationality, cannot fully reveal the mysteries of divine love to the pilgrim. He must therefore look ahead to the great wisdom of Beatrice to fully enlighten the pilgrim. It is interesting that the pilgrim does not feel shortchanged by Virgil's explanation (82), perhaps suggesting the continuing limitations of his own insight.

79–81   *Just continue your effort*   We indirectly learn that the second of the Ps marked on the pilgrim's forehead has been removed. Virgil's description of the workings of penance in Purgatory is also striking; pain is here not a punishment but a source of healing.

85–117   *I seemed to be caught up in a trance*   While the first half of the canto considers physical light and vision, the second half turns inward to visions and experiences that happen within the pilgrim's mind. The visions all show exempla of the virtue of Mildness, the counteraction to the Anger that is purged on this terrace.

87–92   *a number of people in a temple*   The first vision describes an episode related in Lk. 2:42–51. The child Jesus, at that time twelve years old, disappears from his parents' house. Mary and Joseph eventually find him at the temple conversing with the elders. The words referred to in Dante's vision (90–92) are Mary's mild though sad rebuke of her child.

93–105   *there appeared to me another woman*   The second episode is taken from Valerius Maximus' *Facta et dicta memorabilia* V.1, which describes the story of Pisistratus. The daughter of Pisistratus, ruler of Athens, is embraced in the street by a young man who loves her. Pisistratus' wife is outraged by this and insists the youth be executed. Pisistratus mildly responds with the words recorded in lines 104–5.

97–98   *the city whose name was contested*   A reference to a story told in *Met.* VI.70–82 in which there is a dispute between the gods Pallas Athene and Poseidon over the naming of Athens.

106–14   *Then I saw a crowd*   The final dramatic vision shows the martyrdom of St Stephen, the first Christian martyr. After refusing to stop preaching the Christian message, Stephen was stoned to death by an angry mob. In the face of their anger, he prayed to God to have mercy on his attackers (Acts 6:6–15, 7:54–60).

115–17   *When my mind returned*   This tercet encapsulates a central is-
sue of the canto: the contrast between physical and internal forms of truth.
The visions that Dante saw we find had no physical reality in the external
world; they are thus *errors*. However, his experience of them and the validity
of their message is nevertheless absolutely true.

120–38   *What's wrong*   This passage is somewhat ambiguous. It at first
appears that Virgil has been unaware of the visions that have assailed the pil-
grim. This encourages the pilgrim to describe what he has seen. Virgil then
reveals that he is in fact able to read Dante's thoughts and clearly see what
he has seen. The purpose of his initial questioning (120) was instead to stir
the pilgrim into action (136–38). Virgil is the unfailing coach on Dante's
journey, but there is an even more important aspect to this dialogue. Dante
demonstrates his willingness to *speak out* about what he has seen, to share
the internal visions that have been granted to him. In this, he encapsulates
the motivation behind the *Commedia* as a whole.

139–45   *through the evening we journeyed*   The canto closes on a dra-
matic contrast. The blinding light that has prevailed throughout the canto is
ominously threatened by an advancing and inescapable cloud of darkness.

Canto XVI

1–7   *Gloom of hell*   The smoke that facilitates the penance taking place
on this terrace is a manifestation of the nature of Anger itself. In both clas-
sical (see the *Iliad* XVIII.107–10) and biblical (see, e.g., Ps. 17:9; Job 17:7)
sources, Anger is described in terms of smoke and burning. It blinds the
powers of reason, overcoming the senses of the individual experiencing it.
The impenetrable black smoke of the penance forces the souls to turn in-
ward and listen to the voice of reason. The pilgrim too becomes subject to
this penance, thereby becoming further receptive to the reasoned, enlight-
ened discourse of Marco Lombardo.

8–15   *my wise and trusted escort*   Virgil's role becomes increasingly com-
plex as the *Purgatorio* progresses. In these central cantos, however, he still
represents the light of reason, which can guide Dante through moral dark-
ness and intellectual uncertainty.

16–21   *I heard voices*   The souls undergoing penance are invisible in
the thick smoke, only their voices giving evidence of their presence. The
vice of Anger is countered by the virtue of Meekness facilitated by peace in
the mind. The souls communally sing the Agnus Dei (Lamb of God) hymn,
which is a traditional part of Mass: "Lamb of God that takest away the sins

of the world, have mercy on us; Lamb of God that takest away the sins of the world, give us peace."

24 *the knot of their wrath* The vice purged on this terrace is now identified. The image of the knot is a significant one throughout the *Commedia* (see, e.g., *Purg.* XXIII.15, XXIV.56; *Par.* VII.53, XXXIII.91).

25–27 *And who are you* The travelers are accosted by one of the invisible souls, whose abrupt address suggests he is still somewhat swayed by the Anger he purges.

31–33 *O creature cleansing yourself* Dante's courteous and calming address contrasts the spiritual beauty that the soul will attain with the intense blackness under which it currently suffers.

37–42 *Wearing the swaddling clothes* Dante describes his continuing journey in his temporal body and acknowledges the grace that makes his journey possible. As in other encounters, he uses the marvel of his special state to elicit information from the souls.

46–48 *I am a Lombard called Marco* Marco Lombardo, a minor nobleman probably from the province of Venice (c. 1250–1290) described in the *Novellino*. The early commentators identified him as a counselor and diplomat active in some of the courts of northern Italy. His status, similar to that of Dante himself, has led to the character sometimes being read as an alter ego for the poet. Marco's condemnation of the current world's moral laxity (they *aim with unstrung bows*, i.e., without impetus or activity) in these lines leads to the pilgrim's question of why the world is in such decline.

53–63 *But I will burst* The pilgrim asks whether the declining state of human affairs is due to astrological influences or causes originating on Earth. This is one of the *Commedia*'s central questions. Doubt has been raised in the pilgrim by Guido del Duca's comment on earthly goods and reinforced by Marco Lombardo's statement on the decline of the world.

65–126 *Brother the world is blind* Marco Lombardo's extended monologue takes in the centrality of human free will and the need for laws and guidance. The lack of the latter (due to the lack of an emperor and the corruption of the Papacy) is a root cause of the world's moral decline in Lombardo's eyes.

67–75 *You who are still alive* Elsewhere in the *Commedia*, Dante acknowledges the importance of astrological influence (see, e.g., *Par.* XXII.111–17). While the stars may have influence on an individual's initial impulse or desire (73), however, human beings have free will and are thus in control of and responsible for their actions. Human free will is absolutely necessary if human actions are to have any value (72).

76–78   *when it first battles the heavens*   The period of *first battles* is childhood, when the individual is still learning to control its irrational impulses and put them under the government of reason. Free will is not to unrestrainedly follow desire but to exercise the faculty of reason, the best facet of the human soul, in free choice.

79–81   *You, free, are subject to a greater power*   God is the direct Creator of the human intellect, which, since it finds its source in God, is not subject to control by the stars.

85–93   *From the hands of the Creator*   The poet imagines the soul as a child, innocent, unguided, and attracted by trivial delights. It is the joyous creature of a joyous Creator God. Its inborn instinctual desire for pleasurable things needs to be controlled (*reined in*) and guided in order for it to desire what is truly good: God.

94–112   *And so laws had to be imposed*   While laws were created to guide the uncontrolled instincts of the soul, Marco Lombardo here laments the lack of an honest leader to enforce them. By casting the leader as a *shepherd* (98), Dante, through the voice of Lombardo, is making a direct criticism of the contemporary Papacy (the shepherd of the Church), which in assuming the power that should belong to the emperor has corrupted its holy office.

96   *the one true city*   This is the City of God. A good leader must have a vision of this in order to guide his people toward it.

99   *does not have cleft hooves*   The image of the cloven hoof derives from Lev. 11:2–4: "Whatsoever hath the hoof divided and cheweth the cud among the beasts, you shall eat. But whatsoever cheweth indeed the cud, and hath a hoof but divideth it not . . . that shall you not eat, but shall reckon it among the unclean." Christians came to read the passage allegorically to mean that they must be clean rather than unclean. Chewing the cud was interpreted as meditating upon the scriptures. Early commentators and recent scholarship suggest that Dante uses this image to criticize the clergy's mixing of temporal and spiritual power.

100–102   *The people*   Lombardo's speech attributes much of the world's moral decline to the corruption of the Papacy, which, in assuming temporal power, has become embroiled in grasping for temporal goods and has lost its spiritual purpose.

106–8 *Rome, which made the world good once had two suns* Dante felt that Rome was a specially chosen civilization and the model of temporal laws and governance. It was, most importantly, the civilization into which Christ was born and under whose laws he was crucified, thus bringing about the redemption of humankind. In the image of the two suns, Dante is referring to the Empire and the Papacy; the role of the Empire was to guide its citizens toward good worldly ends while the Papacy was to guide their spiritual progress toward God. Dante outlines this view most explicitly in *Mon.* III.11.7–10.

109–10 *the sword is now joined to the crook* The respective symbols of temporal and spiritual power. In Dante's view, the joining of temporal power (the sword) to the spiritual authority of the Church (the crook) is a corruption of the Church's purpose.

113–14 *look at an ear of grain* Continuing the imagery of plants and fertility (or rather infertility) introduced in lines 58–60, these lines are an adaptation of words from the Sermon on the Mount: "By their fruits you shall know them . . . every good tree bringeth forth good fruit and every evil tree bringeth forth evil fruit" (Matt. 7:16–17). The "fruit" of the evil tree of the corrupted Papacy is the sorry state of Italy described in the following lines.

115–29 *In the land* A further example of one of the *Commedia*'s many invectives against the corrupt state of thirteenth-century Italy. The corruption of the land is paradoxically emphasized by the fact that Marco Lombardo can name the only three good men in the whole of northern Italy. Importantly, these figures belong to the older generation, suggesting that it is the generation of the present day that has lost the nobility of its predecessors and fallen into decline.

115 *the Adige and Po* The two rivers that delineate the area of northern Italy.

116–17 *before Frederick met with opposition* Dante identifies the papal opposition to Emperor Frederick II (emperor from 1220 to 1250), starting in the late 1220s, as the point marking the beginning of Italy's decline.

124 *Currado del Palazzo* A political figure from Brescia who served as head of the Guelph party (1277) and *podestà* of Florence and Piacenza.

124 *good Gherardo* Gherardo da Camino of Treviso (c. 1240–1306), a nobleman famed for his generosity to poets. Early commentators suggest that Dante stayed with him in the early days of his exile.

125–26   *Guido del Castel*   A nobleman of the Roberti family of Reggio Emilia (c. 1235 to after 1315). He gained his epithet the "honest Lombard" from his generosity with French nobles.

127–29   *Church of Rome*   A reiteration of the corruption caused by the Papacy assuming temporal as well as spiritual governance.

131–32   *the sons of Levi*   The poet references the biblical story of the tribe of Levi told in Num. 18:20–24. The tribe were appointed priests of the temple and were to receive tithes from other tribes, but they could not own a region of the Promised Land. Dante employs the biblical example to show a biblical precedent for not mixing spiritual with temporal power.

133–40   *But who is this Gherardo*   This rhetorical device (the pilgrim's ignorance and Marco Lombardo's surprise) serves to emphasize the fame of Gherardo.

139–44   *May God go with you*   Marco's brusque adieu is equivalent to his brusque entrance, reminding us that quick-tempered Anger is the sin he is purging.

Canto XVII

1–9   *Recall, reader*   This address to the reader opens the theme of interiority that persists throughout the canto. Shrouded in mist and darkness, the senses are cut off and the focus turns inward to the imagination. The poet encourages his readers to imagine emerging from misty darkness and slowly moving toward the hazy light of the sun.

2–3   *you could not see except as moles do*   It was believed that moles had skin growing over their eyes and were therefore blind (see, e.g., Bruntello Latini's *Tresor* I.197). As with the image of the mist, the mole evokes the idea of sensory deprivation and inward-looking vision.

13–45   *O, imagination*   This passage explores, beneath the exempla of Anger shown, the nature of imagination, its activity, and its origin. Lines 17–18 question whether waking visions come from celestial bodies or from God working through those bodies. Interspersed with the exempla, the poet intercuts metaphors to describe the workings of imagination (*rained down, burst . . . as a bubble*). As in the exempla of Meekness, these internal visions totally overcome the pilgrim's senses, for a time rendering him absent from the sensory world.

19–21   *the impious deed of that woman*   The reference is to the story of Philomela and Procne, told in *Met*.VI.424–674 (see note to canto IX.16–18).The passage refers to Procne's murder of her own son. She and her sister Philomela then fed the child to his father. Precisely which *impious deed*—and therefore which woman—is being referred to is ambiguous.

26–30   *the image of one crucified*   The crucified figure is Haman, minister to the Persian king Ahasuerus. The Jew Mordecai refused to bow to Haman, who, affronted, then persuaded the king to sentence all the Jews to death. Mordecai's niece Esther, the favorite of the king, confronted Haman in the king's presence. The king had Haman hung on the scaffold destined for Mordecai. The story is found in Est. 3 and 4.

34–39   *a young maiden weeping*   A story drawn from Virgil's *Aeneid* (VII.341–53, XII.63–64, 604–6). The young maiden is Lavinia, daughter of Amata the wife of king Latinus of Latium. Amata, who was driven into mad anger by the Fury Allecto, vows that she will never see her daughter married to the Trojan Aeneas instead of the Latian hero Turnus. Believing that Turnus has been killed in battle, Amata hangs herself.

46–51   *I was turning around*   This short passage, in which the pilgrim is filled with focused desire to see the angel, anticipates the discussion on the nature of love and desire that follows in this canto and the next.

58–60   *He treats us*   The poet combines two indirect citations, the first to Mk. 12:31, "Thou shalt love thy neighbor as thyself," and the second to Seneca's *De beneficiis*, which states, "To be slow to wish to give is not to wish it . . . he who delays is unwilling." The angel offers access to the travelers before he is asked, loving them as he loves himself.

67–69   *I felt a wing*   The by now familiar ascent of the pilgrim from one terrace to another: the scar of the P representing Anger is removed from his forehead and a joyful Beatitude is sung, this time *Beati pacifici*, blessed are the peacemakers.

70–75   *Twilight's last rays*   As the sunlight dwindles, the rule of the mountain by which souls cannot ascend at night comes into play (see note to VII.40–60).

85–87   *In this circle is restored*   In response to the pilgrim's question, Virgil tells him that Sloth is the vice purged on this new terrace. Sloth is understood as insufficiently active love.

91–139   *Neither Creator nor creature*   Virgil's discourse here sits at the literal heart of the poem, taking a central place in both the poem's structure and the poem's thought system. Love is what motivates every action, both good and bad. In the light of this, the vices that are purged in Purgatory come to be described by Virgil as love misdirected or misused.

91–93   *Neither Creator nor creature*   Belonging to both God and Creation, love is what negotiates all relationships in the universe. Using the terms "Creator" and "creature," Dante follows Christian Neoplatonist beliefs that God created because of love and that love moves all created things.

94–105   *Natural love*   Virgil compares natural love, in which the creature cannot fail to love its Creator God, and elective love, in which creatures endowed with free will (humans and angels) can choose (for good or ill) the object of their love. Marco Lombardo's discourse on the difficulties surrounding free will gives some context to this question. Because well- or ill-directed love is within the control of rational creatures, their actions can be worthy of reward or punishment.

106–11   *since love can never turn*   In Virgil's reasoning, a subject will always love itself and will always love God as the originator (the first) of its existence.

112–24   *the evil we love*   Since an individual cannot wish evil to itself or God, it must be evil done to one's neighbor that is loved. The poet has already considered the socially destructive nature of sin in the chaotic noncommunities of the *Inferno* as well as the rebuilding of community through virtue in *Purgatorio*. Virgil describes the nature of Pride (115–17), Envy (118–20), and Anger (121–23), of which the pilgrim has witnessed the purgation on the lower terraces of the mountain.

128   *where the mind may rest*   Dante conceives of desire as a motion. Temporal or finite objects of desire are inherently unsatisfying, and it is only in God, the *good where the mind may rest*, that peace from desire can be found.

125–37   *Now I would have you hear*   The capital vices of Pride, Envy, and Anger are characterized as love of the harm of others and therefore love directed toward a bad object. The vices that occupy the higher terraces of Purgatory are examples of excessive love for objects that are not in themselves bad (possessions, food, and people). It is only the nature of Sloth, however, that Virgil describes in any detail here (130–32).

139   *So may you find it yourself*   Virgil, rather than providing an explanation, chooses to leave his pupil's further education to experience.

Canto XVIII

1–9 *After the exalted teacher* The tender relationship between Virgil and Dante, who are teacher and pupil, father and son to each other, is reinforced in this passage. Virgil's role as guide and teacher is at its height in the central cantos of *Purg.* XVII and XVIII, in which he provides his most extended philosophical expositions.

10–18 *my vision becomes so keen* Dante uses the metaphor of physical vision to express his intellectual understanding. This understanding takes place in the light of natural reason, which is provided and represented by Virgil. Virgil continues the metaphor at lines 16–18, encouraging Dante to use the "sharp eyes" of his intellect to lead him away from the blindness of false understanding.

13 *explain to me love* The direct simplicity of the pilgrim's question belies the complexity of the issue and opens the way for one of the poem's most profound and complex poetic-philosophical passages.

19–39 *The mind, ready to love* Virgil's exposition of love is philosophical, rather than theological, in tone as befits his own status as a pagan withheld from the light of divine revelation. Virgil presents an Aristotelian account of *apprehension*, in which his principal influence is Aristotle's *De anima* (On the soul). To paraphrase his argument: the mind is created ready to love and is attracted to pleasing things that it perceives through the bodily senses. The mind takes on the *form* of the pleasing thing that imprints upon the *matter* of the imagination. The mind then forms an intention toward that thing (22–24). If the thing is then truly pleasing to the mind, the latter will turn toward it and this is love. But the account Virgil gives at this stage is of natural, instinctive love, which humans share with animals. It is love undirected by reason. As such, it is not necessarily worthy of praise (34–36), since not everything loved is worthy to be loved. While the internal mechanism of *apprehension* may be good in itself, that does not mean that everything that is *apprehended* is equally good (38–39).

38–39 *not every seal is as good as the wax* The wax is the powers of apprehension that are in themselves good; the seals are the objects that imprint upon those apprehensions, which certainly differ in their worthiness. The image of wax and seal is an important one throughout the *Commedia* (see, e.g., *Purg.* X.44–45; *Par.* XI.106–8). The use of the image here is inspired by Aristotle's *De anima* II.12.42a and later scholastic uses of it.

43–45 *For if love is offered from outside* Dante questions how love can be judged as good or bad based on Virgil's explanation that love is apparently always dictated by outside forces. The question was one that had significantly gained the attention of poets contemporary to Dante and that Dante himself had begun to address in the episode of Francesca, who claims in *Inf.*V that love can overwhelm human reason.

46–48   *As far as reason can go*   Virgil, aware of his own limitations, looks ahead to Beatrice, who will be able to explain these issues to Dante in the light of Christian revelation.

49–75   *Every substantial form*   The second half of Virgil's discourse opens with an explanation of the instinctual kind of love for basic objects of desire that humanity shares with the animal kingdom. This instinctual love *does not admit of either praise or blame* (60). However, humans are distinct from animals in possessing a *sense of judgment* (62). They have rational intellect and free will, which means they do not have to follow every desire that comes to them but can choose which are good and bad. In this choice lies the merit (or blame) of actions (64–66). This is to have free will.

49–54   *Every substantial form*   This passage, like the first half of Virgil's discourse, draws heavily on Aristotelian ideas, in this case substance, form, and virtue. Substance denotes an individual, subsisting thing. Form is what makes a thing what it is; it determines the way a thing is and makes it individual. Virtue ("power" in this translation) is the power a thing has to be what it is. In Virgil's words, virtue can only be revealed in action; thus a plant demonstrates its virtue, its power to be fully itself, in its green leaves.

67–69   *Those who reasoned this through*   Virgil pays homage to his fellow Limbo dwellers, the classical philosophers who developed ethics, in particular Plato and Aristotle.

73–75   *Beatrice understands this noble virtue*   The second mention of Beatrice in the canto reminds us that Virgil's knowledge is necessarily incomplete since he is excluded from the knowledge brought by Christian revelation.

76–81   *The moon, rising just after midnight*   This extended indication of time describes the rising gibbous (bucket shaped) moon, whose light makes the stars invisible. The moon rises at the point where somebody standing in Rome would see the sun set—between Sardinia and Corsica.

82   *Pietola*   The town near Mantua where Virgil was born.

88–105   *But that drowsiness was lifted from me*   The pensive tone of the canto thus far is broken in upon by the running crowd of the slothful penitents. Sloth, defined by Virgil in canto XVII as insufficient love, is counteracted by zeal, which is manifested in the penitents' continual motion, even in the hours of night.

91–93   *just as the Ismenus and Asopus*   The poet compares the group of dashing souls to the worshippers of the god Bacchus, who held wild revels along the banks of the Ismenus and Asopus rivers near the city of Thebes.

96   *with Right Will and Just Love high in the saddle*   Again the poet uses an image of horse riding to express the training of the penitents.

100–102   *Mary ran in great haste*   Two extremely condensed exempla of zeal. The first refers to the story of Mary, who, when she learned she would bear the child of God, ran to tell her cousin Elizabeth (Lk. 1:39–40). The second is taken from Julius Caesar's *De bello civili* (On civil wars) I.34–87 and Lucan's *Pharsalia* III.453–55, which describe an action of Caesar during the civil war against Pompey. Caesar captured the city of Marseilles and then proceeded to march on Pompey's troops in Spain, defeating them. The action took only forty days.

113–17   *Come behind us*   In keeping with the courtesy that marks Purgatory as a whole, the soul asks forgiveness from the travelers for continuing his hasty penance while conversing with them.

118–26   *I was abbot of San Zeno*   This is Gerard, who was abbot of the rich and powerful abbey of San Zeno in Verona during the reign of Emperor Frederick Barbarossa. He died in 1187. It is significant that the individual soul who is an example of Sloth was a monk, since the monastic life was thought to foster the vice of Sloth.

121–26   *there is one with one foot in the grave*   Alberto della Scala, who, the year before he died (1301), had his crippled son Giuseppe appointed as abbot of San Zeno, an act that violated Church law.

134–38   *The people for whom the Red Sea opened*   The examples of Sloth are drawn from the Old Testament and the *Aeneid*. The first refers to the Israelites, who, having been released from Egypt, were tardy and undecided toward God. In response, God commanded that the Israelites could not enter the Promised Land until all those who had crossed the Red Sea during the flight from Egypt had died. The second describes the Trojan women who, weary of the long sea voyage from the destroyed city of Troy, set fire to the Trojan ships to prevent the journey continuing. The fire was put out by a rainstorm sent by Jupiter, and those who did not wish to continue the journey were left behind in disgrace.

Canto XIX

1–6 *At that hour*   The pilgrim's three dreams that take place in Purgatory (here and cantos IX.1–99 and XXVII.94–108) all take place just before dawn, which since antiquity had been believed to be the period of the night that fostered prophetic dreams. The celestial bodies mentioned here—Earth, Saturn, and the moon—were all associated with cold, which by extension was connected to a desire for lesser goods. This setting therefore establishes one of the canto's most important themes: love of false goods.

4–6 *geomancers see their Fortuna Major*   Geomancy is the art of divining the future from Earth signs. Fortuna Major is one of the sixteen geomantic figures and relates to a grouping of stars.

7–33 *There came to me in a dream a woman*   The pilgrim's dream of the Siren continues questions raised in the preceding canto. The pilgrim's unwary unconscious is at first seduced by the Siren, with his own desiring gaze transforming the misshapen crone into a beautiful woman. He is saved by the timely intervention of a mysterious woman and the action of Virgil, who tears away the Siren's clothes to reveal her repellent belly and genitalia. The dream can be interpreted as a meditation on the dangerously seductive power of false goods and the vital role of divine intervention and rational discrimination in controlling human desire.

19–24 *I am, she sang, the sweet Siren*   The myth of the Sirens is told in Homer's *Odyssey* (XII.3.9–54, 158–64, 181–200), in which Ulysses and his band of sailors encounter these creatures. To resist their seductive song that draws men to their doom, Ulysses has his men fill their ears with wax to block out the sound, while he himself is tied to the mast so he can hear them but not be lured toward them. In the myth, the Sirens offer Ulysses knowledge, but in the later tradition they became more associated with sensual pleasure.

25–26 *a lady, holy and alert*   This unidentified lady prefigures the appearance of Beatrice in cantos XXX and XXXI, in which she directly engages the pilgrim in a consideration of his own wayward desires for false goods. The identity of the lady is ambiguous and has been debated in scholarship although it seems likely that she represents an intervention of the divine that stirs the rational judgment (represented by Virgil) into action.

31–33 *rending her clothes to show me her belly*   There is a clear sexual reference here, making this a unique instance in Dante's works of showing sexual disgust.

34   *the stench*   Christian and chivalric traditions often linked a foul stench to the presence of the devil.

43–51   *Come, here is the pass*   The calming appearance of the angel contrasts with the tense and unsettling dream and its aftermath. A further Beatitude (Blessed are they who mourn) confirms the travelers' passage from the terrace of Sloth.

52–63   *Why do you keep staring at the ground*   The appearance of the angel and his exit from the terrace fail to break the pilgrim's preoccupation with his disturbing dream. In lines 58–60 Virgil provides a somewhat cryptic interpretation of the dream designed to allay the pilgrim's fears. Virgil identifies the *ancient witch* with the "love of lesser goods," which is *lamented above us* on the final three terraces of Purgatory. Virgil encourages the pilgrim to focus his attention upon the true good that awaits at the end of his journey to God.

62–66   *your eyes turned to the lure*   Again the image of the training falcon expresses the training that the soul (this time that of the pilgrim) undergoes in Purgatory. Shown the true aim of its desires (*the lure*) the falcon hungrily desires to ascend to it.

70–72   *When I stepped forth*   In contrast to earlier cantos, the travelers are confronted with the penitential souls on this terrace as soon as they arrive.

73   *Adhaesit pavimento anima mea*   The first half of line 25 of Ps. 118, which reads, "My soul has cleaved to the pavement." Augustine in his influential commentary on the psalm took "pavement" to mean earthly goods, and thus the psalm was interpreted as a reflection upon the danger of adhering to earthly things.

76–77   *lightened by both justice and hope*   An important reiteration of the impulses that make the penances of Purgatory bearable.

91–92   *Spirit in whom weeping ripens that state*   Exactly what *that state* is remains ambiguous although it most probably means the focused desire for the things of Heaven as opposed to those of Earth.

99–126   *scias ego fui successor Petri*   A solemn Latin line introduces the soul of Ottobono dei Fieschi (1215–1276), who, only thirty-eight days before his death, became Pope Adrian V. Ottobono foregrounds his short-lived role as Pope since that marked the moment of his true conversion away from the sin of Avarice that he is now purging (106–8). His Latin phrase means "know that I was Peter's successor" and refers to the fact that all Popes are successors of St Peter, the first Pope.

100–102   *Between Sestri and Chiavari*   Sestri and Chiavari are two towns on the Ligurian coast. Ottobono's family, the Fieschi, were counts of the area of the Lavagna river.

106–13   *My conversion—ah me!—was late in coming*   Ottobono's impassioned speech reflects on the nature and consequences of the vice of Avarice. To love earthly goods excessively is to love the unreal, the unessential (108); they can provide no peace from desire (109–10). In this, the poet is echoing a famous line from Augustine's *Confessions*: "Our heart is unquiet until it rests in you" (I.1). Only God can provide the end of desire. To experience excessive love of earthly things is to separate oneself from God by choosing to love what is lesser than Him. Such separation is the worst situation for the soul.

115–17   *the mountain has no penalty more bitter*   While it is clear that Ottobono is speaking from a subjective position, in the process of suffering himself, the identification of the punishment for Avarice as the worst the mountain contains is striking indeed. Arguably, the vice and the punishment go to the very heart of the discussions of love that fill the central cantos of the poem; to be separated from and to lack the sight of God, the only true object of love, is the worst the soul can suffer.

118–26   *Just as our eyes, fixed on earthly things*   While some forms of penance on Mount Purgatory enact the opposite of the vice they purge (the stiff-necked proud are bent over, the envious have their eyes forcibly closed), the vice of Avarice is purged by carrying that vice to its extreme. The souls who chose to fix their eyes on the Earth are now unable to stop doing so.

127–38   *I had kneeled*   On realizing he is speaking to a former Pope, the pilgrim kneels in an attitude of reverence. However, Ottobono rejects the need for his reverence, addressing him as *brother* (133) and reminding him that the Popes are in fact servants of the servants of God (*servi servorum Dei*).

136–38   *Neque nubent*   A reference to the Gospel story of Jesus and the Sadducees (Matt. 22:30). The Sadducees asked Jesus whose wife a woman married seven times would be after the Resurrection. Jesus replied that the marriage bond would no longer apply after the Resurrection. Thus the Pope, symbolically married to his diocese, is loosed from this bond after death, and the pilgrim's reverence to him as a Pope no longer applies.

Canto XX

1–3 *Our wills fight poorly* The close of the previous canto saw the former Pope Adrian V desirous of ending his conversation with Dante in order to return to his penance. These opening lines demonstrate the pilgrim's eagerness to know more.

4–9 *I moved on* The penance of the souls has them laid out facedown upon the pavement. This description indicates that the prostrate souls take up most of the pavement space up to the outer edge, forcing the travelers to hug the cliff face.

10–15 *A curse upon you, wolf of the ages* Dante returns to the image of the she-wolf used in *Inf.* I.91–112, which is now identified specifically with the vice of Avarice. Biblical tradition cites Avarice as the root of all evil (1 Tim. 6:10).

19–33 *I happened to hear* The exempla of liberality, the contrasting virtue to the vice of Avarice. Unusually, these exempla are provided by a single soul calling them out loud.

20–21 *someone call out tearfully* The sound of the individual soul calling out the exempla of liberality is compared to the cries of a woman giving birth. Traditionally, women in labor would invoke the name of Mary for aid and protection. This striking simile introduces the important theme of birth and rebirth that prevails in this and subsequent cantos. Birth is closely associated with conversion to faith and baptism.

20–24 *O sweet Mary* As always, the first exemplum of virtue is an event in the life of the Virgin Mary. This event is the birth of Christ, which took place in a poor stable (Lk. 2:7).

25–27 *O good Fabricius* C. Fabricius Luscius was a Roman consul in 282 BC. He refused to be bribed during a plot to betray Rome and spent the rest of his days in poverty.

31–33 *the dowries bestowed by Nicholas* St Nicholas, bishop of Myra in Asia Minor in the third through fourth centuries. According to legend, to save three sisters from poverty and prostitution, he dropped gold through their window to provide them with dowries.

40–123 *I will tell you* One of the poem's longest monologues, Hugh Capet's account is mostly dedicated to describing the crimes of his own French dynasty, only answering the pilgrim's second question on why he alone speaks the exempla in the final two tercets. The account enters into the minutiae of European history and political machinations in the two centuries before the *Commedia* was written.

43–45 *I was the root of the evil tree* Genealogical trees are a powerful image and objects of frequent pictorial illustration in the medieval period. The evil tree that Hugh describes is a parody of the tree of Jesse (Matt. 1:1–17), which details Christ's genealogy.

46–47 *Douai, Lilla, Ghent and Bruges* The free cities of Flanders. The Capetian king, Philip IV, promised freedom to the Count of Flanders if he surrendered Ghent. Philip went back on his word, imprisoning the count. In response, the free cities defeated Philip in battle at Courtrai in 1302. In relation to the fictional date of the *Commedia* (1300) this event is still in the future.

49–51 *Hugh Capet* Was a lay abbot and died in 996. Hugh founded the line of Capetian kings, the majority of whom were called Philip or Louis (50).

52 *I was the son of a Parisian butcher* While this was a popular legend about the origins of the Capetian family in Dante's period, Hugh and his father were actually dukes of France and counts of Paris and Orleans.

53–54 *the old line of kings* The line of the Carolingian kings. The remaining descendent, who now wears *monk's grey robes*, is Charles of Lorraine, uncle of the last Carolingian king Louis V. According to Godfrey of Viterbo, Hugh forced Charles into a monastery.

55–60 *I found the reins of royal government* With the support of anti-Carolingian factions, Hugh was crowned king in Rheims on Christmas day, 988. His son, Robert I, worked very closely with his father after Hugh's consecration.

61–63 *the great dowry of Provence* The county of Provence came under the possession of the Capetian dynasty when Beatrice of Provence, daughter of Raymond Berenger, married Charles I of Anjou (c. 1246).

66 *Ponthieu, Normandy and Gascony* Territories that had been held by the English but that were reappropriated by the Capetians over the course of the thirteenth century.

67–69 *Charles came into Italy* Charles I of Anjou conducted a military campaign in Italy, defeating Manfred (III.118–29) in 1266. Using treachery, Charles captured Conradino, grandson of Emperor Frederick II, and had him beheaded in Naples in 1268. This ended the Hohenstaufen dynasty. An unfounded story had it that St Thomas Aquinas was poisoned under the order of Charles because he was going to reveal the "truth" about what Charles had done.

70–78   *I see a time*   Hugh foretells events that took place in 1301, when Charles of Valois (1270–1325) marched into Italy intending to reclaim Sicily for the French kingdom. On reaching Florence Charles, allied with Pope Boniface VIII, favored the Black Guelph party and assisted in ousting the White Guelphs, the party to which Dante belonged. Charles at first left his troops outside the city (73), revealing his treachery later. The powerful combined images of the lance of Judas (74) and the burst paunch (75) recall the biblical story of Judas' suicide told in Acts 1:18.

79–81   *The other Charles*   Charles II of Anjou (1248–1309). Overthrown as king of Sicily by Ruggiero di Lauria, admiral of the Aragonese, Charles was held in captivity 1284–1287. Charles gave his daughter Beatrice in marriage to Azzo VIII d'Este in return for a huge sum of money.

82–84   *O Avarice*   Hugh attributes the crimes of his dynasty to the vice of Avarice in their unceasing desire for property, power, and riches.

86–93   *I see the fleur-de-lis*   The event referred to is the arrest of Pope Boniface VIII by order of Philip the Fair, formerly Boniface's ally. Boniface had threatened Philip with excommunication and had issued papal bulls claiming papal authority over French royal prerogatives. Boniface was seized by French agents (the fleur-de-lis is the symbol of France) at his palace in Anagni but was rescued by the townspeople. He died of shock within a month. While Dante is generally extremely critical of Boniface, this passage acknowledges that as Pope he was, nevertheless, Christ's representative on Earth. In this passage, the humiliation of the Pope is figured as a second crucifixion. Following this event, the Papacy came under French control and its seat was moved to the city of Avignon.

91–93   *this new Pilate*   Philip the Fair, who leaves Boniface to his hired agents just as Pilate left Christ to be judged by the Jews.

91–93   *against the Temple*   Referring to events of 1307 in which Philip the Fair ordered the arrest and torture of leaders of the Templar Order. He did this without the sanction of the Pope, the titular head of the order. The order was suppressed in 1312. Philip had been greatly in debt to the Templars but on their suppression acquired much of their vast wealth, in a further instance of the Avarice that so characterizes Hugh's portrayal of the Capetian dynasty.

97–102   *the one and only bride*   Hugh at last returns to the pilgrim's second question about the exempla he alone had been uttering. He tells the pilgrim that during the day the exempla of liberality is spoken, while at night the warning examples of Avarice are told.

103–5 *Pygmalion*   The brother of the Carthaginian queen Dido, Pygmalion murdered Dido's husband Sichaeus in order to acquire his riches. The story is told in *Aen.* I.340–59.

106–8 *avaricious Midas*   King Midas of Phrygia wished that everything he touched might turn to gold. His wish turned sour when his food also turned to gold. The story appears in *Met.* XI.85–179.

109–11 *foolish Achan*   A story told in Jo. 7:1–26. Following the fall of Jericho, the solider Achan steals treasure from the city. When his avaricious action is revealed by Joshua, he is stoned to death.

112 *Sapphira and her husband*   Sapphira and Ananias were members of the early Christian community who kept for themselves part of the proceeds from a land sale. Peter denounced them and they died immediately (Acts 5:1–11).

113 *the trampling of Heliodorus*   Heliodorus was treasurer to the Syrian king Seleucus IV. He was ordered to take money from the Temple of Jerusalem but was prevented from doing so when a mysterious horse and rider in golden armor knocked him to the ground (2 Macc. 3:25).

114–15 *the disgrace of Polymestor*   A second story from the *Aeneid*. King Priam of Troy entrusted his son Polydorus to Polymestor along with a large quantity of gold. When the city of Troy fell, Polymestor murdered Polydorus and took the money (*Aen.* III.55–58).

116–17 *Crassus*   Crassus was the third member of the Roman Triumvirate along with Julius Caesar and Pompey. He was also one of the richest men in Rome. He was defeated and killed by the Parthians and his head was sent to the Parthian king, who ordered that the mouth be filled with molten gold (told in Cicero *De Officiis* I.30).

118–23 *Sometimes one speaks loud*   Hugh at last provides a relatively simple answer to the pilgrim's question of lines 35–36.

127–29 *the whole mountain tremble*   The earthquake that shakes Mount Purgatory recalls the Bible's images of the apocalypse (Lk. 23:28–30; Apoc. 6:16; Is. 2:19).

130–32 *Delos was not shaken so violently*   Delos was the island on which Latona gave birth to the twins Apollo and Diana (132). It was originally a floating island and thus subject to earthquakes; but legend has it that after Latona gave birth, Apollo fixed the island in place (*Aen.* III.73–77).

133–38 *Then there rose up such a cry*   The earthquake is immediately followed by a great singing of "Gloria in excelsis Deo" (Glory to God in the highest). The pilgrim's fearful reaction to the loud cry recalls the traditional connection of this hymn with the Nativity and the fear of the shepherds at the angels' announcement of the birth of Christ (Lk. 2:8–14), and indeed this event is specifically recalled in lines 139–41. The "Gloria" is also traditionally sung at the Easter midnight Mass, accompanied by loud ringing bells. This scene then dramatically brings forward the themes of birth, rebirth, and resurrection.

Canto XXI

1–6 *The natural thirst* The opening of the canto finds the pilgrim assailed by different emotional states: curiosity to understand the cause of the earthquake, physical hurry to progress along the journey, and sadness for the nonetheless just punishment of the souls. In the latter cantos of the *Purgatorio*, the poet frequently employs the metaphor of thirst to express spiritual desire.

1–3 *the poor Samaritan woman* Recalling the meeting of Jesus and the Samaritan woman at a well (Jn. 4:5–15). Jesus' offer of the waters of everlasting life to the Samaritan, a woman from a different group, was taken to be symbolic of the offer of Christianity to Gentiles and Jews alike in response to their "thirst" for God.

7–15 *just as we read in Luke* Dante draws on two biblical scenes to describe the appearance of the as yet unidentified shade, both of which compare the shade to the resurrected Christ. Both events are described in Lk. 24. In the first, two disciples on the road to Emmaus are joined by the resurrected Jesus but do not know him (verses 15–16). In the second, Jesus appears in the midst of the disciples on their return to Jerusalem, saying, "Peace be to you; it is I, fear not" (verses 35–36), echoed in Statius' words at line 13.

16–18 *May the true court* A moving reiteration that the same judgment that saves the newly liberated soul also damns Virgil to Limbo. This tercet opens a central issue of this and the following canto, and indeed the poem as a whole: why cannot Virgil be saved?

25–33 *But since she who spins* Virgil must again explain the unique condition of the pilgrim Dante. Interestingly, Dante's continuing embodiedness is here described as an impediment to clear-sightedness (30). As a man in a body he is out of place in this realm and his bodily perceptions appear unsuited to fully understand it.

25–27   *she who spins the thread*   Three Fates were believed to spin the thread of an individual's life: Clotho allotted the flax, Lachesis spun it, and Atropos cut it. The image reminds us that the pilgrim is not yet dead; his thread of life has not been cut.

28   *His soul, which is your sister and mine*   The Italian word for soul, *anima*, is feminine and so the souls of the three characters are personified as "sisters."

40–72   *And the shade responded*   Statius begins his reply to Virgil's question by explaining that phenomena caused by nature (wind, rain, etc.) do not affect Mount Purgatory (40–57). Therefore, the earthquake that the mountain experienced was not the result of nature but was in fact a response to the liberation of a soul from purgation (58–60). He then explains that a soul in a sense frees itself on feeling its will to be truly liberated from sin (61–66). Finally Statius reveals that it is the liberation of his own soul that aroused the quake and jubilation.

50   *Thaumas' daughter*   Iris, the goddess of rainbows.

53–54   *the vicar of Peter*   The angel who guards the gate of Purgatory.

61–66   *The will alone gives proof of its purity*   The soul in Purgatory is split between two desires: the desire to move toward God and the desire to purge itself in accordance with the sin committed. The issue of a divided will was explored by Augustine in his *Confessions* VIII.8–12, in which his will was torn between a love of God and a love of earthly things.

82–136   *Statius*   The Roman poet Statius (c. 45–96 AD) was from Naples, although Dante (along with many of his contemporaries) confuses him here with Statius Ursulus of Toulouse (89).

82–84   *In the time when the good Titus*   The historical context that Statius gives for his own personal story focuses on the Judean rebellion that took place in 66–73 AD. Along with most medieval Christians, Dante viewed this event as the just punishment of the people who had put Christ to death.

88–90   *So sweet was my poetic voice*   The traditional plant that crowns a great poet is the laurel. Dante's use of myrtle may be a subtle means of retaining the unassigned laurel crown for himself.

92–93   *I sang of Thebes*   Statius mentions two of his major works, the *Thebaid* (which recounts the assault on the city of Thebes by the seven champions of Argos) and the *Achilleid* (an unfinished work recounting the life of the hero Achilles).

94–102   *The seeds of my poetic fire*   The tone of Statius' praise of the *Aeneid* is at once lofty and intimate. The dramatic imagery of fire recalls Virgil's own *Aeneid* (*Aen*.VI.7, 730–32) while the use of the homely *mother and nurse* indicates the personal nourishment that Virgil's poetry provided.

103–36   *These words turned Virgil to me*   One of the most touching and beautifully comic passages of the poem. Virgil does not want his identity to be revealed. The pilgrim, pleased by the praise heaped upon his master, cannot conceal his pleasure and smiles. Statius is confused, perhaps even offended by the pilgrim's smile. And so the pilgrim is caught between two authoritative figures, unable to decide what to do. Facial expressions are important throughout Dante's works, as will be particularly revealed in the pilgrim's forthcoming encounter with Beatrice.

130–36   *Already he was bending*   Virgil insists on the equality between himself and Statius. Statius' excuse is a striking statement on the power of even the memory of great poetry: to make the dead forget they are dead and to live their love again.

Canto XXII

1–6   *The angel*   The encounter with the angel is described briefly and retrospectively this time. The beatitude that celebrates the exit from the terrace of Avarice is referenced elliptically with only *sitiunt*. This is the fourth Beatitude: Blessed are they that hunger and thirst after justice, for they shall have their fill (Matt. 5:6). However, since only *thirsting* (*sitiunt*) is specified, it seems likely that the hunger described in the Beatitude may be reserved for the inhabitants of the next terrace, that of Gluttony.

7–9   *I moved on more lightly*   A subtle reminder of vice as a *weight* that is being progressively removed as the pilgrim climbs the mountain.

10–24   *When Virgil began*   The poet Dante imagines that Virgil has heard about Statius' admiration from the Roman satirist Juvenal and that this inspired an answering affection for Statius in him. A real historical acquaintance between Statius and Juvenal is unlikely but nevertheless provides a charming fiction and an ingenious way of establishing amity between two poets (Virgil and Statius) who never met. Because of this amity, Virgil feels able to question Statius on how he came to succumb to the vice of Avarice.

26–54   *Your every word*   Statius' response to Virgil's question reveals that his vice was not Avarice but its opposite, prodigality. Exclusively in his treatment of avarice/prodigality, Dante uses the Aristotelian definition of vice as a departure from the mean between two extremes of behavior. In the light of this, unrestrainedly to squander money is as bad as to hoard it avariciously. The extreme opposite of a vice can be equally bad.

37–42   *if I had not directed my care*   The first of two passages in which Statius attributes his salvation to the influence of Virgil's works. Statius cites lines from Virgil's *Aeneid* relative to the story of Polymestor and Polydorus (*Aen.* III.55–58; see *Purg.* XX.115): "Quid non mortalis pectora cogis, / auri sacra fames?" (To what will you not drive human hearts, accursed hunger for gold?). Dante's adaptation of these lines, however, is extremely subtle, deriving from the two potential meanings of *sacra*: "accursed" and "sacred." Rather than selecting one or the other, it is likely that Dante wants us to keep this double meaning in mind. Excessive hunger for gold can indeed be destructive, *accursed*; but there is also a right relation to gold, a *sacred* hunger that maintains moderation.

42   *I would be rolling stones now at the grim jousts*   The punishment for Avarice and prodigality described in *Inf.* VII.22–66.

55–63   *Virgil, the singer of bucolic songs*   In his second question to Statius, Virgil asks what made Statius turn to Christianity, having apparently found no Christian tones in his work the *Thebaid* (58–60). Jocasta unwittingly married her own son Oedipus, who fathered two sons by her, Eteocles and Polynices, who go on to kill each other. Clio was the Muse of history, invoked by Statius in *Theb.* I.41–42 and X.628–31.

63   *the Fisherman*   St Peter (Matt. 4:18–20).

64–72   *It was you*   The second instance in which Statius attributes his salvation to the influence of Virgil's work. In one of the most celebrated and saddest images of the *Commedia*, Statius describes Virgil's work as a light that fails to enlighten its own author (67–69). The Virgilian text to which Statius refers in lines 70–72 is the fourth eclogue, which was interpreted by early and medieval Christians as prophesying the birth of Christ.

76–99   *The entire world was already pregnant*   Statius describes the stages of his conversion to Christianity: awakened by Virgil's text, encouraged by the words of Christian preachers, and finally secretly baptized. There is no historical documentation to support his story. Statius refers to the persecution of the early Christians by the Roman emperor Domitian (emperor from 81 to 96 AD) to explain the secrecy around his conversion.

96–114   *Where is our ancient Terence*   Statius' inquiry and Virgil's response come to make up one of the longest catalogues of classical figures in the *Commedia*, extending the list of *Inf.* IV.79–144. The figures are a combination of classical authors and historical/literary figures.

97–98   *Terence, our Caecilius*   Terence, Caecilius, and Plautus were all Roman dramatists whose work was known indirectly by Dante.

100–114   *All those*   Aulus Persius Flaccus was a Roman author who wrote satires. Euripides, Antiphon, Simonides, and Agathon were all dramatists. Antigone, Deiphyle, Argia, Ismene, and *she who revealed Langia* (Hypsipyle) are all figures mentioned in the *Thebaid*. Tiresias' daughter is Manto. Thetis, Achilles' mother, and Deidamia, his wife, are mentioned in the *Achilleid*.

130–53   *a tree*   The first of two trees encountered here on the terrace of Gluttony. The unusual shape of the foliage, like an upside-down pyramid, deters any unwise attempts to climb the tree. This is the first terrace on which the object of the vice (here Gluttony) is presented and indeed presented as sensually tempting. It is in the withholding of the pleasurable object that the punishment lies. The exempla of restraint emanate from the tree itself.

141   *Of this food you shall have a scarcity*   This line derives from the biblical story of Genesis in which God gives the Garden of Eden to Adam and Eve with only the prohibition that they do not eat the fruit from the tree of knowledge (Gen. 2:15–17).

142–44   *Mary gave more thought*   The second exemplum drawn from the episode of the marriage at Cana (Jn. 2:1–11), the first appearing on the terrace of Envy (XIII.28). Here the exemplum emphasizes Mary's concern for others over her pleasure in eating at the feast.

145–46   *The ancient Roman matrons*   Roman women were famed as models of temperate consumption.

146–47   *Daniel scorned feasting*   From Dn. 1:17, in which Daniel encourages the Jews living at the court of Nebuchadnezzar to be satisfied with lentils and water and to hunger instead after knowledge and wisdom.

148–50   *In the Golden Age*   The first age of the world described in Ovid's *Met.* I.89–150.

151–54   *Honey and locusts*   The food consumed by John the Baptist as he wandered in the desert (Matt. 3:4). John was described by Christ as the greatest of the prophets (Lk. 7:28).

Canto XXIII

10–12　*we heard a mournful song*　The travelers hear the souls on this terrace before they see them. The Italian *parturìe* (literally "gave birth"), used by the poet to describe the effect of their singing upon the hearer, is extremely powerful and captures one of the central messages of the canto: penitential suffering (like childbirth) causes both pain and joy.

11　*Labia mea Domine*　This is an extract from Ps. 50 (already referenced in *Purg.* IV.24). Verse 17 of this psalm reads: "O Lord, thou wilt open my lips: and my mouth shall announce thy praise." Souls who sinned through their mouths in the act of Gluttony are now redeemed through using that mouth to praise God.

14–15　*loosening the knot*　The metaphor of the knot is a recurring and central metaphor of the *Commedia*. See, for example, *Purg.* XVI.24, XXIV.56.

22–33　*The eyes of each*　The physical description of the souls of the gluttonous is one of the most elaborate and painful in the *Purgatorio*. They are emaciated, discolored, the image of victims of famine. However, their appearance is also one of the most importantly symbolic. It was believed that the Latin word for man, *omo*, could be read in the human face in the shape of the eye sockets and the eyebrows and cheekbones. Dante tells us that in these starving souls, this word is written extremely clearly. Thus it is that in their penance these souls reveal their essential humanity.

25–30　*I do not believe*　The poet employs two comparisons to describe the famished state of the souls. The first is the story of Erysichthon, told in *Met.* VIII.739–878. Erysichthon cut down an oak that was sacred to the goddess Ceres and was the home of a dryad. The dryad cursed him with insatiable hunger. He went on to consume all his possessions in the attempt to satisfy his hunger, finally consuming his own body. The second comparison is drawn from classical history and the Roman siege of Jerusalem in 70 AD. The starvation of the populace drove one woman, named Mary, to eat her own child (the story appears in *De bello judaico*, book 6 by Flavius Josephus).

40–48　*Forese*　The pilgrim's encounter with the shade of Forese is one of the longest of the *Commedia* and, like the encounter with Brunetto Latini in *Inf.* 15, describes a meeting between Dante and a close personal friend. Forese Donati (c. 1260–1296) belonged to a powerful Florentine family and was a cousin of Dante's own wife, Gemma Donati. Although there is no external historical documentation of their relationship, a close friendship between Dante and Forese is documented by this passage and by a series of reciprocal poems (known as a *tenzone*) that the pair exchanged. These poems are jovially and scandalously insulting in tone, and perhaps the humble morality of the friends' encounter here in Purgatory was written as a counterbalance to their former ribaldry. As in the encounter with Brunetto Latini, Forese's physical appearance at first obscures his identity. It is only by his voice that Dante recognizes him.

49–57 *the dry scabs that discolor my skin* Both Dante and Forese are upset by the disfigurement of Forese's face. On seeing it, Dante movingly recalls Forese's face at his death (55).

58–60 *So in God's name tell me* Dante is unable to respond to Forese's question of how he, a living man, comes to be on Mount Purgatory, because he is distracted by his desire to understand how the souls come to look as they do. This is the first time that the pilgrim has shown an interest in the "mechanics" of the shades' appearance and punishment. Although Forese begins an answer to the question, this will not be fully completed until canto XXV.

61–75 *From the eternal Will* Forese's explanation of the nature of the punishment of the gluttonous. His opening lines stress the connection of this punishment to the Will of God. This connection is powerfully recontextualized toward the end of his speech when he identifies the souls' desire for penance with Christ's dying words on the Cross: "Eli, Eli, lamma sabacthani?" (My God, my God, why have you forsaken me? Matt. 27:46). Both events are connected to the Will of God and are instruments of human redemption and manifestations of God's justice. Through their willing suffering, the souls are imitating Christ. Forese's words at lines 71–72 pick up again the tension expressed in lines 10–12; penance is both suffering and joy (see also the *good sorrow* of line 80 and the *sweet wormwood* of line 86 for a continuation of the bittersweet dichotomy this canto addresses).

76–84 *I responded* The pilgrim is surprised by the speed with which Forese has ascended Mount Purgatory in the space of less than five years since his death.

85–93 *I have been brought so quickly* Forese's speedy ascent of the mountain is thanks to the prayers of his virtuous wife, Nella. Forese uses the good example of Nella to launch an attack on the corruption of other contemporary Florentine women.

94 *the Barbagia of Sardinia* A mountainous region in the center of the island of Sardinia.

98–102   *Already in my vision*   Forese prophesies a piece of legislation that would be put forward by the bishops of Florence in 1310 by which women were prohibited from revealing any part of their torso on pain of excommunication.

115–33   *If you call to mind*   Dante's response to Forese's question has an intimate and informal tone that appears drawn from deep friendship and familiarity. He refers to their shared (and presumably dissolute) life (116–17) in terms that suggest Forese should know what he is talking about. Most importantly he uniquely utters, without ornament or explanation, Beatrice's name. No further information is necessary; Forese, as his friend, must know who he is talking about.

Canto XXIV

8–9   *Perhaps he climbs more slowly*   The reference is somewhat ambiguous and could apply to both Forese, who has slowed his progress to speak to Dante, and Statius, who is eager to continue walking with Virgil.

10–15   *Piccarda*   Forese's sister. Piccarda will appear in person in *Par.* 3.

19–20   *Bonagiunta of Lucca*   Bonagiunta of Lucca was an Italian poet from the mid-thirteenth century. Contemporary documents also show that he was a notary. It is likely that he is responsible for bringing the troubadour style of love poetry developed in Sicily to northern Italy. It is not known for certain whether Dante had met Bonagiunta in life.

21–24   *the face more cracked and withered*   Pope Martin IV, known for his Gluttony. Bolsena is a lake some fifty miles northwest of Rome.

28–29   *Ubaldino dalla Pila*   A member of the Tuscan Ghibelline family of the Ubaldini, Ubaldino was the father of Archbishop Ruggieri, whom the pilgrim encountered in *Inf.* XXXIII.13–18.

29–30   *Bonifazio*   This is the archbishop of Ravenna Bonifazio dei Fieschi. The crozier refers to the traditional distinctive staff carried by the bishops of Ravenna.

31–33   *Messer Marchese*   Marchese degli Argugliosi of Forlì, who, from contemporary accounts, appears to have been known as a drunkard.

43–44   *A woman is born*   This woman is tentatively identified as Gentucca Morla, who may have become known to Dante during his probable visit to the city of Lucca in 1306–1308. That she *does not yet wear the veil* suggests that at this point in 1300 she is not yet married. Bonagiunta's words obliquely prophesy Dante's exile from Florence and his subsequent wanderings.

44–45 *my city* The poet is evoking the continual animosity between Tuscan cities and perhaps recalling his own denunciation of the city of Lucca in *Inf.* XXI.37–49.

49–62 *But tell me* The second half of Bonagiunta's discourse with Dante focuses on the poetic styles of each.

51 *Ladies who have intelligence of love* Bonagiunta aptly picks out as exemplary of Dante's style the first of three canzoni found in Dante's earlier work the *Vita Nova*. The poem "Donne ch'avete intelletto d'amore" is seen as representing a turning point in the text, in which Dante begins what would become his characteristic praise style: poetry that does not focus upon the feelings or sufferings of the lover but finds its satisfaction and inspiration in praising the lady who is the object of love. In this it is a forerunner of the tone of praise (of God, of Beatrice) that so typifies the *Commedia* itself.

52–54 *I am one who* Dante's response to Bonagiunta has become the defining manifesto of the *sweet new style* (57), which Dante and his poetic forerunners Guido Guinizelli and Guido Cavalcanti are credited with developing. On one level, Dante is claiming an emotional authenticity to his poetry: he is the scribe of love; he writes from experience. The term *spirare* (to breathe), however, is also connected to divine breath and the Holy Spirit, particularly in the act of Creation (see *Purg.* X.1–2, XXV.71). As such, Dante is perhaps claiming divine inspiration for his poetry, transforming himself into a *scriba Dei*, a "scribe of God."

55–62 *O brother* Bonagiunta contrasts Dante's poetic success with what he sees as his own poetic failure and that of others. The *Notary* is Giacomo da Lentini (1200 to c. 1250), an early Sicilian poet. *Guittone* is Guittone d'Arezzo (1230–1294). Dante's poetic relationship to the latter has received particular attention, and Dante will return to his criticism of Guittone's style in *Purg.* XXVI. The fault that Bonagiunta seems to particularly identify here is the lack of authenticity and inspiration of these poets. They were too entangled in the *knots* of poetic rhetoric and style.

82–90 *the one who is most to blame* Forese prophesies the downfall of his own brother, Corso Donati. Corso was a leader of the Black Guelph faction. He was suspected of treason, however, and (perhaps while trying to escape) he threw himself from his horse and was stabbed to death by pursuing soldiers.

94–96   *As a horseman*   The chivalric imagery with which Dante imagines Forese's departure contrasts with the doomed ride of his brother Corso Donati.

115–17   *The tree from which Eve ate*   The unidentified voice describes this second tree also as an offshoot of the tree of the knowledge of good and evil from which Adam and Eve plucked the forbidden fruit.

121–23   *those accursed cloud-born creatures*   The first of the examples of Gluttony recalls the story of the hero Theseus' battle against the centaurs (*Met.* XII.210–535). Legend has it that the centaurs were born from the union of Ixion with the goddess Juno, who had taken the form of a cloud. At the wedding of Pirithous (also Ixion's son) the centaurs became drunk and attempted to carry off the women before being defeated by Theseus and Pirithous' warriors, the Lapiths.

124–26   *those Hebrews*   Told in Jgs. 7:1–4. Gideon is told by God to take into battle against the city of Midian only those Hebrews who drink in an appropriate way.

136–50   *Never was glass or metal*   One of the most detailed and striking depictions of an angel in Purgatory. The blinding vision of the angel is contrasted with the sweet scents that come from it, reiterating the tension of pain and pleasure that marks the terrace of Gluttony.

151–54   *Blessed are they*   The second rendering of the fourth Beatitude (Matt. 5:6).

Canto XXV

1–3   *Taurus had reached the day's meridian*   These astrological indications suggest a time just after noon. The travelers are eager to make full use of the hours of daylight that facilitate their journey.

10–18   *like the little stork*   Dante's question and Statius' answer make up the majority of this canto. Here the simile of the baby stork making its first movements toward flight and the strung and taut arrow in the bow are preliminaries to the discourse that will burst forth and enable the *ascent* of the pilgrim's knowledge.

20–21   *How can these spirits grow lean*   Dante's question emerges from his meeting with the souls of the gluttonous. How is it possible that souls who have no *need* of food (no one eats in Purgatory) can become so thin and emaciated by lack of it? His questions open up one of the poem's greatest passages of scientific poetry on the generation and creation of the human soul.

22–27 *If you call to mind* Virgil provides a brief preliminary response to the pilgrim's question using the examples of Meleager and a mirror image. But in Purgatory the pagan Virgil's knowledge is not now sufficient to supply a full answer within this Christian context. He must turn to the Christian convert Statius to provide a fuller answer.

22 *Meleager* From *Met.*VIII.260–525. At his birth, Meleager's mother saved a burning log from a fire. At this point the Fates linked Meleager's life to that of the log. Later, when Meleager killed his mother's brothers, his mother took revenge by throwing the log onto a fire and killing Meleager. The example introduces the idea of a power external to oneself that nevertheless governs the body.

37–108 *The perfect blood* Statius' answer to the pilgrim's question falls roughly into two sections: (1) the development of the human soul, and (2) what happens to that soul after death. From the perspective of modern science (especially the knowledge of the circulation of the blood and the process of conception and pregnancy), Statius' explanation is clearly inaccurate; but in the *Commedia's* intellectual context, Dante presents a daring account that draws on contemporary thought. Commentators and scholars have identified Albert the Great as the clearest influence for this passage (in particular *De natura et origine animae* and *De animalibus*) and the account of human physiology as a whole owes much to Aristotle. The second half of Statius' answer, however, is much more original and imaginative and appears to be invented by Dante to justify the *Commedia's* own poetic constructions concerning the appearance of the souls in the afterlife.

37–51 *The perfect blood* This passage describes the transformation of blood into semen. Following Aristotle's ideas, food enters the stomach and, after being processed there, passes to the liver, where it becomes blood. Some of this blood then goes to the heart, where it becomes *perfect blood*, meaning that it is now active and has formative power (40). Part of this blood is further perfected and increased in transformative potency before descending to the reproductive system (43–44). In females this perfect blood is menstrual blood and, in Aristotelian thought, is passive, able to receive form but not imprint it. In males this perfect blood descends to the testicles and becomes semen, which is active and can imprint form (49–51).

52–60 *The active virtue* Dante, in common with Albert the Great, sees the production of the human soul as a continuous development: semen and menstrual blood combine in the formation of the vegetative soul that becomes the animal soul that is then transformed into—not replaced by—the intellectual soul. The three stages of the soul are drawn from Aristotle. The faculties of the soul increase in stages from those it shares with plant life, to basic organisms (the sea sponge), to animals that can sense and move.

61–66   *a mind wiser than yours*   According to Aristotle, the intellectual soul did not occupy a specific organ within the human body. The great Islamic thinker Averroes (c. 1126–1198) extrapolated from this that, therefore, the active intellect was external and separable from the human soul and, after death, returned to a sort of collective intellect. While this may have been Aristotle's intention, this interpretation was rejected by medieval Christian thinkers since it denied the immortality of the individual soul. Dante, while highly respectful toward Averroes both here and in *Inf.* 4, likewise rejects his interpretation.

67–75   *Open your heart to the truth*   Statius reveals to Dante that once the process of natural generation of the soul is complete, God intercedes directly in the creation of the final human soul. God's joy at Creation is a recurring idea throughout the *Commedia*.

76–78   *look at the sun's heat*   Statius employs the metaphor of the transformation of grape juice into wine through the action of the sun's heat to help the pilgrim understand that the soul generated by nature is transformed into (not replaced by) the soul breathed in by God. The two become inseparable and indistinguishable, like grape juice transformed into wine.

79–108   *the soul is loosed from the flesh*   The second part of Statius' discourse considers the nature of the human soul after death and separation from the physical body. The highly original account that the poet Dante here constructs emphasizes the vital union of a soul with its body; the body is the expression of the soul, and the soul is what forms the body. Dante focuses upon the three central faculties of the soul that it carries with it after death: memory, will, and intellect.

79   *Lachesis*   The Fate who spins the thread of the lives of human beings.

85–86   *one of the two shores*   The disembodied soul after death goes either to Hell or to Purgatory.

88–108   *its formative virtue radiates out*   The soul, on reaching its appointed place, by the force of its own formative virtue reforms an "airy" body for itself with which it will experience the pains and pleasures of the afterlife. The metaphor of the rainbow (91–93) captures beautifully the paradoxical visibility and intangibility of these airy bodies that manifest themselves in the air like sunlight on rain. That the souls have a body, while not necessarily supported by contemporary theology, is nevertheless vital to Dante's own poetic fiction. Without this, the individual encounters and accounts that make up the *Commedia* would be impossible or at least unimaginable.

109–24 *By now we had come to the final circuit* The dramatic appearance of the final terrace of Purgatory immediately changes the canto's mood following the detailed and revelatory tone of Statius' account. The final terrace, that of the lustful, contains a great wall of fire that forces the travelers to walk along the edge of the cliff, dangerously caught between flames and the steep drop. There is a strong sense of physical danger for the pilgrim, who will himself have to pass through the burning flames.

121 *Summae Deus clementiae* An ancient hymn whose text asks for deliverance from sexual urges.

128 *Virum non cognosco* The first of the exempla of Chastity are the words spoken by Mary to the Angel Gabriel at the Annunciation to express her virginity: I know not man (Lk. 1:34).

131–32 *Diana kept to the woods* The second exemplum is drawn from *Met.* II.401–507 and refers to the story of Callisto, a nymph of Diana, who is raped and impregnated by Jupiter. She is banished by Diana when her pregnancy is discovered.

Canto XXVI

7–12 *My shadow* As in earlier instances, it is the pilgrim's shadow that alerts the shades to his special condition and provides the motive for opening conversation. The impact of this trope is heightened when set against Statius' discourse of canto XXV on the nature of the airy bodies of the souls.

28–48 *For down the middle of that burning road* A second group of souls come toward those already speaking to Dante, moving in the opposite direction. The approaching souls (here figured as moving in the *wrong* direction and thus acting against nature) are those of the homosexual lustful; the other group is the heterosexual lustful. The meeting of the two groups is a charming and imaginative picture, comparable to the brief nuzzling meeting of ants intent on their journey.

40–42   *Sodom and Gomorrah*   Each group calls out an example of Lust that rebukes themselves. The homosexual lustful call out the example of the biblical Sodom and Gomorrah (Gen. 18:16 and 19:1), cities that were destroyed by God for their depravity. The heterosexuals refer to the story of Pasiphae, wife of King Minos, who, consumed with lust for a young bull, had a wooden cow made that she could enter in order to copulate with the bull. This union led to the birth of the Minotaur. The example, rather than referring to bestiality per se, describes lust gone beyond reasonable human boundaries and descended to the level of animalistic behavior. This interpretation is backed up by the later explanation at lines 82–84.

44   *Riphean mountains*   Although not recognized in modern geography, this range was traditionally taken to be Europe's northern border.

64   *Tell me, so that I may yet rule it on pages*   A striking autoreference on Dante's part to the fact that the stories he hears will be written down (on the ruled lines of his pages) in the *Commedia*.

76–87   *The souls who do not come with us*   The soul speaking to Dante further explains the examples of Lust that the pilgrim had heard earlier. The group of homosexual souls is described as committing the sin of Caesar. Julius Caesar was believed to have engaged in homosexual relations with the king of Bithynia. On knowing this, his troops taunted him by addressing him as "Queen." It is interesting that in Purgatory Dante does not distinguish between homosexual and heterosexual Lust (compare the separate treatment in *Inf.*V and XV–XVI). It is unregulated desire, both homo- and heterosexual, which is punished here.

91–114   *I am Guido Guinizelli*   The issue of vernacular poets and their poetry that was introduced in cantos XXIII and XXIV is here taken up again in the meeting with the Bolognese poet Guido Guinizelli. Guinizelli formed part of the poetic generation immediately prior to Dante and had a huge influence on his works. Guinizelli, in contrast to his contemporaries, focused upon the ennobling potential of love for a woman. Dante himself builds from this to such an extent that human love becomes not only ennobling but salvific. This imagined meeting with Guinizelli gives Dante the opportunity to acknowledge his debt to the older poet (112–14).

94–95   *in the presence of Lycurgus' grim rage*   A story told in *Theb.*V.534–753. Hypsipyle was nurse to the infant son of King Lycurgus. The baby is killed by a snake while left unattended. Lycurgus condemns Hypsipyle to death, but before the sentence can be carried out she is recognized by two of Lycurgus' soldiers. These turn out to be Hypsipyle's sons, whom she had been forced to abandon. The family is reunited and Hypsipyle is saved.

97 *I heard my father* In describing Guinizelli as "father," Dante is acknowledging him as the originator of the poetic style that he himself went on to develop. This poetic paternity echoes the biological paternity considered in canto XXV. It is also an interesting recontextualization of the relationship between Dante and his other poetic father, Virgil, who is largely silent in this canto.

108 *Lethe* One of the rivers that runs through the Earthly Paradise and removes the memory of sin.

115–48 *O, my brother* Guinizelli courteously diverts Dante's praise toward the Occitan poet Arnaut Daniel.

120 *the troubadour of Limoges* Girault de Bornelh (c. 1160–1210).

124 *Guittone* The second critical reference to the poetry of Guittone d'Arezzo (see XXIV.55–57).

139–47 *he began to speak to me* Dante's encounter with the poet Arnaut Daniel is unique in the *Commedia* since Arnaut speaks to Dante in his native Occitan. Arnaut (c. 1140–1190) was from the Dordogne region of France, which had Occitan as its vernacular language. In this tribute, Dante identifies Arnaut as the best of the poets writing in their own vernacular. While Arnaut's own poetry was self-consciously difficult and convoluted in style, his short speech to Dante is a model of concise eloquence.

Canto XXVII

1–6 *As when it strikes* This unusual indicator of time on Mount Purgatory tells us that sunset is approaching. Instead of the more common astrological references, Dante significantly indicates the time in relation to Jerusalem, which is identified metonymically as the site of Christ's Crucifixion. This is a canto of transition toward the theologically loaded final cantos of Purgatory. A new mood is set in which the pilgrim's experiences are resonant with theological import. Astrological indicators are not absent from the image, however, and the four locations (the Ebro river in Spain, the Ganges, Jerusalem, and Mount Purgatory itself) mark the four cardinal points.

8 *Beati mundo corde* The sixth Beatitude: "Blessed are the pure in heart for they shall see God" (Matt. 5:8).

13–18 *I became like one* On hearing that he too must pass through the burning flames, the pilgrim is overcome with terror and a certain amount of morbid fascination (16). Dante would almost certainly have witnessed public executions by burning, and he himself was sentenced in absentia to be burned alive at the time of his exile from Florence. It is quite possible that a certain amount of Dante's own personal biography and feelings went into creating the intense terror of this moment.

20–36   *My son, there may be torment here*   Virgil's attempt to persuade Dante to enter the flames is carefully constructed. Beginning with reassurance (20–21), he appeals to past experience (23) and further reassurance, even encouraging the pilgrim to test for himself the truth of his words (29–30). His rational arguments, however, are totally ineffectual. It is only when he presents Dante with the object of his desire—the vision of Beatrice—that the pilgrim can overcome his fear (35–36). Virgil's tone of gentle reprimand and fatherly sternness is a moment of particular pathos, given that their relationship in the poem is drawing to its close.

25–27   *You can be sure*   Behind Virgil's words is a subtle reference to the biblical story of the three Israelites Shadrach, Meshach, and Abednego, who were thrown into the fire by King Nebuchadnezzar but who emerged totally unharmed (Dn. 3:27).

37–39   *As Pyramus, dying*   The story of Pyramus and Thisbe appears in *Met.* IV.51–166. Pyramus, believing that Thisbe has been killed by a lion, stabs himself with his own sword. The still-living Thisbe finds her dying lover and it is only at the sound of Thisbe speaking her own name that Pyramus opens his eyes in the moment before death. Pyramus' blood was supposed to have stained red the previously white mulberry. Medieval allegorists interpreted this story as relating to Christ's death on the Cross, providing a further moment in this canto in which the Crucifixion is subtly present.

44–45   *as if at a child*   This charming image has important biblical undertones in the light of a passage in Matt. 18:2–4: "unless you … become as little children, you shall not enter the kingdom of Heaven."

52–54   *I can see her eyes already*   The eyes of the beloved lady, along with her smile, are a central trope of courtly love poetry. In Dante's own *Vita Nova* Beatrice's eyes have amazing power over him, and in the *Commedia* itself her eyes continue to be of vital importance (*Inf.* II.55 and 116–17; below lines 100–108 and 136–37; *Purg.* XXXI.133 and throughout the *Paradiso*).

58   *Venite benedicti Patris mei*   From Matt. 25:34: "Come you, blessed of my Father." These are the words that the Gospel says will be spoken by Christ at the Last Judgment as he welcomes the just into Heaven. Here it

is a second angel that speaks these words as the travelers emerge from the flames.

94–96 *Cytherea* An allusion to Venus; Cytherea was the site of the goddess's birth. The time is just before dawn.

97–108 *I seemed to see in a dream* This is the last of the three dreams that Dante has on Mount Purgatory, and it prefigures the encounters the pilgrim will have in the Earthly Paradise. This shortest of Dante's dreams, it depicts a vision of the Old Testament figure Leah, who describes both her own activity (gathering flowers) and that of her sister Rachel (regarding herself in a mirror). The story of Leah and Rachel appears in Gen. 29–30. Jacob, seeing Rachel, wishes to marry her. Her father Laban agrees to this if Jacob will first serve him for seven years. At the end of this time, Laban tricks Jacob into marrying his elder daughter Leah. Laban then imposes a further seven years of labor before Jacob can finally marry Rachel. The two figures of Leah and Rachel were frequently interpreted by Christian commentators as representing the active and the contemplative life, respectively. Leah delights in activity, working in the world and loving. The contemplative Rachel, however, reflects more closely on knowledge of the truth, thus attaining a higher level of being. The dream is significant at this point in the *Commedia*'s narrative. Although the concerns of the world will be present even in the *Paradiso*, the pilgrim is moving closer to the higher things of God so that the active life of the world becomes recontextualized in the light of divine truths. The dream of Leah and Rachel also marks an important shift from the masculine guides who have accompanied the pilgrim thus far to the feminine guides (culminating in Beatrice herself) who will now take over his progress.

109–11 *the pilgrim soul* Another important moment in which the theme of homecoming emerges in this canto of transition. The wandering pilgrim, excluded from both his natural home (the Earthly Paradise) and his spiritual one (Heaven), is finally returning.

123 *I felt that I was growing wings for flight* The metaphor of flight for spiritual ascent was first introduced in *Purg.* X.124–29.

126–42 *Virgil fixed his eyes on me* This is Virgil's last speech in the *Commedia*, and it announces the end of his authority over Dante and the fulfillment of Dante's authority over himself. Under Virgil's guidance Dante has attained natural justice, the clarifying of his intellect, and the sharpening of his will.

127   *The temporal fire and the eternal*   These are the fires of Purgatory (temporal) and Hell (eternal). The line echoes Virgil's words to the pilgrim in *Inf.* I.112–20.

133–36   *Look at the sun shining*   Dante and his guides stand on the edge of the Earthly Paradise, of which Virgil's words provide the first glimpse.

137–38   *the beautiful eyes*   A recurrence of the image of Beatrice's eyes that first ignited Dante's love for her and that induced Virgil to come to the pilgrim's rescue (*Inf.* II.116–17).

140–42   *Your will is free now*   Virgil's closing lines demonstrate how far the pilgrim has come. He can now exercise his free will unenslaved by wayward passions or bad habits. He is now in control of himself. The two objects that end Virgil's speech of "coronation" are the symbols of king and Pope, the crown and the miter.

Canto XXVIII

1–21   *Eager now to search the environs*   In his description of the Earthly Paradise, Dante engages with the classical myth of the Golden Age and the figurative tradition of the *locus amoenus* (delightful place). There are many examples of this in both classical (see, e.g., Virgil's *Eclogues*) and biblical (e.g., Ps. 22) texts. Dante's delicate and vivid description evokes a forest in springtime in which new life and innocence abound. These physical characteristics are representative of the newfound innocence of the souls who arrive at this place.

20   *Chiassi*   The Roman and medieval port of Ravenna.

21   *Aeolus unleashes the Sirocco*   Aeolus was the classical god of the winds. The Sirocco is the gentle southeasterly wind.

25–30   *a stream*   The as yet unnamed stream is Lethe, whose waters take away the memory of sin. Its characteristic of *concealing nothing* has thus both literal and moral significance.

40–42   *There appeared a lady*   The lady is not named until canto XXXIII.119, where she is referred to as Matelda. Her appearance continues the increasing importance of female figures and guides (beginning with the dream of Leah and Rachel), who will now take over the guidance of Dante's journey. Commentators have speculated over whether Matelda represents a real historical personage. However, as Durling and Martinez have noted, the late introduction of her name suggests that it is her symbolic rather than historical identity that is most important. Her first appearance, singing to herself as she picks flowers, immediately recalls Dante's dream of Leah, the representative of the active life, in canto XXVII. Matelda represents innocent humanity and, like Leah, the service of God in the active life.

43–51 *Ah, beautiful lady* Dante's encounter with Matelda is tinged with both courtly romance and sensual eroticism. His presentation of her and the pilgrim's address to her draw on the pastourelle tradition of poetry in which, typically, a man comes across a beautiful shepherdess and seduces her to love. Eroticism of a more violent kind is also evoked in the reference to Proserpina, who was abducted and raped by Pluto as she picked flowers in the idyllic valley of Enna. One of several sources for this tale is *Met.* V.341–571. The story was interpreted by Christian readers as representing the loss of Eden. The eroticism of Dante's encounter with Matelda, however, is contained and recontextualized. He can only gaze at her across the stream, filled with desire. More importantly, this is a place of innocent desire; as we know from Virgil's final address to the pilgrim, his desires now can only be for the good.

55–69 *She turned toward me* In this passage, the poet focuses on two features of Matelda that were central tropes of medieval love poetry: the lady's eyes (63) and her smile (67).

70–75 *the Hellespont* To describe the keenness of his desire to cross the stream and reach Matelda, Dante refers to two episodes concerning the Hellespont (modern day Dardanelles). The commander Xerxes attempted to invade Greece, crossing the bridges of the Hellespont. As his panicked army retreated, however, the bridges collapsed under them, killing thousands. The second more dominant story is that of the lovers Leander and Hero. The pair lived in cities opposite each other across the Hellespont. To keep their love secret, Leander would swim across every night. One stormy night, however, he was drowned. Hero, unwilling to live without him, also threw herself into the waves. The story is recounted in Virgil's *Georgics* III.258–63.

74 *Sestos and Abydos* The two towns in which Leander and Hero lived that stood opposite each other across the narrowest part of the Hellespont.

80 *Delectasti* Matelda refers to Ps. 91:5–6, the text of which reads: "For thou hast given me, O Lord, delight in thy doings: and in the work of thy hands I shall rejoice. O Lord how great are thy works." Matelda's evocation of this psalm emphasizes the perfection of the place in which the characters find themselves and also the directness of its creation: it is created *by* God *for* humankind. It is the place in which Creation is at its most revelatory.

85–87   *The water*   The pilgrim is confused by the meteorological (the wind) and geographical (the rivers) characteristics of the Earthly Paradise since he had been told by Statius in canto XXI.40–57 that Mount Purgatory was not subject to terrestrial rules.

88–144   *You are newcomers*   The second half of the canto is dedicated to Matelda's explanation of the characteristics of the Earthly Paradise. Matelda explains that the meteorological and geographical characteristics of Eden are entirely connected to the movement of the celestial heavens and the dictates of divine will. Her discourse is scientific and authoritative.

91–102   *The highest Good*   The perfection that the Earthly Paradise enjoys comes from its creation by God as the home for innocent mankind. The place itself was wholly perfect and undisturbed. Only through its own choice (to disobey God's will and eat the apple) did humankind lose Eden.

104   *universe's primal circling*   This is the Primo Mobile, the highest celestial sphere below the empyrean, whose motion contains within itself the whole material universe. The effect of this sphere's motion is transmitted unmediated to the Earthly Paradise, giving this place a privileged and unclouded connection to the Will of God.

109–17   *when a plant is struck*   The plants of the Garden of Eden were believed to be the source of all vegetation on Earth.

127–32   *On this side it descends*   Matelda identifies the two rivers of Eden as Lethe and Eunoe, the first of which removes the memory of sin, while the second restores the memory of good deeds done. Lethe was present in classical literature (see, e.g., *Aen.* VI.748) but Eunoe is Dante's own invention, its name formed from the Greek *eu* (well) and *noesis* (knowledge). That Dante should add a stream that restores the memory of good temporal action is an important statement of his belief in the great value of human activity.

139–44   *The ancient poets*   Dante draws on the classical myth of the Golden Age, which, although it was not known by classical poets, was at least dreamed of.

141   *Parnassus*   A mountain in Greece believed to be the mythical home of the Muses.

Canto XXIX

3 *Beati quorum tecta sunt peccata* The opening of Ps. 31: "Blessed are they whose iniquities are forgiven and whose sins are covered."

12 *I found myself facing East* Continuing upstream and following a bend in the river, the group is now facing east, the direction of the rising sun. This orientation symbolically foreshadows the revelation that is about to take place.

16–18 *a sudden brightness* This is the first of several references in the final cantos of the *Purgatorio* to the imagery of the Apocalypse (see Apoc. 4:5).

37–42 *O Virgins most holy* The poet Dante appeals to the classical Muses to aid him in recording what the pilgrim witnessed. Helicon was a mountain sacred to the Muses and the god Apollo. Urania is the Muse of astronomy.

43–50 *seven trees of gold* The pilgrim's senses are at first confused. What he took to be seven golden trees reveal themselves to be seven candlesticks. The appearance of the candlesticks initiates the solemn procession and liturgical drama that the pilgrim is about to witness.

51 *Hosanna* A term of joyful praise.

73–78 *they left the air behind them painted* The flames of the seven candlesticks leave a visible stream of light behind them, like the trail of a sparkler that does not fade. The seven stripes of light have been interpreted by commentators as representing the seven manifestations of the spirit of God and/or the seven gifts of the Holy Spirit. The image of the candlesticks is drawn from the Apocalypse (see 1:12 and 1:19).

82–154 *Beneath a sky as beautiful as I describe* This dramatic scene has been interpreted as representing the stages of the revelation of divine truth. The procession is in three sections: the first group of figures representing the books of the Old Testament; the griffin representing Christ, who stands in the middle of the procession just as he stands in the middle of history; and the figures who come after the griffin representing the books of the New Testament.

83–84 *twenty-four elders* These figures represent the twenty-four books of the Old Testament. The lilies they wear symbolize their faith in a future Redeemer. The lily is also a symbol of the Virgin Mary.

86–87   *Blessed are you*   Part of the greeting with which the angel Gabriel greets the Virgin Mary at the Annunciation (Lk. 1:28). Mary herself does not appear in the procession, and the chanting here is a salutation to Beatrice.

92–105   *four living creatures*   These are the symbols of the four evangelists that are described in Apoc. 4:6–8. Traditionally these are Mark represented by a lion, Luke by a calf, Matthew by a man, and John by an eagle. The account in John's Apocalypse describes the creatures as each having six wings, a description Dante here replicates; but Dante appeals to the description of these creatures in Ez. 1:10–11 for other details of their appearance. With a bold poetic move, Dante states in line 105 that rather than drawing from the biblical accounts, John's account is in agreement with his own rendering.

95   *Argus*   Argus was a creature with one hundred eyes. Juno set him to guard Io from the lustful Jupiter. Argus was charmed to sleep by Mercury, who then decapitated him. Juno then took Argus' eyes and used them to decorate the tail feathers of peacocks (*Met.* I.622–723).

106–14   *a triumphal chariot*   The chariot is drawn by a griffin, a mythical creature with the head and wings of an eagle and the body of a lion. This creature with two natures has been interpreted by commentators as representing the dual nature of Christ (both God and man). Its eagle parts are gold, representing the indestructible purity of the divine; its lion body is white and red, representing the combined fragility and nobility of man.

115–20   *so splendid a chariot*   Dante describes the glorious chariot through comparisons. The first two compare the chariots of the Roman triumphs of Scipio Africanus and the emperor Augustus. The third comparison refers to the chariot of the sun god Helios, stolen by Phaeton. Phaeton lost control of the chariot, causing the Earth to be scorched. At prayers from those on Earth, Jupiter destroys Phaeton with a thunderbolt.

121–29   *Three ladies came dancing*   These three figures represent the three theological virtues: red for charity, green for hope, and white for faith. Charity, the greatest of all virtues, leads the dance of the others (128–29).

130–32   *four other ladies*   Representations of the four moral virtues: Justice, Prudence, Temperance, and Fortitude. The virtue of Prudence (both a moral and intellectual virtue) is represented with three eyes, indicating her ability to see past, present, and future.

133–50   Behind the whole group   The procession closes with figures representing the remaining books of the New Testament: the book of Acts (136–38); Paul's letters (139–41; Paul is traditionally depicted with a sword);

the epistles of James, Peter, John, and Jude (142); and finally the Apocalypse (143–44; traditionally presented as a sleeping figure). These figures wear roses that represent charity and Christ's passion.

Canto XXX

1–9   *the Seven Stars of the first heaven*   The heavenly stars are the lights of the seven candles representing the gifts of the Holy Spirit that had led the procession. These are compared to the seven stars that make up the constellation Ursa Minor (the bear), which includes the polestar used by sailors to navigate.

10–11   *Veni, sponsa de Libano*   An adapted quotation from Sg. 4:8: "Come, bride from Lebanon." These wedding songs were interpreted as expressing different relationships of love: between God and the chosen people of Israel; Christ and the Church; God and Mary; God and the individual soul. Christ and God take the role of bridegroom, while the Church, soul, or Mary are the bride. It can be presumed that the singer leading this chorus is the figure representing the book of the Song of Songs.

13–15   *As the blessed at the last trumpet blast*   This allusion to the resurrection of the body that will come on the Day of Judgment gives an important aspect to the imminent arrival of Beatrice. The Resurrection of the dead will occur with the Second Coming of Christ. Beatrice's appearance is thus staged as a foreshadowing of this event. The coming judgment of the pilgrim himself that will reduce him to insensibility before he is "reborn" continues this important analogy.

17   *ad vocem tanti senis*   (At the voice of so great an elder). This appears to be a Latin phrase of Dante's own invention rather than a quotation.

19   *Benedictus qui venis*   An adaptation from Ps. 117:26, meaning "Blessed are you who come." The words are shouted by the crowds during Christ's Triumphal Entry into Jerusalem (see Matt. 21:9) and would have been familiar to Dante's readers from their use in the Mass. It is important to note that "Benedictus" is masculine and therefore addresses not Beatrice but Christ.

21   *Manibus, oh, date lilia plenis!*   The first of this canto's important allusions to Virgil's *Aeneid*: "O give lilies with full hands." The line appears in *Aen.* VI.883, in which Aeneas' father Anchises gives a long lament for the death of the Emperor Augustus' nephew Marcellus (*Aen.* VI.868–70, 882–86).

31–33   *above a white veil, a lady mantled in green*   Beatrice appears clothed in the three colors of green, white, and red, which represent the three theological virtues of Hope, Faith, and Charity, respectively. These colors also recall the clothes in which Dante first saw Beatrice as described in the *Vita Nova* II.

34–42   *my spirit*   The pilgrim feels the effect of Beatrice's presence upon him before having visual confirmation of her identity. The overwhelming nature of her effect upon his body and spirits is well documented in the *Vita Nova* (see in particular chapter 14).

46–48   *Not a drop of blood*   The pilgrim echoes (with slight adaptation) the words spoken by Dido on confessing her feelings of love for Aeneas, the first reawakening of love since her husband's death (*Aen.* IV.23). Although Dante presents Dido's love for Aeneas as a betrayal of her first husband, the context of the quotation here focuses it on the reestablishment of love in spite of death.

52–54   *all that our ancient mother lost*   The joy of being in Eden (the space lost by the sin of Eve) cannot compensate for Dante's misery on losing his beloved guide Virgil.

55   *Dante*   The only point in the *Commedia* at which Dante names himself. This indeed is a canto of naming; the tragic repeated naming of the lost Virgil, Dante's own autoreference, and the ringing declaration of Beatrice's own name (74).

55–81   *Dante, do not weep yet*   The long-awaited appearance of Beatrice is one of the most dramatic moments of the entire poem. As opposed to a loving and tender reunion, Beatrice appears as a stern judge, reducing the pilgrim to self-deprecating tears of remorse. Ultimately, however, only through tears can his salvation come.

73–74   *I am indeed Beatrice*   Beatrice emphatically stamps her name upon the episode. It has been suggested that the form in which she identifies herself echoes Is. 43:11 and 25: "Ego sum, ego sum Dominus" (I am, I am the Lord).

82–84   *In te, Domine, speravi*   This abridged quotation (In you Lord, I have hoped) comes from Ps. 30:2–8. *Pedes meos* means "my feet" and closes verse 9 of the psalm. The psalm calls on God for protection and asserts hope in his mercy.

85–99   *Just as snow*   This evocative simile describes how the pilgrim, stunned by Beatrice's harsh reception, melts into tears at the sound of the angels' compassion. These tears of shock and remorse are an important step in the process of contrition that the pilgrim has embarked upon.

103–8   *You keep watch in the everlasting day*   Beatrice introduces her speech, which takes up all the remaining lines of the canto, with an address to the angels. They are sleepless, all-knowing beings who have no need of hearing the events she is about to recount. Their recitation is for the benefit of the pilgrim. But, of course, they are also a necessary and subtle device of the poem; we the readers also need to hear.

109–45   *Not only by the work of the celestial wheels*   Beatrice enumerates the pilgrim's failings and the steps by which he fell into sin. At birth he was endowed with every good potential by the heavens (109–11) and by divine grace (112–14). Beatrice explains, however, that this naturally fertile beginning, rather than fostering goodness, enabled bad tendencies to grow (118–20). She herself helped the pilgrim turn toward the good (121–23), but at her death and the removal of her physical form from his sight, he turned away to become distracted by false and empty objects of desire (124–32). The dreams with which Beatrice attempted to draw Dante back to herself may be those described in the latter chapters of the *Vita Nova*. This work is a vital intertext for Beatrice's speech.

Canto XXXI

1–90   *You on the other side of the sacred stream*   The first half of the canto continues Beatrice's rebuke of the pilgrim, his remorse, and his confession. The passage is full of violent emotions that eventually reduce the pilgrim to unconsciousness. The main elements of their discourse are as follows: (1) Beatrice, continuing her discourse of canto XXX, demands that Dante admit the truth of her accusations (1–15); (2) Dante confesses and bursts into tears under the relief of confession (16–21); (3) Beatrice demands from Dante the cause of his straying (22–30); (4) Dante attributes his faults to a desire for "false pleasures" that presented themselves to him after Beatrice's death (31–36); (5) Beatrice acknowledges the value of his confession but goes on to explain how the pilgrim's desire should have followed her even after death (37–63); (6) to increase the pilgrim's remorse yet further, Beatrice demands that he raise his face to her and see her beauty (67–84); (7) the extreme consciousness of his past sins causes Dante to faint (85–90).

64–75   *As children who are ashamed*   The tone of parental rebuke is extremely strong in this and the preceding canto. In Beatrice's order to *lift your beard* (68), however, she is reminding Dante of his maturity. In turning away from her, he acted not as an innocent and ignorant child but as an adult responsible for his actions. In the light of this, the seriousness of his sins is accentuated.

71 *Iarbas' land* Iarbas was the king of Libya who unsuccessfully wooed the Carthaginian queen Dido.

77 *primordial creatures* Referring to the angels, the first of God's creations.

79–84 *And my eyes* Despite Beatrice's invitation for the pilgrim to look directly at her, she continues to be separated from him. Her gaze is focused upon the (more important) griffin, and view of her is obscured by her veil. The delay in the pilgrim's attainment of the full and clear sight of Beatrice adds to the dramatic tension of the passage.

92–102 *the lady I had found alone* Matelda draws the pilgrim through the river of Lethe, which will remove his memory of sin. The imagery suggests he is undergoing a second baptism.

98 *Asperges me* Taken from Ps. 50: "Thou shalt sprinkle me with hyssop and I shall be cleansed."

103–11 *Then she drew me out* Matelda leads the pilgrim into the dance of the four nymph-virtues. The scene is allegorically laden; the four moral virtues prepared the world to receive divine revelation (107–8); before the pilgrim can approach Beatrice (a symbol of divine revelation) he must first acquire the moral virtues (the four nymphs) and the theological virtues (the other three nymphs). Kirkpatrick has suggested that "Confession, as Dante pictures it here, is a public act concerning the reconciliation of the individual with the wider community of the Church" (491). The entering of the pilgrim into the dance seems to be an enactment of his being welcomed back into the community of the virtuous.

119–20 *those eyes that flashed light* The fixity of Beatrice's contemplation of the griffin (the symbol of Christ) recalls the pilgrim's dream of Rachel (symbol of the contemplative life focused upon divine truth) in canto XXVII.

121–26 *Just as the sun shines forth* This dramatic image is laden with theological and personal meaning. The two simultaneous natures of the griffin, which the pilgrim is able to see reflected in Beatrice's eyes, are emblematic of the two natures of Christ joined in hypostatic union. It is only by contemplating the creature *in Beatrice's eyes* that the pilgrim can awaken to the wonder of its dual nature. The scene makes a powerful comment on the personal significance of Beatrice for the pilgrim; it is through her that the nature of Christ can be revealed to him.

130–32 *The other three* The three nymphs representing the three theological virtues take over from the cardinal virtue-nymphs, representing a development to a higher order of spiritual enlightenment and activity.

133–38 *Turn, Beatrice* While Beatrice's eyes appear to have been the focus of the pilgrim's desire up to this point, the singing nymphs now encourage her to reveal her mouth, which conceals *deeper beauty*. The greater significance of the mouth is explored in the *Vita Nova* XIX: "I speak of her eyes which are the beginning of love . . . and of her mouth, which is the goal of love." It is from the mouth that wisdom and praise can issue forth.

Canto XXXII

2 . *a ten-year thirst* The poet refers to the ten years since Beatrice's death.

8–9 *those goddesses* The three nymphs representing the theological virtues who stand on the chariot's right side. It has been suggested that the nymphs criticize Dante's overfixation with Beatrice's physical beauty or that they criticize his attempt to see things that he is not yet prepared to understand.

16–24 *the glorious army* The procession of the Church is here cast as the Church Militant; their organized movements are described as military maneuvers.

31–32 *her who trusted the snake* Dante attributes the emptiness of the Earthly Paradise to Eve's mistake in trusting the tempting words of the snake that led her and Adam to eat of the forbidden fruit and lose Paradise.

37–42 *a tree stripped of its leaves* Commentators have interpreted this as the tree of the knowledge of good and evil, despoiled by Adam and Eve's sin in eating the forbidden fruit. Like the tree found on the terrace of the gluttonous, the tree's branches form an upside-down pyramid, growing wider as the tree grows higher.

48 *So is the seed of justice preserved* The griffin's words paraphrase those spoken by Christ to St John the Baptist when he asks for baptism: "For so it becomes us to fulfill justice" (Matt. 3:15).

49–51 *Turning to the yoke-pole* The wooden structure of the chariot, with its stave and crossbeam shape, forms a cross and thus recalls the cross of the Crucifixion. Here, in a moment loaded with symbolism, the cross of the chariot (around which the whole liturgical drama had been played) is tied to the tree of the knowledge of good and evil, indicating that the sin that was initiated with the tree was redeemed by Christ's sacrifice. Medieval legends even suggested that the wood of the Cross on which Christ was crucified came from an offshoot of the tree of knowledge (see, e.g., the *Legenda Aurea* of Jacobus Voragine).

54   *the constellation that follows Pisces*   Aries, the zodiac sign of March–April and thus the sign of spring and rebirth, as the image of the tree bursting into life suggests.

58–60   *a hue less red than rose*   The new leaves of the tree are crimson, the color of blood. This further connects this scene with Christ's Crucifixion and the shedding of his blood, which brought about new life and redemption.

64–66   *If I could describe how those pitiless eyes*   A second reference to the myth of Argus recounted in the *Metamorphoses*.

72–81   *As, when brought to the blossoming apple tree*   Dante compares his own moment of awakening to the event of the Transfiguration described in Matt. 17, in which Jesus leads the apostles Peter, James, and John up a mountain. There, he is transfigured before them appearing in bright white and flanked by the prophets Moses and Elijah. Matelda's words to the pilgrim, "Arise; what are you doing?" echo Jesus' words to the apostles as they fall down in terror before the vision: "Arise and fear not."

77–78   *the word by which deeper slumbers*   A reference to the raising of the dead Lazarus, who comes back to life at Christ's words (Jn. 11:43–44).

94–96   *She was sitting there alone*   Against the background of the allegory of the Church that these cantos perform, the symbolism of Beatrice is rich and enigmatic at this point. Sitting alone on the bare Earth she may represent the correct and apostolic poverty of the Church. With the griffin who represents Christ now absent, she may represent the wisdom that should sustain the Church on Earth even when the Savior is not present.

99   *Aquilo and Auster*   The north wind and the south wind, respectively.

100–102   *that Rome where Christ Himself is Roman*   Here Dante compares Heaven to the "chosen city" of Rome. Just as the earthly Rome was, in Dante's political theology, divinely predestined to bring about the Augustan peace into which Christ was born, so the *pax Romana* can even function as an image for the peace of Heaven. The extent to which this ideal is not being lived up to in Dante's own Italy has been made clear already in this *cantica*, not least in cantos VI and XVI.

103–5   *what you see, make sure you write down*   Beatrice imposes upon Dante the task of writing down what he witnesses during his journey. She calls his particular attention to the scene about to take place, which will consider the corruption of the contemporary Church. We are reminded of the immense didactic force that Dante's *Commedia* claims for itself. His is a mission to write a work that can heal the *ailing world*.

109–60   *Never has lightning descended so swiftly*   The drama that occupies the final seventeen tercets of the canto displays the seven stages of tribulation that the Church had undergone, up to the corruptions that beset it in Dante's own day.

109–17   *Never has lightning*   The scene depicting the first tribulation of the Church represents the early persecution of Christians under the Roman Empire. The eagle, the symbol of the Roman Empire, descends like lightning on the chariot, which, in the allegory, represents the Church.

118–23   *a vixen*   Based on biblical imagery (Ez. 13:4 and Cant. 2:5), the starving vixen's insidious entry into the chariot has been interpreted as representing the divisive heresies (e.g., those of the Gnostics, Arians, and Donatists) that beset the early Church. Beatrice, here symbolizing orthodox theology, drives out the vixen from the chariot (121–23).

124–29   *I saw the eagle dive*   The second descent of the eagle represents the *Donation of Constantine* by which it was believed the Emperor Constantine had given power over the Western Empire to the Popes. Dante believed that this donation (which was found in the fifteenth century to have been forged) was a central source of corruption of the Church since it embroiled the institution in temporal power struggles.

130–35   *I saw a dragon rise*   The fourth tribulation has been interpreted as representing the rise of Islam, which drew away followers from Christianity to its new belief. Dante, along with his medieval contemporaries, viewed Islam as a heresy and a schism from the true faith. The imagery of the dragon and the rise of a beast is drawn from Apoc. 12:4, 13:1, and 13:11.

136–41   *What remained was again covered over*   This strange image of the broken chariot covered with plumage (again suggesting the intervention of the eagle) has been interpreted as later political donations of privileges and property to the Church by the French kings Pepin and Charlemagne.

142–47   *Transformed in this way*   The seven heads that sprout from the chariot of the Church have been read as the seven capital vices. Dante is making a radical and highly critical comment on the state of corruption into which the contemporary Church has fallen. The imagery of the seven heads recalls the first beast of the Apocalypse (Apoc. XIII.1).

148–60   *Sitting on it, secure as a fortress*   The final tribulation is a faux prophecy, relating to events after the fictional date of the *Commedia* (1300) but before the point at which it was written. Commentators generally agree that the whore represents the corrupt contemporary Papacy (perhaps specifically Boniface VIII) while the giant represents the French monarchy, in particular Philip the Fair. Through this evocative image, Dante is commenting on the corruption that has been brought about by the embroiling of the spiritual institution of the Church in politics and struggles for power and wealth. The image of the Whore of Babylon is also drawn from Apoc. 17:1. The removal of the chariot of the Church from its allotted place at the base of the tree may represent the removal of the seat of the Papacy from Rome to Avignon in 1305.

Canto XXXIII

1–12   *Deus, venerunt*   The opening of canto XXXIII is a lament on the corruption of the Church, symbolized by the separation of the chariot (representing the Church) from the tree (representing Christ's Cross). Dante compares Beatrice's mourning at this separation with Mary's mourning at the Crucifixion.

1   *Deus, venerunt gentes*   (God, the heathens have come.) The opening of Ps. 78, which laments the destruction of the temple in Jerusalem by Nebuchadnezzar.

10–12   *Modicum et non videbitis me et iterum*   A quotation from Jn. 16:16–19: "A little while and you shall not see me; and again a little while and you shall see me."

34–78   *the vessel the serpent broke*   Beatrice's obscure and challenging speech is made to remind the pilgrim of his intellectual limitations; he still has much to learn.

37–39   *The eagle that feathered the chariot*   Recalling the visions of canto XXXII, the *eagle that feathered the chariot* represented the *Donation of Constantine*. Beatrice suggests here that an heir to the Empire is coming (39) who will destroy the Church that has become corrupted (38). Sixty-two years had passed between the death of Emperor Frederick II and the coronation of Henry VII.

43   *When a Five Hundred Ten and Five*   This enigmatic line has long intrigued interpreters of the *Commedia*. Attempts have been made to interpret it through gematria (decoding numbers), with no definitive explanation

being offered. At the simplest level, the number in Roman numerals (500, D; 10, X; 5,V) seems to point to a leader (in Latin "dux" or "DVX"). The prophecy may refer to Emperor Henry VII. Dante had high hopes that Henry VII would restore a stable and just empire; another interpretation suggests the Second Coming of Christ.

46–47   *words as dark as those of Themis or of the Sphinx*   Beatrice compares her enigmatic words to the riddles of Themis, a consort of Jupiter (*Met.* I.375–415), and the Sphinx (*Theb.* I.66–67).

52–57   *Take note of them*   Beatrice again endows Dante with the mission to write down what he has seen in order to improve the moral and spiritual life of those still on Earth.

61–63   *the first soul pined*   Eusebius of Caesarea calculated the exact number of years according to the Bible between the expulsion of Adam from Paradise and the Crucifixion, after which Adam's soul was released from Limbo: 5,232 years. Dante adopts this calculation here.

64–66   *Your wits are asleep*   This is a canto much concerned with the limits of human knowledge and the need to recognize them. The difficulty of ascent represented by the inverted tree that gets wider as it gets higher, represents the restrictions placed by God upon human knowledge.

67   *Elsa's water*   The Elsa is a mineral-rich river in Tuscany whose waters cause a crust to form on objects immersed in them.

69   *like Pyramus staining the mulberry*   Another of the many references to the story of Pyramus, whose dying blood was said to have transformed the originally white berry of the mulberry to red. Beatrice compares the pilgrim's clouded mind to the objects hardened in the Elsa and the white mulberry stained.

91–96   *I do not remember*   The fact that the pilgrim cannot now remember having been estranged from Beatrice emphasizes the sin that he committed in doing so. Having drunk of the river Lethe, it is his bad actions that he cannot remember.

112–14   *Tigris and Euphrates*   Two of the traditional four rivers of Eden described in Gen. 2:11–14. Augustine identified the other pair as the Gihon and the Nile (*De genesi ad litteram* I.160).

119   *Matelda*   The lady who first appeared to the pilgrim in canto XXVIII is at last named as Matelda.

Index of the Penitent

Denizens of Purgatory according to Dante. Names in Roman type denote characters referred to by name in the translation at least once; names in *italics* denote characters referred to in the translation only by locution. Angels are listed in a separate section below the penitents.

Abbot of San Zeno: XVIII.118
Adrian V, Pope: XIX.88
Alfonso III of Aragon: VII.115
Arnaut Daniel: XXVI.142

Belacqua: IV.123
Benincasa da Laterina: VI.13
Bonagiunta Orbicciani: XXIV.19
Bonifazio of Ravenna: XXIV.29
Buonconte da Montefeltro: V.88

Casella: II.91
Cato the Younger: I.31, II.118
Currado Malaspina II: VIII.65, VIII.118

Farinata degli Scornigiani: VI.17
Federico Novello: VI.16
Forese Donati: XXIII.40

Guido del Duca: XIV.81

Henry III of England: VII.131
Henry I of Navarre: VII.104
Hugh Capet: XX.49

Jacopo del Cassero: V.64

Manfred: III.112

Marchese di Forlì: XXIV.31
Marco Lombardo: XVI.46
Martin IV, Pope: XXIV.21

Nino Visconti: VIII.53

Oderisi: XI.79
Omberto Aldobrandesco: XI.67
Orso degli Alberti, Count: VI.19
Ottokar II of Bohemia: VII.100

Peter III of Aragon: VII.112
Philip III of France: VII.103
Pia dei Tolomei: V.133
Pierre de la Brosse: VI.22
Provenzan Salvani: XI.121

Rinieri da Calboli: XIV.88
Rudolph I of Hapsburg: VII.94

Sapìa: XIII.109
Sordello: VI.74, VII.52, VIII.94
Statius: XXI.91, XXII.25, XXV.31,
XXVII.47, XXXII.28, XXXIII.134

Ubaldino dalla Pila: XXIV.29

William of Monferrat: VII.134

Angel of Chastity: XXVII.6
Angel of the Church: IX.78
Angel of Generosity: XV.34
Angel of Humility: XII.79
Angel of Liberality: XXII.1

Angel of Meekness: XVI.144, XVII.47
Angel-Pilot: II.43
Angel-Sentinels: VIII.25
Angel of Temperance: XXIV.136
Angel of Zeal: XIX.46